Energy Developments
in the Middle East

Other Books by Anthony H. Cordesman

The Iraq War: Strategy, Tactics, and Military Lessons (Westport, CT: Praeger, 2003)
Saudi Arabia Enters the Twenty-first Century: The Political, Foreign Policy, Economic, and Energy Dimensions (Westport, CT: Praeger, 2003)
Saudi Arabia Enters the Twenty-first Century: The Military and International Security Dimensions (Westport, CT: Praeger, 2003)
The Lessons of Afghanistan: War Fighting, Intelligence, and Force Transformation (Washington, DC: CSIS, 2002)
Iraq's Military Capabilities in 2002: A Dynamic Net Assessment (Washington, DC: CSIS, 2002)
Strategic Threats and National Missile Defenses: Defending the U.S. Homeland (Westport, CT: Praeger, 2002)
A Tragedy of Arms: Military and Security Developments in the Maghreb (Westport, CT: Praeger, 2001)
Peace and War: The Arab-Israeli Military Balance Enters the 21st Century (Westport, CT: Praeger, 2001)
Terrorism, Asymmetric Warfare, and Weapons of Mass Destruction: Defending the U.S. Homeland (Westport, CT: Praeger, 2001)
Cyber-threats, Information Warfare, and Critical Infrastructure Protection: Defending the U.S. Homeland, with Justin G. Cordesman (Westport, CT: Praeger, 2001)
The Lessons and Non-Lessons of the Air and Missile Campaign in Kosovo (Westport, CT: Praeger, 2000)
Iran's Military Forces in Transition: Conventional Threats and Weapons of Mass Destruction (Westport, CT: Praeger, 2000)
Transnational Threats from the Middle East: Crying Wolf or Crying Havoc? (Carlyle, PA: Strategic Studies Institute, 1999)
Iraq and the War of Sanctions: Conventional Threats and Weapons of Mass Destruction (Westport, CT: Praeger, 1999)
U.S. Forces in the Middle East: Resources and Capabilities (Boulder, CO: Westview, 1997)
Perilous Prospects: The Peace Process and Arab-Israeli Military Balance (Boulder, CO: Westview, 1996)
The Lessons of Modern War, Volume IV: The Gulf War, with Abraham R. Wagner (Boulder, CO: Westview, 1995; paperback, 1999)
U.S. Defence Policy: Resources and Capabilities (London: RUSI Whitehall Series, 1993)
After the Storm: The Changing Military Balance in the Middle East (Boulder, CO: Westview, 1993)
Weapons of Mass Destruction in the Middle East (London: Brassey's, 1991)
The Lessons of Modern War, Volume I: The Arab-Israeli Conflicts, with Abraham R. Wagner (Boulder, CO: Westview, 1990)
The Lessons of Modern War, Volume II: The Iran-Iraq Conflict, with Abraham R. Wagner (Boulder, CO: Westview, 1990)
The Lessons of Modern War, Volume III: The Afghan and Falklands Conflicts, with Abraham R. Wagner (Boulder, CO: Westview, 1990)
The Gulf and the West: Strategic Relations and Military Realities (Boulder, CO: Westview, 1988)

Energy Developments in the Middle East

ANTHONY H. CORDESMAN

Published in cooperation with the
Center for Strategic and International Studies,
Washington, D.C.

PRAEGER

Westport, Connecticut
London

Library of Congress Cataloging-in-Publication Data

Cordesman, Anthony H.

    Energy developments in the Middle East / Anthony Cordesman.
    p. cm.
    "Published in cooperation with the Center for Strategic and International Studies,
Washington, D.C."
    Includes bibliographical references and index.
    ISBN 0-275-98398-6 (alk. paper)
    1. Petroleum industry and trade—Middle East. 2. Gas industry—Middle East.
3. Energy policy—Middle East. I. Center for Strategic and International Studies
(Washington, D.C.) II. Title.
    HD9576.M52C67 2004
    333.8'23'0956—dc22   2004052306

British Library Cataloguing in Publication Data is available.

Library of Congress Catalog Card Number: 2004052306
ISBN: 0-275-98398-6

First published in 2004

Praeger Publishers, 88 Post Road West, Westport, CT 06881
An imprint of Greenwood Publishing Group, Inc.
www.praeger.com

Printed in the United States of America

The paper used in this book complies with the
Permanent Paper Standard issued by the National
Information Standards Organization (Z39.48–1984).

10 9 8 7 6 5 4 3 2 1

Contents

Illustrations

Acknowledgments

I would like to thank Jennifer Moravitz, Mehmet Emre Furtun, Stephen Lanier, Adam Whetsone, Daniel Berkowitz, Paul Famolari, and Ghada Elnajjar for their help in researching and editing prior work on energy developments in the Middle East and North Africa during past years, and Jennifer Moravitz, M. Emre Furtun, and Stephen Lanier for work drawn upon in this study. I would also like to thank my colleagues James R. Schlesinger and Robert Ebel for their advice and help over many years.

This book would also have been impossible to write without the efforts of the Energy Information Administration (EIA) of the U.S. Department of Energy, and particularly of its country and area analysts. Much of the country and regional analysis is taken from this work by the EIA, and its analysts deserve great credit for consistently excellent reporting over the years. Their work can be readily accessed at www.eia.doe.gov/emeu/cabs/cabsme.html.

The work of the International Energy Agency was also of great value, especially in writing the sections on energy investment in Chapter 5. Credit should also be given to the many press sources used in researching this book, and particularly to four publications that provide consistently excellent reporting on regional political, economic, and energy developments: the *Economist,* the *Estimate, Middle East Economic Digest,* and *Middle East Economic Survey.* While this book relies primarily on official U.S. government sources, and international organizations like the International Energy Agency and World Bank, for its data and citations, extensive use was made of press sources in researching this analysis.

Chapter 1

The Growing Importance of Middle Eastern Energy Exports

The Iraq War has removed a tyrant, but it has had little impact on the overall importance and security of energy supplies in the Middle East and North Africa (MENA) except to cut short-term Iraqi production and create new uncertainties about Iraq's midterm export capacity. Similarly, for all the talk of new U.S. energy policies, and energy discoveries in other areas of the world, there have been no meaningful reductions in global and U.S. strategic dependence on Middle Eastern energy exports since the early 1970s, and virtually all projections call for a sharp increase in such dependence between 2004 and 2030.

The MENA region dominates world energy exports today, and will almost certainly do so for decades to come. This is true even if one assumes steady progress in conservation, major improvements in the supply of renewables, and major increases in energy supplies from gas, coal, nuclear power, and renewables. There are many sources of global energy estimates, they use many different models, and their results differ in detail. There are also many major uncertainties as to the size of the oil and gas reserves in a given country, the cost of extracting them, future energy demand, future energy costs, and virtually every other aspect of energy analysis and forecasting.

Most energy experts do, however, agree in broad terms with the data produced by the Energy Information Administration (EIA) of the U.S. Department of Energy (DOE), and the International Energy Agency (IEA). The forecasts and estimates of the work the EIA and IEA also represent the results of one of the few modeling efforts that receive public review and that is supported by large analytic resources. The EIA also annually recalibrates its forecasts and estimates based on its past degree of accuracy.

There are serious limits even in these forecasts. The EIA estimates for the period 2001–2025 are based on demand-driven models, and they tend to exaggerate the increases in world energy use and to understate the costs of providing energy at the projected level of supply. In effect, they estimate the amount of energy the global economy would like, and then find ways to show how energy supplies could increase to meet market needs without becoming unaffordable. The modeling efforts of most governments and international agencies—such as the International Energy Agency and the Organization of Petroleum Exporting Countries (OPEC)—present the same problems. Supply-driven models generally project far slower rates of increase in energy supply, or substantially higher prices. Unfortunately, such models are generally funded by major oil companies and are proprietary. Their results are not available for public use.

The EIA estimates are likely to be realistic in terms of the role petroleum will play in the world's future energy supply, however, because they assume that future demand for oil and gas will be limited by the impact of other sources of energy, advances in technology, advances in energy efficiency, and the impact of conservation. These estimates forecast a substantial average annual growth in the global consumption of natural gas (1.6–2.7 percent), coal (1.0–2.1 percent), nuclear energy (0.4–0.6 percent), and renewables (1.4–2.4 percent). They expect major improvements in global efficiency and conservation, and in oil and gas experts from other regions—especially in the developing world, the former Soviet Union, and Eastern Europe. Even so, they still project an annual increase of 1.2–2.6 percent in the use of oil, and the reference case estimate is 1.9 percent.

The International Energy Agency makes the same estimate of an average annual increase in world oil consumption: 1.7 percent. Two other respected modeling efforts do not go as far into the future, but make estimates through 2015. The PIRA Energy Group estimates that oil consumption will go up by 1.8 percent per year, and Petroleum Economics Ltd. (PEL) estimates a rise of 1.6 percent. All assume major increases in energy from natural gas, coal, and renewables, although the IEA, PIRA, and PEL all estimate that the gain in nuclear energy will be much lower than the EIA projections.[1]

There is never any certainty to such estimates of the future role of given sources of energy. It is always possible that some massive technological breakthrough will occur that will sharply reduce the need for oil, or some massive new source of energy resources will be found outside the Middle East. However, ever since the United States first sought to reduce its dependence on foreign oil—which took place as part of Project Independence, beginning in the early 1970s—various experts have promised the solution could come from offshore oil reserves outside the MENA region, or from other sources of energy like fuel cells, shale oil, nuclear power, fusion, geo-thermal energy, biomass, wind, conservation, and a host of other means.

None of these promises has paid off by altering the fundamental balance of world energy supplies, or by reducing global economic dependence on exports from the MENA region. In fact, thirty years of efforts to find sub-stitutes for MENA energy resources and exports have raised estimates of the percentage of the world's proven oil reserves located in the MENA area, and increased projection of global dependence on MENA exports. One can argue the validity of the way that proven oil reserves are estimated, but BP Amoco estimated that the world had a total of 648.3 billion barrels of re-serves in 1978, and that the Middle East and North Africa accounted for 405.7 billion barrels of this total (63 percent). BP Amoco estimated that the world had a total of 917.8 billion barrels of reserves in 1988, and that the MENA area accounted for 608.1 billion barrels of this total (66 per-cent). In 1998, BP Amoco estimated that the world had a total of 1,052.9 billion barrels of reserves, and that the MENA area accounted for 716.2 billion barrels of this total (68 percent). At the end of 2002, BP Amoco estimated that the world had a total of 1,047.7 billion barrels of reserves, and that the MENA area accounted for 728.3 billion barrels of this total (70 percent).[2]

OIL VERSUS OTHER SOURCES OF ENERGY

It is notable that the highest risks in terms of the gains in the various pro-jections of future sources of energy are in nuclear (because of the perceived safety risk), and in coal (environmental problems). While renewables are often seen as desirable in terms of emissions, virtually all of the projected gain in current projections comes from large hydroelectric plants, which is increas-ingly seen as posing major environmental risks of a different kind.

Put differently, if any shortfall occurs in the highest risk areas in global energy supply, the demand for oil will actually be much higher than mod-els presently estimate, particularly because oil remains by far the most ef-ficient way of transporting energy flexibly over long distances. Similarly, the higher the rate of global economic growth and the more developing nations actually develop, the higher the demand for oil and oil imports.

Such trends only become clear, however, when they are both quantified and portrayed in graphic form. They are too complex to describe in prose alone and the interactions between the trends involved can only be under-stood by taking the time to compare the numbers and trends developed in different estimates and projections. Like many areas of economics, this may make energy analysis a "dismal science" for those who dislike numbers. As this book illustrates, however, there is no other way to approach the problem and to illustrate both what estimates predict and the major un-certainties in such estimates.

The following charts and tables illustrate these points, as well as provide an overview of the possible trends in world energy supplies and consumption:

- Chart 1.1 shows an estimate by the Energy Information Administration of the U.S. Department of Energy of world energy consumption by type of fuel through 2025. It projects major increases in the use of hydroelectric and renewable energy (shown as "other"), a more than 100 percent increase in the use of natural gas, and a roughly 50 percent increase in the use of coal. The world still, however, nearly doubles its use of oil.

Chart 1.1
EIA Projection of World Energy Consumption by Type of Fuel: 1970–2025

(EIA Reference Case in Quadrillions of BTUs)

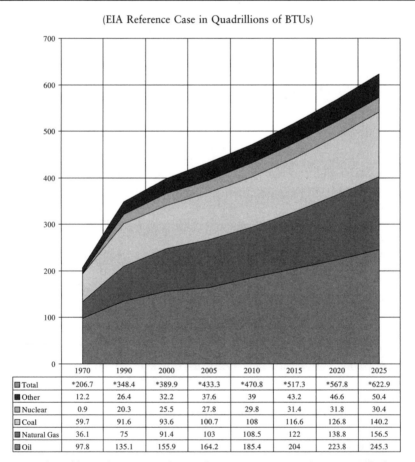

	1970	1990	2000	2005	2010	2015	2020	2025
�◪ Total	*206.7	*348.4	*389.9	*433.3	*470.8	*517.3	*567.8	*622.9
■ Other	12.2	26.4	32.2	37.6	39	43.2	46.6	50.4
▣ Nuclear	0.9	20.3	25.5	27.8	29.8	31.4	31.8	30.4
▢ Coal	59.7	91.6	93.6	100.7	108	116.6	126.8	140.2
■ Natural Gas	36.1	75	91.4	103	108.5	122	138.8	156.5
▣ Oil	97.8	135.1	155.9	164.2	185.4	204	223.8	245.3

Source: Adapted by Anthony H. Cordesman from EIA, *International Energy Outlook 2003*, DOE/EIA-0484 (2003), March 2003, Table A24, p. 182; and EIA, *International Energy Outlook 2004*, www.eia.doe.gov/oiaf/ieo/index.html, April 2004, Table A2, p. 165.

- Chart 1.2 shows a similar projection to 2030 by the International Energy Agency. Hydro increases by nearly 50 percent in spite of environmental concerns, and renewables nearly triple. Coal use increases by over 50 percent and the use of natural gas more than doubles. Nevertheless, oil use increases by over 60 percent.
- Chart 1.3 shows that the IEA projects a significantly smaller increase in oil use than the EIA. Nevertheless, oil use is still 39 percent of all world primary energy consumption in 2030, versus 38 percent in 2000.

Chart 1.2
IEA Projection of World Primary Energy Consumption by Type of Fuel: 1971–2030

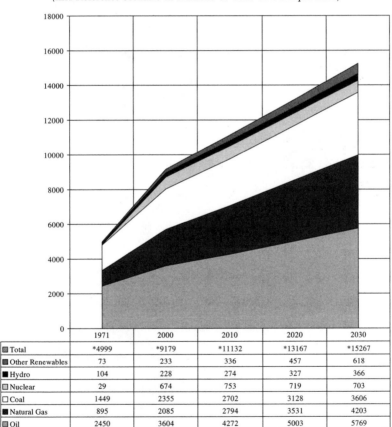

(IEA Reference Scenario in Millions of Tons of Oil Equivalent)

	1971	2000	2010	2020	2030
▨ Total	*4999	*9179	*11132	*13167	*15267
▨ Other Renewables	73	233	336	457	618
■ Hydro	104	228	274	327	366
☐ Nuclear	29	674	753	719	703
☐ Coal	1449	2355	2702	3128	3606
■ Natural Gas	895	2085	2794	3531	4203
▨ Oil	2450	3604	4272	5003	5769

Source: Adapted by Anthony H. Cordesman from International Energy Agency (IEA), *World Energy Outlook 2002*, Paris: IEA, 2002, p. 411.

Chart 1.3
IEA Projection of World Consumption of Primary Energy by Source as Percentage of World Total

(In Percent of World Total)

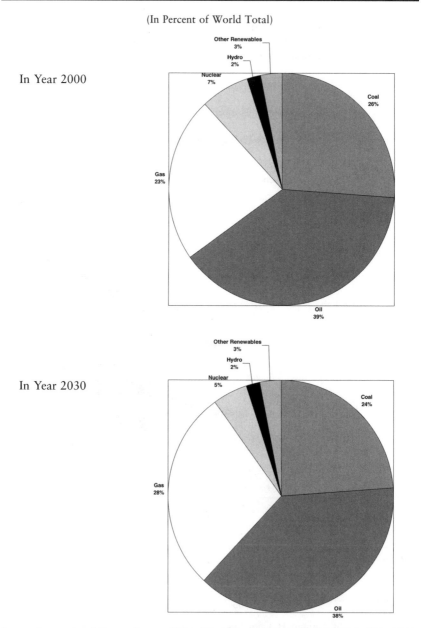

In Year 2000

Other Renewables 3%
Hydro 2%
Nuclear 7%
Coal 26%
Gas 23%
Oil 39%

In Year 2030

Other Renewables 3%
Hydro 2%
Nuclear 5%
Coal 24%
Gas 28%
Oil 38%

Source: International Energy Agency (IEA), *World Energy Outlook 2002*, Paris: IEA, 2002, p. 410.

- Chart 1.4 shows that the EIA and IEA both model a significant drop in the future rate of increase in oil consumption relative to the past, but that both estimate there will still be a 1.7–1.8 percent annual increase in oil use over the next twenty-two to twenty-seven years.

In terms of actual oil consumption, the EIA estimates that world consumption will rise from 66.1 million barrels per day (MMBD) in 1990, and 76.9 MMBD in 2000, to 81.1 MMBD in 2005, 89.7 MMBD in 2010, 98.8

Chart 1.4
Comparative EIA and IEA Estimates of Average Annual Percentage of Future Growth of World Energy Consumption by Type of Fuel: 1971–2030

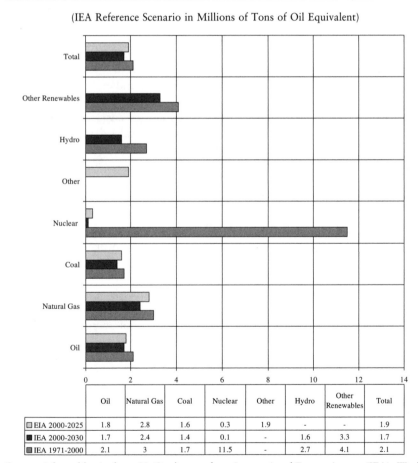

(IEA Reference Scenario in Millions of Tons of Oil Equivalent)

	Oil	Natural Gas	Coal	Nuclear	Other	Hydro	Other Renewables	Total
☐ EIA 2000-2025	1.8	2.8	1.6	0.3	1.9	-	-	1.9
■ IEA 2000-2030	1.7	2.4	1.4	0.1	-	1.6	3.3	1.7
■ IEA 1971-2000	2.1	3	1.7	11.5	-	2.7	4.1	2.1

Source: Adapted by Anthony H. Cordesman from International Energy Agency (IEA), *World Energy Outlook 2002*, Paris: IEA, 2002, p. 411 and EIA, *International Energy Outlook 2004*, www.eia.doe.gov/oiaf/ieo/index.html, April 2004, Table A2, p. 165.

MMBD in 2015, 108.2 MMBD in 2002, and 118.8 MMBD in 2015. While this is only an average annual increase of 1.8 percent per year, it amounts to a total increase of 41.9 MMBD between 2000 and 2025—a cumulative increase of 54 percent.[3] The EIA's *Annual Energy Outlook 2004 (AEO2004)* does not provide all of the same detail, but indicates that world oil demand is projected to increase from 78 million barrels per day in 2002 to 121 million barrels per day in 2025.[4]

The actual future will, of course, be different. As has been touched upon earlier, these estimates are based on demand-driven modeling techniques that tend to assume incremental supply is available at moderate prices. Even if they were more realistic in estimating how quickly supply will increase, real-world historical trends are never smooth or consistent. By definition, no one can predict a technological breakthrough. No one can predict economic growth or environmental developments with any precision, and extrapolating existing trends in known sources of energy over more than two decades is certain to produce substantial errors.

The world's economy does, however, have tremendous momentum. Drastic shifts in the global balance of different types of energy supply involve massive investments in production, transportation, and end-use equipment that are expensive and difficult to accomplish. The world is hard to change in broad structural terms, and most shifts in energy cost, availability, export methods, and technology are incremental and take decades to have a major global impact. It seems doubtful that any of the forces now at work could produce major short-term (2003–2010) changes in the broad structure of global energy balances, and there are many reasons why the Middle East will probably continue to dominate the world oil market for the next two decades even if substantial changes take place in global demand.

The MENA area has been, and will continue to be, a critical factor in meeting global demand and in providing oil exports for simple and straightforward reasons. It has more oil, its oil is cheaper to produce, and it has the infrastructure to export energy cheaply and in large amounts. Its cost for additional production are low by comparative standards, and domestic demand for oil in the MENA region is low relative to total production capacity. In fact, if some major breakthrough in other sources of energy or conservation should reduce global demand for oil, higher-cost producers in other areas would probably have to cease producing or reduce production first.

THE SIZE OF MIDDLE EASTERN AND NORTH AFRICAN OIL RESERVES

There are a number of different ways to estimate oil reserves, and there are many debates over the size of probable oil reserves and future discoveries, how to count heavy oil and tar sands, and the rate of future advances in recovery technology. As has been discussed earlier, estimates of the share of the world's total oil reserves that are in the MENA area have increased steadily for a quarter of a century, but some experts question how realistic current estimates of proven and potential reserves really are, and how long the gains from new exploration, drilling, and production technologies can be sustained.

There are also serious debates over how given countries are characterizing and managing their oil reserves, and these involve such key MENA countries as Iraq, Kuwait, Saudi Arabia, and the United Arab Emirates (UAE). Matthew R. Simmons, for example, has challenged current calculations of Saudi oil reserves, and is correct in pointing out that estimates of proven and potential reserves are often issued for political and financial reasons. Certainly, there was a race among Gulf states to increase their claims to proven reserves during the Iran-Iraq War, both to obtain outside aid and to gain political status. Kuwait, for example, claimed its reserves suddenly jumped from estimates of around 65.4 billion barrels in the early 1980s (1982), to around 90.0 billion in 1985. Iran claimed an increase from 58.0 billion barrels in 1982 to 100.0 billion in 1987. Abu Dhabi increased its claims from 58.0 billion to 92.9 billion during this same period. Iraq responded with claims that its reserves increased from 31.0 billion in 1982 to 100.0 billion in 1988, and Saudi Arabia increased its claims from 163.4 billion in 1982 to 257.5 billion in 1989.[5]

In broad terms, however, most experts would agree that the further increases that have taken place in the estimates of the reserves of given Middle Eastern countries since 1990 have large validated such claims, and usually have significantly increased them, based on normal practices in calculating such figures. Such estimates still leave important gaps—since few MENA countries provide meaningful technical data and key countries like Iran and Iraq have had their exploration and reservoir technology efforts disrupted by war and sanctions—but such uncertainties affect all forms of international statistics and are simply a fact of life. Few in the world's major oil companies would argue with the broad accuracy of BP's estimate that the Middle East has some 65.4 percent of the world's total reserves of 1.047 billion barrels—or 69.6 percent in the North African states of Egypt, Algeria, Libya, and Tunisia are included.

Once again, the vast majority of these reserves are held in the Gulf. The Gulf and Yemen have 65.2 percent of the world's reserves, the Levant has 0.2 percent, and North Africa has 4.2 percent.[6] Moreover, if one uses the conventional method of estimating proven oil reserves, the broad patterns in the distribution of the world's oil reserves by country have not changed in more than a decade. In fact, unless one counts recent efforts to reclassify Canadian tar sands as part of proven oil reserves, the end result of more than thirty years of exploration since the oil embargo of 1973 has been to increase the Middle East's percentage of proven total world oil reserves.

- Table 1.1 shows a BP estimate of the trends in Middle Eastern reserves over the last two decades. It is clear that they have increased consistently over time.
- Chart 1.5 shows how Middle Eastern nations rank relative to other leading oil producers in terms of total proven reserves. It illustrates the critical importance of key producers like Saudi Arabia, Iraq, Iran, Kuwait, and the UAE.
- Chart 1.6 shows the same kind of data, but by region rather than by country. One striking point is that all reserves in the former Soviet Union (FSU)—Russia, Caspian, and Central Asia—still total far less than one-tenth of the total Middle Eastern and North African reserves. This shows that the FSU cannot act as a substitute for Middle Eastern reserves.

Table 1.1
Middle East and World Petroleum Reserves (Billions of Barrels)

Nation	End 1982	End 1992	End 2002	Percent of World Reserves	R/P Ratio %	Production in 2002– of World
Bahrain	n/a	n/a	n/a	n/a	n/a	n/a
Iran	55.3	92.9	89.7	8.6	73.8	4.7
Iraq	41.0	100.0	112.5	10.7	>100.0	2.8
Kuwait	67.2	96.5	96.5	9.2	>100.0	2.6
Oman	2.7	4.5	5.5	0.5	16.8	1.3
Qatar	3.4	3.7	15.2	1.5	57.6	1.0
Saudi Arabia	165.3	260.3	261.8	25.0	86.0	11.8
Syria	1.5	1.7	2.5	0.2	11.9	0.8
UAE	32.4	98.1	97.8	9.3	>100.0	3.0
Yemen	—	4.0	4.0	0.4	23.4	0.6
Other	0.2	0.1	0.1	<0.05	7.8	0.1
Total Middle East	369.0	661.8	685.6	65.4	92.0	28.5
Algeria	9.4	9.2	9.2	0.9	16.5	2.0
Egypt	3.3	6.2	3.7	0.4	14.1	1.0
Libya	21.5	22.8	29.5	2.8	59.4	1.8
Tunisia	1.9	1.7	0.3	<0.05	11.2	0.1
Total MENA	405.1	701.7	728.3	69.5	193.2	33.4
Russia	n/a	48.5	60.0	5.7	21.7	10.7
U.S.	35.1	32.1	30.4	2.9	10.8	9.9
Europe/Eurasia	88.8	26.5	35.5	3.6	17.0	11.3
Asia/Pacific	39.2	44.6	38.7	3.7	13.7	10.7
World Total	676.6	1006.7	1047.7	100.0	40.6	100.0

Source: The reserve and production data are adapted by Anthony H. Cordesman from British Petroleum, *BP Statistical Review of World Energy 2003*, London: 2003, pp. 6–8.

Chart 1.5
Key Nations in Percent of Total Proven World Oil Reserves in 2002

(Quantity in Billions of Barrels; Percent is Percent of Total World Reserves)

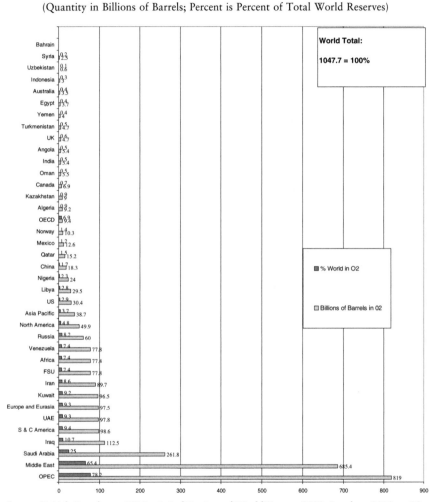

Source: British Petroleum, *BP Statistical Review of World Energy 2002*, London: 2003, p. 20.

Most departures from the conclusions reached in the BP estimate are the possibility of including Canadian tar sands in estimates of world reserves. Canada has proposed this on the grounds that they can be produced at cost of $16 to $26 per barrel, less transportation. The U.S. Geological Service (USGS) indicates that recoverable tar sands could be only 20 percent to 33 percent of what the Canadian Energy Board claims.[7]

Chart 1.6
The Role of Middle East Oil Reserves in Total World Reserves

(In Billions of Barrels)

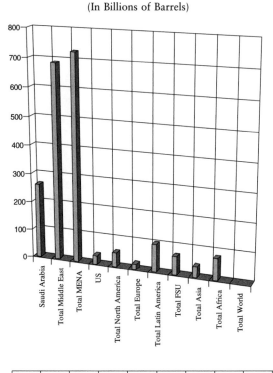

	Saudi Arabia	Total Middle East	Total MENA	US	Total North America	Total Europe	Total Latin America	Total FSU	Total Asia	Total Africa	Total World
▨ Billions of Barrels	261.6	685.6	725.5	30.4	49.9	19.1	98.6	65.3	38.7	77.4	1047..7
■ % of World	*25.0	*65.4	*69.3	*2.9	*4.8	*1.9%	*9.4	*6.4	*3.7	*7.4	*100
☐ R/P Ratio	*86	*92	-	*10.8	*10.3	*7.7	*42.0	*22.7	*13.7	*27.3	*40.4

Source: BP Amoco, *Statistical Review of World Energy 2003*, 2003, p. 6.

The EIA has made less ambitious estimates of total oil reserves that consider this issue, and if such sands are included in the pool of proven reserves,
the EIA estimates that the share of world reserves would be reduced from
some 65 percent to around 57 percent. The EIA analysis indicates that the
commercialization of Canadian tar sands at this price spread *may* prove
to be commercial over time, but that this will take years to fully conform
and requires a massive new production and transportation infrastructure.
Accordingly, the DOE estimates that even if such a revised estimate proves
of world oil reserves does prove valid in real-world economic terms, it will
only lead to 2.2 MMBD worth of actual production by 2025, and 1 MMBD

of exports to the United States.[8] This makes it an interesting possibility, but one that at best has minimal short- to midterm impact.

- Chart 1.7 shows how the Middle East's reserves change as a percentage of total reserves if Canadian tar sands are counted as proven oil reserves.

The USGS provides another way of considering how estimates of world reserves might change in the future. It estimates not only proven reserves—which are recoverable with today's technology and today's costs—but also

Chart 1.7
EIA Estimate of Proven Oil Reserves with Canadian Tar Sands Classified as Crude Oil

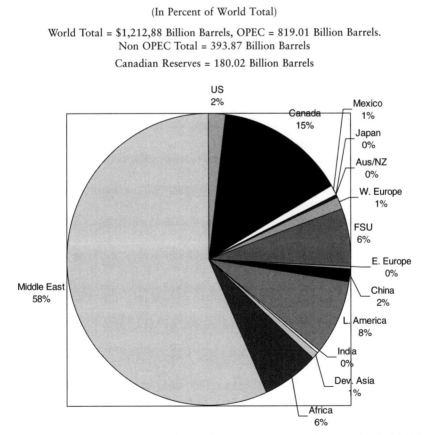

(In Percent of World Total)

World Total = $1,212,88 Billion Barrels, OPEC = 819.01 Billion Barrels.
Non OPEC Total = 393.87 Billion Barrels

Canadian Reserves = 180.02 Billion Barrels

Source: Adapted by Anthony H. Cordesman from EIA, *International Energy Outlook 2003*, DOE/EIA-0484 (2003), March 2003, Table 11, p. 318.

the potential growth in reserves in known fields and the probable size of undiscovered fields. According to the USGS, the present total size of proved reserves in 1,212.9 billion barrels—substantially higher than the BP estimate. The Middle East has 685.64 billion barrels, or 58 percent of the total.[9]

If one looks at potential discoveries through 2025, the USGS estimates that known reserves and fields will be found to have another 730.5 billion barrels by 2025, and that the Middle East will then have 252.5 billion barrels, or 34.6 percent of these new discoveries. If one combined proved reserves and reserve growth, the Middle East would have a total of 938.1 billion barrels, or 48 percent of 1,943 billion barrels. This indicates that the Middle East could shrink as a percentage of future world production after 2025.

This would be truer if one considers the USGS estimate of undiscovered fields and reserves. The USGS estimates that undiscovered fields and reserves could amount to another 939.9 billion barrels, and that the Middle East could have 269.2 billion barrels, or 28.7 percent of this total. If one combines proved reserves, reserve growth, and undiscovered reserves, the Middle East would have 1,207.3 billion barrels, or 42 percent of a global total of 2,882.9 billion barrels. In short, the Middle East would remain of critical strategic importance but could lose its present level of dominance at some point between 2020 and 2030. An important long-term possibility, but one with little practical importance for current and midterm energy policy.

- Table 1.2 shows the IEA estimate of known and estimated reserves. It should be noted that this estimate differs significantly from the estimate by the EIA. This is an area of major debate and uncertainty, although none of the debates have a material impact on the relative importance of the Middle East.
- Chart 1.8 provides similar data based on an EIA estimate, this time by region and subregion.

The International Energy Agency uses a mixture of its own databases and the USGS estimates. The IEA calculates total world oil production to date at 718 billion barrels, and annual production in 2001 at 75.8 MMBD. It projects 959 billion barrels of remaining reserves and 939 billion barrels of undiscovered reserves. Saudi Arabia has an estimated 221 billion barrels in remaining reserves, and 136 billion barrels in undiscovered reserves. Russia ranks second with 137 billion barrels in remaining reserves, and 115 billion barrels in undiscovered reserves. Other Middle East states dominate the rest of the picture.[10]

If one looks at the IEA estimate of the reserves of other major MENA oil producers, they reach the following levels:

- Iraq is estimated to have 78 billion barrels in remaining reserves, and 61 billion barrels in undiscovered reserves. (Estimates of Iraq's oil reserves and re-

Table 1.2
IEA Estimate of Oil Reserves, Resources, and Production by Country

Rank	Country	Remaining Reserves (billion barrels)	Undiscovered Resources (billion barrels)	Total Production (billion barrels)	2001 Production (million barrels)
1	Saudi Arabia	221	136	73	8.5
2	Russia	137	115	97	7.0
3	Iraq	78	51	22	2.4
4	Iran	76	67	34	3.8
5	UAE	59	10	16	2.5
6	Kuwait	55	4	26	1.8
7	U.S.	32	83	171	7.7
8	Venezuela	30	24	46	3.0
9	Libya	25	9	14	1.4
10	China	25	17	24	3.3
11	Mexico	22	23	22	3.6
12	Nigeria	20	25	4	0.8
13	Kazakhstan	20	25	4	0.8
14	Norway	16	23	9	3.4
15	Algeria	15	10	10	1.5
16	Qatar	15	5	5	0.8
17	UK	13	7	14	2.5
18	Indonesia	10	10	15	1.4
19	Brazil	9	55	2	1.4
20	Neutral Zone*	8	0	5	0.6
	Others	73	220	91	16.2
TOTAL		959	939	728	75.8

*Kuwait/Saudi Arabia.
Note: Estimates include crude oil and NGLs; estimates are taken from the IEA and USGS
   databases.
Source: International Energy Agency (IEA), *World Energy Outlook 2002*, Paris: IEA, 2002,
   p. 97.

sources vary widely since only 10 percent of the country's resources have been
explored. Various reports—by the Baker Institute, the Center for Global Energy Studies, the Federation of American Scientists, among others—indicated
that the main deep oil-bearing formations of Iraq located in the Western Desert
region, which could contribute addition resources up to 100 million barrels.
These resources, however, have not been explored.)

• Iran is estimated to have 78 billion barrels in remaining reserves, and 67 billion barrels in undiscovered reserves.

• The UAE is estimated to have 59 billion barrels in remaining reserves, and
   10 billion barrels in undiscovered reserves.

Chart 1.8
EIA Estimate of World Oil Resources

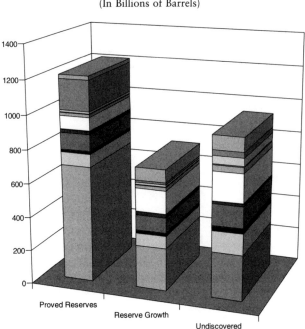

(In Billions of Barrels)

	Proved Reserves	Reserve Growth	Undiscovered
▨ INDUSTRIALIZED			
▨ US	22.45	76.03	83.03
▪ Canada	180.02	12.48	32.59
▫ Mexico	12.62	12.48	45.77
▪ Japan	0.06	0.09	0.31
▪ Aus/NZ	3.52	2.65	5.93
▨ W. Europe	18.1	19.32	34.58
▪ EURASIA			
▫ FSU	77.83	137.7	170.79
▪ E. Europe	1.53	1.46	1.38
▪ China	18.25	19.59	14.62
▨ DEVELOPING			
▨ C&S America	98.55	90.75	125.31
▪ India	5.37	3.81	6.78
▪ Other Asia	11.35	14.57	23.9
▫ Africa	77.43	73.46	124.72
▨ ME	685.64	252.51	269.19
▫ TOTAL	*1,212.88	*730.05	*939.9
▨ OPEC	*819.01	*395.57	*400.51
▪ Non-OPEC	*393.87	*334.48	*538.39

Source: Adapted by Anthony H. Cordesman from U.S. Department of Energy, *International Energy Outlook 2004*, Washington, DC: Energy Information Administration, www.eia.doe.gov/oiaf/ieo/index.html, April 2004, Table 5, p. 36; and www.usgs.gov/energy/World Energy/DDS-60.

- Kuwait is estimated to have 55 billion barrels in remaining reserves, and 4 billion barrels in undiscovered reserves.
- Libya is estimated to have 25 billion barrels in remaining reserves, and 9 billion barrels in undiscovered reserves.
- Algeria is estimated to have 15 billion barrels in remaining reserves, and 10 billion barrels in undiscovered reserves.
- Qatar is estimated to have 15 billion barrels in remaining reserves, and 5 billion barrels in undiscovered reserves.
- The Kuwaiti-Saudi Neutral Zone is estimated to have 8 billion barrels in remaining reserves, and 0 billion barrels in undiscovered reserves.
- The U.S. is estimated to have 32 billion barrels in remaining reserves, and 83 billion barrels in undiscovered reserves.

Other factors need to be considered in evaluating such estimates of the near and midterm impact of new discoveries on the world oil market. The cost of production from outside the MENA region varies sharply from region to region once one considers reserve growth and undiscovered reserves. Much of the production would have to come from the former Soviet Union, and from Latin American and African states, where production costs are often at least twice those in the Middle East. The estimates of reserve growth require major advances in enhanced oil recovery to make production economically viable outside the Middle East, and it can take decades to create the production and export infrastructure necessary to exploit undiscovered reserves.

PROJECTED INCREASES IN MENA OIL PRODUCTION CAPACITY THROUGH 2030

Given these factors, it is hardly surprising that most estimates indicate that the MENA region will steadily expand its oil production increase its share of world production, and increase its impact on the global economy through 2030. There are major uncertainties in such estimates, and it must again be stressed that they are based upon demand-driven models that can exaggerate the ease with which major long-term increases can be made in supply at moderate prices. Nevertheless, the reference case of the Energy Information Administration provides what seems to be the most realistic model publicly available, and it does include forecast production from Canadian tar sands and substantial exploitation of enhanced oil recovery and new discoveries outside the Middle East.

As a result it is striking that the EIA still estimates that total oil production capacity of the OPEC states of the Persian Gulf alone will increase from 22.4 MMBD in 2001 to 24.5 MMBD in 2005, 28.7 MMBD in 2010, 33 MMBD in 2015, 38.96 MMBD in 2020, and 45.2 MMBD in 2025.[11]

Put differently, Gulf OPEC oil production capacity will increase from 26.9 percent of total world capacity in 1990, and 28.3 percent of world capacity in 2001, to 32 percent of world capacity in 2015 and 36.3 percent of world capacity in 2025.[12] These figures would be even higher if other non-OPEC "Gulf" oil-producer powers like Oman and Yemen were included. Moreover, the EIA's *Annual Energy Outlook 2004* estimates that total OPEC oil production will reach 56 million barrels per day in 2025, almost 80 percent higher than the 30 million barrels per day produced in 2002.

Reference Case Estimates of the Increase in Production Capacity

While the Gulf dominates the increase in MENA oil production capacity, the EIA estimates also projects significant increases in oil production capacity in North Africa. Algeria and Libya are estimated to increase their production from 3.3 MMBD in 2001 to 3.4 MMBD in 2005, 4 MMBD in 2010, 4.3 MMBD in 2015, 5 MMBD in 2020, and 5.7 MMBD in 2025.[13]

If the entire MENA region is considered, oil production capacity is projected to increase from 22.9 MMBD in 1990 and 27.5 MMBD in 2001 to 29.9 MMBD in 2005, 34.9 MMBD in 2010, 37.2 MMBD in 2015, 46.4 MMBD in 2020, and 53.6 MMBD in 2025. This would mean that total MENA oil production capacity would increase from 33 percent of total world capacity in 1990, and 34.7 percent of world capacity in 2001, to 35.5 percent of world capacity in 2005, 39.8 percent in 2010, 40.1 percent in 2015, and 43 percent of world capacity in 2025.[14]

- Chart 1.9 shows the estimated trend in increased oil consumption by region, illustrating the trend in "demand pull" for Middle Eastern exports, particularly in China and developing Asia.
- Charts 1.10 and 1.11 show the historical trend in Middle Eastern oil production, and reveal the differences in annual level that can result from changes in world economic demand.
- Chart 1.12 shows the EIA's projection of future increases in oil production by region. It is clear that the projected increases in Middle Eastern capacity shape the curve.
- Chart 1.13 shows the EIA's projection of increases in Middle Eastern oil production capacity by country, illustrating the critical importance of Saudi Arabia, and the role of Iran, Iraq, Kuwait, and the UAE.
- Chart 1.14 illustrates the impact of different economic and oil price conditions on the estimated rate of increase in Middle Eastern oil production capacity, illustrating one of the key uncertainties involved.

The IEA makes generally similar projections, although it uses different time periods and definitions of the regions to be assessed. It estimates that global oil demand will increase by an average of 1.6 percent during 2000–

Chart 1.9
EIA Projection of Growth in World Oil Demand: 1990–2025

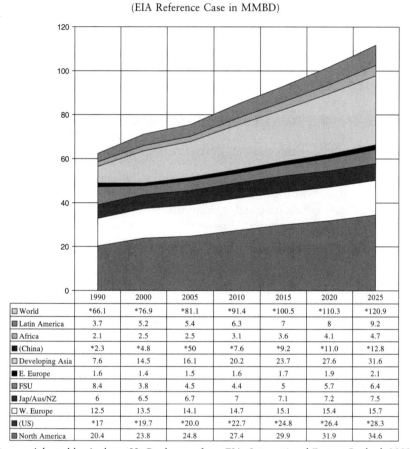

(EIA Reference Case in MMBD)

	1990	2000	2005	2010	2015	2020	2025
☐ World	*66.1	*76.9	*81.1	*91.4	*100.5	*110.3	*120.9
▨ Latin America	3.7	5.2	5.4	6.3	7	8	9.2
☐ Africa	2.1	2.5	2.5	3.1	3.6	4.1	4.7
▪ (China)	*2.3	*4.8	*50	*7.6	*9.2	*11.0	*12.8
☐ Developing Asia	7.6	14.5	16.1	20.2	23.7	27.6	31.6
▪ E. Europe	1.6	1.4	1.5	1.6	1.7	1.9	2.1
▨ FSU	8.4	3.8	4.5	4.4	5	5.7	6.4
▪ Jap/Aus/NZ	6	6.5	6.7	7	7.1	7.2	7.5
☐ W. Europe	12.5	13.5	14.1	14.7	15.1	15.4	15.7
▪ (US)	*17	*19.7	*20.0	*22.7	*24.8	*26.4	*28.3
▪ North America	20.4	23.8	24.8	27.4	29.9	31.9	34.6

Source: Adapted by Anthony H. Cordesman from EIA, *International Energy Outlook 2002*, DOE/EIAA4 D1; and EIA, *International Energy Outlook 2004*, www.eia.doe.gov/oiaf/ieo/index.html, April 2004, Table A4, p. 167.

2030. This compares with 1.8 percent for the EIA over the period 2000–2030.[15] Other sources do reflect more serious differences in the estimate of the coming shifts in demand for oil. For example, similar estimates by Shell call for 1.1 percent average annual growth, and by DRI/WEFA for 2.2 percent growth.[16]

The IEA estimates that total OPEC Middle Eastern production will increase by an annual average rate of 3 percent per year from 2000 to 2030, and will grow by 1.4 percent a year as a share of total world production.

Chart 1.10
Middle Eastern Petroleum Production by Country: Part One—BP Estimate for 1992–2002

(MMBD of Crude Oil, Tar Sands, Shale Oil, and NGLs)

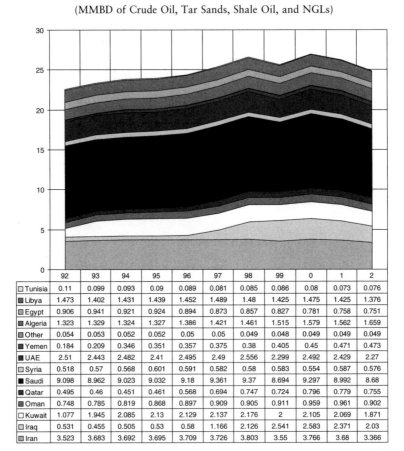

	92	93	94	95	96	97	98	99	0	1	2
☐ Tunisia	0.11	0.099	0.093	0.09	0.089	0.081	0.085	0.086	0.08	0.073	0.076
▣ Libya	1.473	1.402	1.431	1.439	1.452	1.489	1.48	1.425	1.475	1.425	1.376
▣ Egypt	0.906	0.941	0.921	0.924	0.894	0.873	0.857	0.827	0.781	0.758	0.751
▣ Algeria	1.323	1.329	1.324	1.327	1.386	1.421	1.461	1.515	1.579	1.562	1.659
▣ Other	0.054	0.053	0.052	0.052	0.05	0.05	0.049	0.048	0.049	0.049	0.049
▪ Yemen	0.184	0.209	0.346	0.351	0.357	0.375	0.38	0.405	0.45	0.471	0.473
▪ UAE	2.51	2.443	2.482	2.41	2.495	2.49	2.556	2.299	2.492	2.429	2.27
☐ Syria	0.518	0.57	0.568	0.601	0.591	0.582	0.58	0.583	0.554	0.587	0.576
▪ Saudi	9.098	8.962	9.023	9.032	9.18	9.361	9.37	8.694	9.297	8.992	8.68
▣ Qatar	0.495	0.46	0.451	0.461	0.568	0.694	0.747	0.724	0.796	0.779	0.755
▣ Oman	0.748	0.785	0.819	0.868	0.897	0.909	0.905	0.911	0.959	0.961	0.902
☐ Kuwait	1.077	1.945	2.085	2.13	2.129	2.137	2.176	2	2.105	2.069	1.871
☐ Iraq	0.531	0.455	0.505	0.53	0.58	1.166	2.126	2.541	2.583	2.371	2.03
▣ Iran	3.523	3.683	3.692	3.695	3.709	3.726	3.803	3.55	3.766	3.68	3.366

Source: Adapted by Anthony H. Cordesman from British Petroleum, *BP Statistical Review of World Energy 2001*, London: 2003, p. 7.

The IEA estimates that total Middle Eastern OPEC production will grow from 21 MMBD in 2000 (28.1 percent of the world oil supply) to 26.5 MMBD in 2010 (40.4 percent), 37.8 MMBD in 2020 (36.4 percent), and 51.4 MMBD (54.1 percent) in 2030. The rest of the Middle East is projected to cut production from 2.1 MMBD in 2000 to 1.8 MMBD in 2010, 1.5 MMBD in 2020, and 0.9 MMBD in 2030.

- Chart 1.15 shows the IEA's estimate of the increase in oil production by region through 2030. It is measured by a different model and set oil definitions

Chart 1.11
Middle Eastern Petroleum Production by Country: Part Two—CEA Estimate of Historical Trends in Middle Eastern Oil Production: 1970–2001

($Current Billions)

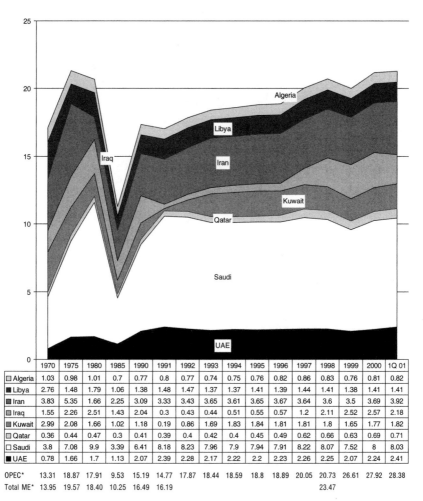

	1970	1975	1980	1985	1990	1991	1992	1993	1994	1995	1996	1997	1998	1999	2000	1Q 01
□ Algeria	1.03	0.98	1.01	0.7	0.77	0.8	0.77	0.74	0.75	0.76	0.82	0.86	0.83	0.76	0.81	0.82
■ Libya	2.76	1.48	1.79	1.06	1.38	1.48	1.47	1.37	1.37	1.41	1.39	1.44	1.41	1.38	1.41	1.41
▦ Iran	3.83	5.35	1.66	2.25	3.09	3.33	3.43	3.65	3.61	3.65	3.67	3.64	3.6	3.5	3.69	3.92
▨ Iraq	1.55	2.26	2.51	1.43	2.04	0.3	0.43	0.44	0.51	0.55	0.57	1.2	2.11	2.52	2.57	2.18
▦ Kuwait	2.99	2.08	1.66	1.02	1.18	0.19	0.86	1.69	1.83	1.84	1.81	1.81	1.8	1.65	1.77	1.82
□ Qatar	0.36	0.44	0.47	0.3	0.41	0.39	0.4	0.42	0.4	0.45	0.49	0.62	0.66	0.63	0.69	0.71
□ Saudi	3.8	7.08	9.9	3.39	6.41	8.18	8.23	7.96	7.9	7.94	7.91	8.22	8.07	7.52	8	8.03
■ UAE	0.78	1.66	1.7	1.13	2.07	2.39	2.28	2.17	2.22	2.2	2.23	2.26	2.25	2.07	2.24	2.41

OPEC*	13.31	18.87	17.91	9.53	15.19	14.77	17.87	18.44	18.59	18.8	18.89	20.05	20.73	26.61	27.92	28.38
Total ME*	13.95	19.57	18.40	10.25	16.49	16.19							23.47			

*Pre-1992 data: CEA, *World Oil Trends, 1998*, Cambridge, MA: 1998, pp. 26–27. 1992–1998: IEA, *Oil Market Report*, May 11, 2000, p. 45. After 1998: IEA, *Oil Market Report*, May 11, 2001, p. 52.

Source: Adapted by Anthony H. Cordesman from Cambridge Energy Associates, *World Oil Watch, 2000*, Cambridge, MA: 2000, p. 26.

Chart 1.12
EIA Projection of World Production Capacity by Region: 1990–2025

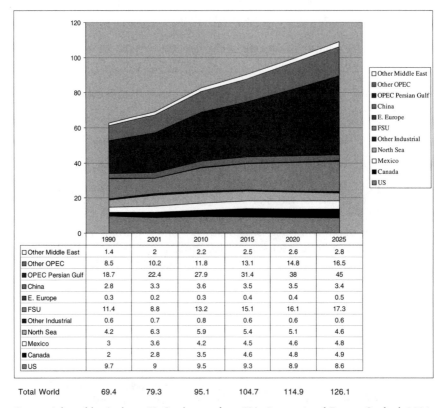

(EIA Reference Case in MMBD)

	1990	2001	2010	2015	2020	2025
□ Other Middle East	1.4	2	2.2	2.5	2.6	2.8
■ Other OPEC	8.5	10.2	11.8	13.1	14.8	16.5
■ OPEC Persian Gulf	18.7	22.4	27.9	31.4	38	45
■ China	2.8	3.3	3.6	3.5	3.5	3.4
■ E. Europe	0.3	0.2	0.3	0.4	0.4	0.5
▨ FSU	11.4	8.8	13.2	15.1	16.1	17.3
■ Other Industrial	0.6	0.7	0.8	0.6	0.6	0.6
▨ North Sea	4.2	6.3	5.9	5.4	5.1	4.6
□ Mexico	3	3.6	4.2	4.5	4.6	4.8
■ Canada	2	2.8	3.5	4.6	4.8	4.9
▨ US	9.7	9	9.5	9.3	8.9	8.6

| Total World | 69.4 | 79.3 | 95.1 | 104.7 | 114.9 | 126.1 |

Source: Adapted by Anthony H. Cordesman from EIA, *International Energy Outlook 2004,*
April 2004, Table D1, p. 238.

than the EIA estimate, but clearly reveals the same increase in Middle Eastern
capacity relative to the rest of the world.

Key Uncertainties in Estimates of Increases in Production Capacity

It should be stressed that it is highly likely that the MENA area will not
make all of these production increases at the level that the EIA and IEA
estimate and that their estimates of future energy costs may provide a better

Chart 1.12
EIA Projection of World Production Capacity by Region: 1990–2025

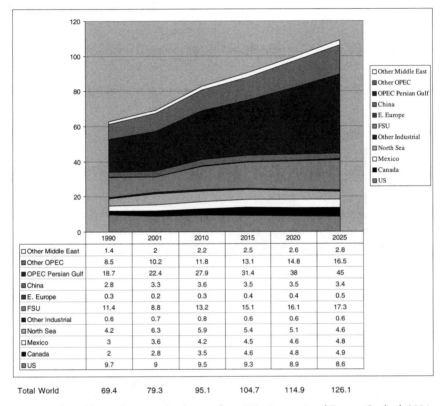

(EIA Reference Case in MMBD)

	1990	2001	2010	2015	2020	2025
□ Other Middle East	1.4	2	2.2	2.5	2.6	2.8
■ Other OPEC	8.5	10.2	11.8	13.1	14.8	16.5
■ OPEC Persian Gulf	18.7	22.4	27.9	31.4	38	45
■ China	2.8	3.3	3.6	3.5	3.5	3.4
■ E. Europe	0.3	0.2	0.3	0.4	0.4	0.5
▨ FSU	11.4	8.8	13.2	15.1	16.1	17.3
■ Other Industrial	0.6	0.7	0.8	0.6	0.6	0.6
▨ North Sea	4.2	6.3	5.9	5.4	5.1	4.6
□ Mexico	3	3.6	4.2	4.5	4.6	4.8
■ Canada	2	2.8	3.5	4.6	4.8	4.9
▨ US	9.7	9	9.5	9.3	8.9	8.6

Total World	69.4	79.3	95.1	104.7	114.9	126.1

Source: Adapted by Anthony H. Cordesman from EIA, *International Energy Outlook 2004*,
April 2004, Table D1, p. 238.

than the EIA estimate, but clearly reveals the same increase in Middle Eastern
capacity relative to the rest of the world.

Key Uncertainties in Estimates of Increases in Production Capacity

It should be stressed that it is highly likely that the MENA area will not
make all of these production increases at the level that the EIA and IEA
estimate and that their estimates of future energy costs may provide a better

Chart 1.11
Middle Eastern Petroleum Production by Country: Part Two—CEA Estimate of
Historical Trends in Middle Eastern Oil Production: 1970–2001

($Current Billions)

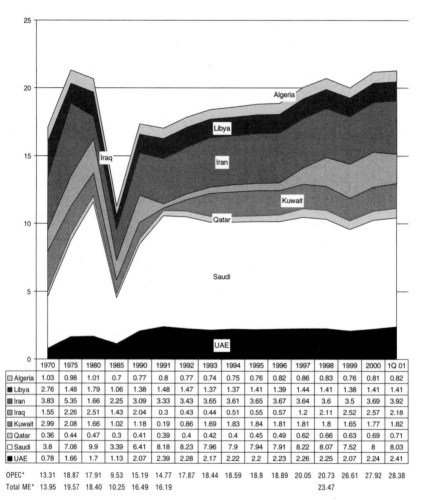

	1970	1975	1980	1985	1990	1991	1992	1993	1994	1995	1996	1997	1998	1999	2000	1Q 01
☐ Algeria	1.03	0.98	1.01	0.7	0.77	0.8	0.77	0.74	0.75	0.76	0.82	0.86	0.83	0.76	0.81	0.82
■ Libya	2.76	1.48	1.79	1.06	1.38	1.48	1.47	1.37	1.37	1.41	1.39	1.44	1.41	1.38	1.41	1.41
■ Iran	3.83	5.35	1.66	2.25	3.09	3.33	3.43	3.65	3.61	3.65	3.67	3.64	3.6	3.5	3.69	3.92
☐ Iraq	1.55	2.26	2.51	1.43	2.04	0.3	0.43	0.44	0.51	0.55	0.57	1.2	2.11	2.52	2.57	2.18
■ Kuwait	2.99	2.08	1.66	1.02	1.18	0.19	0.86	1.69	1.83	1.84	1.81	1.81	1.8	1.65	1.77	1.82
☐ Qatar	0.36	0.44	0.47	0.3	0.41	0.39	0.4	0.42	0.4	0.45	0.49	0.62	0.66	0.63	0.69	0.71
☐ Saudi	3.8	7.08	9.9	3.39	6.41	8.18	8.23	7.96	7.9	7.94	7.91	8.22	8.07	7.52	8	8.03
■ UAE	0.78	1.66	1.7	1.13	2.07	2.39	2.28	2.17	2.22	2.2	2.23	2.26	2.25	2.07	2.24	2.41

	1970	1975	1980	1985	1990	1991	1992	1993	1994	1995	1996	1997	1998	1999	2000	1Q 01
OPEC*	13.31	18.87	17.91	9.53	15.19	14.77	17.87	18.44	18.59	18.8	18.89	20.05	20.73	26.61	27.92	28.38
Total ME*	13.95	19.57	18.40	10.25	16.49	16.19							23.47			

*Pre-1992 data: CEA, *World Oil Trends, 1998*, Cambridge, MA: 1998, pp. 26–27. 1992–
1998: IEA, *Oil Market Report*, May 11, 2000, p. 45. After 1998: IEA, *Oil Market Report*,
May 11, 2001, p. 52.

Source: Adapted by Anthony H. Cordesman from Cambridge Energy Associates, *World Oil
Watch, 2000*, Cambridge, MA: 2000, p. 26.

Chart 1.13
EIA Projection of Middle Eastern Petroleum Production Capacity by Country Relative to World Capacity: 1990–2025

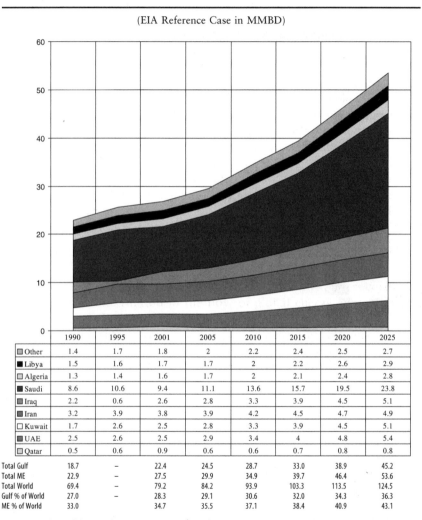

(EIA Reference Case in MMBD)

	1990	1995	2001	2005	2010	2015	2020	2025
☐ Other	1.4	1.7	1.8	2	2.2	2.4	2.5	2.7
■ Libya	1.5	1.6	1.7	1.7	2	2.2	2.6	2.9
☐ Algeria	1.3	1.4	1.6	1.7	2	2.1	2.4	2.8
■ Saudi	8.6	10.6	9.4	11.1	13.6	15.7	19.5	23.8
■ Iraq	2.2	0.6	2.6	2.8	3.3	3.9	4.5	5.1
■ Iran	3.2	3.9	3.8	3.9	4.2	4.5	4.7	4.9
☐ Kuwait	1.7	2.6	2.5	2.8	3.3	3.9	4.5	5.1
◼ UAE	2.5	2.6	2.5	2.9	3.4	4	4.8	5.4
☐ Qatar	0.5	0.6	0.9	0.6	0.6	0.7	0.8	0.8
Total Gulf	18.7	–	22.4	24.5	28.7	33.0	38.9	45.2
Total ME	22.9	–	27.5	29.9	34.9	39.7	46.4	53.6
Total World	69.4	–	79.2	84.2	93.9	103.3	113.5	124.5
Gulf % of World	27.0	–	28.3	29.1	30.6	32.0	34.3	36.3
ME % of World	33.0		34.7	35.5	37.1	38.4	40.9	43.1

Source: Adapted by Anthony H. Cordesman from EIA, *International Energy Outlook 1997*, DOE/EIA-0484 (1997), April 1997, pp. 157–160; EIA, *International Energy Outlook 2002*, DOE/EIA-0484 (2002), March 2002, Table D1; and EIA, *International Energy Outlook 2003*, DOE/EIA-0484 (2003), March 2003, Table D1.

Chart 1.14
Variations in EIA Estimate of Middle Eastern Oil Production Capacity in 2025 by Economic Case

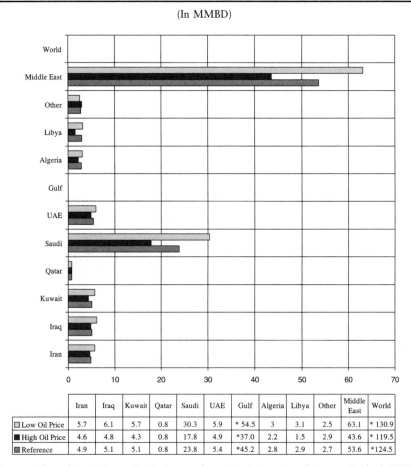

(In MMBD)

	Iran	Iraq	Kuwait	Qatar	Saudi	UAE	Gulf	Algeria	Libya	Other	Middle East	World
☐ Low Oil Price	5.7	6.1	5.7	0.8	30.3	5.9	* 54.5	3	3.1	2.5	63.1	* 130.9
■ High Oil Price	4.6	4.8	4.3	0.8	17.8	4.9	*37.0	2.2	1.5	2.9	43.6	* 119.5
▨ Reference	4.9	5.1	5.1	0.8	23.8	5.4	*45.2	2.8	2.9	2.7	53.6	*124.5

Source: Adapted by Anthony H. Cordesman from EIA, *International Energy Outlook 1997*, DOE/EIA-0484 (1997), April 1997, pp. 157–160; EIA, *International Energy Outlook 2003*, DOE/EIA-0484 (2003), June 2003, Tables D1 to D4.

model of what the market wants than what countries are capable of supplying or are willing to sell at such prices. As has been noted from the start, these projected increases in production capacity are based on economic models that assume MENA states can and will expand production capacity to meet market demand. They are not based on country plans to actually fund and implement such increases. This makes any such estimates—and the related projections of increases in exports—much more uncertain than they would be.

Chart 1.15
IEA Projection of Petroleum Production Capacity by Region: 2000–2030

(EIA Reference Case in MMBD)

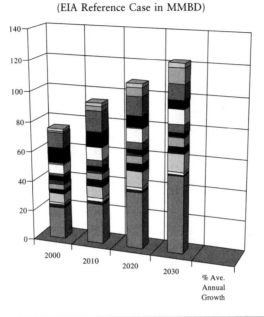

	2000	2010	2020	2030	% Ave. Annual Growth
☐ Processing Gains	1.7	2.2	2.6	3.1	* 1.9
▦ Non-Conventional Oil	1.1	3	5.6	9.9	* 7.7
▪ US/Canada	10.1	14	12.3	9.9	* -1.1
▪ Mexico	3.5	4.1	4	2.7	* -0.8
▦ OEC Europe	6.7	5.2	3.5	2.5	* -3.3
▦ OECD Pacific	0.9	0.5	0.5	0.5	* -1.8
☐ Russia	6.5	8.6	9	9.5	* 1.3
▪ Transition	1.6	4.1	4.9	5.4	* 4.1
▪ China	3.2	2.8	2.5	2.1	* -1.4
▦ India	0.7	0.5	0.4	0.3	* -2.5
▪ Other Asia	1.6	1.4	1.1	0.7	* -2.8
▦ Latin America	3.6	4.3	5.2	5.8	-
▪ Africa	2.8	4.5	4.9	4.4	* 1.5
▦ Other OPEC	6.3	7.9	10.7	11.8	* 1.9
☐ Indonesia	1.4	2.5	1.7	1.7	* 0.6
▪ Other Middle East	2.1	1.8	1.5	0.9	* -2.7
▦ OPEC Middle East	21	26.5	37.8	51.4	* 3

	2000	2010	2020	2030	% Ave. Annual Growth
Total World	75.0	88.8	104.0	120.03	1.6
OPEC	28.7	35.9	50.2	64.9	2.8
Non-OPEC	43.4	47.8	45.7	42.1	−1.7
ME OPEC as Percent of World	28.1	29.8	36.4	42.9	1.4

Note: Transition = Central Asia, Caspian, E. Europe, Cyprus, and Malta.
Source: International Energy Agency (IEA), *World Energy Outlook 2002*, Paris: IEA, 2002,
  p. 96.

There are dangers in estimating and modeling the behavior of countries before the countries involved have made any clear decision about their future plans. Most countries in the region have only limited long-range plans to would be if the countries involved had either declared they would make such increases of that it was in response to market forces. At the same time, most countries in the region have never made serious long-range plans to expand production capacity and most have reacted to market forces although few have risked anticipating them. A country-by-country review of current plans and energy strategies also shows that no MENA country has a credible long-term (2005+) energy plan. There simply is no valid basis for making "supply-based" estimates as distinguished form "market-driven" or "demand-based" estimates.

There are many technical uncertainties in estimating the size and character of oil reserves, and the cost of maintaining and expanding production. Errors of 20 percent or more can easily occur in projecting the mid- and long-term nature and behavior of a given field, particularly when countries have not updated their exploration, testing, and management techniques. Abu Dhabi, Iran, Iraq, Kuwait, Libya, Oman, and Yemen are all examples of MENA states that have demonstrated in the past that they have questionable capability to accurately characterize their reserves and execute oil field development and increase production on a "best practices" basis, although most of these countries do at least approach international standards.

It is equally important to note that market forces are only one of the factors that have shaped MENA behavior. The MENA region has been the scene of more than ten conflicts and major internal security struggles over the last two decades, and the production capacity and exports of several states have been affected by UN and U.S. sanctions. As a result, it is important to review the assessments of estimated increases in production by country and understand that the expansion in each country involves both economic aid and some security risks.

Even if one only considers economic factors, one can produce very different estimates. The EIA reference case projection for 2025 does estimate increases by OPEC country under different economic conditions, which are summarized as the "high oil price" (high demand, lesser supply) and "low oil price" (lower demand, higher supply) cases. The resulting EIA projections can be summarized as follows (the minimum and maximum range provided in other projection is shown in parentheses):[17]

- Algeria is projected to increase production capacity from 1.6 MMBD in 2001 to 2.8 MMBD in 2025, or by 75 percent (2.2 MMBD to 3.0 MMBD).

- Iran is projected to increase production capacity from 3.7 MMBD in 2001 to 4.9 MMBD in 2025, or by 32 percent (4.6 MMBD to 5.7 MMBD).

- Iraq is projected to increase production capacity from 2.8 MMBD in 2001 to 5.2 MMBD in 2025, or by 75 percent (4.8 MMBD to 6.1 MMBD).
- Kuwait is projected to increase production capacity from 2.4 MMBD in 2001 to 5.1 MMBD in 2025, or by 113 percent (4.3 MMBD to 5.7 MMBD).
- Libya is projected to increase production capacity from 1.7 MMBD in 2001 to 2.9 MMBD in 2025, or by 71 percent (2.4 MMBD to 3.1 MMBD).
- Qatar is projected to increase production capacity from 0.6 MMBD in 2001 to 0.8 MMBD in 2025, or by 0.0 percent (0.8 MMBD to 0.8 MMBD).
- Saudi Arabia is projected to increase production capacity from 10.2 MMBD in 2001 to 23.8 MMBD in 2025, or by 133 percent (17.6 MMBD to 30.3 MMBD).
- The UAE is projected to increase production capacity from 2.7 MMBD in 2001 to 5.4 MMBD in 2025, or by 100 percent (4.9 MMBD to 5.9 MMBD).

As is touched upon previously, the variations shown in parentheses reflect the impact of different projections of market forces. The lower production capacity is the result of high oil prices that ease the revenue and cash flow problems of exporting states. The high production capacity estimate is the result of low oil prices and the need to increase production to increase export earnings.

To put these differences in perspective, the reference case estimates project the OPEC Gulf nations to have a total production capacity of 45.2 MMBD in 2025—a rise of over 100 percent above the 2001 level. The low-end estimate would be 37.0 MMBD and the high-end estimate would be 54.5 MMBD. If North Africa and the rest of the Middle East are considered separately, they would increase in the reference case from 4.7 MMBD in 2001 to 8.4 MMBD in 2025—a rise of 78 percent. The low estimate in 2025 would be 7.9 MMBD. The high estimate would be 8.6 MMBD. The reference case estimate for the entire MENA area would be 53.6 MMBD. The range would be from a low of 44.9 MMBD to a high of 63.1 MMBD.

Once again, simply modeling uncertainty does not mean that the resulting conclusions establish the boundaries of the problem. Many in the oil industry feel that all of the EIA and IEA estimates of future production capacity are too high and that the countries in the region will be much slower to increase production. It should also be noted that several real-world trends do not conform to the EIA and IEA projections even in the short term. Iraqi oil production was only 800,000–1,200,000 MBPD in August 2003 because of the impact of the Iraq War and its aftermath. Iran and Libya have failed to modernize and increase production for more than half a decade because of internal political developments and external sanctions. Kuwait has fallen badly behind in field development and technology because its National Assembly has blocked suitable investment reforms. Algeria continues a civil war, and the problem of terrorism has become more serious in the Gulf region and Saudi Arabia in particular. This does not mean that the EIA and IEA projections will not prove accurate over time, but it does mean that there are security as well as market risks and that future production and export capacity is as much an energy risk as embargoes or temporary interruptions in production.

Yet such uncertainties have little strategic impact on the importance of the MENA region. The sources of current and increased oil production in other regions—the FSU, Latin America, and West Africa—are all subject to the same general uncertainties as those in the MENA area. The countries involved have been at least as affected by poor state planning and development, and conflict and internal instability, as has the MENA area. Energy comes from a risk-filled worlds, and only truly massive and lasting shifts in the pattern of regional oil exports have true strategic importance.

PROJECTED INCREASES IN MENA OIL EXPORTS THROUGH 2025

The past and projected trends in oil exports follow a different pattern from increases in oil production because many producers consume most or large portions of their domestic production. The MENA region, however, retains massive surplus capacity relative to domestic demand, and this explains why its share of world exports is much higher than its share of total production or production capacity.

According to estimates in the BP's *Statistical Review of World Energy,* the Middle East produced an average of 20.97 MMBD in 2002.[18] This was 28.5 percent of the world total of 73.94 MMBD. The Middle East exported an average of 18.1 MMBD in 2002, or 41.4 percent of the total world average of 43.63 MMBD in exports.[19]

If the four oil exporters in North Africa are added to the total to create a figure for the MENA region, Egypt, Algeria, Libya, and Tunisia would add an average annual production of 3.86 MMBD in 2002.[20] This was 4.9 percent of a world total of 73.94 MMBD. The North African states exported an average of 3.1 MMBD in 2002, or 0.7 percent of the total world average of 43.63 MMBD in exports. The total MENA region produced 24.83 MMBD, or 33.6 percent of the world total. The total average oil exports were 21.2 MMBD in 2002, or 48.6 percent of the world total.

If one uses the EIA, rather than the BP estimates referenced earlier, the Gulf OPEC states exported an average of 16.9 MMBD, or 30 percent of a world total of 56.3 MMBD. If one includes the North African states, the exports climb to 19.5 MMBD, or 35 percent.[21] The DOE projects that Gulf OPEC exports will reach 36.4 MMBD by 2025, or 40.737 percent of the world total of 89.4 MMBD. If one includes North Africa, the level of exports climbs to 41.7 MMBD, or 46.64 percent of the world total. This is a climb of 10–11 percent in the Middle East's share of global oil exports between 2001 and 2025.[22]

The EIA, in its *Annual Energy Outlook 2003 (AEO2003)*, summarizes the trends in Gulf oil exports as follows:

> Considering the world market in crude oil exports, the historical peak for Persian Gulf exports (as a percent of world oil exports) occurred in 1974, when they made up more than two-thirds of the crude oil traded in world markets (Figure 35). The most recent historical low for Persian Gulf oil exports came in 1984 as a result of more than a decade of high oil prices, which led to significant reductions in worldwide petroleum consumption. Less than 40 percent of the crude oil traded in 1984 came from Persian Gulf suppliers. Following the 1985 oil price collapse, the Persian Gulf export percentage again began a gradual increase, but it leveled off in the 1990s at 40 to 45 percent when non-OPEC supply proved to be unexpectedly resilient.
>
> In the *AEO2003* reference case, Persian Gulf producers are expected to account for 45 percent of worldwide trade by 2007—for the first time since the early 1980s. After 2007, the Persian Gulf share of worldwide petroleum exports is projected to increase gradually to 66 percent by 2025. In the low oil price case, the Persian Gulf share of total exports is projected to reach 76 percent by 2025. All Persian Gulf producers are expected to increase oil production capacity significantly over the forecast period, and both Saudi Arabia and Iraq (assuming the lifting of United Nations export sanctions after 2003) are expected to nearly triple their current production capacity.

While estimates of export trends are no more able to predict the future with any precision than estimates of oil production capacity, it is again clear that it would take a massive breakthrough in technology or discoveries of reserves outside the Middle East to change these trends. These totals also understate the true importance of the MENA region because the EIA does not issue an estimate for the entire Middle East or MENA region as distinguished form the Gulf, and OPEC country estimates for the region exclude exports from Oman, Yemen, and the Levant.

THE DIRECTION OF MENA OIL EXPORTS AND ITS IMPORTANCE IN A GLOBAL ECONOMY

Under most conditions, the normal day-to-day destination of MENA oil exports is strategically irrelevant. Oil is a global commodity, which is distributed to meet the needs of a global market based on process bid by importers acting in global competition. With the exception of differences in price because of crude type and transportation costs, all buyers compete equally for the global supply of available exports, and the direction and flow of exports changes according to marginal price relative to demand. As a result, the percentage of oil that flows from the MENA region to the United States under normal market conditions has little strategic or economic importance. If a crisis occurs, or drastic changes take place in prices, and the United States will have to pay the same globally determined price as any other nation, and the source of U.S. imports will change accordingly. Moreover, the United States is required to share all imports with other countries of the Organization of Economic Cooperation and Development (OECD) in a crisis under the monitoring of the International Energy Agency.

Dependence on Indirect Imports

The size of direct imports of petroleum is also only a partial measure of strategic dependence. The U.S. economy is dependent on energy-intensive imports from Asia and other regions, and what comes around must literally go around. While the EIA and IEA do not make estimates of indirect imports of Middle Eastern oil in terms of the energy required to produce the finished goods—the United States imports them from countries that are dependent on Middle Eastern exports—analysts guess that they would add at least 1 MMBD to total U.S. oil imports. To put this figure in perspective, direct U.S. oil imports increased from an annual average of 7.9 MMBD in 1992 to 11.3 MMBD in 2002, and 2.6 MMBD worth of U.S. petroleum imports came directly from the Middle East in 2002.[23] If indirect U.S. imports, in the form of manufactured goods dependent on imports of Middle Eastern oil, were included, the resulting figure might well be 30–40 percent higher than the figure for direct imports.

Dependence on the Flow of Oil to the Global Economy

Moreover, the United States and other industrialized states are increasingly dependent on the health of the global economy. U.S. economic activity and growth are dependent on how well the economies of Europe, Asia, and Latin American function. With the exception of Latin America, Mexico, and Canada, all of America's major trading partners are critically dependent on Middle Eastern oil exports. In 2002, the Middle East and North Africa supplied 5 MMBD of 11.9 MMBD of European imports (42 percent). MENA exporters supplied 4 MMBD of Japanese imports of 5.1 MMBD (79 percent). MENA countries supplied 0.8 MMBD out China's imports of 2.0 MMBD (39 percent and growing steadily in recent years), 0.2 MMBD of Australia's imports of 0.6 MMBD (33 percent), and 6.5 MMBD of some 8.6 MMBD in imports by other Asian and Pacific states (76 percent).[24]

The EIA and IEA project that the global economy will also grow far more dependent on the Middle East and North Africa in the future. The EIA's *International Energy Outlook 2004* projects that North American imports of MENA oil will increase from 3.3 MMBD in 2001 to 6.3 MMBD in

2025—an increase of 91 percent, almost all of which will go to the United States. The increase in exports to Western Europe will be from 4.7 MMBD to 7.6 MMBD, an increase of 62 percent. This assumes major increases in oil exports from the FSU and conservation will limit the scale of European imports from the Middle East. Industrialized Asia—driven by Japan—will increase its imports from 4.1 MMBD to 6 MMBD, or nearly 50 percent. China will increase its imports from 0.9 MMBD to 6 MMBD, or by nearly 570 percent; and Pacific Rim states will increase imports from 5 MMBD to 10.2 MMBD, or by 104 percent.

- Chart 1.16 shows the EIA's estimate of just how critical increases in Gulf exports—only part of the MENA total—will be to the global economy in 2025.
- Table 1.3 shows the EIA's estimate of the shifts in oil exports between 2001 and 2025 in more detail. Showing both the importance of increases to North America and the industrial economies, and the critical importance of such increases in meeting demand from developing economies.
- Chart 1.17 provides similar data in graphic form.

These trends reflect the impact of the high rate of economic development in Asia, the limits to Asian oil reserves, and the fact the Middle East is the most economic supplier. In fact, total Asian imports are projected to increase from 18.2 MMBD in 2001 to 36.2 MMBD in 2025, an increase of nearly 100 percent, almost all of which will go to developing Asian states.[25] Furthermore, the EIA's *Annual Energy Outlook 2004* indicates that the developing countries of Asia will have the largest growth in demand for oil, and this demand will increase at an average rate of 3.0 percent per year.[26]

The trends projected by the IEA are very similar to the trends projected by the EIA. The IEA projects that total interregional trade in oil will increase from 32 MMBD in 2000 to 42 MMBD in 2010 and 66.1 MMBD in 2030, Middle Eastern exports (less North Africa) will increase from 19 MMBD in 2000 to 46 MMBD in 2030. Most of these additional exports will go to Asia, with China emerging as the largest market, followed by India. The rise in U.S. imports will be limited by increased exports from Canada, because of production from tar sands, from Mexico, and from sub-Saharan Africa.[27]

The IEA also provides the longest-term estimate of the share of Middle Eastern exports relative to other regions: It provides estimates to 2030 versus 2025 for the EIA. It estimates the interregional oil trade at 66.1 MMBD in 2030. The Middle East would provide 70 percent of that total. If another 4 MMBD were added for North Africa, the MENA region would provide 76 percent. In contrast, Central Asia and the Caspian would provide 4 MMBD. Russia would provide 5 MMBD, the rest of Africa would provide 4 MMBD, Brazil would provide 0.1 MMBD, and the rest of Latin America would provide 3 MMBD.[28]

Chart 1.16
U.S. Projections of Gulf Petroleum Exports: 2001 versus 2025

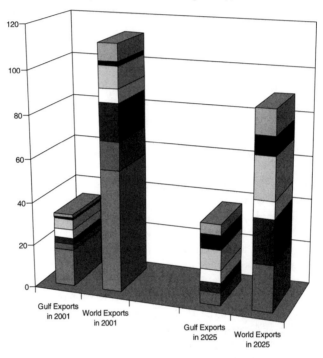

(In Millions of Barrels per Day)

	Gulf Exports in 2001	World Exports in 2001		Gulf Exports in 2025	World Exports in 2025
▨ Rest of World	1.5	7.8		4.9	11.4
■ China	0.9	2		6.6	8.6
▨ Pacific Rim	4.8	10		9.4	19.5
□ Industrial Asia	4.1	6.2		5.9	8.1
■ Western Europe	2.7	17.3		4.5	20.4
■ North America	2.9	13		5.8	21.4
▨ TOTAL	16.9	56.3		*36.4	*89.4

Gulf as % of World   30.1%   40.71%

Source: Adapted by Anthony H. Cordesman from U.S. Department of Energy, *International Energy Outlook 2003*, Washington, DC: Energy Information Administration, March 2003, Table 13, p. 38; and. U.S. Department of Energy, *International Energy Outlook 2003*, Washington, DC: Energy Information Administration, March 2003, Table 14, p. 42.

Chart 1.17
The Rising Importance of Gulf Exports Relative to Other Exports in Meeting World Demand: 2001 versus 2025

(EIA Reference Case in MMBD)

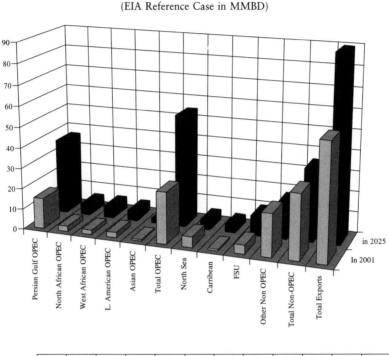

	Persian Gulf OPEC	North African OPEC	West African OPEC	L. American OPEC	Asian OPEC	Total OPEC	North Sea	Carribean	FSU	Other Non OPEC	Total Non-OPEC	Total Exports
In 2001	14.8	2.6	2.2	2.6	0.7	24.9	5.2	0.8	4.5	20.8	31.4	56.3
in 2025	36.4	5.3	5.6	4.9	2.3	54.4	4.7	3.7	9.6	17.1	35	89.4

Source: Adapted by Anthony H. Cordesman from EIA, *International Energy Outlook 2002*, DOE/EIA-0484 (2002), March 2002, Table 11, p. 38; EIA, *International Energy Outlook 2003*, DOE/EIA-0484 (2003), March 2003, Table 14, p. 42; and EIA, *International Energy Outlook 2004*, www.eia.doe.gov/oiaf/ieo/index.html, April 2004, Table 8, p. 40.

Table 1.3
EIA Estimate of Trends in World Oil Exports by Supplier and Destination: 2001–2025 (Millions of Barrels per Day)

| | Importing Region | | | | | | | |
| | Industrialized | | | | Non-Industrialized | | | |
Exporting Region	North America	Western Europe	Asia	Total Industrial	Pacific Rim	China	Rest of World	Total Non-Industrial
2001								
OPEC								
Persian Gulf	2.9	2.7	4.1	9.7	4.8	0.9	1.5	7.2
North Africa	0.4	2.0	0	2.4	0.2	0	0.0	0.2
West Africa	0.9	0.6	0	1.5	0.7	0	0.1	0.8
South America	1.8	0.2	0.2	2.2	0.1	0	0.3	0.4
Asia	0.1	0	0.3	0.4	0.2	0	0	0.2
Total OPEC	6.1	5.5	4.6	16.1	6.0	0.9	1.9	8.8
Non-OPEC								
North Sea	0.6	4.5	0	5.2	0	0	0	0
Caribbean Basin	0.6	0.1	0	0.7	0.1	0	0.1	0.2
FSU	0.2	3.6	0.3	4.2	0.2	0	0.1	0.3
Other Non-OPEC	5.5	3.6	1.2	10.3	3.7	1.1	5.8	11.0
Total Non-OPEC	6.9	11.8	1.6	20.4	4.0	1.1	5.8	11.0
World Total	**13.0**	**17.3**	**6.2**	**36.5**	**10.0**	**2.0**	**7.8**	**19.7**

2025

OPEC								
Persian Gulf	6.3	4.5	5.9	16.3	9.4	5.7	4.9	20.1
North Africa	0.5	3.1	0.1	3.6	0.8	0.3	0.5	1.6
West Africa	1.6	1.1	0.3	2.9	1.9	0.5	0.2	2.6
South America	3.9	0.1	0.4	4.3	0.1	0.0	0.4	0.6
Asia	0.1	0.0	0.3	0.4	1.5	0.1	0.2	1.9
Total OPEC	*11.9*	*8.8*	*6.9*	*27.6*	*13.8*	*6.6*	*6.3*	*26.8*
Non-OPEC								
North Sea	0.7	3.4	0.0	4.2	0.3	0.0	0.2	0.5
Caribbean Basin	1.6	0.5	0.2	2.3	0.6	0.0	0.8	1.4
FSU	0.5	4.7	0.6	5.7	0.7	1.7	1.5	3.8
Other Non-OPEC	6.8	3.0	0.4	10.1	4.2	0.3	2.5	6.9
Total Non-OPEC	*9.5*	*11.6*	*1.2*	*22.3*	*5.7*	*2.0*	*5.0*	*12.7*
World Total	**21.4**	**20.4**	**8.1**	**49.9**	**19.5**	**8.6**	**11.4**	**39.5**

Source: Adapted by Anthony H. Cordesman from estimates in EIA, *International Energy Outlook 2002*, DOE/EIA-0484 (2001), March 2002, Table D1, p. 38; EIA, *International Energy Outlook 2003*, DOE/EIA-0484 (2003), March 2003, Table 14, p. 42; EIA, *International Energy Outlook 2004*, www.eia.doe.gov/oiaf/ieo/index.html, April 2004, Tables 8, p. 40 and D1, p. 38; and EIA, *International Energy Outlook 2003*, DOE/EIA-0484 (2003), March 2003, Table 14, p. 42.

• Chart 1.18 shows the IEA's estimate of the interregional oil trade in 2030. The estimated total of Middle Eastern oil exports is notably higher than the EIA estimate, but the period is five years later, and the IEA estimate covers the entire Middle East and not just Gulf OPEC countries.

CHANGES IN THE NATURE OF PETROLEUM IMPORTS FROM THE MENA REGION

More is involved in analyzing the importance of MENA oil exports than estimating the export of crude oil. The Middle Eastern states and North Africa are steadily attempting to increase profit margins by producing and exporting refined oil products, rather than selling crude. At the same time, some countries—such as the United States—have created major permitting and environmental barriers to creating new refineries. As a result, the nature of Middle East exports will shift sharply from crude oil to product over the coming decades.

Middle Eastern refinery capacity has already increased from 5 MMBD in 1990 (8 percent of world capacity) to 5.9 MMBD in 2000 (7 percent). The IEA projects that it will increase to 10 MMBD in 2010 (11 percent), 12.6 in 2020 (12 percent), and 15.6 in 2030 (13 percent). These figures do not include North Africa because the IEA does not break out its estimates to show the difference between North and sub-Saharan Africa.[29]

The IEA projects that total OECD demand for imports of refined product will increase from 2 percent of total product demand in 2000 to 11 percent by 2030. The IEA also projects that the Middle East (less North Africa) will export some 7 MMBD in refined oil products by 2030, versus 2 MMBD for all of Africa, 3 MMBD for all of the FSU, and 0.2 MMBD for Latin America. By this time, North America (virtually all going to the United States) is projected to import 7 MMBD in refined product, China to import 2 MMBD, and the rest of Asia 3 MMBD.[30]

A shift to product imports does not necessarily alter dependence in strategic terms. It can, however, lead to greater dependence on a given Middle Eastern supplier because a given exporter produces the products given importers need for their economy and industries. It can reduce the flexibility of global markets in substituting for Middle Eastern oil because there may be no source of similar refinery or production capacity that can provide substitutes. A shift to product exports also reduces the total volume of product shipped, although it increases its value, making MMBD a less valid measure of dependence on oil imports.

• Chart 1.19 shows the IEA's estimate of the interregional trade in refined products in 2030. The estimated total for Middle Eastern (less North African) exports approaches 7 MMBD. This is not critical in terms of total world refinery capacity, but will be critical to ensuring the stable flow of refined product at moderate prices.

Chart 1.18
IEA Projection of Interregional Oil Trade in 2030

(in MMBD)

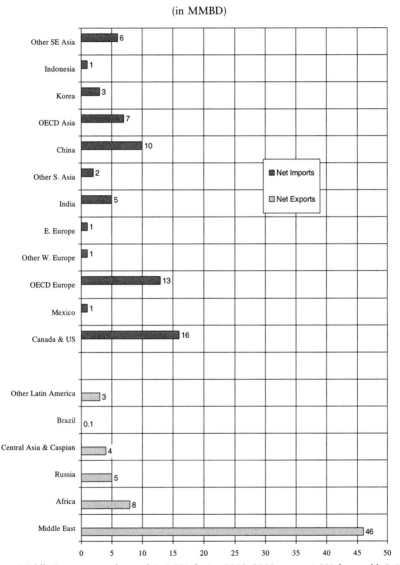

Note: Middle Eastern annual growth is 3.3% during 2000–2030, versus 1.3% for world, 0.6% for OECD North America, 0.4% for OECD Europe.
Source: International Energy Agency (IEA), *World Energy Outlook 2002*, Paris: IEA, 2002, pp. 102–104.

Chart 1.19
IEA Projection of Interregional Trade in Refined Oil Products: 2030

(in MMBD)

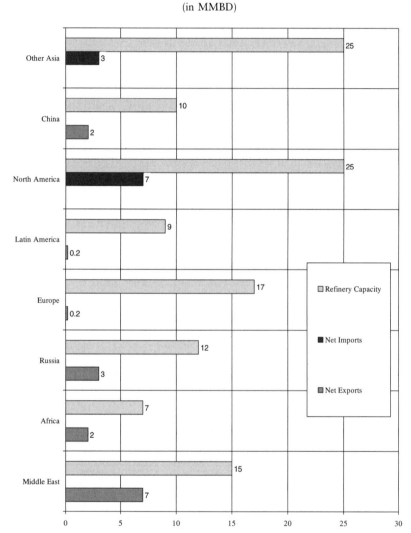

Note: Middle Eastern annual growth is 3.3% during 2000–2030, versus 1.3% for world, 0.6% for OECD North America, 0.4% for OECD Europe.
Source: International Energy Agency (IEA), *World Energy Outlook 2002*, Paris: IEA, 2002, p. 109.

- Chart 1.20 shows how critical financing and executing increases in Middle Eastern (less North African) refinery capacity will be in meeting this future demand.

THE TRENDS IN U.S. PETROLEUM IMPORTS

U.S. oil imports are only a subset of U.S. strategic dependence on Middle East oil exports. As has been noted earlier, the United States is dependent on the overall health of the global economy, and on large amounts of indirect energy imports in the form of manufactured goods from Asia and other nations that are dependent on Middle East oil. The United States must also compete for the global supply of oil exports on market terms in any short-term crisis, or longer-term shortfall in MENA exports, and it is the global supply of oil exports relative to global demand, not where the United States gets oil at any given time, that determines availability and price to the United States as well as all other importing nations.

These realities are reflected in the past patterns of U.S. dependence on oil imports from the Middle East. The EIA reports wide fluctuations in U.S. oil imports over time. If one looks only at total U.S. imports of crude oil, imports from all sources reached 3.2 MMBD in 1973. They rose to a temporary peak of 6.6 MMBD in 1979, and then slowly declined until 1985, when they reached 3.2 MMBD. They then rose consistently, reaching 5.1 MMBD in 1988, 6.1 MMBD in 1992, 7.1 MMBD in 1994, 8.2 MMBD in 1997, 9.1 MMBD in 2000, and 9.6 MMBD in 2003.[31]

Imports include product as well as crude oil, however; and if both crude oil and product are counted, U.S. net imports were 6 MMBD in 1973, rising to 8.6 MMBD in 1977, and then dropping to 4.3 MMBD in 1984. They then rose to 5.4 MMBD in 1986, 6.5 MMBD in 1988, 7.2 MMBD in 1989, 8.1 MMBD in 1994, 9.1 MMBD in 1997, 10.4 MMBD in 2000, and averaged over 10.5 MMBD in 2001–2003.[32] It should be noted that some estimates of import dependence only count crude—a method that has little meaning in real-world economic terms.

The EIA does not report on U.S. dependence on crude oil and product imports from the Middle East per se, or from the entire MENA region. It does, however, measure U.S. dependence on imports from the Gulf—which dominate the vast majority of U.S. imports from the MENA area.

The share Persian Gulf imports have of the U.S. market at any given time is determined not by the price of crude in some abstract sense, but rather by the real-world market value of a given type of oil or product from a given exporter delivered to the U.S. market versus the same or similar crude or product delivered from any other source. In practice, even the smallest price differential—some times a few cents per barrel—leads a U.S. importer to buy from the Middle East, Africa, or any other source.

Chart 1.20
IEA Projection of Middle Eastern Growth in Crude Oil Distillation Capacity:
1990–2025

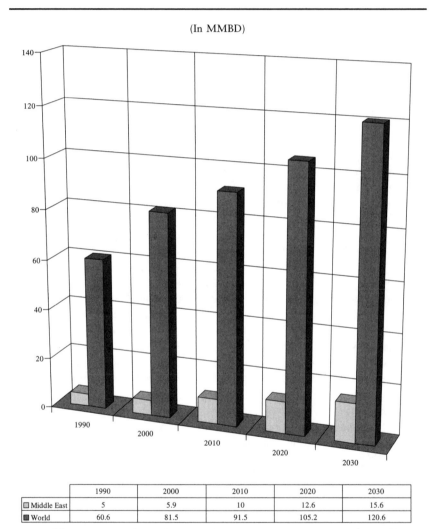

(In MMBD)

	1990	2000	2010	2020	2030
▢ Middle East	5	5.9	10	12.6	15.6
■ World	60.6	81.5	91.5	105.2	120.6

Note: Middle Eastern annual growth is 3.3% during 2000–2030, versus 1.3% for world, 0.6% for OECD North America, 0.4% for OECD Europe.

Source: International Energy Agency (IEA), *World Energy Outlook 2002*, Paris: IEA, 2002, pp. 102–104.

It should not be surprising, therefore, that the patterns in U.S. imports from the Persian Gulf (Bahrain, Iran, Iraq, Kuwait, Qatar, Saudi Arabia, and the UAE) do not reflect the same pattern as total U.S. oil imports, particularly as Asian demand leads Asian countries to take advantage of the lower shipping costs from the Middle East, and the United States seeks oil with lower transportation costs from Africa and Latin America. According to the EIA, U.S. petroleum imports (crude oil, lease condensate, unfinished oils, petroleum products, natural gas plant liquids, and hydrocarbon compounds blended into finished products) from the Persian Gulf have fluctuated as follows over time:[33]

- U.S. imports from the Gulf totaled 0.85 MMBD in 1973. They were 4.8 percent of total products supplied, and 13.6 percent of total imports.

- U.S. imports from the Gulf rose steadily during 1974–1977. They totaled 2.44 MMBD in 1977. They then were 13.3 percent of total products supplied, and 27.8 percent of total imports.

- U.S. imports from the Persian Gulf declined steadily after that time from 1978 to 1983. They totaled 1.5 MMBD in 1980, 1.2 MMBD in 1981, and then dropped sharply to 0.7 MMBD in 1982. They reached a low of 0.442 MMBD in 1982. They then were 2.9 percent of total products supplied, and 8.8 percent of total imports. They "bottomed out" at only 0.311 MMBD in 1985, with 2 percent of product and 6.1 percent of total imports.

- Changes in Saudi and OPEC price strategy in 1986 led to an increase in U.S. imports from the Gulf to 0.91 MMBD in 1986, 1.1 MMBD in 1987, and 1.87 MMBD in 1989. They were 10.7 percent of total product imports and 23.1 percent of total U.S. imports in 1989.

- U.S. imports from the Gulf fluctuated from 1.57 MMBD to 1.8 MMBD during 1990–1997, and ranged from 8.8 to 11 percent of total products supplied, and from 16.9 to 24.5 percent of total imports.

- From 1998 onward, U.S. imports from the Gulf have been above 2 MMBD, reaching 2.1 MMBD in 1998, 2.5 MMBD in 1999, 2.5 MMBD in 2000, 2.8 MMBD in 2001, 2.3 MMBD in 2002, and averaging 2.8 MMBD in 2003. They totaled 2.44 MMBD in 1977. They have ranged from 11.5 to 14.1 percent of total products supplied, and from 19.7 to 23.5 percent of total imports.

Once again, it must be stressed that such shifts in the source of U.S. exports reflect the volatility of transportation costs, world demand and supply, and small margins of difference in the delivered price of oil and product. Moreover, market-driven patterns apply only as long as no major interruption takes place in the exports of given regions and states, and that it is the trend in both total global export, and in total U.S. imports from all sources, that counts in terms of strategic dependence.

It is important to note in this regard that neither the Bush energy policy nor any recent congressional energy bills is projected to have any meaningful strategic impact on U.S. import dependence if it is ever passed into law and transformed into action. It takes massive shifts in U.S. energy consumption and supply over extended periods of time to accomplish this and there are good reasons that both the Bush administration and congressional advocates of different policies either have failed to make meaningful analysis of the impact of their proposals on U.S. import dependence or have provided "blue sky" estimates that are little more than intellectual rubbish.

If one turns to the EIA estimates made since the Bush administration came to office, it is clear that realistic models of U.S. energy needs will lead to steady increases in U.S. energy imports, although no one can predict the exact trends. In the short term, the EIA predicts that total U.S. petroleum imports were 10.9 MMBD in 2001 and 10.54 MMBD in 2002, and will reach 11 MMBD in 2003 and 11.3 MMBD in 2004. Largely because of a dip in U.S. economic activity, U.S. imports dropped by 3.3 percent during 2001–2002, but they are projected to rise by 3.8 percent in 2002–2003 and by 3.3 percent in 2003–2004.[34]

What is most important, however, is the mid- and long-term picture where temporary economic conditions have less impact, and trends tend to be more consistent over time. The EIA's *Annual Energy Forecast 2003* reports that net imports of petroleum accounted for 55 percent of domestic petroleum consumption in 2001. U.S. dependence on petroleum imports is projected to reach 68 percent in 2025 in the reference case. This is a rise in U.S. net imports from 10.9 MMBD in 2021 to 19.8 MMBD in the reference case (+82 percent). In the low oil price case, net imports would rise to 21.1 MMBD. They would be 18.2 MMBD in the high oil price case, 17.8 MMBD in the low economic growth case, and 22.3 MMBD in the high economic growth case.[35]

The EIA's annual forecast for 2004 predicts that imports will be even higher. It reports that net imports of petroleum accounted 53 percent of domestic petroleum consumption in 2002. U.S. dependence on petroleum imports is estimated to reach 70 percent in 2025 in the reference case, versus 68 percent in the 2003 forecast. Imports are expected to be 65 percent of total consumption. In the low oil price case this number is estimated to be 75 percent.[36] (The *AEO2003* report indicated that estimated imports as a share of total oil consumption would be 65 percent in high price case in 2025, and 70 percent in the low price case.)

The share of U.S. imports as a share of total consumption is expected to range from 65 percent in the high oil price case and 70 percent in the low oil price case by 2025. Crude oil is expected to continue as the major component of petroleum imports, but refined products are projected to growing as a share of total imports because the projected growth in demand for refined products will exceed the expansion of U.S. domestic refining capacity. The EIA projects that refined products will increase from a 15 percent share of imports in 2001 to 34 percent in 2025 in the reference case, with 27 percent of net petroleum imports in 2025 in the low economic growth case and 39 percent in the high growth case.[37] In practice, this would mean that U.S. imports of petroleum product would rise from 1.6 MMBD in 2021 to 6.7 MMBD in the reference case (+82 percent). In the low oil price case, net imports would rise to 7.1 MMBD. They would be 5.7 MMBD in the high oil price case, 4.8 MMBD in the low economic growth case, and 8.6 MMBD in the high economic growth case.[38]

Once again, the EIA does not estimate the share that MENA countries will provide of these U.S. imports. Its forecast does indicate, however, that the share of U.S. imports from OPEC countries will increase substantially during 2003–2025. As for other sources of imports, the EIA indicates that:[39]

[c]rude oil imports from the North Sea are projected to increase slightly through 2007, but decline gradually as the United Kingdom's North Sea production ebbs. Significant imports of petroleum from Canada and Mexico are expected to continue, while West Coast refiners are expected to import crude oil from the Far East to replace the declining production of Alaskan crude oil. Imports of light products are expected to more than triple by 2025, to 5.3 million barrels per day. Most of the projected increase is from refiners in the Caribbean Basin, North Africa, and the Middle East, where refining capacity is expected to expand significantly. Vigorous growth in demand for lighter petroleum products in developing countries means that U.S. refiners are likely to import smaller volumes of light, low-sulfur crude oils.

It should be stressed that these projections of a growth in imports are based on overall estimates of the trends in U.S. energy supply and demand that include relatively high estimates of U.S. domestic oil and gas production, nuclear power, coal use, increases in energy efficiency, increases in renewable energy, and increases in the domestic production of ethanol. They are conservative in nature, and may well underestimate the need for imports.

- Chart 1.21 shows the EIA estimate of the rise in U.S. imports since 1973, and the estimated level of U.S. imports in 2025, depending on different economic conditions.

THE IMPORTANCE OF MENA GAS, RESOURCES, AND EXPORTS

At present, Middle Eastern gas reserves are more important as a means of meeting local energy needs and reducing domestic MENA consumption of crude oil, than as a source of global energy exports. This may change in the future, however, as world demand for gas rises, and gas is used more often to provide the raw material for gas-based petrochemicals. The EIA estimates that global demand for natural gas has increased from 36 trillion cubic feet (TCF) in 1970 to 53 TCF in 1980, 73 TCF in 1990, and 87

Chart 1.21
EIA Estimate of Trend in U.S. Oil Imports

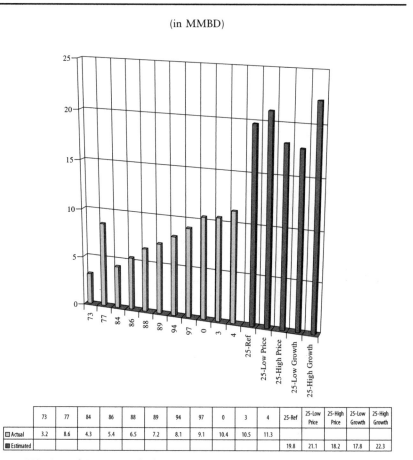

(in MMBD)

	73	77	84	86	88	89	94	97	0	3	4	25-Ref	25-Low Price	25-High Price	25-Low Growth	25-High Growth
☐ Actual	3.2	8.6	4.3	5.4	6.5	7.2	8.1	9.1	10.4	10.5	11.3					
■ Estimated													19.8	21.1	18.2	17.8	22.3

Source: EIA, *Annual Energy Outlook, 2003*, pp. 80–84.

TCF in 2000 to 90 TCF in 2001. It is projected to rise to 151 TCF in 2025, nearly 70 percent higher than 2001.[40]

MENA Gas Reserves

The Middle East and North Africa now have a total of 40.8 percent of the world's proven gas reserves (36 percent in the Middle East and the rest in Algeria, Egypt, and Libya). These MENA reserves have more than doubled since 1982, and increased from 26 trillion cubic meters (TCM) in

1982, to 49 TCM in 1992, and to 63 TCM (2,244 TCF) in 2002.[41] They did so in spite of major limitations in oil and gas exploration and development because of war and internal conflict in such critical states as Algeria, Iran, Iraq, and Libya. EIA estimates that the Middle East production of natural gas will be 18.8 TCF in 2025.[42]

There is no firm consensus as to how to estimate proven gas reserves. Many MENA countries are just beginning to make serious efforts to fully characterize their gas reserves, and have little experience with the costs of real-world development of massive gas production efforts and the necessary distribution systems. Estimates of proven gas reserves are significantly more controversial than estimates of proven oil reserves, and estimates of potential and undiscovered reserves are too uncertain to be used for the purposes of this analysis.

It is clear from virtually all sources, however, that several MENA states have a large share of the world's reserves. According to both the EIA and BP. Bahrain has 0.90 TCM (3.3 TCF) or 0.1 percent of the world total, Iran has 23 TCM (812.3 TCF) or 14.8 percent, Oman has 0.83 TCM (29.35 TCF) or 0.5 percent, Qatar has 14.4 TCM (508.5 TCF) or 9.2 percent, Saudi Arabia 6.4 TCM (224.7 TCF) or 4.1 percent, the UAE has 6.01 TCM (212.1 TCF) or 3.9 percent, Iraq has 3.1 TCM (109.83 TCF) or 2.0 percent, and Yemen has 0.48 TCM (16.9 TCF) or 0.3 percent.[43]

Syria has 0.24 TCM (8.5 TCF) or 0.2 percent and the rest of the Middle East has 0.05 TCM (1.65 TCF). In North Africa, Algeria has 4.52 TCM (159.7 TCF) or 2.9 percent, Egypt has 1.66 TCM (58.5 TCF) or 1.1 percent, and Libya has 1.31 TCM (46.4 TCF) or 0.8 percent.[44]

- Table 1.4 shows the BP estimate of Middle Eastern gas reserves and their share of the world total. As well as of world production in 2000. It indicates that MENA countries have some 40 percent of all world reserves.
- Chart 1.22 shows the recent trend in estimates of MENA gas reserves and the growth in estimates of the resources of many countries.
- Chart 1.23 shows how MENA gas reserves are distributed by country and how they compare to the reserves in states outside the region.
- Chart 1.24 shows how proven MENA reserves compare to probable total world reserves. The Middle East's share is smaller, but still extremely significant.

The EIA and IEA do not provide detailed projections of probable discoveries of new gas reserves by country, but many Middle Eastern states have only begun to fully explore their gas reserves, and most are likely to make major additional discoveries. The EIA also does indicate that total global reserves now total 5,501 TCF and undiscovered reserves total another 4,839 TCF—almost all in the developing world. If these estimates are right, the Middle East and North Africa have another 20–25 percent of the world's undiscovered reserves. Some 2,347 TCF in reserves are expected to

Table 1.4
MENA and World Gas Reserves and Production

Nation	Reserves in 2000		Percent of World Reserves	Production in 2000 (% of World)
	TCM	TCF		
Bahrain	0.09	3.3	0.1	0.4
Iran	23.00	812.3	14.6	2.65
Iraq	3.11	109.8	2.0	0.3
Kuwait	1.49	52.7	1.0	0.6
Oman	0.82	29.3	0.5	0.4
Qatar	14.40	508.5	9.2	1.2
Saudi Arabia	6.36	224.7	4.1	2.2
Syria	0.24	8.5	0.2	0.2
UAE	6.01	212.1	3.9	1.8
Yemen	0.48	16.9	0.3	—
Other	0.05	1.6	—	0.1
Total Middle East	**56.06**	**1,979.7**	**36.0**	**9.3**
Algeria	4.52	159.7	2.9	3.2
Egypt	1.66	58.5	1.1	0.9
Libya	1.31	46.4	0.8	0.2
Total MENA			**40.8**	**12.7**
Russia	47.57	1680.0	30.5	22.0
U.S.	5.19	183.5	3.3	21.7
EU	3.14	111.0	2.0	8.3
Asia/Pacific				11.9
World Total	**155.78**	**5501.5**	**100**	**100**

Source: The reserve and production data are adapted by Anthony H. Cordesman from British Petroleum, *BP Statistical Review of World Energy, 2003*, London: 2003, pp. 20–23.

be discovered during 2000–2025, and more than one-half is estimated to be found in the FSU and MENA areas.[45]

IEA estimates that the Middle East has 34 percent of the world's remaining reserves and probably has at least 19 percent of its undiscovered reserves.[46] CEDIGAZ, a respected source of energy estimates, indicates that the Middle East has 53.9 TCM of proven gas reserves, and some 115–136 TCM of the world's ultimate reserves are in the Middle East. This is 34 percent of the worlds proven reserves, and 25.4–25.8 percent of its undiscovered reserves.[47]

Chart 1.22
Total Proven Gas Reserves of the MENA States, 1979–2002: BP Estimate

(In Trillions of Cubic Meters)

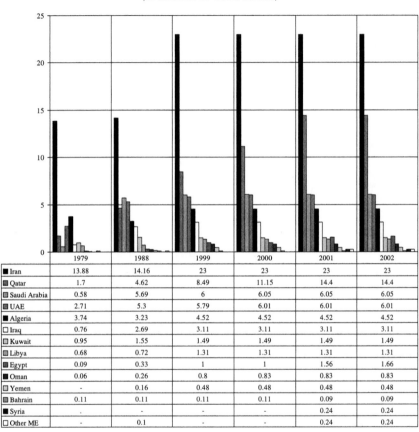

	1979	1988	1999	2000	2001	2002
■ Iran	13.88	14.16	23	23	23	23
▨ Qatar	1.7	4.62	8.49	11.15	14.4	14.4
▨ Saudi Arabia	0.58	5.69	6	6.05	6.05	6.05
▨ UAE	2.71	5.3	5.79	6.01	6.01	6.01
■ Algeria	3.74	3.23	4.52	4.52	4.52	4.52
☐ Iraq	0.76	2.69	3.11	3.11	3.11	3.11
▨ Kuwait	0.95	1.55	1.49	1.49	1.49	1.49
▨ Libya	0.68	0.72	1.31	1.31	1.31	1.31
■ Egypt	0.09	0.33	1	1	1.56	1.66
■ Oman	0.06	0.26	0.8	0.83	0.83	0.83
☐ Yemen	-	0.16	0.48	0.48	0.48	0.48
▨ Bahrain	0.11	0.11	0.11	0.11	0.09	0.09
■ Syria	.	-	-	-	0.24	0.24
☐ Other ME	-	0.1	-	-	0.24	0.24

Source: British Petroleum, *BP Statistical Review of World Energy 2001*, London: 2001, pp. 20–21, and *BP Statistical Review of World Energy 2003*, London: 2003, p. 20.

In contrast, the United States is one of the world's largest gas consumers, but is estimated to have less than 10 percent of the world's remaining reserves. It will become steadily more dependent on imports—largely from Canada and Mexico. Europe is one of the fastest growing consumers of gas, but is depleting its reserves and will become steadily more dependent on imports from the FSU and MENA. Some sources indicate that Europe will have to import 60 percent of its natural gas by 2020.[48] Japan and most developing Asian states have little or no significant reserves.

Chart 1.23
Key Nations in Percent of Total Proven World Gas Reserves in 2002

(Quantity in Trillion Cubic Meters; Percent is Percent of Total World Reserves)

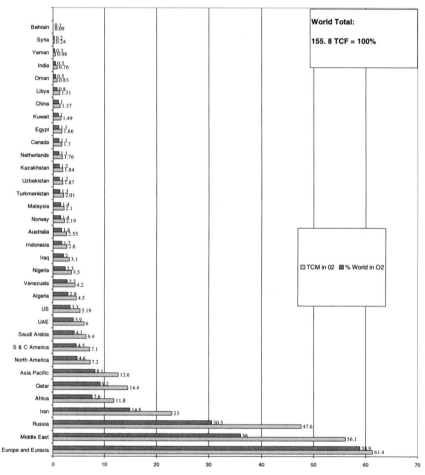

Source: British Petroleum, *BP Statistical Review of World Energy 2003*, London: 2003, p. 20.

MENA Gas Consumption and Oil Exports

The importance of MENA gas reserves is illustrated in part by their ability to limit the growth of Middle Eastern consumption of crude oil. During the decade between 1992 and 2002, regional consumption increased from roughly 1 MMBD to 1.3 MMBD, although this still left the Middle

Chart 1.24
IEA Projection of Remaining Proven Natural Gas Reserves and Total Resources

(In Trillions of Cubic Meters)

Reserves = 165 TCM

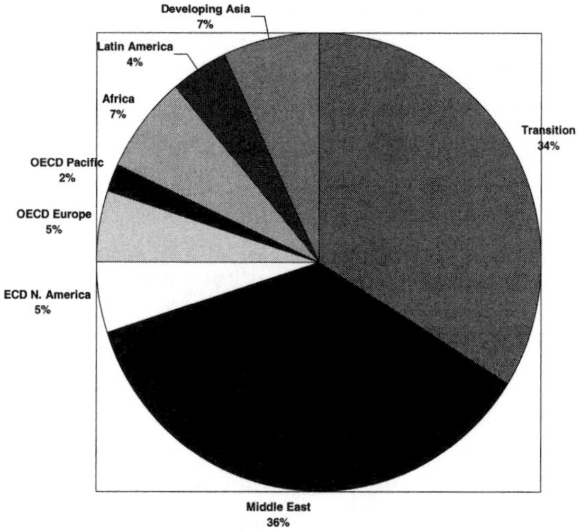

Developing Asia
7%
Latin America
4%
Africa
7%
OECD Pacific
2%
OECD Europe
5%
ECD N. America
5%
Transition
34%
Middle East
36%

Resources = 500 TCM

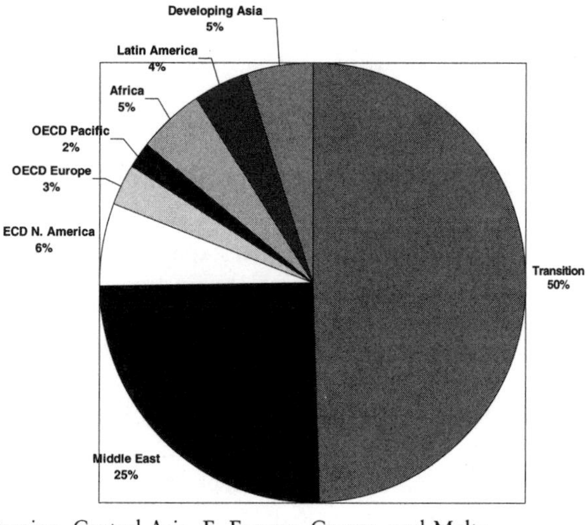

Developing Asia
5%
Latin America
4%
Africa
5%
OECD Pacific
2%
OECD Europe
3%
ECD N. America
6%
Transition
50%
Middle East
25%

Note: Transition = Russia, Caspian, Central Asia, E. Europe, Cyprus, and Malta.
Source: International Energy Agency (IEA), *World Energy Outlook 2002*, Paris: IEA, 2002, p. 114.

East consuming only 5.9 percent of the world's use of oil. North African consumption increased from 0.67 MMBD to 0.77 MMBD.[49] This consumption of oil would have been far greater if Middle East oil exporters had not steadily increased their use of local gas as a substitute for oil. Middle Eastern states increased their use of natural gas from 110.6 BCM in 1992 to 205.7 BCM in 1992, and this increase was driven by the creation of more effective national gas distribution systems in key exporters like Iran, Kuwait, and Saudi Arabia.[50] Similarly, key North African states like Algeria and Egypt increased their use of national gas from 29.1 BCM in 1982 to 47.4 BCM in 2002.

Current plans call for major further increases in domestic use of gas in most of the Gulf states. The IEA also projects that total Middle East use of gas will increase from 3.6 TCF in 1990, and 6.8 TCF in 2000, to 8.8 TCF in 2010, 11.1 TCF in 2020, and 13.9 TCF in 2025. This is an average annual increase in consumption of 2.3 percent.[51] In contrast, the EIA projects that MENA will increase domestic oil consumption from 3.4 MMBD in 1990 and 5.2 MMBD in 2000 to 5.2 MMBD in 2010, 6.7 MMBD in 2020, and 7.6 MMBD in 2025.[52] This is an average annual increase in consumption of 2 percent, and would be at least 4 percent higher without regional domestic use of gas.

- Chart 1.25 shows the steady increase in MENA gas production in recent years.
- Chart 1.26 shows how critical gas is to future MENA energy needs and to allowing the Middle East to maximize oil exports.

MENA Gas Exports

An analysis of the MENA region's role in gas exports is more speculative than an analysis of its role in oil exports. While the MENA area has long exported some gas, gas exports are just beginning to become a major part of world energy exports and projections must be based on highly uncertain data as to future export capacity, future demand, and future price. The EIA and IEA do, however, project world demand for gas as one of the most rapidly growing areas of energy demand.

The reference case of the EIA projects that world use of gas will rise from 75 TCF in 1990, 91.4 TCF in 2000, and 93.1 TCF in 2001, to 108.5 TCF in 2010, 1138.8 TCF in 2020, and 156.5 TCF in 2025. This is an average annual increase in consumption of 2.2 percent versus 1.9 percent for oil.[53] Much of this increase will be met by an increase in domestic production or by major increases in exports from the FSU.

The United States may well, however, have to make major increases in gas imports by ship, Korea and Japan already rely heavily on tankers to deliver MENA gas exports, and total developing Asian nation consumption is projected to rise from 3.0 TCF in 1990 and 6.6 TCF in 2000, to 10.4 TCF in

Chart 1.25
MENA Natural Gas Production by Country: 1992–2002

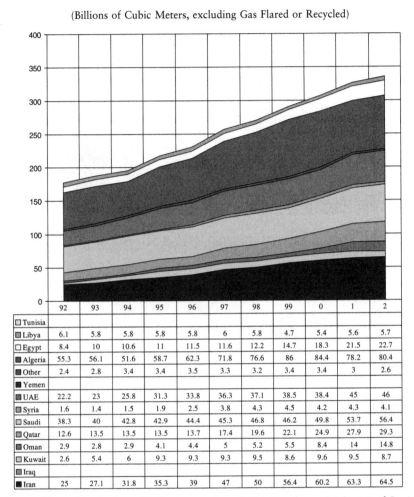

(Billions of Cubic Meters, excluding Gas Flared or Recycled)

	92	93	94	95	96	97	98	99	0	1	2
☐ Tunisia											
■ Libya	6.1	5.8	5.8	5.8	5.8	6	5.8	4.7	5.4	5.6	5.7
☐ Egypt	8.4	10	10.6	11	11.5	11.6	12.2	14.7	18.3	21.5	22.7
■ Algeria	55.3	56.1	51.6	58.7	62.3	71.8	76.6	86	84.4	78.2	80.4
■ Other	2.4	2.8	3.4	3.4	3.5	3.3	3.2	3.4	3.4	3	2.6
■ Yemen											
■ UAE	22.2	23	25.8	31.3	33.8	36.3	37.1	38.5	38.4	45	46
■ Syria	1.6	1.4	1.5	1.9	2.5	3.8	4.3	4.5	4.2	4.3	4.1
☐ Saudi	38.3	40	42.8	42.9	44.4	45.3	46.8	46.2	49.8	53.7	56.4
■ Qatar	12.6	13.5	13.5	13.5	13.7	17.4	19.6	22.1	24.9	27.9	29.3
■ Oman	2.9	2.8	2.9	4.1	4.4	5	5.2	5.5	8.4	14	14.8
☐ Kuwait	2.6	5.4	6	9.3	9.3	9.3	9.5	8.6	9.6	9.5	8.7
■ Iraq											
■ Iran	25	27.1	31.8	35.3	39	47	50	56.4	60.2	63.3	64.5

Source: Adapted by Anthony H. Cordesman from British Petroleum, *BP Statistical Review of World Energy 2001*, London: 2003, p. 22.

2010, 17.7 TCF in 2020, and 2.16 TCF in 2025. This is an average annual increase in consumption of 4.5 percent and much of it will have to come from the MENA area.[54] The projections of the IEA are somewhat different, but estimate a 2.1 percent annual average increase in OECD Europe consumption between 2000 and 2030, a 2.3 percent average increase in OECD Asia, and a 5.5 percent average annual increase in China, a 3.7 percent increase in East Asia, and a 4.7 percent increase in South Asia.[55]

Chart 1.26
Diversification of MENA Energy Consumption: 1990–2025

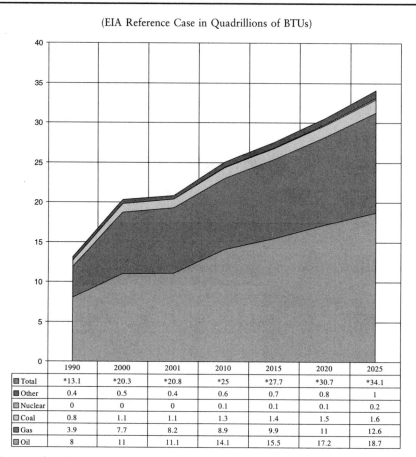

(EIA Reference Case in Quadrillions of BTUs)

	1990	2000	2001	2010	2015	2020	2025
■ Total	*13.1	*20.3	*20.8	*25	*27.7	*30.7	*34.1
■ Other	0.4	0.5	0.4	0.6	0.7	0.8	1
■ Nuclear	0	0	0	0.1	0.1	0.1	0.2
□ Coal	0.8	1.1	1.1	1.3	1.4	1.5	1.6
■ Gas	3.9	7.7	8.2	8.9	9.9	11	12.6
□ Oil	8	11	11.1	14.1	15.5	17.2	18.7

Source: Adapted by Anthony H. Cordesman from EIA, *International Energy Outlook 2002*, DOE/EIAA4 D1; and EIA, *International Energy Outlook 2004*, www.eia.doe.gov/oiaf/ieo/ index.html, April 2004, Table A.2, p. 165.

At present, MENA gas production lags far behind the level of production by the FSU and Eastern Europe. The MENA region has one-third of their total production, although the MENA region has slightly larger total gas reserves. All Gulf gas exports are also in the form of liquefied natural gas (LNG), although Iran is exploring shipping gas to Europe by pipeline through Turkey, and several Gulf states have considered pipelines through the Indian Ocean, Pakistan, or to India across Afghanistan. Qatar has much larger gas reserves than oil reserves, and has aggressively expanded its LNG facilities. It is seeking to triple its LNG capacity to 45 million metric tons per year by

2010, plus new gas-to-liquid plants, and is a key force behind the creation of the first long distance pipeline to serve customers in the Gulf area—the Dolphin project. (The UAE's production of gas is largely associated gas and is limited by oil production, and its consumption of gas is outstripping supply.)[56] Saudi Arabia has planned a massive new Gas Initiative, and while its efforts to find foreign investment have been delayed and scaled-back, it too is likely to become a major exporter over the coming years.

The situation is somewhat different outside the Gulf. Algeria is already the second largest LNG producer in the world, and has significant exports by pipeline. It is Western Europe's second largest supplier of exports and delivers supplies by pipeline to Italy, Spain, and Portugal, and by LNG tanker to France, Spain, Italy, Belgium, Greece, and Portugal. Algeria is seeking to add a new 4 million metric ton LNG train to its production, and is trying to diversify exports to new markets in the United States. It exports about 0.8 TCF via the Transmed pipeline through Tunisia to Italy, and Algeria and Italy are exploring the possibility of a new pipeline through Sardinia and Corsica. Another "Medgaz" pipeline may be built to Spain, with a capacity growing from 0.3 to 0.6 TCF. Egypt is creating gas trains to export to France and Spain, and Libya is planning to increase its export capability by building a pipeline from Melita to Sicily with a capacity of 0.3 TCF.[57]

The IEA does project a massive increase in world dependence on gas imports. It is projects an increase in Middle Eastern exports from 23 BCM in 2000 to 365 BCM in 2030.[58] While it is careful to qualify the major uncertainties involved, the IEA projects that interregional flows from the Middle East will increase as follows between 2000 and 2030: 1.7 BCM to 104 BCM to North America, 0.4 BCM to 160 BCM to Europe, 0 BCM to 27 BCM to South Asia, 21 to 60 BCM to Japan and Korea, and 0 to 13 BCM to China. To put these estimates in perspective, they do not include North Africa, because the IEA only provides totals for all of Africa. If only total Middle Eastern exports are included, however, they will increase fifteen-fold from 23.1 billion cubic feet (BCF) in 2000 to 351 BCF in 2030. In comparison, the FSU's gas exports will increase 2.5 times from 112 BCF in 2000 to 277 BCF in 2030.[59]

- Chart 1.27 shows the IEA estimate of massive increases in global gas imports between 2000 and 2030.

- Chart 1.28 shows how critical Middle Eastern exports will be to meeting this demand.

DEALING WITH AN UNCERTAIN FUTURE

Details and facts often seem boring. So do statistics and tables, and the results of complex models. The moment one actually looks in detail at the

Chart 1.27
IEA Estimate of World Gas Import Dependence: 2000–2030

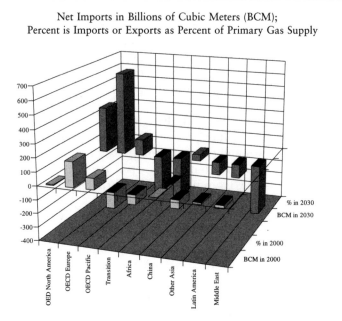

Net Imports in Billions of Cubic Meters (BCM);
Percent is Imports or Exports as Percent of Primary Gas Supply

	OED North America	OECD Europe	OECD Pacific	Transition	Africa	China	Other Asia	Latin America	Middle East
BCM in 2000	5	186	83	-112	-69	0	-60	-10	-23
% in 2000	* 1	* 36	* 67	* -18	* -130	0	* -36	* -9	* -11%
.									
BCM in 2030	345	625	121	-277	-299	47	-94	-103	-365
% in 2030	* 26	* 63	* 50	* -29	* -125	* 29	* -19	* -28	* -85

Note: Transition Economics include Russia, other nations of FSU including Central Asia and
  Caspian, Baltic nations, Eastern Europe, Balkan states, Cyprus, Gibraltar, and Malta.
Source: Adapted by Anthony H. Cordesman from IEA, *World Energy Outlook 2002*, Paris:
  International Energy Agency, 2002, p. 117.

numbers projected by the most respected sources of energy data and future
estimates, however, it becomes clear that such details really count. Such
estimates and models make it clear that there are no near or midterm developments in the real world that will reduce a growing global dependence
on Middle Eastern energy exports, or the world's dependence on the ability and willingness of the Middle East to increase its energy production and
export capability.

Time and technology will almost certainly change this situation, but not
in a few years or even a few decades—barring some massive, unanticipated

Chart 1.28
IEA Projection of Interregional Gas Trade in 2030

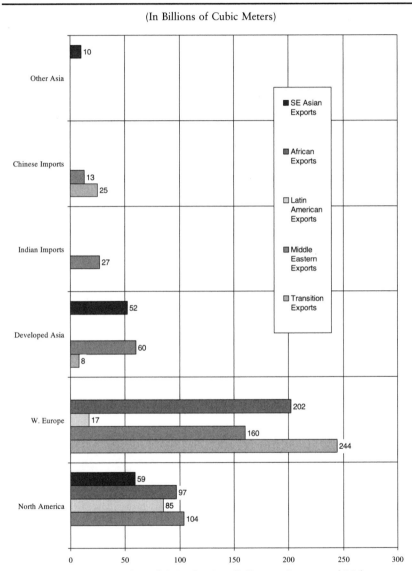

(In Billions of Cubic Meters)

Note: Transition = Russia, Central Asia, Caspian, E. Europe, Cyprus, and Malta.
Source: International Energy Agency (IEA), *World Energy Outlook 2002*, Paris: IEA, 2002, p. 119.

breakthrough in alternative energy supplies. In fact, even if dramatic changes did take place in the cost alternative energy supplies, it might well take a decade for such changes to really have a decisive global impact. The world has simply invested too much in vehicles, facilities, homes, and industrial processes that use oil, and few breakthroughs could take the form of supplies that could be cheaply and quickly produced on a global basis.

These realities may not be apparent when the numbers that lie behind global energy balances are ignored, or when policymakers and analysts look at only part of the problem—such as the size of today's direct U.S. imports of crude oil from the Middle East. It is clear from the previous analysis, however, that the real world is far more complicated and that any honest analysis must reflect that complexity. It should be equally clear that major changes in the future projected by groups like the IEA and EIA might change the numbers, but are unlikely to change the broad trend in ways that radically affect the pattern of world energy consumption, world energy exports, or global dependence on the Middle East.

Chapter 2

The Geopolitics and Security Dimension of Middle Eastern and North African Energy Exports

The many uncertainties affecting the international energy market, the discovery and exploitation of energy reserves, and the competition between fuels are only part of the forces shaping Middle East energy supply. The analysis in the preceding chapter discussed estimates that assume that market forces will dominate the future development of energy exports in the Middle East and North Africa. The Middle East and North Africa (MENA) as a region, however, has been the scene of many internal crises and external conflicts. There have been several past occasions on which these crises have affected both the flow of MENA energy exports, and the development of Middle Eastern energy production and export capacity.

The MENA region is anything but stable today, and there are a wide range of external and internal forces that may become major future threats to Middle Eastern energy exports. The politics, economics, and social dynamics that shape these threats are complex. They are driven by political and security issues, but they are also driven economic and demographic factors, and a wide range of cultural factors. It is also dangerous to generalize. The MENA area includes at least twenty-two nations, located in an arc that sweeps from North Africa to the edge of Central Asia and the Red Sea. As of 2000, these states had a total population of some 295 million, and a gross national product (GNP) of some $651 billion, and each had different political, economic, demographic, and security conditions and needs.[1]

Most MENA states are Arab and Muslim, but a common ethnic and religious background has never meant that they do not go to war with each other or do not have internal sectarian, ethnic, and political conflicts. The MENA region is also divided into at least four subregions, each of whose nations have different interests and present different risks. These four subregions include the Maghreb, with Mauritania, Morocco, Algeria, Libya, and Tunisia; the Levant and the Arab-Israeli confrontation states: Egypt, Israel, Jordan, Lebanon, and Syria; the Gulf: Iran, Iraq, Kuwait, Bahrain, Qatar, Saudi Arabia, the United Arab Emirates (UAE), and Oman; and the Red Sea states like Yemen, the Sudan, and Somalia.

Each subregion includes states that have been the source of recent terrorism or conflicts, although many states have been comparatively stable and have regimes with a long history of friendship to the West. The economics of every MENA state relies on strong trading partners outside of the region, and these links also differ by subregion and nation. The nations of North Africa are linked closely to southern Europe, and also have ties to the sub-Saharan states. The states of the Levant trade primarily with Europe and the United States. The Southern Gulf states trade with the West and increasingly with Asia and the developing world. Iran is in many ways a Central Asian state that exports through the Gulf. It has good reason to be deeply concerned about security issues in Afghanistan and proliferation in India and Pakistan.

Treating the Middle East as a "region," rather than as a group of disparate actors, often conceals far more than it reveals. The future development of energy supply in each nation and subregion will be affected by exporting different political, security, ethnic, and sectarian fault lines. The internal character and strategic interests of given nations differ sharply from state to state. In many cases, regional or national tensions have already led to war or could lead to future conflicts. In other cases, internal tensions have already produced civil conflicts. Violent religious extremism is an ongoing problem in many MENA countries, and the events of September 11, 2001, have only dramatized internal security problems and terrorism on global level that long existed on a national and regional level.

A HISTORY OF CONFLICT AND TENSION

MENA nations have a long history of violence and conflict. The Arab-Israeli wars of 1948, 1956, 1967, 1970, 1973, 1982, and the first and second intifadas are all cases in point. So are the Iran-Iraq War, the Iraqi invasion of Kuwait, the Gulf War, and the Iraq War. There is little chance that the region will avoid new conflicts between the present and 2020. Many Middle Eastern states still dispute at least one border with one of its neighbors, and most countries have serious religious and/or ethnic divisions. Low-level conflicts and internal unrest are virtual certainties.

In several cases, Middle Eastern states are either currently at war, or there is a serious risk of future conflict. Mauritania has long been the scene of a low-level race war between Arabs and Black Africans. Morocco is still in the process of a long war with the Polisario for control of the Western Sahara. Algeria is involved in a bitter civil war between its ruling military junta and Islamic extremists. Tensions have grown between Libya's leader, Muammar Qadhafi, and Libya's Islamists, and there has been low-level fighting in a number of areas. The Egyptian government and a number of other regional governments are fighting low-level wars against Islamic terrorists.

A "war process," or "second intifada," has replaced the Arab-Israeli peace process. Israel is still formally at war with Syria and Lebanon, and faces a serious potential threat from outside terrorists. Israel may become involved in a broader conflict with its Arab neighbors and Iran, and has clashed on its northern border with Hezbollah—a Shiite Islamic movement with strong Iranian and Syrian sponsorship. Lebanon remains under Syria, and its factions still present the threat of another round of civil war.

The Southern Gulf states are relatively stable, and have resolved many of their border disputes in recent years, but there has been civil violence in Bahrain between Sunni and Shiite. Saudi Arabia has growing problems with Al-Qaeda and Islamic extremists, and there are extremist elements in every Southern Gulf state. Islamic extremism and terrorism are at least low-level problems in Yemen, and many southern Gulf states are heavily dependent on foreign workers to the extent that this raises serious issues about their future stability.

While Iran may be becoming more moderate, there is little sign that the Khatami faction or Iranian moderates will gain firm control of the country. Khatami expressed deep dissatisfaction about his ability to accomplish meaningful reform in August 2003, and there is still a serious risk of internal clashes between its "moderates" and "traditionalists." Iran also presents major problems in terms of proliferation, its opposition to the Arab-Israeli peace process, and continued hostility to any U.S. presence in the Gulf.

The fall of Saddam Hussein in 2003 has removed one major source of instability in the region, but the war and the looting that followed have seriously damaged some aspects of Iraq's oil industry. There is also a risk that the aftermath to Saddam's repressive regime could be some form of lingering civil conflict or a long period of internal instability. Iraq is divided along sectarian lines between Sunni and Shiite, and Arab, Kurd, and Turkmen. Nation building in Iraq presents major challenges and risks, and there is a threat that the United States and Britain will face a growing threat from guerrilla attacks and sabotage. The Iraq War has already serious cut Iraq's oil exports and there is no current way to predict the future development of its Petroleum industry and exports.

The civil war in the Sudan has entered its second decade, and the death toll from fighting and starvation will probably exceed well over one million.

Yemen faces tensions between its government and key political and tribal groups in the South, and has clashed with Eritrea over the control of islands in the Red Sea.

None of these tensions and conflicts poses immediate threats to the flow of MENA oil exports, but they have affected the development of energy supply in Algeria, Iran, Iraq, Libya, and Yemen, and new outbreaks of violence could occur in many MENA states with little or no warning. Most MENA states suffer from internal political, economic, and demographic problems that compound intraregional conflicts and tensions. Virtually all Middle East states have regimes with a high degree of authoritarianism—regardless of whether the ruler is called a king, shaikh, sultan, president, general, or ayatollah. Virtually all suffer from weak or failed economic development, high rates of population growth and a virtual youth explosion, aging and largely authoritarian regimes, and serious problems with internal stability.

The MENA region also suffers from a process of creeping proliferation that may ultimately change the nature of conflicts and the balance of power, in the region. Algeria, Egypt, Iraq, Iran, Israel, Libya, Syria, and Yemen have all created missile programs and have at least conducted research into weapons of mass destruction. Israel is a major regional nuclear power and has chemical and biological programs. Egypt has chemical and biological research programs. Iran, Libya, and Syria are either trying to develop biological and chemical weapons or have already deployed them, and Iran seems to have made a major effort that it may or may not have halted in late 2003. Iraq continues to seek nuclear weapons. So far, such weapons have only been used in the Yemeni civil war and the Iran-Iraq War, but there is little doubt that the Middle East is acquiring far more lethal chemical, biological, radiological, and nuclear (CBRN) weapons and delivery systems than it has possessed in the past.

MILITARISM, MILITARY EXPENDITURES, AND ARMS IMPORTS

One of the problems in analyzing trends in the MENA area is the tendency to separate the analysis of the overall trends in the economy and state spending from the trends in energy spending and from military spending and arms imports. This often suits the regimes involved, who do not want serious public or external debate over their use of energy revenues or military spending and arms purchases, and who often seek to avoid close examination of any aspect of their overall level of state spending or "statism." The fact remains, however, that their failure to invest in economic development, to modernize their economies and to privatize state industry, often interacts in embarrassing ways with a lack of any clear mid- to long-term energy investment strategy and their overspending on military forces and arms imports.

The level of waste in MENA military efforts, and the burden they place on economic and energy development, is difficult to put in perspective—particularly because reliable data are not always available for recent years. It has long been clear, however, that the region's militarism poses serious dangers to its peoples as well as to its stability as an energy supplier.

Several factors are involved. One is the history of crises escalating into serious conflicts, some of which have led to energy interruptions. Another is a level of total expenditure—often without a clear threat and/or producing any effective defense capability—that is so high that it seriously limits the funds available for development, including energy investment. Finally, many MENA countries are finding it harder and harder to sustain their present conventional force structures. At least in some cases, this adds to the pressures to acquire weapons of mass destruction and proliferate. Such weapons present a major potential future threat to MENA energy facilities and exports.

The Overall Level of Military Efforts

There has been a decline in MENA military expenditures and arms imports since the end of the Cold War. Middle Eastern military expenditures dropped from \$93.0 billion in 1985 to \$38.4 billion during 1997–2000.[2] Nevertheless, the region still spends nearly 6.8 percent of its gross national product (GNP) on military expenditures, and this compares with an average of only 2.3 percent and for the developed world and 2.7 percent for the developing world. Militarism remains a serious problem in the MENA area. It remains the largest arms market in the developed world. It currently accounts for roughly half of the world's conventional weapons purchase agreements.[3]

Once again, numbers and trends often speak louder than words:

- Table 2.1 illustrates the scale of MENA military efforts in terms of demographics. This table also provides some of the best data currently available on the number of males entering the labor forces, and in the age groups most needing jobs and most prone to terrorism and violent political action.
- Table 2.2 summarizes the present strength of MENA military forces.
- Chart 2.1 shows why the MENA region is described in various assessments as the most militarized area in the world. While current data are not available in a directly comparable form, the CIA's *World Factbook* indicates that the basic trends shown in this chart, and the other charts based on U.S. State Department, Bureau of Verification and Compliance, *World Military Expenditures and Arms Transfers, 1989–1999,* do reflect valid current trends.
- Chart 2.2 shows that the overall level of military effort in the region has dropped since the end of the Gulf War. This chart does not reflect the impact of the Israeli-Palestinian conflict that began in September 2000, but other data

Table 2.1
The Military Demographics of the Greater Middle East

Country	Total Population	Males Reaching Military Age Each Year	Males between the Ages of			Males between 15 and 49	
			13 and 17	18 and 22	23 and 32	Total	Medically Fit
Egypt	70,712,345	712,983	3,707,000	3,313,000	5,150,000	19,030,030	12,320,902
Gaza	1,225,911*	—					—
Israel	6,029,529	51,666	284,000	272,000	535,000	1,542,835	1,262,973
Jordan	5,307,470	57,131	280,000	247,000	454,000	1,517,751	1,073,991
Lebanon	3,677,780	—	216,000	194,000	397,000	1,003,174	618,129
Palestine	2,900,000*	—	163,000	140,000	233,000	—	—
Syria	17,155,814	200,859	1,076,000	883,000	1,274,000	4,550,496	2,539,342
West Bank	2,163,667*	—				—	—
Iran	66,622,704	823,041	4,735,000	3,960,000	5,959,000	18,868,571	11,192,731
Iraq	24,001,816	274,035	1,472,000	1,270,000	1,899,000	6,135,847	3,430,819
Bahrain	656,397	5,926	35,000	26,000	40,000	222,572	121,955
Kuwait	2,111,561	18,309	124,000	107,000	148,000	812,059	486,906
Oman	2,713,462	26,470	163,000	140,000	233,000	780,292	434,026
Qatar	793,341	6,797	26,000	22,000	38,000	316,885	166,214

Saudi Arabia	23,513,330	233,402	1,391,000	1,177,000	1,725,000	6,007,635	3,359,849
UAE	2,445,989	25,482	87,000	87,000	143,000	773,938	419,851
Yemen	18,701,257	238,690	1,008,000	803,000	1,328,000	4,272,156	2,397,914
Algeria	32,277,942	388,939	1,986,000	1,834,000	2,962,000	9,016,048	5,513,317
Libya	5,368,585	61,694	387,000	320,000	492,000	1,503,647	890,783
Morocco	31,167,783	348,380	1,780,000	1,612,000	2,726,000	8,393,772	5,289,283
Tunisia	9,815,644	105,146	529,000	505,000	869,000	2,806,881	1,597,565
Chad	8,997,237	82,003	408,000	332,000	518,000	1,881,769	985,094
Mauritania	2,828,858	—	149,000	121,000	194,000	644,294	312,276
Western Sahara	256,177	—	—	—	—	—	—
Afghanistan	27,755,775	252,869	1,499,000	1,194,000	2,053,000	6,896,623	3,696,379
Djibouti	472,810	—	42,000	35,000	57,000	110,221	64,940
Eritrea	4,465,651	—	252,000	210,000	320,000	—	—
Ethiopia	67,673,031	703,625	3,977,000	3,172,000	4,780,000	14,925,883	7,790,977
Somalia	7,753,310	—	626,000	511,000	726,000	1,881,634	1,040,662
Sudan	37,090,298	398,294	1,990,000	1,693,000	2,542,000	8,739,982	5,380,917
Turkey	67,308,928	674,805	3,264,000	3,251,000	6,242,000	19,219,177	11,623,675

Note: Totals include non-nationals, total population, males reaching military age, and males between 15 and 49 and are generally CIA data; the rest are IISS data.

*Totals for Palestinians are IISS, totals for Gaza and West Bank are CIA.

Source: Adapted by Anthony H. Cordesman, CIA, *World Factbook 2002*; and IISS, *The Military Balance*, various editions.

Table 2.2
The "Perceptual Balance": Military Forces of the Greater Middle East

Country	Total Active Manning	Total Active Army Manning	Tanks	OAFVs	Artillery	Combat Aircraft	Armed Helicopters
Egypt	443,000	320,000	3,860[a]	4,179	1,415[a]	608	128
Israel	161,500	120,000	3,750	7,808	1,653	454	135
Jordan	100,240	84,700	1,101[a]	1,545	531	101	22
Lebanon	71,830	70,000	327	1,463	183	0	0
Palestine[b]	(35,000)	(35,000)	—	—	—	—	—
Syria	319,000	215,000	3,500	5,025	2,560	611	106
Iran[c]	520,000	450,000	1,565	1,455	3,284	306	69
Iraq	389,000	350,000	2,600	3,400	2,300	316	62
Bahrain	10,700	8,500	140	306	93	34	40
Kuwait	15,500	11,000	293	561	95	81	20
Oman[c]	41,700	31,400	117	349	126	40	0
Qatar	12,400	8,500	35	302	44	18	19
Saudi Arabia[c]	199,500	150,000	710	5,057	390	294	33
UAE	41,500	35,000	381	1,305	343	101	49
Yemen[a]	66,500	60,000	790	1,040	695	76	8

Algeria	136,700	1,089	1,964	729	222	63
Libya	76,000	985	2,383	1,921	400	48
Morocco	175,000	520	1,279	452	95	24
Tunisia	35,000	84	391	117	29	15
Chad	30,350	60	203	5	2	2
Mauritania	15,750	35	75	75	8	0
Afghanistan[b]	—	—	—	—	—	—
Djibouti	8,000	0	31	6	0	0
Eritrea	172,200	100	80	155	17	0
Ethiopia	252,500	300	400	360	55	30
Somalia[b]	(35,900)	—	—	—	—	—
Turkey	514,850	4,205	4,543	2,990	485	53

Notes: Totals count all "active" equipment, much of which is not operational. They do not include stored equipment, but are only approximate estimates of combat-ready equipment holdings. Light tanks, APCs, AIFVs, armored recce vehicles, and misc. AFVs are counted as OAFVs (Other Armored Fighting Vehicles). Artillery counts towed and self-propelled tube weapons of 100-mm+ and multiple rocket launchers, but not mortars. Only armed or combat-capable fixed wing combat aircraft are counted, not other trainers or aircraft.

[a]Egypt has 100 additional M-1A1 Abrams MBT, 179 M-109A2/A3 SP ARTY on order. Jordan is awaiting 47 additional Challenger 1 MBT. Yemen has an additional 5 MiG-29S/UB on order.

[b]No current data available for Palestine, Afghanistan, and Somalia due to recent combat.

[c]Iranian totals include Revolutionary Guard Corps; Saudi totals include the Saudi National Guard and Omani totals include the Royal Household Guard.

Source: Adapted by Anthony H. Cordesman, CIA, *World Factbook*, various editions; and IISS, *The Military Balance*, various editions.

Chart 2.1
"The Most Militarized Region in the World"

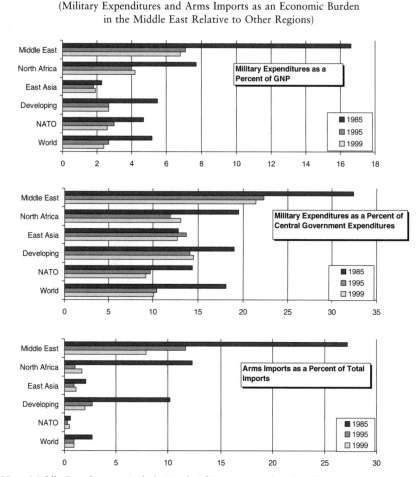

(Military Expenditures and Arms Imports as an Economic Burden
in the Middle East Relative to Other Regions)

Note: Middle East does not include North African states other than Egypt.
Source: Adapted by Anthony H. Cordesman from U.S. State Department, Bureau of Verification and Compliance, *World Military Expenditures and Arms Transfers, 1989–1999*.

indicate that the decline in overall regional military efforts has continued and even accelerated in some cases. The fall of Saddam Hussein's regime in April 2003 is also likely to result in further cuts in military efforts in the Gulf area.

- Chart 2.3 shows that economic growth and overall central government expenditures are outpacing military expenditures and arms imports.
- Chart 2.4 shows that military expenditures represent far too large a portion of central government expenditures in many MENA states, limiting the funds

Chart 2.2
Middle Eastern Military Efforts Have Also Dropped Sharply as a Percentage of GNP, Government Expenditures, Total Population, and Arms Imports: 1984–1999

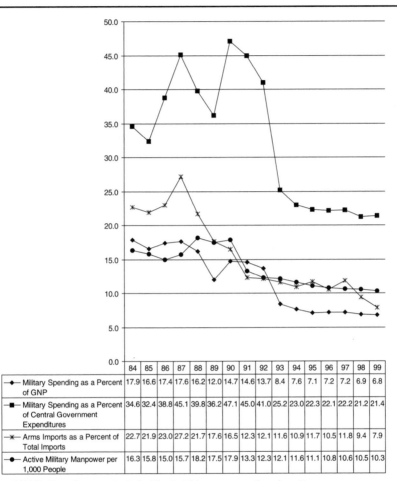

	84	85	86	87	88	89	90	91	92	93	94	95	96	97	98	99
Military Spending as a Percent of GNP	17.9	16.6	17.4	17.6	16.2	12.0	14.7	14.6	13.7	8.4	7.6	7.1	7.2	7.2	6.9	6.8
Military Spending as a Percent of Central Government Expenditures	34.6	32.4	38.8	45.1	39.8	36.2	47.1	45.0	41.0	25.2	23.0	22.3	22.1	22.2	21.2	21.4
Arms Imports as a Percent of Total Imports	22.7	21.9	23.0	27.2	21.7	17.6	16.5	12.3	12.1	11.6	10.9	11.7	10.5	11.8	9.4	7.9
Active Military Manpower per 1,000 People	16.3	15.8	15.0	15.7	18.2	17.5	17.9	13.3	12.3	12.1	11.6	11.1	10.8	10.6	10.5	10.3

Note: Middle East does not include North African states other than Egypt.
Source: Adapted by Anthony H. Cordesman from U.S. State Department, *World Military Expenditures and Arms Transfers,* various editions.

available for development and energy investment. In some cases, military expenditures are so large that they either compound the burden excessive state spending puts on the entire economy or come close to dominating that burden as the largest single aspect of "statism." This combination of excessive military spending, state spending, and inefficient state industrial blocks the growth and diversification of the economy as well as the work of market forces.

Chart 2.3
Middle Eastern Military Expenditures and Arms Imports Dropped Sharply Relative to Economic Growth and Government Spending During 1989–1999

(1989 = 100, and all following years are percentages of 1989 as base year. All expenditure totals are measured in constant 1989 U.S. dollars)

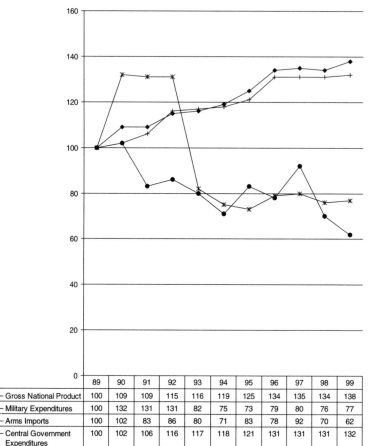

	89	90	91	92	93	94	95	96	97	98	99
Gross National Product	100	109	109	115	116	119	125	134	135	134	138
Military Expenditures	100	132	131	131	82	75	73	79	80	76	77
Arms Imports	100	102	83	86	80	71	83	78	92	70	62
Central Government Expenditures	100	102	106	116	117	118	121	131	131	131	132

Note: Middle East does not include North African states other than Egypt.
Source: Adapted by Anthony H. Cordesman form U.S. State Department, Bureau of Verification and Compliance, *World Military Expenditures and Arms Transfers, 1999–2000*.

- Chart 2.5 shows a declassified U.S. estimate of the long-term trend in Middle Eastern (less North African) military spending and arms imports in current dollars. It reflects the massive swings that can occur in a time of war, but also a trend toward smaller defense expenditures and more limited arms imports.

Chart 2.4
Military Expenditures and Arms Transfers as an Aspect of "Statism" in Individual Middle Eastern Countries in 1999

(Military spending as a percent of Central Government Expenditures [CGE] and Gross National Product [GNP], and Arms Imports as a Percent of Total)

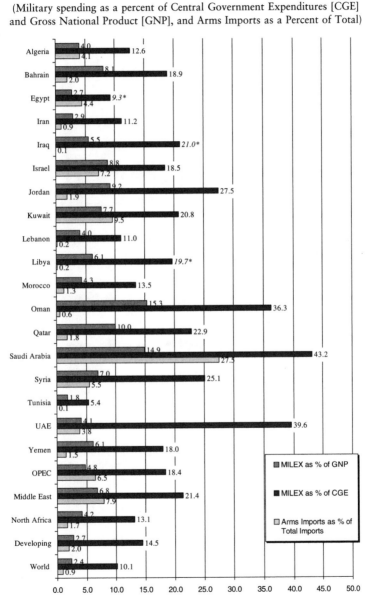

Note: Figures marked with asterisks are estimated or older data.

Source: Adapted by Anthony H. Cordesman from U.S. State Department, Bureau of Verification and Compliance, *World Military Expenditures and Arms Transfers*, various editions.

Chart 2.5

The Trend in Middle Eastern Military Expenditures and Arms Transfers since the October War

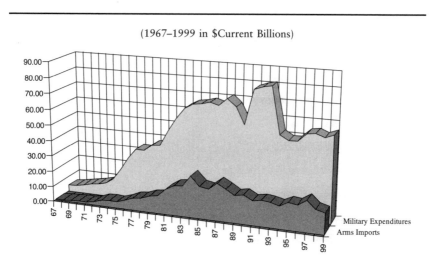

(1967–1999 in $Current Billions)

Note: Middle East does not include North African states other than Egypt.
Source: Adapted by Anthony H. Cordesman from U.S. State Department, Bureau of Arms Control, *World Military Expenditures and Arms Transfers*, various editions.

- Chart 2.6 shows more recent trends in current dollars. The capping of military expenditures and limits to arms imports emerge more clearly. One key implication of these data, however, is that most Middle Eastern states are not spending enough to recapitalize their force structures and maintain modern forces at anything like their present equipment strength. The slope of arms imports would have to have risen steadily from 1991 onward and spending levels would have had to nearly double in constant dollars to maintain both the force size shown in Table 2.2 and force quality.

- Chart 2.7 shows the trends in current dollars for military expenditures and arms transfers in North Africa. It is clear from the decline in North African arms imports that North African countries have not come close to spending what they need to replace the equipment in their military forces. The end result is large, wasteful force structures that are incapable of fighting any advance enemy—although the low overall standard of military modernization means that fighting can be sustained among North African states. The rise in military spending toward the end of the 1990s reflects the growing internal threat in several states, and the cost of the ongoing civil war in Algeria.

- Chart 2.8 shows how these trends in North Africa spending relate to the overall trends in the regional economy. There has been a decline in the burden of military spending, but it is still high. The burden of arms imports is far lower, but has been heavily offset by internal security spending.

Chart 2.6
The Trend in Middle Eastern Military Expenditures and Arms Transfers in Constant Dollars since 1989

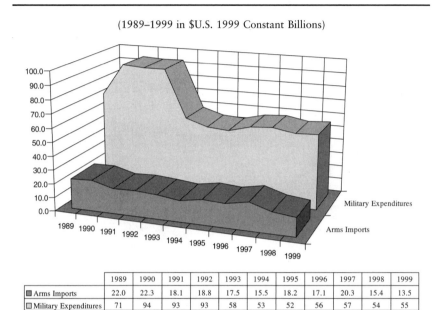

(1989–1999 in $U.S. 1999 Constant Billions)

	1989	1990	1991	1992	1993	1994	1995	1996	1997	1998	1999
■ Arms Imports	22.0	22.3	18.1	18.8	17.5	15.5	18.2	17.1	20.3	15.4	13.5
▢ Military Expenditures	71	94	93	93	58	53	52	56	57	54	55

Note: Middle East does not include North African states other than Egypt.
Source: Adapted by Anthony H. Cordesman from U.S. State Department, Bureau of Verification and Compliance, *World Military Expenditures and Arms Transfers, 1999–2000*.

The Problem of Arms Imports

The decline in MENA arms imports summarized in the previous charts often has not been a matter of choice on the part of the individual nations involved. It has been forced on by them by the need to spend far more on internal security and counterterrorism, the end of concessionary arms transfers by the former Soviet Union (FSU), growing regional economic problems, and a range of sanctions on key states like Iran, Iraq, and Libya.

The recent drop in spending on arms imports must also be kept in careful perspective. Spending on arms is still high enough to divert important sums away from economic and energy development. The cumulative impact of the resulting drop in force quality is broad enough so that it limits the ability of MENA countries to fight powers like the United States, but it does not affect their ability to fight each other, since most regional states are left at nearly the same level of force quality. Moreover, the more the

Chart 2.7
North African Military Expenditures and Arms Transfers in Constant Dollars Have Dropped to Low Levels by Global Standards

(Algerian, Libyan, Moroccan, and Tunisian spending in Constant $U.S. 1999 Billions)

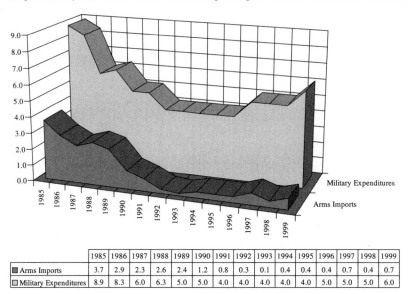

	1985	1986	1987	1988	1989	1990	1991	1992	1993	1994	1995	1996	1997	1998	1999
▣ Arms Imports	3.7	2.9	2.3	2.6	2.4	1.2	0.8	0.3	0.1	0.4	0.4	0.4	0.7	0.4	0.7
▢ Military Expenditures	8.9	8.3	6.0	6.3	5.0	5.0	4.0	4.0	4.0	4.0	4.0	5.0	5.0	5.0	6.0

Source: Adapted by Anthony H. Cordesman from Bureau of Arms Control in the U.S. State Department (formerly U.S. State Department, Bureau of Arms Control), *World Military Expenditures and Arms Transfers*, various editions.

trend in arms imports is analyzed, the more clear it is why the problems in modernizing conventional forces have been a factor leading some nations to shift their resources away from conventional forces to the acquisition of weapons of mass destruction, long-range delivery systems, and carefully selected advanced conventional weapons.

- Chart 2.9 puts the MENA level of arms imports in global perspective. It should be noted, however, that this table also shows that MENA arms deliveries still cost some $15 billion a year, and these figures do not include the cost of military related imports of civilian and dual-use equipment likes trucks, communications, and the like. The true cost is clearly in excess of $20 billion that could otherwise be used for economic or energy development.

- Chart 2.10 shows how cumulative trends relate to the impact of given wars. Presumably, the fall of Saddam Hussein will cause a further cut in regional arms imports, although no Gulf country has yet announced since plans. It should also be noted that the data are somewhat skewed by the fact the Israeli-

Chart 2.8

North African Military Efforts Declined Sharply as a Percentage of GNP, Government Expenditures, Imports, and Total Population: 1985–1999

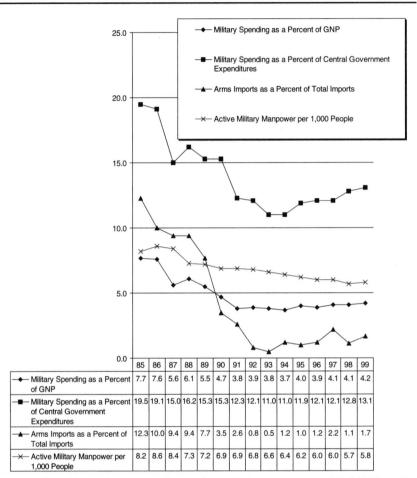

	85	86	87	88	89	90	91	92	93	94	95	96	97	98	99
◆ Military Spending as a Percent of GNP	7.7	7.6	5.6	6.1	5.5	4.7	3.8	3.9	3.8	3.7	4.0	3.9	4.1	4.1	4.2
■ Military Spending as a Percent of Central Government Expenditures	19.5	19.1	15.0	16.2	15.3	15.3	12.3	12.1	11.0	11.0	11.9	12.1	12.1	12.8	13.1
▲ Arms Imports as a Percent of Total Imports	12.3	10.0	9.4	9.4	7.7	3.5	2.6	0.8	0.5	1.2	1.0	1.2	2.2	1.1	1.7
✕ Active Military Manpower per 1,000 People	8.2	8.6	8.4	7.3	7.2	6.9	6.9	6.8	6.6	6.4	6.2	6.0	6.0	5.7	5.8

Source: Adapted by Anthony H. Cordesman from U.S. State Department, *World Military Expenditures and Arms Transfers*, various editions, GPO, Washington. Middle East does not include North African states other than Egypt.

Palestinian War does not involve major arms imports, and Israel's true level of imports is grossly understated in any case because only complete weapons sales—not components for military industries—are counted. Similarly, Algeria's imports relating to its civil war are often civilian or dual-use goods. The graph also sharply understates spending for nations like Iran and Syria because the costs do not include proliferation and imports for weapons of mass destruction (WMD).

Chart 2.9
MENA Arms Deliveries Are Declining: 1985–1999

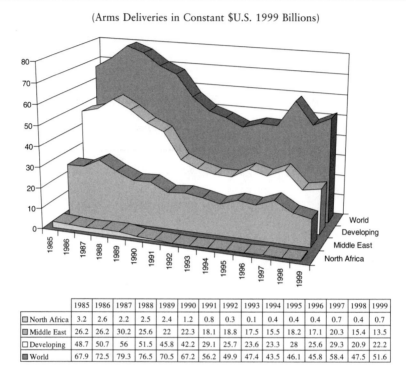

(Arms Deliveries in Constant $U.S. 1999 Billions)

	1985	1986	1987	1988	1989	1990	1991	1992	1993	1994	1995	1996	1997	1998	1999
☐ North Africa	3.2	2.6	2.2	2.5	2.4	1.2	0.8	0.3	0.1	0.4	0.4	0.4	0.7	0.4	0.7
▨ Middle East	26.2	26.2	30.2	25.6	22	22.3	18.1	18.8	17.5	15.5	18.2	17.1	20.3	15.4	13.5
☐ Developing	48.7	50.7	56	51.5	45.8	42.2	29.1	25.7	23.6	23.3	28	25.6	29.3	20.9	22.2
▉ World	67.9	72.5	79.3	76.5	70.5	67.2	56.2	49.9	47.4	43.5	46.1	45.8	58.4	47.5	51.6

Note: Middle East does not include North African states other than Egypt.
Source: Adapted by Anthony H. Cordesman from Bureau of Arms Control in the U.S. State
  Department, *World Military Expenditures and Arms Transfers*, various editions.

- Chart 2.11 shows in more detail just how dramatic the impact of end of the
  Iran-Iraq War, and the sanctioning of Iraq and Libya, was in leading to the
  cuts in arms imports. The data for Syria do not reflect the real nature of its
  arms transfers because it was obtaining arms at concessionary price or through
  loans through most of the 1980s, and these ceased to be available after the
  start of the 1990s. As a result, the number of arms per dollar dropped pre-
  cipitously.

- Chart 2.12 uses declassified U.S. data on arms sales to show the trend by major
  Middle Eastern country for both new arms orders and deliveries. The dominant role of two critical energy exporters—Saudi Arabia and the UAE—is
  clearly apparent. The Saudi data are particularly striking because many of the
  nation's economic and energy development problems could be solved if it cut
  its arms imports to more rational levels.

Chart 2.10
The Cumulative Impact of the Arab-Israeli Peace Accords, Sanctioning of Libya, End of the Iran-Iraq War, the Cold War, the Gulf War, and Economic Recession: 1985–1999

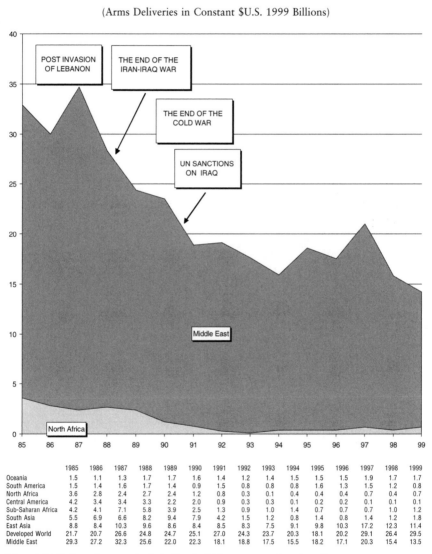

(Arms Deliveries in Constant $U.S. 1999 Billions)

	1985	1986	1987	1988	1989	1990	1991	1992	1993	1994	1995	1996	1997	1998	1999
Oceania	1.5	1.1	1.3	1.7	1.7	1.6	1.4	1.2	1.4	1.5	1.5	1.5	1.9	1.7	1.7
South America	1.5	1.4	1.6	1.7	1.4	0.9	1.5	0.8	0.8	0.8	1.6	1.3	1.5	1.2	0.8
North Africa	3.6	2.8	2.4	2.7	2.4	1.2	0.8	0.3	0.1	0.4	0.4	0.4	0.7	0.4	0.7
Central America	4.2	3.4	3.4	3.3	2.2	2.0	0.9	0.3	0.3	0.1	0.2	0.2	0.1	0.1	0.1
Sub-Saharan Africa	4.2	4.1	7.1	5.8	3.9	2.5	1.3	0.9	1.0	1.4	0.7	0.7	0.7	1.0	1.2
South Asia	5.5	6.9	6.6	8.2	9.4	7.9	4.2	1.5	1.2	0.8	1.4	0.8	1.4	1.2	1.8
East Asia	8.8	8.4	10.3	9.6	8.6	8.4	8.5	8.3	7.5	9.1	9.8	10.3	17.2	12.3	11.4
Developed World	21.7	20.7	26.6	24.8	24.7	25.1	27.0	24.3	23.7	20.3	18.1	20.2	29.1	26.4	29.5
Middle East	29.3	27.2	32.3	25.6	22.0	22.3	18.1	18.8	17.5	15.5	18.2	17.1	20.3	15.4	13.5

Note: Middle East does not include North African states other than Egypt.

Source: Adapted by Anthony H. Cordesman from U.S. State Department, Bureau of Verification and Compliance, *World Military Expenditures and Arms Transfers*, various editions.

Chart 2.11
The Cumulative Decline in Military Spending by Selected Major Buyers in Constant Dollars: 1984–1999

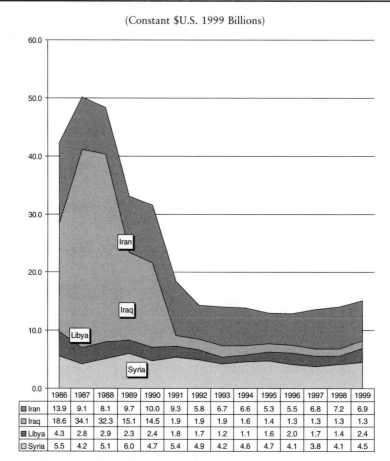

(Constant $U.S. 1999 Billions)

	1986	1987	1988	1989	1990	1991	1992	1993	1994	1995	1996	1997	1998	1999
▣ Iran	13.9	9.1	8.1	9.7	10.0	9.3	5.8	6.7	6.6	5.3	5.5	6.8	7.2	6.9
▣ Iraq	18.6	34.1	32.3	15.1	14.5	1.9	1.9	1.9	1.6	1.4	1.3	1.3	1.3	1.3
■ Libya	4.3	2.8	2.9	2.3	2.4	1.8	1.7	1.2	1.1	1.6	2.0	1.7	1.4	2.4
☐ Syria	5.5	4.2	5.1	6.0	4.7	5.4	4.9	4.2	4.6	4.7	4.1	3.8	4.1	4.5

Note: Some data adjusted or estimated by author.
Source: Adapted by Anthony H. Cordesman from U.S. Arms Control and Disarmament Agency, *World Military Expenditures and Arms Transfers*, various editions.

- Chart 2.13 shows similar data on North African arms imports. The militaristic character of Algeria is clearly apparent. So is the impact of UN sanction in producing a sharp decline in Libyan arms imports, effectively putting an end to Qadhafi's dreams of becoming a serious regional military power.

Chart 2.12
Middle Eastern Agreements and Deliveries by Country: 1994–2002

(Arms Agreements and Deliveries to North African nations in $U.S. Current Millions)

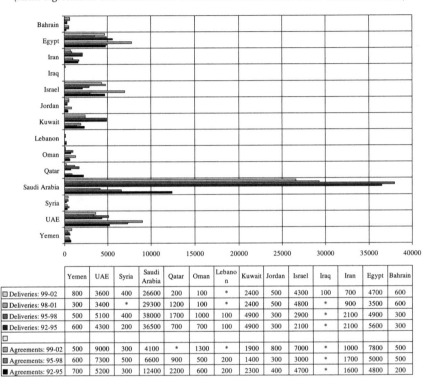

	Yemen	UAE	Syria	Saudi Arabia	Qatar	Oman	Lebano n	Kuwait	Jordan	Israel	Iraq	Iran	Egypt	Bahrain
☐ Deliveries: 99-02	800	3600	400	26600	200	100	*	2400	500	4300	100	700	4700	600
▨ Deliveries: 98-01	300	3400	*	29300	1200	100	*	2400	500	4800	*	900	3500	600
▪ Deliveries: 95-98	500	5100	400	38000	1700	1000	100	4900	300	2900	*	2100	4900	300
■ Deliveries: 92-95	600	4300	200	36500	700	700	100	4900	300	2100	*	2100	5600	300
☐														
▨ Agreements: 99-02	500	9000	300	4100	*	1300	*	1900	800	7000	*	1000	7800	500
▪ Agreements: 95-98	600	7300	500	6600	900	500	200	1400	300	3000	*	1700	5000	500
■ Agreements: 92-95	700	5200	300	12400	2200	600	200	2300	400	4700	*	1600	4800	200

0 = Data less than $50 million or nil. All data rounded to the nearest $100 million.
Source: Richard F. Grimmett, *Conventional Arms Transfers to the Developing Nations*, Congressional Research Service, various editions.

The Threat to Energy Facilities

War and military forces have long affected the development and security of MENA energy supplies. The Arab-Israeli wars of 1956 and 1967 each affected the flow of exports to some degree, although at a time when the world was far less dependent on the MENA region. The October War of 1973 triggered an oil embargo that led to a drastic strategic reappraisal of the importance of energy exports and imports. The Iran-Iraq War of 1980–1998, and the closely related U.S.-Iranian tanker war of 1997–1998, involved deliberate and systematic attempts to target energy production and export capabilities in a prolonged conflict. Iraq burned Kuwait's oil fields

Chart 2.13
Trend in North African Agreements and Deliveries by Country: 1986–2002

(Arms Agreements and Deliveries to North African nations in $U.S. Current Millions)

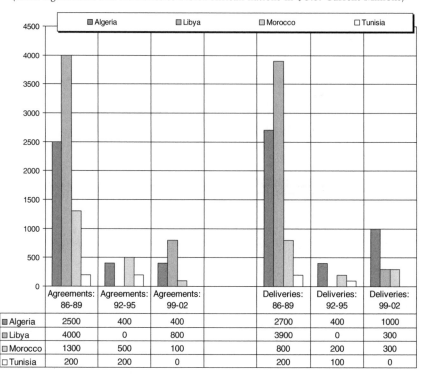

	Agreements: 86-89	Agreements: 92-95	Agreements: 99-02	Deliveries: 86-89	Deliveries: 92-95	Deliveries: 99-02
Algeria	2500	400	400	2700	400	1000
Libya	4000	0	800	3900	0	300
Morocco	1300	500	100	800	200	300
Tunisia	200	200	0	200	100	0

0 = Data less than $50 million or nil. All data rounded to the nearest $100 million.
Source: Richard F. Grimmett, *Conventional Arms Transfers to the Developing Nations*, Congressional Research Service, various editions.

and looted the country during its withdrawal, oil, and sabotage and looting seriously reduced Iraq's oil production and export capacity during the Iraq War of 2003.

The net impact of such wars, however, has so far been relatively limited. As yet, no country has had both the motive and capability to launch well-planned precision strikes against an opponent's energy facilities and exports, although Iran and Iraq at least attempted to carry out such attacks during 1980–1988. The overthrow of Saddam Hussein's regime has removed one of the few governments in the MENA region that was willing to conduct such attacks without extreme provocation, and it is unclear that any other government has an incentive to conduct some form of energy war in the near future. If anything, it is terrorism, not state-versus-state conflicts, that is likely to be the future threat.

The downward trend in MENA military forces, spending, and arms transfers does not, however, mean that MENA energy facilities and exports are necessarily becoming safer. Both MENA nations and extremist movements are learning a great deal more about asymmetric war with time, and states are using their remaining funds to acquire more precision weapons and better platforms to launch them from. These weapons include air launched weapons that can be used against such key targets as export facilities, major energy processing and distribution facilities and gas-oil separators, desalination and war injection facilities, power plants, gas train refineries, and petrochemical plants. MENA countries are also buying better maritime surveillance systems and longer range antiship missiles, better mines, and submarines also allow MENA states to do a better job of attacking tankers and offshore facilities.

The history of war is also the history of sudden explosive crises, and unplanned escalation. There is no way to predict whether one MENA state will launch such attacks on another's energy facilities, or whether such attacks will then be well planned and well executed. What does need to be understood, however, is that the broader trends in MENA military forces do not necessarily affect the security of energy facilities. In fact, it is at least possible that MENA nations with limited overall capability for conventional war would lash out at high value targets to try to defeat, intimidate, or punish their neighbors. If so, they will continue to acquire the means to conduct such attacks over time.

PROLIFERATION

Proliferation is serious problem in the Middle East, and one that is not likely to diminish in the near future. There is a complex pattern of proliferation in the region, and the range of delivery systems is steadily expanding. Algeria, Egypt, Iran, Iraq, Israel, Libya, the Sudan, and Yemen have all been involved in past efforts to acquire weapons of mass destruction— albeit at very different levels and with different goals and intentions. Algeria, Iraq, the Sudan, and Yemen are no longer part of the list of serious proliferators, but Iran, Israel, and Syria are. Israel has large nuclear forces, and Iran has a rapidly maturing nuclear program; Iran and Syria have significant biological warfare programs; and Egypt and Israel have conducted significant research and development activity. All of the proliferators in the Middle East are working on—or have—chemical weapons. Iran, Libya, and Syria probably have a stockpile of such weapons. Algeria, Egypt, and Israel have the technical capability to produce them. Egypt, Iran, Iraq, Israel, Libya, and Saudi Arabia have long-range missiles or programs to acquire them.

Terrorist movements like Al-Qaeda have also sought weapons of mass destruction and there is no way to predict how asymmetric wars or terrorism using CBRN weapons could damage oil and gas production and petroleum export facilities, or the level and duration of any interruption in exports. It is all too clear, however, that the threat posed by future wars and terrorism is becoming far more serious than in the past.

Proliferators in the Middle East

Table 2.3 shows the list of MENA proliferators and the current estimated status of their efforts. The nations listed in Table 2.3 are so different in terms of regime, goals, and behavior that it is obvious that there is no regional threat to the West, but rather the possibility that individual states might pose a threat to individual Western nations or interests. Two major proliferators—Iran and Libya—are of special interest. These are nations that have posed a threat to the West in the past and that have also sponsored attacks of state terrorism against Western targets and/or on Western soil.

Iran currently poses the most significant near-term threat in terms of acquiring biological and nuclear weapons, and long-range missiles that might strike Europe or the United States. In spite of Iranian denials, there is little doubt that Iran has an active nuclear and biological weapons program, and has already begun to test long-range missiles. Iran's capabilities, however, will remain highly limited for the next decade, and Iran faces a strong regional threat from Israel. While Iran's regime may or may not become truly moderate in character, it has become more pragmatic since the death of Khomeini, and it is far from clear that it would take "existential" risks of the kind posed by such an attack on the West.

There has, however, been growing international pressure on Iran to cutback on its nuclear program. The discovery of two major undeclared underground facilities in 2003 that included a centrifuge plant suitable for producing fissile Uranium, and a heavy water plant for a reactor fuel cycle that could produce weapons-grade plutonium, led to broad international pressure on Iran to permit full-scale inspection on the terms provided to the protocol for the Nuclear Non-Proliferation Treaty (NNPT). So did a follow up analysis by the International Atomic Energy Agency (IAEA) that investigated Iran's nuclear program in depth and reported a number of forbidden research and development activities; and confirmation of the fact that Pakistan had secretly sold nuclear weapons technology to Iran. The protocol to the NNPT that allows the IAEA broader rights of access to sites in the country on December 18, 2003, but this does not preclude Iran from going on with covert research and development activity. Iran is also proceeding with long-range missile developments that have little military meaning unless the missiles are armed with weapons of mass destruction, and there are no effective limits on its chemical and biological weapons programs.[4]

Table 2.3
Nations with Weapons of Mass Destruction

Country	Type of Weapon of Mass Destruction		
	Chemical	Biological	Nuclear
East-West			
Britain	Breakout	Breakout	Deployed
France	Breakout	Breakout	Deployed
Germany	Breakout	Breakout	Technology
Sweden	—	—	Technology
Russia	Residual	Residual	Deployed
U.S.	Residual	Breakout	Deployed
Middle East			
Algeria	Technology	Technology	Interest
Egypt	Residual	Breakout	—
Israel	Breakout	Breakout	Deployed
Iran	Deployed?	Breakout	Technology
Iraq	?	?	Technology
Libya	Deployed	Research	—
Syria	Deployed	Technology?	—
Yemen	Residual	—	—
Asia and South Asia			
China	Deployed?	Breakout?	Deployed
India	Breakout?	Breakout?	Deployed
Japan	Breakout	Breakout	Technology
Pakistan	Breakout?	Breakout?	Deployed
North Korea	Deployed	Deployed	Deployed (?)
South Korea	Breakout?	Breakout	Technology
Taiwan	Breakout?	Breakout	Technology
Thailand	Residual	—	—
Vietnam	Residual	—	—
Other			
Argentina	—	—	Technology
Brazil	—	—	Technology
South Africa	—	—	Technology

Libya has the dubious distinction of being the only MENA state to have fired a long-range missile on a Western target—it fired on the Italian island of Lampadusa following the U.S. raid on Tripoli. At the same time, a lot of Libya's grandiose military plans have so far ended in failure. Libya has some chemical weapons capability, but has failed to develop ballistic missiles with longer ranges than the Scud. It has explored biological and nuclear weapons programs, but there is little evidence of success. Moreover, the interception of a ship carrying nuclear centrifuge and weapons technology to Libya in the fall of 2003 led to political pressure that resulted in Libya's declaration in December 2003 that it would give up all its programs for developing missiles and weapons of mass destruction and allow unconditional inspections. This was followed by both U.S. and IAEA inspections, and the transfer of much of Libya's technology to the United States.

Given this background, it currently seems unlikely that even the most radical MENA power would readily take the risk of directly confronting a combination of its neighbors, the United States, and other Western states, given the relative military weakness of key potential threats, and the risk of massive retaliation. No Middle Eastern state can disregard the fact that any use of a biological or nuclear weapon that produced massive casualties could trigger devastating conventional strategic strikes or even the use of nuclear weapons by the West.

At the same time, there are dangers in assuming that Middle Eastern states will always behave as "rational actors," and terrorist and extremist movements are far harder to deter than states. The history of the region is filled with miscalculations, erratic behavior, and risk-taking. Behavior can alter rapidly in a crisis, and the most threatening states have rulers or ruling elites who may choose to escalate in ways that are far less conservative than what Western planners would consider under similar conditions. Extremist movements like Al-Qaeda have also shown that they will take extreme risks to take extreme action, and they may either cooperate with proliferating states or act as their covert proxy.

The following scenarios could involve either the more radical proliferators in the region or terrorist attacks and may not represent even moderate probability cases, but they are possible enough so they deserve serious consideration:

- Weapons of mass destruction might be used against key energy and energy export facilities in intraregional conflicts to pose a major economic threat to a regime or put pressure on the West.

- Attacks might be carried out on Western power projection forces in the region, or the threat of such attacks might be used to try to force a regional power to expel Western power projection forces, or deprive regimes of Western support.

- Threats against the West, demonstrative long-range missile attacks against targets in the West, or low-level use of weapons of mass destruction might be used against targets in the region or the West to try to force Western nations to support the policies of a given Middle Eastern state, or intervene in a regional conflict. The escalation of an Israeli-Syrian conflict, or a future Iranian-Iraqi conflict, might lead to such a threat.

- A regional power might set up a launch on warning or launch-under-attack system targeted on the West in an effort to deter Western intervention or military action. Such a system might be created to prevent Western counterproliferation strikes.

- The threat, demonstrative use, or larger scale use of such weapons might be utilized in an effort to force an end to sanctions or containment.

- A regime on the edge of collapse might lash out, feeling it had nothing to lose and accepting the risk of broader retaliation against the nation. Alternatively, a nation under nuclear attack by Israel might feel that attacks were justified against Western targets, particularly U.S. bases.

- Terrorists could use such weapons in the West to try to further divide the West and Arab world, building on the tensions caused by the second intifada and hostility growing out of September 11, 2001.

- Middle Eastern states are not limited to conventional forms of warfare. While a great deal of attention focuses on long-range missiles, a Middle Eastern state might use unconventional delivery means or a terrorist proxy to deliver such weapons—hoping that it would not be identified as the source or that enough ambiguity would exist to prevent a decisive response.

- Technology or fissile material transfers might suddenly destabilize the balance. This might include the transfer of long-range missiles or fissile material, or key components and technology for missiles and weapons. This could suddenly alter the regional balance and the perceived risk in threatening the West or Western interests.

Once again, the problem is to balance possible risks against probable risks over a period as long as 2003–2030, knowing that new proliferators can emerge and many regional powers could acquire missiles, cruise missiles, or better strike aircraft. Most MENA states and leaders are normally cautious and self-preservation is normally the highest single priority. There is no question, however, that a combination of creeping proliferation, and having to rely on the judgment and stability of at least five major proliferators, presents risks.

The Threat to Energy Facilities

Proliferation represents the most serious potential threat to MENA energy facilities in terms of lethality. Even a small nuclear weapon could destroy any energy production or export complex in the Middle East, although oil and gas fields are too dispersed and "hardened" for such attacks to have much effect. Radiological weapons are far harder to produce in effective lethal form than many analysts seem to understand, but are probably within the state of the art of the more advanced Middle Eastern economies, and even small, relatively nonlethal, radiological weapons might keep workers from entering a site or facility.

Biological weapons can be more lethal than nuclear weapons, and have the advantage of leaving facilities intact. Persistent biological weapons are possible, and can be used to contaminate facilities in much the same way as radiological weapons. Once again, their psychological effect might be more important than their lethality or killing effect.

Large amounts of chemical weapons are needed to achieve high lethality against large energy facilities, but such attacks are within the state of the art for countries like Syria and Iran—which seem to have cluster munitions and persistent nerve gas. Advances in warhead and weapons design are also improving the capability to disseminate both chemical and biological weapons from missiles, cruise missiles, bombs, and UCAVs. There is no way to know how advanced MENA countries now are or how much progress they will make in the future, but it is clear that some could have a limited capability now and that they could all potentially acquire relatively sophisticated capabilities during 2005–2010.

Proliferating MENA nations may never use weapons of mass destruction against energy facilities, but there are incentives that could lead to making such threats or to actually using such weapons in a crisis. Energy facilities are a natural hostage in a strategic confrontation, and involve far less provocation than attacks on civilian populations. The threat of such attacks might offset a major conventional advantage on the part of an opponent or be used to deter military action or the support/basing of outside powers like the United States. The effective destruction of a key energy facility could also produce a serious mid- to long-term blow in economic terms.

In any case, it is dangerous to assume that crises and escalation are handled in rational terms or from a common set of perceptions. Proliferating nations know that even the threat of such strikes can have a powerful deterrent or intimidating impact, and threats can lead to use. Moreover, world energy markets might well panic at the very threat of the use of WMD and might take days or weeks to stabilize after even a token use of a weapon whose effects would be difficult to estimate and understand.

Independent or proxy action by terrorist groups presents a further problem, as does the risk of covert attack. Extremist groups cannot present the same range of military threats as states, but this might not matter if they picked the right target. State use of a terrorist group as a proxy, or covert attack, could achieve significant results in some scenarios with far less fear of retaliation or some kind of serious action by the international community.

TERRORISM AND STATE TERRORISM

Many of the regimes in the region are repressive, and state terrorism is endemic. A lack of representative government, a failure to establish a sound rule of law, and human rights abuses have led human rights groups and the U.S. State Department to cite a continuing pattern of arbitrary arrests, abuse of internal security efforts, and corruption. These problems have often helped to breed extremist and terrorist opposition groups.

Many other forces are at work, however; and terrorism is scarcely limited to attacks on the most repressive regimes. As Chapter 3 describes, the MENA area is filled with serious economic, cultural, and demographic problems. Many moderate regimes face problems with internal and external terrorism, much of it directed against their secular character and often against progressive change and reform.

The Problem of Islamic Extremism and Violence

Islamist extremist violence has proved to be exceptionally dangerous and destabilizing. Every nation in the Middle East, no matter how moderate, faces some level of internal and external threat from such movements. Active internal fighting has taken place in Algeria, Libya, Egypt, Lebanon, Syria, Saudi Arabia, and Yemen. Iran is torn between Islamic "hard-liners" and "moderates," and the fall of Saddam Hussein has unleashed new Islamist forces in Iraq. Every other MENA country has had to establish new security procedures, and cope with its own Islamist extremists. The problem is also an international one that reaches far outside the MENA area. It now involves Central Asia, South Asia, the Islamic countries of Southeast Asia, and movements in Europe and North America.

While militarism and proliferation pose potential threats to the region's development and energy exports, the most active threat of violence now comes from this violent extremism. It does not, however, have one source or represent one cause. Some have arisen in response to state terrorism, in response to regional conflicts like the Israeli-Palestinian War, but other elements have developed in part due to the pressures of social change. The end result is a complex mix of threats mixes national movements, regional movements, and truly international movements like Al-Qaeda.

The ideology and goals of these movements differ from group to group, but there are often loose alliances of groups with different goals. What most do have in common is that their ideology is based on an extremist version of Shiite, Sufi, Salafi, and Wahhabi Islam and that the religious goals of each movement are mixed with an antisecular political agenda and a rejection of modern economic priorities and reform. So far, they are all small extremist groups that do not represent the views and hopes of the vast majority of the people in their country of the MENA region, but several have already proven to be dangerous both inside and outside the Middle East.

The Regional and Global Impact of Islamic Extremist Terrorism

Long before September 11, 2001, the attacks on Al-Khobar, the U.S.S. *Cole,* and the World Trade Center showed that terrorism posed a threat to the moderate regimes in the Middle East and a transnational threat to the West. There have been many serious terrorist attacks on Western targets in the Middle East in the past, such as the bombing of the U.S. Marine Corps barracks in Beirut.[5]

The November 13, 1995, truck bombing of the National Guard Headquarters in Riyadh killed five U.S. servicemen and two Iranians. The June 25, 1996, bombing of the Khobar Towers killed nineteen U.S. servicemen. The attacks on the U.S. embassies in Kenya and Tanzania involved large numbers of innocent casualties—247 dead and over 5,000 wounded in the case of Kenya, and 10 dead and more than 75 wounded in the case of Tanzania. These attacks involved truck bombs with 600–800 pounds of explosives.

Civil tension in the Middle East has made tourists a target. For example, the worst terrorist attack in Egypt's history occurred on November 17, 1997. Six gunmen belonging to the Egyptian terrorist group Al-Gama'at al-Islamiyya (Islamic Group [IG]) entered the Hatsheput Temple in Luxor. For nearly half an hour, they methodically shot and knifed tourists trapped inside the Temple's alcoves. Fifty-eight foreign tourists were murdered, along with three Egyptian police officers and one Egyptian tour guide. The gunmen then fled the scene, although Egyptian security forces pursued them and all six were killed. Terrorists launched a grenade attack on a tour bus parked in front of the Egyptian National Antiquities Museum in Cairo on September 18, 1997, killing nine German tourists and an Egyptian bus driver, and wounding eight others.

The West began to respond long before September 11. The U.S. cruise missile attacks on targets in Afghanistan and the Sudan on August 20, 1998, reflected the fact that U.S. intelligence had reliable information that Osama bin Laden, a leading sponsor and financier of terrorism, planned large-scale attacks on U.S. targets. The U.S. attack on the Shifa Pharmaceutical Plant in Khartoum was a preemptive attempt to prevent the production and use of VX nerve gas by bin Laden's organization. These attacks, however, show that the wrong use of military power can do more to provoke than deter.

Nevertheless, the attack that truly globalized Middle Eastern terrorism was the series of attacks on the World Trade Center and the Pentagon on September 11, 2001. There have been many previous attempts at such attacks, and many smaller successful attacks on targets in Europe. It was September 11, however, that showed the United States that its territory and civil population could be as vulnerable as the nations of the Middle East.

While Al-Qaeda emerged as the most important current threat, there were many causes of transnational terrorism in the Middle East, and many different targets:

- The United States is a major target because it projects the most power into the region, because of its close ties to Israel, because attacks on the United

States produce the most worldwide publicity, and because the United States can often be used as a proxy for less popular attacks on Middle Eastern regimes.

- The breakdown in the Arab-Israeli peace process has triggered a wave of Palestinian "terrorism" in response to steadily escalating Israeli "excessive force." It is a tragedy that could trigger a broader Arab-Israeli conflict and make Americans a target, both out of frustration and in an effort to break up the peace process.

- The failures of Middle Eastern secular governments, state terrorism and authoritarianism, economic hardship, social dislocation, and the alienation of youth combine to create extremist groups that not only attack their governments, but use Western targets as proxies. Motives can include attempting to drive out the Western military forces that provide Middle Eastern countries with security, cripple the economy to weaken governments, or win public recognition in the region. While some of these groups are secular, most are Islamic in character. Some totally reject both secularism and any ties to the West or Western values.

- The West can be attacked on the basis of its values, and for corrupting Islamic countries and supporting secular regimes. While the United States is the primary target of such attacks, figures like the Saudi terrorist financier Osama bin Laden want to drive the West out of the region. Unlike more conventional forms of terrorism, such attacks deliberately seek to create a "clash of civilizations" and to build on other regional problems and tensions to divide the West and Arab worlds.[6]

- European nations can become the scene of attacks by opposition groups on the Embassies of Middle Eastern regimes, or by opposition groups attacking each other. Iran has sponsored state terrorist attacks on the People's Mujahidin and Kurdish opposition groups in France, Germany, Switzerland, and Turkey. Israel has killed Palestinians in nations like Norway. France has become the scene of fighting between Algerian factions.

- Western tourists and businessmen can be the targets of terrorists in the Middle East, as such groups seek to put economic pressure on local regimes, or prove their status and power. For example, an Algerian terrorist group called the Armed Islamic Group (GIA) killed seven foreigners in Algeria in 1997, bringing the total number of foreigners the GIA has killed in Algeria to 133 (since 1992). Bombs have been used in civilian areas in Bahrain, although Westerners have not been major targets. Four U.S. employees of Union Texas Petroleum and their Pakistani driver were shot and killed in Karachi on November 12, 1998, when the vehicle they were riding in was attacked by terrorists who seem to have been affiliated with Middle Eastern extremist groups.

The Clash Within a Civilization, the Arab-Israeli Conflict, and the Western Counterreaction

It is still unclear how Islamic extremism and the aftermath of September 11 will play out in the MENA area. What is clear is that Al-Qaeda launched a new series of bloody attacks of Saudi Arabia, that such attacks have taken place in Iraq, that the Algerian civil war continues, and that extremist Islamic movements exist at some level on every MENA state. Extremism and terrorism remain a major threat to MENA governments, and the end result is more a clash within an Islamic civilization than a clash between Islam and the Arab world and the West. The primary goal of most Islamic extremist movements is not to attack the West but to create Islamic regimes, based on ill-defined concepts of religious Puritanism, radical socialism or economic change, and conservative social customs. Such an extremism is an attack on secularism per se, and explains why such movements oppose MENA secular governments and social and economic modernization without clearly articulating the kind of government, society, and economy that should replace them. Islamic extremists know what they are against. They have only vague and impractical ideas of what they are for.

There are, however, other forms of terrorism and extremist violence. The fact that the Arab-Israeli peace process has given way to an Israeli-Palestinian War has led to a new wave of violence on both sides. The Israeli side has used conventional forces to occupy and attack the Palestinians. The Palestinians have used asymmetric and guerrilla warfare, and terrorism—most notably in the form of suicide bombings. The Palestinian terrorist attacks have been overwhelmingly by Islamist groups like Hamas and Palestinian Islamic Jihad (PIJ), but have increasingly involved support from the hard-line elements of secular Palestinian groups as well.

The lines between Islamic extremism and the Arab-Israeli conflict have been further blurred by the role Shiite groups like Hezbollah played in driving Israel out of Lebanon, and the role Iran and Syria have played in supporting Hezbollah. Syria at least tolerates terrorist groups on its soil that oppose Israel. Iran has increasingly funded non-Shiite groups like Hamas and the PIJ, and money has flowed to such groups from the Gulf and other Arab states—partly to support their charities and partly to support the groups in attacking Israel.

Unlike most forms of Islamic extremism and terrorism, the Israeli-Palestinian conflict also polarizes the Arab world at a popular level. If the Israeli image is one of Palestinian terrorism, the Arab image is one of excessive Israeli use of force, continued occupation, and continued settlements. It allows extremist and terrorist groups to exploit the conflict to win popular support and to exploit the image of the United States as Israel's ally and supporter. More generally, it allows them to exploit the image of the West as exploiting the Arab world.

The West, and particularly the United States, has often reacted by confusing Islamist extremism and terrorism with Islam, the Arab world, and Iran. U.S. officials have tried to avoid such stereotypes and dangerous generalizations, but many U.S. Western media and analysts have not. One of the ironies of September 11 is that Osama bin Laden and Al-Qaeda have succeeded in part in producing a Western counterreaction that does to some extent reflect a "clash between civilizations." The U.S. and British invasion and occupation of Iraq has increased such tensions as have the failures to bring effective security and development to Afghanistan, and U.S. talk of broad regime change along lines where its concept of future "democracies" is as vaguely defined as of the future desired by most Islamist extremists.

State Support of Terrorism and the Use of Terrorist Proxies

The regional security problems created by independent terrorist movements are further compounded by the state support of terrorism or state use of terrorist proxies. Several states have actively sponsored external terrorist movements, or have conducted acts of terrorism outside their own territory. These states have included Iran, Iraq, Libya, and Syria.

Such states may help extremist movements acquire weapons of mass destruction in the future, and the most serious challenge proliferation poses to MENA energy facilities may well prove to be the risk that proliferation interacts with terrorism. At present, this is only a possibility, but terrorist attacks using weapons of mass destruction would present a fundamentally different kind of threat. They would be a far more lethal kind of terrorist threat than the region and the West have yet faced.

Under many conditions, a single act of terrorism can kill thousands of people and/or induce levels of panic and political reaction that governments cannot easily deal with. Under some conditions, the use of weapons of mass destruction can pose an existential threat to the existing social and political structure of a small country—particularly one where much of the population and governing elite are concentrated in a single urban area.

Terrorism and Middle East Energy

Both MENA energy exporters and global energy consumers need a smooth flow or energy exports that must be delivered reliably on a day-by-day basis and expanded over time to meet global demand. Chapter 1 has shown that the world needs the Middle East and North Africa to both make massive increases in its energy exports, and sustain these at moderate market prices provided by reliable daily deliveries, and to avoid any interruptions in supply. The next chapter shows that MENA states face immense demographic and economic challenges that require them to earn as much from energy exports as possible, although the era of "oil wealth" has ended and stability can only come from both energy export and a much more diversified pattern of overall economic development.

So far, terrorism and extremism have rarely made direct attacks on energy facilities. This may be because most Islamic extremist movements act largely as national groups or subgroups and see energy export earnings as serving national needs and not just these of the regime or Western interests. There has, however, been a history of minor sabotage in Bahrain and Saudi Arabia, and Al-Qaeda has attacked foreign compounds in Saudi Arabia in ways that could have a future impact on the foreign expertise Saudi Arabia still needs for some aspects of its energy production. There have been occasions in the Algerian civil war when terrorists attacked energy targets and workers in energy facilities. Pipelines and energy facilities were sabotaged during the Iran-Iraq War, although conventional attacks dominated the damage to energy facilities. There has also been a consistent pattern of systematic terrorist attack and sabotage of Iraq's nation's energy facilities since the U.S. and British occupation of Iraq.

It is difficult to generalize from such a unique case, and particularly one that is still in progress, but the Iraq War has at least shown that such attacks can have a powerful political and economic success and that pipelines and export facilities are vulnerable. The attacks to date have also shown that much of the reaction is a matter of how the target is then perceived as a reliable supplier and country for investment, rather than determined by the success of the attack or its impact on exports.

Middle Eastern states are also becoming steadily more vulnerable to sabotage and terrorist attacks. Economies of scale lead to the procurement of highly specialized facilities whose equipment involves long lead times for manufacture and repair. Increases in pipeline capacity increase vulnerability, and petrochemical plants often make lucrative targets as do refineries. Attacks on desalination facilities offer extremely lucrative targets that affect the workers in energy facilities. The creation of large, heavily automated gas trains is creating a new target mix in many countries, and electric power is necessary for oil and gas field operations, export facilities, petrochemical production, and civil life. Even comparatively low value targets like individual oil and gas wells can be attacked in ways that can lead to importer panic or overreaction and force states to deploy large forces to protect entire fields.

There is no present way to know how these various forces will play out, or how much they will affect energy development and supply from the MENA region. It is clear, however, that they already have significantly increased the risk premium many Western companies see as necessary to invest and do business in the MENA area. They have increased the reluctance to provide foreign investment to an area whose nations have long created legal and economic barriers to such investment, and they have led a number of Western businessmen and technical personnel to leave key MENA energy exporting nations like Saudi Arabia. The Arab world, in turn, is increasingly more reluctant to deal with the United States and there have been minor boycotts of U.S. companies over U.S. support of Israel. There has been much less reluctance to deal with Europe, but Islamic extremists continue to attack outside investment and secular influences in broad terms, and not just U.S. influence.

There does, therefore, seem to be a growing risk that the forces of extremism and terrorism will present a growing direct threat to energy exports and facilities. The target is extremely tempting. It is one of the few areas where attackers can easily threaten the fiscal stability of the MENA regimes they are seeking to overthrow, and have significant leverage against the West. At the same time, Saudi Arabia has already been the scene of broader attacks on Western businessmen, and the guerrilla war in Iraq is demonstrating how attacks on Western workers can affect nation building as well as energy supply.

REGIONAL SELF-DEFENSE AND THE ROLE OF THE WEST AND WESTERN POWER PROJECTION

The overall military stability of the MENA region is heavily dependent on Western power projection capabilities, and particularly the United States. The United States has shown in the Iraq War just how well it can project conventional military power, although it has also shown just how many difficulties it can encounter in dealing with asymmetric warfare. While the fall of Saddam has removed a key threat to the region's military stability, threats like Iran remain. The United States may be Israel's ally but it is also seen as a major restraining influence and an ally of moderate regimes—most of which have shown they can do a far better job of buying arms than create effective self-defense capabilities.

As a result, the present security structure of the MENA region is still dependent on de facto alliance between the moderate states in the Middle East and the West, and their access to help from Western power projection capabilities. The United States is the key to such power projection, but this makes it the target of many opposition movements and Islamic extremists as well. The high profile of U.S. forces in the Gulf has also interacted with the tensions caused by the second intifada to cause sufficient political backlash so that the United States is now a major target for terrorists and presents growing political problems for U.S. allies, like Egypt, Jordan, and Saudi Arabia.

European power projection forces cannot substitute for those of the United States. The European members of the North Atlantic Treaty Organization (NATO) have never developed to the capability for large-scale power projection in the MENA region and are unlikely to do so. Iraq has deeply divided the United States and Europe. Europe itself is deeply divided over the attention and role it should play in dealing with the problems in Algeria and North Africa, and the European Union's efforts to create power projection forces have so far been more political than real. Britain and France are the only NATO powers capable of meaningful power projection to the Gulf, but they have minimal strategic lift, and only about half the potential pool of forces they had in 1990.

The end result is that the United States continues to play the critical role in defending the major energy exporters in the Gulf, and this is compounded by the fact that the United States is the only power that now can play a major role in securing the global lines of communication to the MENA region and the flow of tankers and other oil exports.

At the same time, major changes are taking place in the regional role of the United States and other Western states in projection power in the Middle East. U.S. and other Western power projection will be made steadily more complicated by proliferation and the development of more dangerous forms of asymmetric warfare.

The Israeli-Palestinian War, the Iraq War, and the problems the United States has had in dealing with allies like Saudi Arabia since September 11 have made it progressively harder for it to maintain a presence and operate in the MENA region. The United States still maintains major forces in the region and many countries depend upon it, but U.S. and regional military relations are troubled and uneasy. Europe talks about power projection capability, but it is not buying it or the systems to ensure broad inter-operability with the United States.

The wars in Afghanistan and Iraq have also reinforced the lessons of Lebanon and Somalia that the United States is far from ready to fight asymmetric warfare and highly political conflicts in ways that effectively terminate wars and deal with the issues of peacemaking and nation building. The United States has not shown it can properly characterize and target forces with weapons of mass destruction. Perhaps most important, the United States has never planned to help regional states deal with internal security or save a regime from its own people. U.S. and Western capabilities cannot play a military role in dealing with what may be the most serious threat to MENA stability and energy exports.

The United States, its Western allies, and its allies in the region do not yet have a clear counterproliferation option or surplus funds to pay for such an option. They have no common strategy for dealing with terrorism and asymmetric warfare. Moreover, none of the moderate Arab states has power projection forces that can substitute for Western ones. Even Egypt and Syria have only tenuous power projection capabilities and little current willingness to use them.

ENERGY VULNERABILITY AND MARITIME CHOKEPOINTS

Oil moves in many different ways. Oil and gas pipelines connect North Africa to Europe, and may eventually connect Middle Eastern states to South Asia. During 2002, the Energy Information Administration (EIA) estimated that some 1.9–2.2 million barrels per day (MMBD) (12–14 percent) of the oil export from the Persian Gulf was shipped via various pipelines, rather than by tanker through the Strait of Hormuz. Most of MENA oil and gas, however, are directly or eventually moved by sea. For example, oil was exported out of maritime ports in the Gulf and Indian Ocean and Indian Ocean and through the Saudi East-West pipeline to the port of Yanbu on the Red Sea (about 1 MMBD); via pipeline from Iraq's Kirkuk oil region to the Turkish port of Ceyhan (about 0.5–0.8 MMBD); and by pipeline via Syria (around 0.2 MMBD). Only comparatively small amounts to their ultimate destination moved by land, largely by truck to destinations like the Kurdish areas of northern Iraq, Turkey, Jordan, and Iran.[7]

It is easy to focus on the security of oil and gas fields, energy facilities, and pipelines in the MENA area and to forget that most energy exports ultimately move by sea. Moreover, Chapter 1 has indicated that Gulf exports alone will require something like 2.5 times the tanker traffic by 2025 than exists today, as well as vastly expanded ports and loading facilities. Much of this increase in tanker traffic will go to Asia and through the Indian Ocean and Pacific, but a substantial portion will go to Europe and the United States.

The flow of oil exports can be attacked at any point during a tanker voyage. However, there are several key maritime chokepoints that could have a critical impact on the flow of oil in the Middle East:[8]

- *The Strait of Hormuz* is the only shipping channel in and out of the Persian Gulf. Over 14 MMBD of oil flow through this strait to Japan, the United States, Western Europe, and other countries and regions. It is the world's most important oil chokepoint. At its narrowest, it consists of two-mile wide channels for inbound and outbound tankers within the Omani side of the strait, and a two-mile wide buffer zone. The exits on both sides of the strait are close to Iranian waters and air space. Iran and the UAE have also long quarreled over sovereignty over three islands on the western side of the strait that are near the main tanker channels. These islands include Abu Musa, Greater Tunb, and Lesser Tunb, all strategically located in the Strait of Hormuz. Iranian troops occupied the islands in 1992, and the Iranian Foreign Ministry claimed that the islands were "an inseparable part of Iran" in 1995. The UAE has sought mediation and Iran rejected proposal by the Gulf Cooperation Council (GCC) for the dispute to be resolved by the International Court of Justice in 1996. Iran also took action to demonstrate its control over the islands. It started up a power plant on Greater Tunb, opening an airport on Abu Musa, and announced plans for construction of a new port on Abu Musa. Iran did state its willingness to hold talks with the UAE on the dispute in September 2000 and reports that Iran had fortified the islands seem to be untrue. However, no talks have taken place, and the GCC issued a statement reiterating its support for the UAE's sovereignty over Abu Musa and the Tunbs on December 31, 2001. It declared Iran's claims on the islands as "null and void," and backed "all measures . . . by the UAE to regain sovereignty on its three islands peacefully."[9]

The 13.6 MMBD or so of oil that transit the Strait of Hormuz go all over the world, eastward to Asia (especially Japan, China, and India) and westward (via the Suez Canal, the Sumed Pipeline, or around the Cape of Good Hope in South Africa) to Western Europe and the United States. The

EIA reference case indicates that exports through the strait must nearly double by 2020, reaching around 42 MMBD. This implies that up to three times more tankers will transit the strait in 2020 than at present. Alternative routes cannot move anything close to current export levels, much less the much higher production levels forecast by the U.S. Department of Energy (DOE).

- *The Red Sea.* Tankers moving west from the Gulf toward the Suez Canal or Sumed Pipeline must pass through the Bab al-Mandab. This strait is located between Djibouti and Eritrea in Africa, and Yemen on the Arabian Peninsula. It connects the Red Sea with the Gulf of Aden and the Arabian Sea. Any closure of the Bab al-Mandab would keep tankers from reaching the Suez Canal/Sumed Pipeline complex, diverting them around the southern tip of Africa. This would add greatly to transit time and cost, and effectively tie up spare tanker capacity.[10]

There has not been any major fighting in this area, but Yemen fought a brief battle with Eritrea over Greater Hanish Island, located just north of the Bab al-Mandab, in December 1995. The Bab al-Mandab can be bypassed by utilizing the east-west oil pipeline. However, southbound oil traffic, closure addition, and closure of the Bab al-Mandab would effectively block nonoil shipping from using the Suez Canal, except for limited trade within the Red Sea region.

- *The Suez/Sumed Pipeline complex.* This is a chokepoint at the western end of the Red Sea. Oil passing through the Bab al-Mandab or shipping toward the west from Yemen or the Red Sea coast of Saudi Arabia must move by tanker through the Suez Canal or be shipped through the Sumed Pipeline complex in Egypt. Both of these routes connect the Red Sea and Gulf of Suez with the Mediterranean Sea. The EIA reports that over 3 MMBD of Gulf oil exports currently transit the Suez Canal/Sumed Pipeline complex. Any closure of the Suez Canal and/or Sumed Pipeline would divert tankers around the southern tip of Africa (the Cape of Good Hope), sharply increasing transit time and the required tanker capacity.[11]

Chokepoints like the Strait of Hormuz remain critical areas of risk where U.S. power projection and alliances with friendly nations are critical to energy security. At the same time, the proliferation of long-range naval strike aircraft, antiship missiles, smart mines, submarines, and guided missile ships is extending the range at which threats can strike at the movement of energy exports.

These changes in military technology and in the flow of Gulf exports are changing the definition of "chokepoint." One key example is the acquisition of long-range missiles and weapons of mass destruction by nations like Egypt, India, Iran, Iraq, Israel, Libya, and Syria. Another is Iran's development of bases on islands near the Strait of Hormuz and the shipping channels in the Gulf, and its acquisition of advanced antiship missiles, submarines, long-range strike aircraft, and missile patrol boats. The same weapons and technologies allow any nation along the shipping lanes to Asia to create new "chokepoints" at ranges up to several hundred kilometers.

OIL INTERRUPTION AND EMBARGOES

These threats show that the risk of a serious interruption in Middle Eastern oil exports, and particularly Gulf Exports, cannot be ignored. As Table 2.4 shows, there has been a long history of oil interruptions since 1951. Virtually all of these interruptions have taken place in the MENA region, and some have been serious.

The oil embargo of 1973–1974, for example, triggered a massive rise in oil prices that reshaped the energy costs of the global economy, and made dependence on energy imports a major strategic issue for the first time. The fall of the Shah in 1979, and the Iran-Iraq War that followed, created a global panic in the oil market and again dramatized strategic dependence on the Gulf. The period of 1979–1980 also marked the height of MENA energy export revenues in constant dollars. Iraq's invasion of Kuwait and the Gulf War of 1990–1991 marked another major rise in oil prices, although its affects were much less serious than the interruptions of 1973–1974 and 1979–1980.

The Importance of MENA Energy Exports

Conflicts and instability affecting other major energy exporters could also cause a serious interruption in the flow of global energy exports. These countries include Russia, Nigeria and Angola, and Venezuela. The MENA region, however, is the most critical region because it is both unstable and will remain the center of world oil beyond 2030. The region's importance as an energy exporter has been discussed in detail in Chapter 1, and the threat posed by a new interruption in MENA energy exports can be summarized as follows:

- World crude oil flows averaged around 35 MMBD in the early 2000s.
- The Gulf has roughly 65 percent of all world oil reserves. The flow of exports from the Gulf averages over 15 MMBD versus 1.8 MMBD from North Africa, 2.7 MMBD from Latin America, and 1.6 MMBD from Mexico.
- In 2002, Gulf countries had estimated net oil exports of 15.5 MMBD. Saudi Arabia exported the most oil of any Persian Gulf country in 2002, with an estimated 7.0 MMBD (45 percent of the total). Also in 2002, Iran had estimated net exports of around 2.3 MMBD (15 percent), followed by the United Arab Emirates (2.1 MMBD, 13 percent), Kuwait (1.7 MMBD, 11 percent), Iraq (1.6 MMBD, 10 percent), Qatar (0.8 MMBD, 5 percent), and Bahrain (0.01 MMBD, 0.1 percent).[12]
- The peak for Persian Gulf oil exports as a percentage of world oil exports was in 1974, when they accounted for more than two-thirds of the oil traded in

Table 2.4
Global Oil Supply Disruptions since 1951

Date of Net Oil Supply Disruption	Duration (Months of Net Supply Disruption)	Average Gross Supply Shortfall (MMBD)	Reason for Oil Supply Disruption
3/51-10/54	44	0.7	Iranian oilfields nationalized May 1, following months of unrest and strikes in Abadan area
11/56-3/57	4	2.0	Suez War
12/66-3/67	3	0.7	Syrian Transit Fee Dispute
6/67-8/67	2	2.0	Six Day War
5/70-1/71	9	1.3	Libyan price controversy; damage to Tapline
4/71-8/71	5	0.6	Algerian-French nationalization struggle
3/73-5/73	2	0.5	Unrest in Lebanon; damage to transit facilities
10/73-3/74	6	2.6	October Arab-Israeli War; Arab oil embargo
4/76-5/76	2	0.3	Civil war in Lebanon; disruption to Iraqi exports
5/77	1	0.7	Damage to Saudi oil field
11/78-4/79	6	3.5	Iranian revolution
10/80-12/80	3	3.3	Outbreak of Iran-Iraq War
8/90-10/90	3	4.6	Iraqi invasion of Kuwait/Desert Storm
4/99-3/00	12	3.3	OPEC (ex. Iraq) cuts production in effort to increase prices

Source: Adapted from work by the EIA.

world markets. The Persian Gulf share of world oil exports has risen since the oil price collapse of the mid-1980s, but it is not expected to surpass the 1974 level until after 2020.

- U.S. imports from the Gulf slowly rose from an annual average of 1.5 MMBD in 1988 to 2.1 MMBD in 1998, and ranged from 2.2 to 2.8 MMBD in 2001–2003. They rose from 8.7 percent of U.S. demand in 1997 to 13.9 percent in 2002, and from 70 percent to 75 percent of U.S. imports.[13]

- West European imports from the Gulf ranged from 15 percent to 29 percent of total demand during 1990–2002, and from 29 percent to 45 percent of total imports.

- Japanese imports from the Gulf ranged from 64 percent to 76 percent of total demand during 1990–2002, and from 65 percent to 76 percent of total imports.

- DOE projects the MENA region will provide well over 50 percent of world oil exports by 2020. The EIA's *International Energy Outlook 2002* projects that Gulf oil production is expected to rise from 22.4 MMBD in 2001 to 28.7 MMBD in 2010, 38.9 MMBD in 2020, and 45.2 MMBD in 2025. This would increase Persian Gulf oil production capacity to 36.2 percent of the world total by 2025, up from 28 percent in 2000.[14]

- Gulf exports are critical in terms of preserving a margin of surplus or swing production. The EIA estimates that they normally maintain around 90 percent of the world's excess oil production capacity.

- Total MENA production capacity was 23.9 MMBD of production capacity in 2000 (29.7 percent). The EIA estimates that it will be 34.9 MMBD in 2010, 46.4 MMBD in 2020 and 53.6 MMBD in 2020 (43.1 percent).[15]

- The Southern Gulf states alone (through the GCC) provided 17.1 MMBD worth of world production capacity in 2000 (21.3 percent of world capacity), which is estimated to reach 35.1 MMBD by 2025 (28.25 percent).[16]

- The IEA projects that Middle Eastern oil production by the Organization of Petroleum Exporting Countries (OPEC) will increase from 21.0 MMBD in 2000 to 26.5 MMBD in 2010, 37.8 MMBD in 2020, and 54.4 MMBD in 2030. Total Middle Eastern oil production will increase from 24.1 MMBD in 2000 to 28.3 MMBD in 2010, 39.3 MMBD in 2020, and 52.3 MMBD in 2030.[17] The IEA projects that Middle East oil exports will reach 46 MMBD by 2030.

- The EIA estimates that Gulf oil exports will rise from 16.9 MMBD in 2001 to 36.4 MMBD in 2025. They will rise from 30 percent of world exports to 41 percent.[18]

- The IEA projects that Middle Eastern refined oil product exports will increase to 7 MMBD by 2030.[19]

- The Gulf is a major gas exporter with 32.8 percent of world reserves.

- The IEA projects that Middle Eastern gas exports will increase from 23.1 BCM in 2000 to 364 BCM in 230. Flows to North America will increase from 17 to 104 BCM, flows to Europe will rise from 0.4 to 160 BCM, flows to South Asia will increase from nearly 0 to 27 BCM, and flows to East Asia will increase from 21 to 73 BCM.[20]

The Problem of Guessing at Future Scenarios

There is no consensus as to what kind of interruptions might take place in the flow of MENA oil exports, in part because there is no current set of contingencies or threats that appears probable enough to merit detailed planning. The preceding analysis has shown that such interruptions could have a wide range of causes and take a wide range of forms. Future interruptions, however, could include a new oil embargo, a civil war in a key MENA country, the impact of a local war, the result of a series of terrorist attacks, or the closing of a major export route like the Strait of Hormuz.

A major new embargo now seems less likely. The MENA oil-exporting states have a steadily growing need for cash flow, and most have shown little solidarity with the Palestinians since Arafat supported Iraq in 1990. The world has also learned to adapt better to oil interruptions when they occur. The embargo of 1973–1974 led the world market to increase oil production in other areas, but world markets were not capable of tracking what was happening or effectively identifying and distributing the oil available. As a result, the seriousness of the crisis was caused as much by the world's inability to track supply in real time as by any shortfall in supply. These problems continued through the late 1970s, but tracking and reporting improved after the crisis following the fall of the Shah of Iran. Neither the "tanker war" between Iran and Britain and the United States in 1987–1998 nor the Gulf War in 1990–1991 led to the same level of panic, price rises, and hoarding.

The most likely interruptions seem to be ones that are short or limited in scope, and many could be dealt with by production increases by other countries. The impact of the loss of Iraq and Kuwait oil production during the Gulf War in 1990–1991, for example, was limited by increases in Saudi and other production. Increases in production by other exporters largely compensated for a political crisis that led to Venezuelan production cuts in 2002, and the same was true when Iraq ceased to export during the Iraq War of 2003. While each interruption did produce price rises, and had some impact on global economic growth, the impact was too limited to have a major impact on the global economy.

The steady increases in world demand for MENA energy exports projected through 2030 do mean, however, that the global economy will become steadily more vulnerable to major interruptions. The Gulf alone is projected to more than double its flow of exports during 2000–2025. Five Gulf countries—Saudi Arabia, the UAE, Iraq, Iran, and Kuwait—will become steadily more important producers and exporters. At the same time, the gap between the normal production of oil and total production capacity is expected to shrink steadily, leaving less and less surplus production capacity that MENA and other nations can bring online in the event of a major interruption in exports from one or more Gulf states.

The cases that seem to merit most consideration—more because of the seriousness of their impact than their probability—are some form of war involving Iran that could at least temporarily close the Strait of Hormuz, a major attack on Saudi Arabia or a civil conflict that disrupted production, or some new war involving Iraq or a civil conflict.

- Chart 2.14 shows that is possible to make rough estimates of how the impact of interruption scenarios might change over time, based on the changes in estimated production capacity, although major differences exist in such estimates between sources and according to the economic conditions assumed.

- Chart 2.15 provides similar data in a form where it is possible to see how a major embargo, the closing of Strain of Hormuz, the loss of production from Saudi Arabia or another key Gulf country, or the loss of Algerian or Libyan production might impact on world supply. The problem is that not only are such estimates uncertain, but there is no way to know market conditions and the level of surplus production capacity relative to demand, how much of a region or nation's output would actually be lost, or how long the interruption would take place.

- Chart 2.16 shows the importance of the Gulf, North Africa, and entire MENA region in terms of current and projected world oil exports. While the particular numbers involved are as uncertain as the estimates of production capacity, it is obvious that a true MENA embargo or loss of most Gulf oil exports would have a massive impact on the world economy today and that this impact will grow steadily with time.

These charts do not include gas exports, which will have growing importance over time. The risk of any interruption would be compounded by any problems that reduced the supply of nuclear power or use of coal for environmental reasons.

Charts 2.14 to 2.16 show how dangerous a major and lasting Arab embargo could be if Arab states would actually be willing to give up their oil export revenues. It is clear how critical the Gulf is to world production capacity, and it is clear just how much the world will come to depend on a steady and stable increase in Saudi production and exports. In fact, Russia is the only major exporter outside the MENA area where a major interruption could have a critical impact on the global economy, particularly because it is both a major oil and gas exporter.

At the same time, the next chapter shows that MENA states already desperately need the cash flow from their energy exports and this need will grow over time. The demographic and economic pressures on the region are so severe that no regime in an exporting country can ignore the consequences of an embargo and the factions in any civil fighting must consider the popular reaction to an attack on such facilities. Wars tend to do limited damage of limited duration and do not produce catastrophic interruptions, and any belligerents in the region must consider the fact that U.S.

Chart 2.14
Trends in Middle Eastern Petroleum Production Capacity That Could Be Affected by a Future Oil Interruption Scenario by Country Relative to World Capacity: 1990–2025

(EIA Reference Case in MMBD)

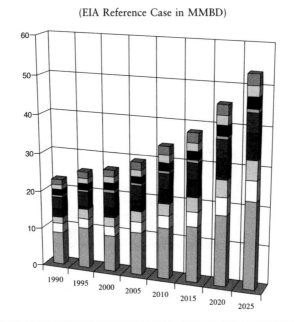

	1990	1995	2000	2005	2010	2015	2020	2025
▨ Other	1.4	1.7	1.8	2	2.2	2.5	2.6	2.8
▢ Algeria	1.3	1.4	1.6	1.7	2	2.1	2.4	2.7
■ Libya	1.5	1.6	1.7	1.7	2	2.2	2.6	2.9
▨ Qatar	0.5	0.6	0.9	0.6	0.7	0.7	0.8	0.8
■ Iran	3.2	3.9	3.8	3.9	4	4.3	4.7	4.9
■ Iraq	2.2	0.6	2.6	2.8	3.7	4.4	5.3	6.6
▢ Kuwait	1.7	2.6	2.5	2.8	3.1	3.7	4.4	5
▢ UAE	2.5	2.6	2.5	2.9	3.3	3.9	4.6	5.2
▨ Saudi	8.6	10.6	9.4	11.1	13.2	14.4	18.2	22.5

Total Gulf	18.7	—	22.4	24.5	27.9	31.4	38.0	45.0
Total ME	22.9	—	27.5	29.9	34.1	38.2	45.6	53.4
Total World	69.4	—	79.2	84.2	95.1	104.7	114.9	126.1
Gulf % of World	27.0	—	28.3	29.1	29.3	29.9	33.07	35.6
ME % of World	33.0		34.7	35.5	35.8	36.4	39.7	42.3

Source: Adapted by Anthony H. Cordesman from EIA, *International Energy Outlook 1997*, DOE/EIA-0484 (1997), April 1997, pp. 157–160; EIA, *International Energy Outlook 2002*, DOE/EIA-0484 (2002), March 2002, Table D1; EIA, *International Energy Outlook 2003*, DOE/EIA-0484 (2003), March 2003, Table D1; and EIA, *International Energy Outlook 2004*, www.eia.doe.gov/oiaf/ieo/index.html, April 2004, p. 213.

Chart 2.15
Range of MENA Contribution to World Oil Production Capacity: 2001–2025

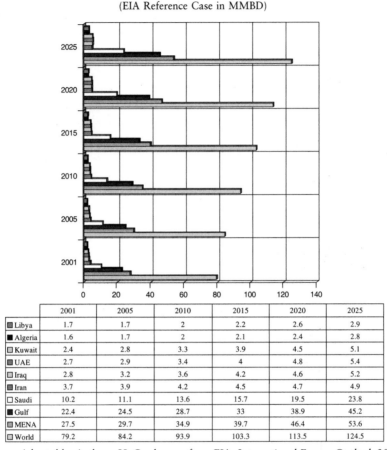

(EIA Reference Case in MMBD)

	2001	2005	2010	2015	2020	2025
Libya	1.7	1.7	2	2.2	2.6	2.9
Algeria	1.6	1.7	2	2.1	2.4	2.8
Kuwait	2.4	2.8	3.3	3.9	4.5	5.1
UAE	2.7	2.9	3.4	4	4.8	5.4
Iraq	2.8	3.2	3.6	4.2	4.6	5.2
Iran	3.7	3.9	4.2	4.5	4.7	4.9
Saudi	10.2	11.1	13.6	15.7	19.5	23.8
Gulf	22.4	24.5	28.7	33	38.9	45.2
MENA	27.5	29.7	34.9	39.7	46.4	53.6
World	79.2	84.2	93.9	103.3	113.5	124.5

Source: Adapted by Anthony H. Cordesman from EIA, *International Energy Outlook 2003*,
DOE/EIA-0484 (2003), June 2003, p. 235

and outside intervention would almost certainly occur in the event of a
major interruption, just as it did during the Iran-Iraq War when the United
States "reflagged" tankers and defended Gulf shipping against Iran.

In short, there are so many different real-world ways in which an interruption could develop and play out in terms of its politics, the use of military force, the actual level of cuts in exports, in the duration of such cuts,
in the way other exporters can compensate, and in terms of the global economic climate and level of demand that such scenario analysis can be little
more than a matter of informed guesswork.

Chart 2.16
Range of MENA Contribution to World Oil Exports: 2001–2025

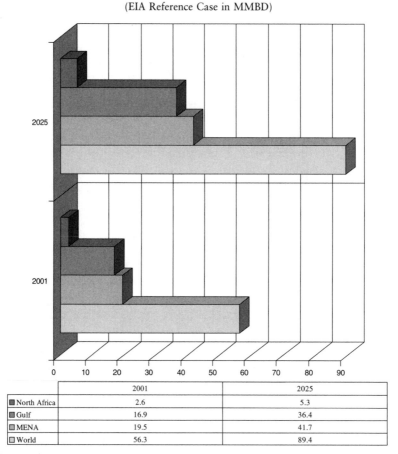

(EIA Reference Case in MMBD)

	2001	2025
■ North Africa	2.6	5.3
▨ Gulf	16.9	36.4
▤ MENA	19.5	41.7
☐ World	56.3	89.4

Source: Adapted by Anthony H. Cordesman from EIA, *International Energy Outlook 2003*, DOE/EIA-0484 (2003), June 2003, Table 14, p. 42; and EIA, *International Energy Outlook 2004*, www.eia.doe.gov/oiaf/ieo/index.html, April 2004, Table 8, p. 40.

- Chart 2.14 shows the relative size of each MENA country's oil export capacity during 2000–2025, and illustrates the maximum impact any combination of MENA states could have in an oil interruption scenario.

- Chart 2.15 shows similar data, but is organized to show the impact of an oil interruption in a single state.

- Chart 2.16 shows how the flow of Gulf, North African, and total MENA exports relates to total world exports in 2001 and 2025, and provides a rough picture of the impact of "worst cases" like a total closing of the Gulf or comprehensive regional oil embargo.

The Economic Impact of Energy Interruptions

There is no reliable way to measure the economic impact any given interruption in MENA energy exports would have, and such an impact would vary sharply according to scenario and duration. Under many conditions, an interruption might be limited enough—and of be such short duration—that it would actually have less impact than the normal fluctuations in oil prices than grow out of market conditions.

For example, the EIA reports that the world oil price in nominal dollars per barrel fell from $21.02 in the first quarter of 1997 to a low of $10.86 in the first quarter of 1999. Then, in the second quarter of 1999, the world oil price began to rise dramatically, ultimately almost tripling to a high of $29.11 in the third quarter of 2000.

The EIA's *Annual Economic Outlook 2004* forecast indicates that the average crude oil price in the lower 48 will be $23.61 per barrel in 2010 and $26.72 per barrel in 2025 in the reference case. In the high world oil price case, the price increases to $32.80 in 2010 and $34.90 per barrel in 2025. In the low oil price case, this number declines to $16.36 per barrel in 2010 then rises to $16.49 per barrel in 2025.[21]

The path for the wellhead natural gas price was less volatile than for oil between 1997:1 and 2000:1, fluctuating between a high of $2.63 per thousand cubic feet to a low of 1.76. At the start of the second quarter of 2000, however, the wellhead price of natural gas increased dramatically. From the first quarter to the second quarter of 2000, the price rose from $2.26 to $3.06 and by the fourth quarter to $5.19 per thousand cubic feet.[22]

The EIA has made a rough estimate of the impact of the alternative price and supply levels. During the two-year period from 1997:1 to 1999:1, falling energy prices boosted the U.S. economy. If energy prices had remained at their 1997 levels instead, the growth rate of gross domestic product (GDP) might well have been reduced by 0.3 percentage points. The opposite case occurred in the years that followed: during the next two-year period, from 1999:1 to 2001:1, energy prices first rose dramatically, then began to decline. If this rapid rise in energy prices had not occurred, there may have been as much as 0.7 percentage points of additional GDP growth. Over the entire four-year period, a steady energy price path could have potentially boosted GDP growth by 0.2 percentage points.

This price volatility may at first seem so massive that it must have dramatic effects, but its not atypical of the impact of "normal" market conditions in energy exports. In fact, any analysis of the past ups and downs in oil prices caused by market forces shows that it would take a very serious interruption to have more serious effects. It is important to note, however, that the shifts in prices during 1997–2001 occurred over an extended period of time and avoided panic buying. It is almost impossible, however, to estimate the psychological impact of sudden interruptions on the market, and it is clear that major market-driven changes in energy prices—which would be similar to the impact of a major oil interruption—had a real but moderate impact on the U.S. economy.

The economic impact of an interruption could also be reduced if the United States made timely and effective use of its Strategic Petroleum Reserves (SPR) and the interruption was not serious enough to trigger the sharing of available oil imports called for under the security agreements the United States and its allies signed in creating the International Energy Agency. The SPR currently has a storage capability of 700 million barrels, and President George W. Bush ordered the SPR to be filled to its maximum capacity on November 13, 2001.

This fill is being carried out by continuing to use the royalty-in-kind program carried out jointly between the Department of Energy and the Department of the Interior. The royalty-in-kind program applies to oil owed to the U.S. government by producers who operate leases on the federally owned Outer Continental Shelf. These producers are required to provide from 12.5 percent to 16.7 percent of the oil they produce to the U.S. government. The government can either acquire the oil itself or receive the equivalent dollar value. The SPR reached 600 million barrels in May 2003, about fifty-three days of inventory at current U.S. consumption rates.[23]

The EIA "Rules of Thumb" for Calculating the Impact of Energy Interruptions

The EIA has established some rough "rules of thumb" for estimating the impact of major interruptions. The EIA rules estimate that oil prices increase by $3–5 per barrel for every one million barrel per day of oil disrupted, and that the growth rate of U.S. GDP will be reduced by 0.3–0.5 percentage points. In other words, if U.S. GDP is expected to increase and a 3.0 percent and a 1 million barrel per day oil supply disruption occurred, U.S. GDP would be expected to grow by only 2.5–2.7 percent (a reduction of 0.3–0.5 percentage points).[24]

As the EIA notes, these rules of thumb are subject to important qualifications:[25]

- These estimates represent price pressure on the economy, but the actual pass through will be determined by a number of other factors, such as the financial and operating position of firms and industries comprising the economy.
- If the price of oil were $30 per barrel, the price and GDP rules-of-thumb could be combined in the following way to estimate the impacts of a disruption. For every 1 million barrels per day of oil disrupted, the price rule-of-thumb suggests that oil prices could increase by $3–5 per barrel, or by 10 percent–17 percent. The GDP rule-of-thumb suggests that if these price increases were sustained, the U.S. GDP growth rate could be reduced by 0.05–0.08 percentage points (likely first year impacts), with the U.S. GDP growth rate reduc-

tion ranging as high as 0.10–0.17 percentage points (likely second-year impacts).

• The effects of an oil supply disruption are directly related to the size of the disruption. First, estimate how much oil was being produced in the disrupted countries that is no longer available. The EIA defines this as the "gross disruption size." However, to better estimate price and economic impacts, an adjustment to the gross disruption size is necessary. To better estimate the impacts of an oil supply disruption, subtract from the gross disruption size how much more oil unaffected countries are likely to produce to help offset the loss of oil to the market. As the initial supply disruption occurs, prices are likely to increase immediately. However, this higher price increases the incentive for other producing countries, where possible, to increase their oil production. Once you have subtracted an assumed amount of excess production that will be utilized from the gross disruption size, your result is what EIA labels the "net disruption size." Using the net disruption size in the rules of thumb listed earlier should better estimate the impacts of the disruption. Other factors, such as the availability of oil inventories and the use of strategic oil inventories such as the Strategic Petroleum Reserve, can also affect the impacts of an oil supply disruption.

• The basic economic data used in formulating these EIA rules are now badly out of date, and have not been updated since at least 1997. As a result, they understate the real-world economic impact of any interruption even if the basic rules are valid. It should also be understood that these additional rules do not consider the psychological impact of a given crisis on world markets or the impact of any conflict that may cause them. At the same time, they are no weaker than far more sophisticated models because so many complex factors are involved, and so many uncertainties, that no method of modeling or estimation can have more than low credibility as a predictive tool.

The grim truth is that the nature and economic impact of any given energy interruption is likely to be known only as it develops. It is always possible to speculate using both the scenarios discussed earlier and the EIA rules of thumb, but the chances of their coinciding with reality are negligible. This does not, however, make the risks less real. The fact that no one can predict the impact of regional conflict and instability thirty years into the future, or even the nature and outcome of the most likely cases, has never prevented them from occurring.

Chapter 3

Political, Economic, and Demographic Pressures on Middle Eastern Energy Production and Exports

Internal political and economic instability pose problems and uncertainties as great as those affecting military security. The Middle East and North Africa (MENA) as a region has many regimes that have an uncertain ability to govern, internal religious and ethnic tensions, succession problems, and semiauthoritarian characteristics or lack a stable popular base. Most regimes need political reform and need to develop more pluralistic and representative governments that serve the nation, not the ruling class. The rule of law needs to be strengthened, in terms of both human rights and the protection of property and basic civil and economic operations. In practice, this means that the political structure and internal stability of every MENA energy exporter must be the subject of constant review. This is particularly true in view of the threat posed by Islamic extremism and terrorism.[1]

Politics, however, are only the most volatile aspect of internal instability. In spite of its energy export earnings, the MENA region has not succeeded in developing modern and competitive economics and virtually all the countries in the region take major demographic problems. For most energy-exporting states, "oil wealth" is a myth dating back to the late 1970s and early 1980s. Energy exports now sustain faltering economies that are not yet on the road to diversified and stable development. Major increases in population are destroying traditional social structures, creating hyperurbanization and a "youth explosion" in terms of rapid, massive additions to work forces that already have high levels of disguised unemployment.

THE POLITICAL DIMENSION

MENA political structures remain fragile and largely authoritarian regardless of the formal structure of government, and all regional governments are repressive to some extent. In broad terms, no state in the region has managed to create a secular political culture that provides effective pluralism. In fact, traditional monarchies often interfere less in human rights and normal social conduct than titular democracies. All of the competing secular ideologies of the postcolonial have so far failed: pan-Arabism, socialism, capitalism, Marxism, statism, and paternalism have not provided lasting political cohesion, given development adequate momentum, or met social needs. As for Islam, the fact that much of the population of the region has turned back to more traditional social structures and religion is scarcely surprising. At the same time, it is unclear that even the most moderate and pragmatic Islamists have meaningful solutions to the region's problems.

The region is scarcely without hope. Leaders have emerged in some MENA countries who are pressing for serious reform. Far too often, however, MENA societies are so static that they may be moving toward revolution or civil war when they should be moving toward evolutionary political and economic reform. The tragedy of the Middle East is that so many opportunities are being wasted and the region is steadily falling behind the cutting edged of political, economic, and social development in areas like Asia and Latin America.

AGING LEADERS, UNSTABLE REGIMES, UNCERTAIN REPLACEMENTS, AND ISLAMIC EXTREMISM

The age of many of the region's leaders is a cliché in the political analysis of the Middle East. Age and ill-health have already led to a transfer of power in Bahrain, Jordan, and Morocco, and are leading to one in Saudi Arabia. They may soon lead to a transfer of power in the United Arab Emirates (UAE). Age is a growing factor in any calculation about the future leadership of Kuwait. Unstable leadership elites are another serious problem, affecting Algeria, Iran, Iraq, Libya, and Syria. Even a ruler's track record of long-term survival—as is the case in Yemen—is no promise of what will happen when President Salah goes, and Sultan Qabus has left serious uncertainties regarding the succession in Oman.

One has to be careful, however, about drawing any "après moi le déluge" conclusions about succession in the MENA states. For all of its problems, the region is now more stable than it was at the time of pan-Arabism and Nasser, and during much of the Cold War. While Islamic extremism is a serious problem, the fact is, however, that there is no guarantee of stability for a future that extends out to the year 2020. The key succession/domestic political issues affecting oil and gas exportation include:

- The success of the new leaders in Bahrain, and divisions within the royal family over how to govern, the political divisions between Shiite and Sunni, and the much higher birthrates of the Shiites.

- The near senility of the emir and prime minister of Kuwait, growing divisions within the Kuwaiti royal family, and deep political divisions within a National Assembly more interested in ideology, Islam, and service politics than creating a stable structure of government.

- The uncertain balance of power between the "moderates" of President Khatami and the "traditionalists" of the Ayatollah Khamenei in Iran, and the future impact of low export revenues, low economic growth, and high population growth on the political stability of an aging and somewhat dysfunctional revolution.

- The problems of replacing the regime of Saddam Hussein present in Iraq, and the less obvious problems of creating a stable postautocratic regime in a state with massive internal economic problems, high population growth, and deep divisions between Sunni, Shiite, and Kurd. These problems are compounded by the fact that the Shiite and Kurdish population is growing much more quickly than the Sunni population.

- The lack of formal heir to Sultan Qabus in Oman, other internal political problems and rivalries, and the fear the Sultan is increasingly isolated from the people and is not getting effective technocrat advice.

- Residual divisions within Qatar's royal family and a tendency to provoke "generational" quarrels with Bahrain, Egypt, Saudi Arabia, and the UAE.

- Saudi Arabia now seems to have a smooth succession process from Fahd to Abdullah to Sultan, but may face a generational succession problem much sooner depending on their actual longevity. It certainly faces continuing problems with its Islamic extremists and "youth explosion."

- Divisions within the UAE, questions about the post-Zayed unity of the seven emirates, and rivalries within Abu Dhabi's ruling family.

- The uncertain ability of Bashir Asad to govern in Syria, and the problems of creating a stable postautocratic regime in Syria with an unreformed economy, very high population growth, and divisions between Alawite and Sunni, and secularist and Islamist. These problems are compounded by the slow progress in the peace process and the uncertain future of Syria's presence in Lebanon.

- Mubarak's age and the lack of a formally designated vice president in Egypt.

- President Zine El Abidine Ben Ali's health, and failure to build a stable base of pluralism for his regime, raises serious questions about the future of Tunisia.

- Growing Islamist challenges to Qadhafi from Islamists in Libya and the lack of any modern state structure of government whether or not his sons replace him.

- Islamic extremism and secular corruption and authoritarianism have proven to be an explosive mix in Algeria.

- King Mohamed VI of Morocco has emerged as a more popular leader than his father, and has eased much of the repression in the country. There are so many demographic and economic problems in the country, however, that his efforts at reform may fail to bring stability.

Given this list, there is no reason to assume that a broad-ranging succession crisis will occur in the region, whether it is a matter of aging leaders or aging regimes. It would be equally unrealistic, however, to assume that all of these succession and leadership issues will be resolved peacefully and lead to stable new governments and will affect the energy security of at least one Middle Eastern state between now and 2020.

THE NEXT CLASS OF TECHNOCRATS

Western risk analysis often focuses on the "corruption" of MENA ruling elites, military and arms spending, and human rights issues. Practical governance and energy development, however, are heavily dependent on the quality of the region's technocrats. The present generation presents a major problem because it has not learned to control costs, to properly plan and manage projects on the basis of realistic ROI calculations, and often seeks to create very large-scale projects on a first of a kind basis for national and personal prestige. The end result has often been a vast drain on national budgets, a waste of resources on unprofitable ventures and investments, and a resistance to private investment and realistic national budgets and five-year plans. The region's technocrats have accomplished a great deal and have much to be proud of, but they have cumulatively cost more, and created more problems, than corruption and military forces.

Many MENA technocrats have not adapted rapidly enough to deal with the decline in state revenues and investment income. Worse, many have no clear pattern of succession, and the authoritarian and personal nature of many governments has retained aging technocrats with too little turnover and too little delegation of responsibility. This may be least true in the energy sector, where the need for global competitiveness demands a high degree of competence. The problems still exist, however, and the problems in the energy sector cannot be separated from the overall management of the national budget.

A number of countries have also seen a major drop in the Western education of their future technocrats without replacing it with high-quality domestic education. Local education overemphasizes rote learning, Islam, and politics in a way that means the pool of future talent with realistic public administration, economic, and business skills is too small to meet future needs. At the same time, many countries are cutting their numbers of foreign managers and advisers or relegating them to less influential roles. The demands on the next generation of technocrats will also be much higher than in the past for one simple reason: there is far less money and surplus capital.

THE CHALLENGE OF LIMITED DEVELOPMENT AND ECONOMIC GROWTH

Important as politics are, it is economics and demographics that may prove to present the most serious challenges to the region's stability. Economic development has been poor since the end of the oil boom in the late 1970s. The Middle East only averaged 1.5 percent annual economic growth from 1990 to 2000, only half of its average annual population growth. This situation has improved since 1990, but growth averaged less than 3 percent before the economic collapse in Asia and similar collapse in world oil prices in late 1997. Population growth slightly outpaced real economic growth throughout the 1990s.

The World Bank's *Global Economic Development Report* for 2003 shows a sharp decline in economic growth in gross domestic product (GDP) in constant prices from 6.5 percent during 1971–1980 to 2.5 percent during 1981–1990. While growth rose to 3.2 percent during 1991–2000, it still barely kept pace with population growth. This is reflected in the fact that growth in per capita income in constant prices dropped from 3.6 percent during 1971–1980 to –0.6 percent during 1981–1990, and was only 1 percent from 1991 to 2000—reflected static income over nearly twenty years in a region with extremely poor equity of income distribution.

While interregional comparisons may be somewhat unfair, the economic growth in East Asia and the Pacific was 6.6 percent during 1971–1980, 7.3 percent during 1981–1990, and 7.7 percent during 1991–2000. The growth in real per capita income was the economic growth in East Asia and the Pacific was 3.0 percent during 1971–1980, 4.8 percent during 1981–1990, and 5.4 percent during 1991–2000.

Some states like Kuwait, Qatar, and the UAE have so much oil and gas wealth per capita that they maybe able to buy their way out of their mistakes indefinitely. Most Middle Eastern states, however, suffer severely from economic mismanagement and excessive state control of the economy. Structural economic reform has begun in Algeria, Morocco, Tunisia, Egypt, Jordan, Saudi Arabia, Lebanon, and Bahrain. This reform, however, remains highly uncertain and no country has yet carried out such reform to the point where it has a serious prospect of success.

The other Middle Eastern states have uncertain near- to midterm economic prospects, and this is true of most oil exporters as well. The Israeli and Palestinian economies have been crippled by war; Egypt, Jordan, Lebanon, and Syria are all experiencing serious economic and demographic problems; and the Iraqi economy is weak and may soon face the shock of a new war. The Iranian economy is in a serious crisis, compounded by deep ideological conflicts over how to deal with the issue.

Algeria's efforts at economic reform have been partially blocked by corruption and civil war. Qadhafi's mismanagement and UN sanctions have

Chart 3.1
The Middle East and North Africa Have Had a Steadily Declining Share of the Global Economy

(The GNP of the Middle East Relative to World Total in $U.S. Current Billions)

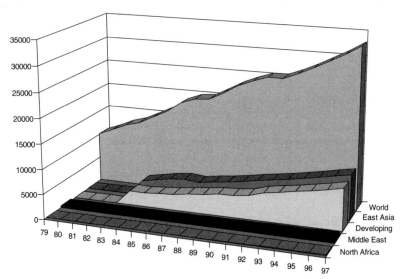

Note: Middle East does not include North African states other than Egypt.
Source: Adapted by Anthony H. Cordesman form ACDA, *World Military Expenditures and Arms Transfers*, various editions.

blocked much of Libya's development. Bahrain no longer has significant oil reserves. Saudi Arabia has experienced over a decade of budget deficits and has only about 40 percent of the real per capita income it had at the peak of the oil boom. Oman is also experiencing serious development problems. While sources differ according to report, work by the World Bank shows that many Middle Eastern states have had rates of economic growth that lag behind their population growth, and that Middle East development has fallen badly behind the rate of growth in East Asia and China.

Once again, these trends become clearer when quantified:

- Chart 3.1 shows a U.S. State Department estimate of the trends in global economic growth in the Middle East and in the developing world as a whole and East Asia in particular.
- Chart 3.2 shows the same data only for the developing world.
- Chart 3.3 compares World Bank data on GDP growth by region and key MENA country. It is clear that Middle Eastern growth rates have dropped from parity with East Asia in the 1970s to rates that have been level ever since.

Chart 3.2

Comparing Total Middle Eastern and North African GNP Growth to the Overall Trend in Developing States

(\$Current Billions)

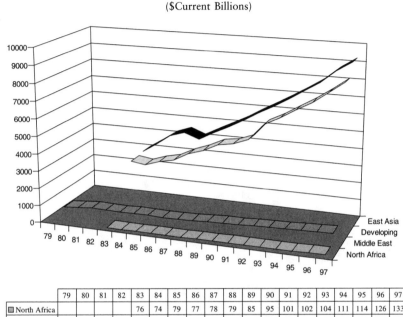

	79	80	81	82	83	84	85	86	87	88	89	90	91	92	93	94	95	96	97
▨ North Africa					76	74	79	77	78	79	85	95	101	102	104	111	114	126	133
▨ Middle East	281	355	408	403	384	402	409	381	402	410	446	491	498	544	565	588	629	657	692
▢ Developing					2895	2773	3053	3244	3680	3970	4390	4520	4850	5780	6230	6750	7240	7850	8460
■ East Asia					3005	3526	4109	4400	4070	4540	4960	5420	5930	6390	6890	7420	7960	8650	9210

Note: Middle East does not include North African states other than Egypt.
Source: Adapted by Anthony H. Cordesman form ACDA, *World Military Expenditures and Arms Transfers*, various editions.

It is also clear that major oil powers like Saudi Arabia have had growth rates far lower than their population growth rates for more than two decades.

- Chart 3.4 shows similar data for per capita population growth.
- Chart 3.5 compares World Bank data on GDP growth by region and key MENA country. It is again clear that Middle Eastern growth rates have dropped from parity with East Asia in the 1970s to rates that have been level ever since. It is also clear that major oil powers like Saudi Arabia have had growth rates far lower than their population growth rates for more than two decades.

POPULATION GROWTH, DEMOGRAPHIC PRESSURES, AND A "YOUTH EXPLOSION"

The total population of the Middle East and North Africa has grown from 78.6 million in 1950 to 101.2 million in 1960, 133.0 million in 1970,

Chart 3.3
GDP Growth of the Gulf and MENA States: The Lag Behind East Asia

(Percent of Real Annual Change during 1980–2000)

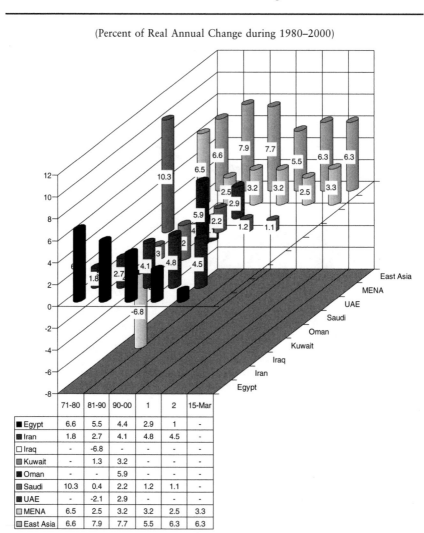

	71-80	81-90	90-00	1	2	15-Mar
■ Egypt	6.6	5.5	4.4	2.9	1	-
■ Iran	1.8	2.7	4.1	4.8	4.5	-
□ Iraq	-	-6.8	-	-	-	-
▨ Kuwait	-	1.3	3.2	-	-	-
■ Oman	-	-	5.9	-	-	-
▨ Saudi	10.3	0.4	2.2	1.2	1.1	-
■ UAE	-	-2.1	2.9	-	-	-
□ MENA	6.5	2.5	3.2	3.2	2.5	3.3
▨ East Asia	6.6	7.9	7.7	5.5	6.3	6.3

Source: Adapted by Anthony H. Cordesman from World Bank, *World Development Indicators 2002*, pp. 204–206; and *Global Economic Prospects 2003*, p. 204.

177.9 million in 1980, 244.8 million in 1990, and 307.1 million in 2000. Conservative projections put it at 376.2 million in 2010, 449.3 million in 2020, 522.3 million in 2030, 592.1 million in 2040, and 656.3 million in 2050. This growth will exhaust natural water supplies, force permanent dependence on food imports, and raise the size of the working population

Chart 3.4
Average Per Capita Income Remains High by Developing Country Standards in PPP Terms

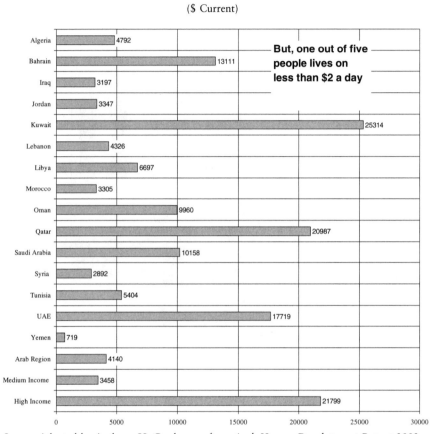

($ Current)

Algeria	4792
Bahrain	13111
Iraq	3197
Jordan	3347
Kuwait	25314
Lebanon	4326
Libya	6697
Morocco	3305
Oman	9960
Qatar	20987
Saudi Arabia	10158
Syria	2892
Tunisia	5404
UAE	17719
Yemen	719
Arab Region	4140
Medium Income	3458
High Income	21799

But, one out of five people lives on less than $2 a day

Source: Adapted by Anthony H. Cordesman from *Arab Human Development Report 2002*, pp. 5, 143.

aged fifteen to thirty from 20.5 million in 1950 to 87.8 million in 2000, and 145.2 million in 2050. The fact that the age group of fourteen years or younger now totals over 40 percent of the population of the region creates an immense bow wave of future strain on the social, educational, political, and economic system.

The end result is that a combination of fluctuating oil revenues, high population growth rates, and a failure to modernize and diversify the overall economy threatens to turn the past oil wealth of the oil-exporting states into oil poverty. The Southern Gulf states have only about 40 percent of

Chart 3.5
Trend in GDP Per Capita of Gulf and MENA States

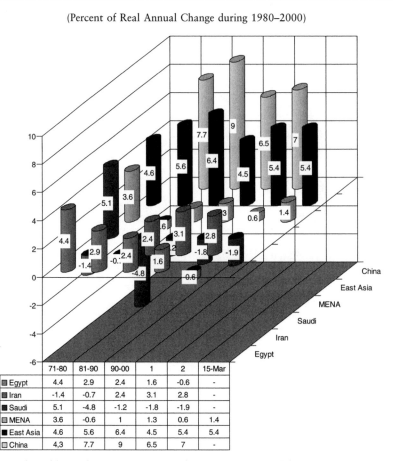

(Percent of Real Annual Change during 1980–2000)

	71-80	81-90	90-00	1	2	15-Mar
▦ Egypt	4.4	2.9	2.4	1.6	-0.6	-
▤ Iran	-1.4	-0.7	2.4	3.1	2.8	-
■ Saudi	5.1	-4.8	-1.2	-1.8	-1.9	-
▦ MENA	3.6	-0.6	1	1.3	0.6	1.4
■ East Asia	4.6	5.6	6.4	4.5	5.4	5.4
▢ China	4,3	7.7	9	6.5	7	-

Source: Adapted by Anthony H. Cordesman from World Bank, *Global Economic Prospects 2003*, p. 205.

the real per capita income they had at the peak of the oil boom in the early 1980s, and little prospect for anything other than a slow decline. Kuwait, Qatar, and the UAE maintain high per capita incomes, but Saudi Arabia's "oil wealth" is becoming increasingly marginal, as its population is growing far more quickly than its economy.

The resulting social turbulence is compounded by the region's extremely young population, overstretched and outdated educational systems, and the failure of the labor market to create productive jobs, or any jobs at all for many of the young men entering the labor force. Emigration creates another source of social turbulence, while religious and cultural barriers to the effective employment of women compound other problems in productivity and competitiveness with other developed regions.

Political structures remain fragile and largely authoritarian regardless of the formal structure of government. Traditional monarchies often interfere less in human rights and normal social conduct than supposed democracies. In broad terms, however, no state in the region has managed to create a secular political culture that provides effective pluralism, and most competing secular ideologies have failed: pan-Arabism, socialism, capitalism, Marxism, statism, and paternalism have all failed to provide adequate development and meet social needs, and all governments are to some extent repressive. The fact that so many in the region have turned back to more traditional social structures and religion is scarcely surprising, but it is unclear that this offers any meaningful solution to the problems involved. Theocracies seem to be the common enemy of man, economic development, and God.

- Chart 3.6 shows the trends for the entire Middle East and North Africa.
- Chart 3.7 shows the even steeper rate of population increase in the Gulf region, driven by higher average rates of birth than that in the entire MENA area.
- Chart 3.8 shows how the "youth explosion" will dominate total population growth until 2030, but that a sharp rise in the postwork part of the population over sixty-five years of age will provide a new source of demographic pressure after that time.
- Chart 3.9 reveals that these estimates of population growth do reflect a sharp decline in the growth rate in most countries over time. This is projected on the basis of experience in Europe and Asia. If Middle Eastern societies react differently, the rate of population growth will be much steeper much longer.
- Chart 3.10 shows the impact of the demographic bulge and "youth explosion" by major MENA country.
- Chart 3.11 shows similar data for smaller MENA countries.

TRADE, OIL WEALTH, AND OIL NONWEALTH

The world's dependence on MENA energy exports often disguises the fact that the region's overall role in world trade has shrunk just as steadily as its share of the world's GDP. In broad terms, MENA trade has shrunk as a share of world exports for nearly half a century. The only exceptions are a few years, like 1974 and 1980, of sudden massive peaks in the value of oil exports. This drop in the importance of MENA trade reflects a drop in overall regional competitiveness relative to the industrialized world, Asia, and Latin America. It also reflects the inefficiency of state industries and

Chart 3.6
Living in a Crowded Desert: Massive Ongoing Population Growth in the Total Middle East and North Africa (MENA)

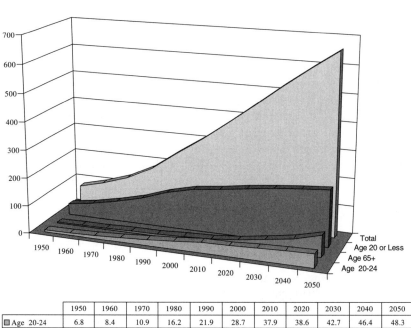

(UN Estimate—Population in Millions)

	1950	1960	1970	1980	1990	2000	2010	2020	2030	2040	2050
■ Age 20-24	6.8	8.4	10.9	16.2	21.9	28.7	37.9	38.6	42.7	46.4	48.3
■ Age 65+	3.1	3.6	5.1	6.4	8.2	11.3	15.5	24.6	38	53.9	77.9
■ Age 20 or Less	39.9	53.6	73.1	96.2	128.4	151	161.7	175.7	187.6	196.5	203.6
□ Total	78.7	101.2	133	177.9	244.8	307.7	376.2	449.3	522.4	592.1	656.3

Source: Adapted by Anthony H. Cordesman from data provided by the U.S. Census Bureau.

MENA financial systems, a comparative inability to attract foreign investment, and a growing dependence on imports from other regions. MENA nations produce fewer and fewer goods and services that are competitive within each country or on an intraregional basis. All MENA nations now trade primarily with trading partners outside the region, and efforts to break down regional trade barriers can accomplish little at best.

- Chart 3.12 shows the broad decline in Middle East and North Africa trade as a share of world trade and relative to other developing countries.
- Chart 3.13 shows that the trend in North Africa is even less competitive than the trend in the Middle East.

Chart 3.7
Population Growth in the Gulf

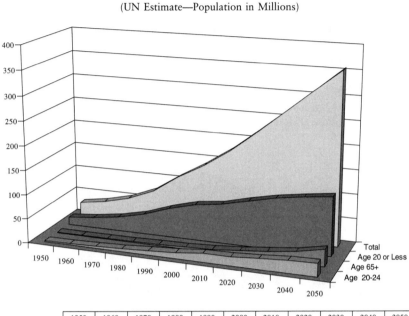

(UN Estimate—Population in Millions)

	1950	1960	1970	1980	1990	2000	2010	2020	2030	2040	2050
Age 20-24	2.5	3.2	4.5	6.5	9.4	12.6	18.2	18.7	22.4	26.2	27.8
Age 65+	1.3	1.4	1.7	2.2	3	4.3	6.5	10.9	16.5	23.1	34.5
Age 20 or Less	15.4	20.9	28.8	40.9	59	73.7	80.9	94	106	114.1	121.2
Total	30.4	39	52.3	74	109.6	140.2	176.1	219.4	264.6	310.3	355.4

Source: Adapted by Anthony H. Cordesman from data provided by the U.S. Census Bureau.

- Chart 3.14 shows that oil revenues have not, in general, led to high rates of growth among oil exporters, and that diversified economies have outperformed petroeconomies.

- Chart 3.15 shows the same is true in terms of per capita income.

- Chart 3.16 shows that the fiscal balances of diversified MENA economies have done better than those of oil economies except in boom years.

- Chart 3.17 shows that the same is true for terms of trade.

- Chart 3.18 shows, however, that trade flows and balances do differ sharply by MENA country and that regional trends do not apply in many individual cases.

Chart 3.8
MENA Youth Explosion and the Pensioner Burden

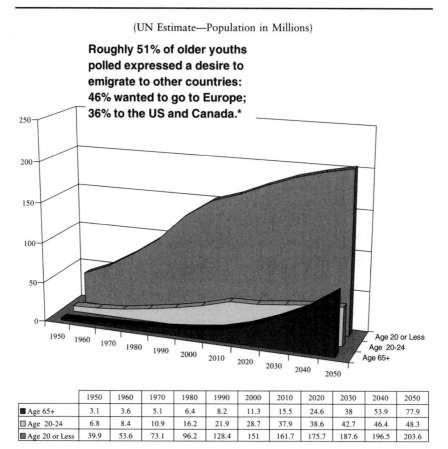

(UN Estimate—Population in Millions)

Roughly 51% of older youths polled expressed a desire to emigrate to other countries: 46% wanted to go to Europe; 36% to the US and Canada.*

	1950	1960	1970	1980	1990	2000	2010	2020	2030	2040	2050
■ Age 65+	3.1	3.6	5.1	6.4	8.2	11.3	15.5	24.6	38	53.9	77.9
□ Age 20-24	6.8	8.4	10.9	16.2	21.9	28.7	37.9	38.6	42.7	46.4	48.3
■ Age 20 or Less	39.9	53.6	73.1	96.2	128.4	151	161.7	175.7	187.6	196.5	203.6

*From *Arab Human Development Report 2202*, p. 30.
Source: Adapted by Anthony H. Cordesman from data provided by the U.S. Census Bureau.

THE IMPACT OF OIL AND GAS EXPORT REVENUES

If oil revenues are a blessing in terms of past and present income and development, the previous charts have shown they can also be a curse if nations rely on oil rather than diversified development. This will be even truer in the future. In spite of the projected rises in MENA energy exports, the resulting export revenues will not meet the needs of Middle Eastern states with high population growth and economies with limited diversification. Violent swings between "oil crash" and "oil boom" have not helped

Chart 3.9
Population Growth Rates Do Decline

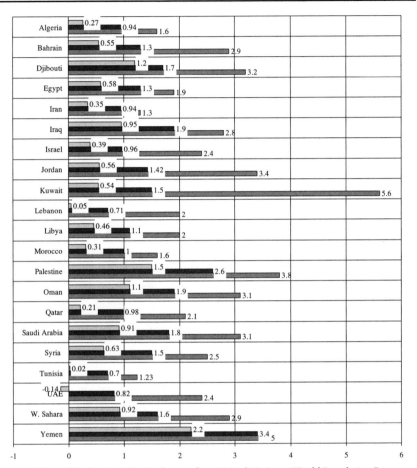

Source: Adapted by Anthony H. Cordesman from United Nations, *World Population Prospects: The 2002 Revision*, New York: United Nations, ESA/WP 180, 2003.

the situation. They tend to undercut economic reform in "boom" years and make it unaffordable or politically impossible in bust years.

One such "oil bust" took place in 1997–1999 only to be followed by a short "oil boom" in 200–200, which has been followed by relatively high prices ever since. The "oil crash" that began in 1997 led to a series of unexpected cuts in oil prices that reached lows of $10 a barrel and cuts in annual oil revenues that approached 30–40 percent. As a result, OPEC oil

Chart 3.10
Population Momentum Continues: Total Population by Larger MENA Country in 2003

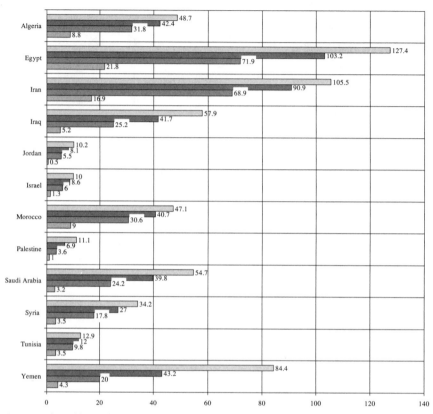

Source: Adapted by Anthony H. Cordesman from United Nations, *World Population Prospects: The 2002 Revision*, New York: United Nations, ESA/WP 180, 2003.

revenues swung from $148.7 billion in 1997 to $99.9 billion in 1998. These cuts in oil revenues affected every major oil and gas producer in the Middle East and have reduced the region's ability to maintain both welfare payments and entitlements, and short-term investment. The "oil crash" of 1997–1998 had a particularly dire impact on those MENA economies that had failed to modernize and diversify, and/or were affected by the impact of sanctions on several critical suppliers. They led to sharp cuts in the estimated size of the future demand for exports, in national policies to increase production and export capacity, and the ability to obtain the investment necessary to implement those policies. They affected political stability and

Chart 3.11
Total Population by Smaller MENA Country in 2003

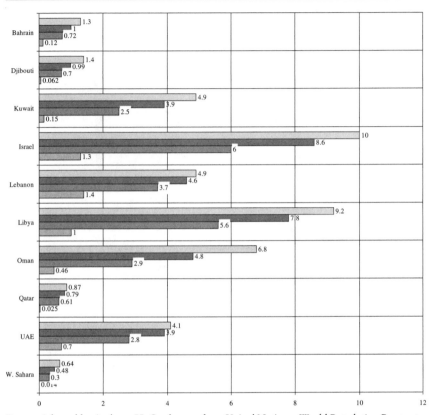

Source: Adapted by Anthony H. Cordesman from United Nations, *World Population Prospects: The 2002 Revision*, New York: United Nations, ESA/WP 180, 2003.

influenced a wide range of social problems, most importantly the impact of very high rates of population growth, the inability to sustain past welfare and entitlement programs, and the need to create new economic structures that offer suitable employment and incentives for investment.

The cycle soon swung back in the other direction. Upward swings in oil revenues began to ease the situation in the spring of 1999. In March 1999, OPEC's member countries, together with some important outside producers, settled on a program of stringent oil production cuts. Following the implementation of cutbacks, the price of crude oil rose sharply over the course of 1999 and eventually reached levels in 2000 that had not been seen since the 1990–1991 Persian Gulf crisis. They were then dropped back to

Chart 3.12A
Trends in MENA Trade as a Share of World Trade: Part One—The Middle East and North Africa Badly Lagged in the Growth of World Trade: 1986–1997

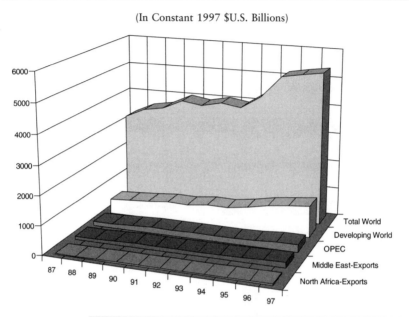

(In Constant 1997 \$U.S. Billions)

	87	88	89	90	91	92	93	94	95	96	97
North Africa-Exports	27.8	26.3	29	39.8	36	32.2	27.6	26.7	32.2	35.7	36.4
Middle East-Exports	114	110.3	134.1	157.1	143	152.4	140.3	144.7	158.9	183.2	189.5
OPEC	157.2	149.8	177.8	221.9	201.8	209.7	193.2	195.6	214.9	254.3	262.4
Developing World	519.1	558.5	607.1	667.2	648	717.8	714.7	810.1	957.7	1035	1107
Total World	3240	3552	3674	3990	3884	4037	3917	4367	5119	5242	5348

Note: Middle East does not include North African states other than Egypt.
Source: Adapted by Anthony H. Cordesman from U.S. State Department, *World Military Expenditures and Arms Transfers*, various editions.

\$190.7 billion in 2001, and \$187 billion in 2002, with an estimated total of \$223 billion in 2003.[2]

These swings in oil revenues are typical of other cycles in oil revenues that have long contributed to the problems in past Middle Eastern economic growth and the problems the region faces in dealing with its youth explosion and in funding both future development and expanded petroleum production and exports.

OPEC oil revenues were worth around \$102.8 billion in constant 2000 dollars in 1972. After the October War and the 1974 oil embargo, they leapt to levels of around \$443.4 billion and then dropped back to an average of

Chart 3.12B
Trends in MENA Trade as a Share of World Trade: Part Two—Growth in Middle
East and North Africa Trade Relative to Other Regions: 1992–2001

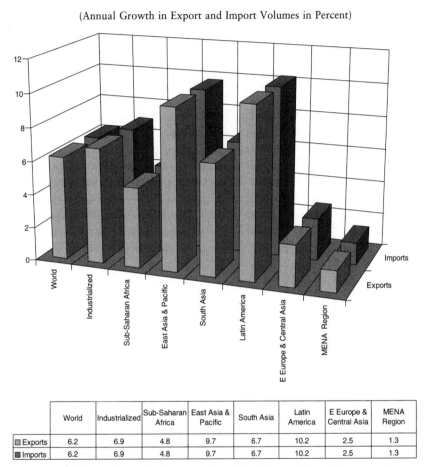

(Annual Growth in Export and Import Volumes in Percent)

	World	Industrialized	Sub-Saharan Africa	East Asia & Pacific	South Asia	Latin America	E Europe & Central Asia	MENA Region
Exports	6.2	6.9	4.8	9.7	6.7	10.2	2.5	1.3
Imports	6.2	6.9	4.8	9.7	6.7	10.2	2.5	1.3

Source: Adapted by Anthony H. Cordesman from World Bank, *Global Economic Prospects 2003*, Washington, DC: World Bank, 2003, pp. 208–211.

$365.5 billion during 1975–1978. The fall of the Shah of Iran and the start
of the Iran-Iraq War drove them to a new peak in 1980, when they were
worth $597.5 billion. An oil price collapse began in 1985, and revenues
dropped to $117.2 billion in 1986. They gradually rose back to levels of
around $171.46 billion a year in early 1997, but a new "oil crash" began
late that year. Major production cuts led to a rise in oil prices in 1999, but
total revenues in nominal dollars still only reached $143.9 billion in 1999

Chart 3.13

The Middle East Has Exhibited Consistent Growth in Exports; North Africa Has Not

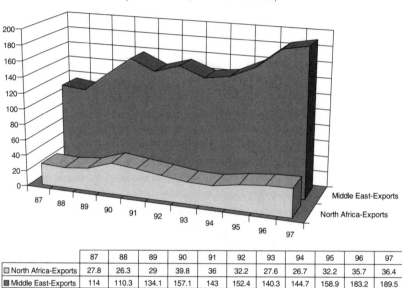

(In Constant $1997 U.S. Billions)

	87	88	89	90	91	92	93	94	95	96	97
☐ North Africa-Exports	27.8	26.3	29	39.8	36	32.2	27.6	26.7	32.2	35.7	36.4
■ Middle East-Exports	114	110.3	134.1	157.1	143	152.4	140.3	144.7	158.9	183.2	189.5

Note: Middle East does not include North African states other than Egypt.
Source: Adapted by Anthony H. Cordesman form ACDA, *World Military Expenditures and Arms Transfers*, various editions.

and $226.6 billion in 2000. They were $117.2 billion in 2002 (in 2000 $U.S.) and projected to be $208.7 billion in 2003.[3] Many countries are beginning to rethink their plans to increase production capacity and their attitudes toward private and foreign investment.

The region's economic and budget problems have been shaped by years of overreliance on oil wealth, economic mismanagement, massive population growth, mismanaged government spending, and the failure of regional governments to realistically plan and budget for the future. Some key Middle Eastern governments have had a decade of nearly continuous budget deficits. Saudi Arabia and Iraq are key cases in point. Other countries are in major structural crisis. They cannot afford to implement their five-year plans, and cannot fund both their present levels of entitlements and investment. Cases in point include Algeria, Syria, Bahrain, Iran, Oman, and Yemen. Most Middle Eastern governments now face a major short-term budget crisis, and this seems to include even states with relatively high ratios of exports to population: Kuwait, Qatar, and the emirates other than Abu Dhabi and possibly Dubai.

Chart 3.14
The GDP Growth of MENA Fuel Exporters Lagged Behind That of Diversified
Exporters and Was Far More Vulnerable to Changes in Oil Prices

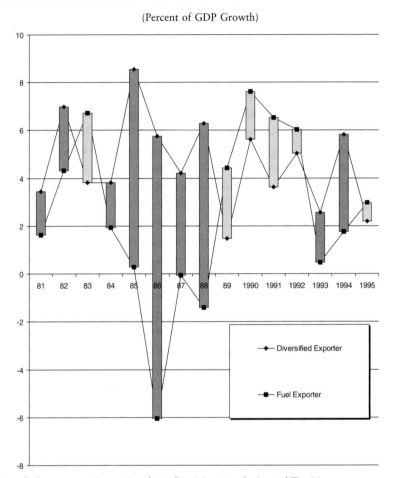

(Percent of GDP Growth)

Diversified exporter = Egypt, Israel, Jordan, Morocco, Syria, and Tunisia.
Fuel exporter = Algeria, Bahrain, Iran, Kuwait, Oman, Qatar, Saudi Arabia, and the UAE.

Source: Adapted by Anthony H. Cordesman from IMF, *World Economic Outlook*, Washington, DC: IMF, 1996, pp. 98–105.

Past drops in oil revenue and the resulting budget problems have already led to underinvestment in infrastructure, economic diversification, and state industries other than the petroleum sector in many states. Even the petroleum sector has been underfunded in some cases, although "starving the hand that feeds you" presents obvious enough problems for most

Chart 3.15
The Per Capita Income Growth of MENA Fuel Exporters Lagged Behind That of Diversified Exporters and Was Far More Vulnerable to Oil Prices

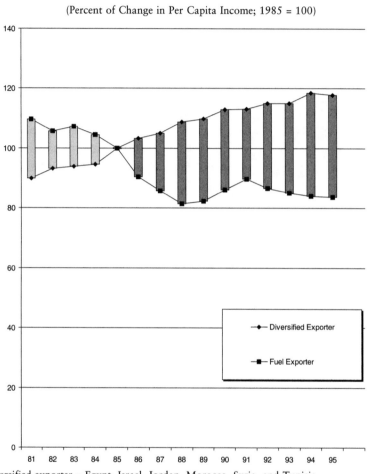

(Percent of Change in Per Capita Income; 1985 = 100)

Diversified exporter = Egypt, Israel, Jordan, Morocco, Syria, and Tunisia.
Fuel exporter = Algeria, Bahrain, Iran, Kuwait, Oman, Qatar, Saudi Arabia, and the UAE.
Source: Adapted by Anthony H. Cordesman from IMF, *World Economic Outlook*, Washington, DC: IMF, 1996, pp. 98–105.

Middle Eastern states to think twice. In short, the traditional rentier patriarchy of most MENA oil-exporting states no longer has all the money it needs to function, and cannot attract enough outside or internal investment to meet national needs, and many are further crippled by a reliance on inefficient state industries.

Chart 3.16
The Fiscal Balances of MENA Fuel Exporters Deteriorated Relative to Those of Diversified Exporters

(Budget Deficits as a Percent of GNP)

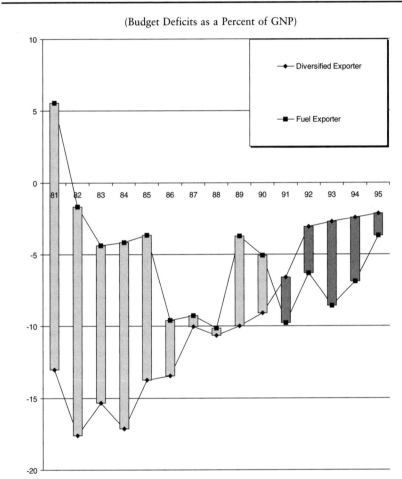

Diversified exporter = Egypt, Israel, Jordan, Morocco, Syria, and Tunisia.
Fuel exporter = Algeria, Bahrain, Iran, Kuwait, Oman, Qatar, Saudi Arabia, and the UAE.

Source: Adapted by Anthony H. Cordesman from IMF, *World Economic Outlook*, Washington, DC: IMF, 1996, pp. 98–105.

Chart 3.17A
Trade Conditions Do Not Favor Energy Exporters: The Terms of Trade of MENA
Fuel Exporters Deteriorated Relative to Those of Diversified Exporters

(1985=100)

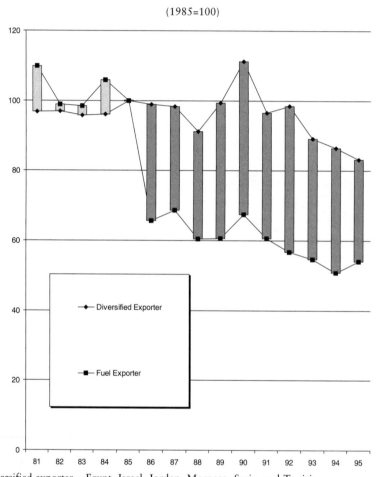

Diversified exporter = Egypt, Israel, Jordan, Morocco, Syria, and Tunisia.
Fuel exporter = Algeria, Bahrain, Iran, Kuwait, Oman, Qatar, Saudi Arabia, and the UAE.

Source: Adapted by Anthony H. Cordesman from IMF, *World Economic Outlook*, Washington, DC: IMF, 1996, pp. 98–105.

Chart 3.17B
Trade Conditions Do Not Favor Energy Exporters: Comparative Trend in Energy
Commodity Prices versus Nonenergy Commodities

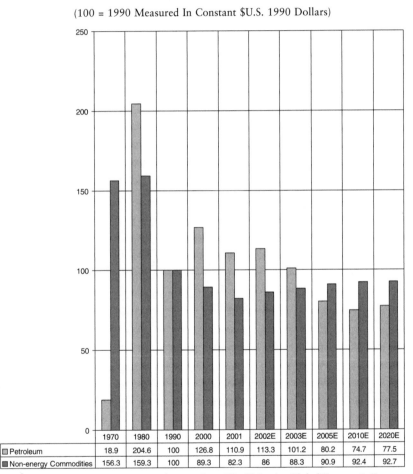

(100 = 1990 Measured In Constant $U.S. 1990 Dollars)

	1970	1980	1990	2000	2001	2002E	2003E	2005E	2010E	2020E
Petroleum	18.9	204.6	100	126.8	110.9	113.3	101.2	80.2	74.7	77.5
Non-energy Commodities	156.3	159.3	100	89.3	82.3	86	88.3	90.9	92.4	92.7

Source: Adapted by Anthony H. Cordesman from World Bank, *Global Economic Prospects
2003,* Washington, DC: World Bank, 2003, pp. 208–211.

Chart 3.18
Countries Differ Radically in Volume of Trade and Trade Balances Are Uncertain Except in Years with High Oil Revenues

(Exports and Imports in 2000 in $U.S. Current Billions)

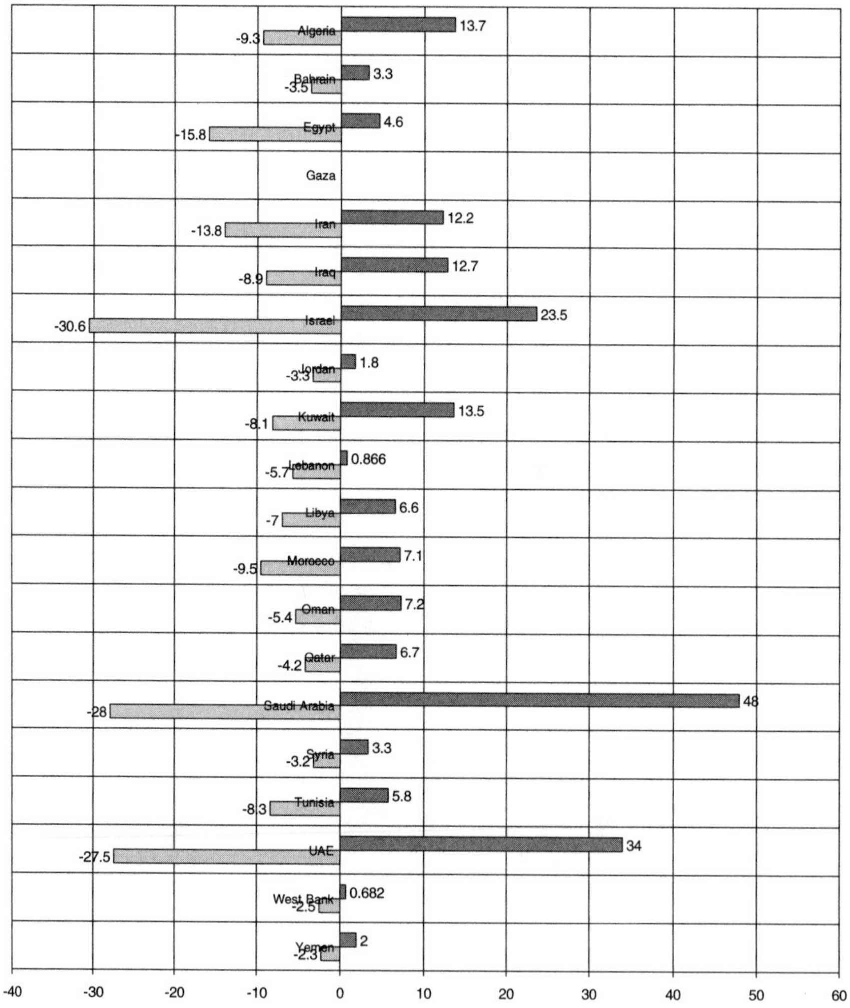

Country	Imports	Exports
Algeria	-9.3	13.7
Bahrain	-3.5	3.3
Egypt	-15.8	4.6
Gaza		
Iran	-13.8	12.2
Iraq	-8.9	12.7
Israel	-30.6	23.5
Jordan	-3.3	1.8
Kuwait	-8.1	13.5
Lebanon	-5.7	0.866
Libya	-7	6.6
Morocco	-9.5	7.1
Oman	-5.4	7.2
Qatar	-4.2	6.7
Saudi Arabia	-28	48
Syria	-3.2	3.3
Tunisia	-8.3	5.8
UAE	-27.5	34
West Bank	-2.5	0.682
Yemen	-2.3	2

Source: Adapted by Anthony H. Cordesman from CIA, *World Factbook 2000*.

Chart 3.19
OPEC Oil Export Revenues: Investment and Stability versus Interruptions: Total

(In $U.S. Current and 2000 Constant Billions)

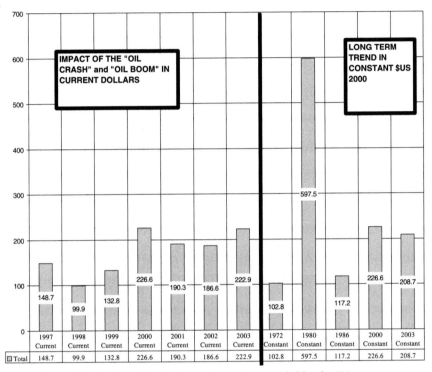

	1997 Current	1998 Current	1999 Current	2000 Current	2001 Current	2002 Current	2003 Current	1972 Constant	1980 Constant	1986 Constant	2000 Constant	2003 Constant
Total	148.7	99.9	132.8	226.6	190.3	186.6	222.9	102.8	597.5	117.2	226.6	208.7

Source: Adapted by Anthony H. Cordesman from data provided by the EIA.

THE INTERACTION AMONG OIL REVENUES, ECONOMIC DEVELOPMENT, AND DEMOGRAPHICS

Demographics compound the impact of low oil and gas export revenues on regional economies, and increase the risk of political unrest. Oil income per capita drops because of the "youth explosion" discussed earlier. At the same time, some 40 percent of the region's population is now under fifteen years of age, and rates of population growth are projected to be high enough in a number of countries so that the number of people entering the labor force will often double over a period of a decade. The region's educational system is already under extreme stress, and real and disguised unemployment for males between eighteen and twenty-five years probably averages over 20 percent.[4] The ratio of urbanization in the total population rose from

Chart 3.20

Demographics and Oil Wealth "Oil Crash" to "Oil Boom" in 1992–2001: Even in Peacetime, Oil Revenues Are Unpredictable and Have Massive Regional Macroeconomic Impacts

(In $U.S. Current Billions)

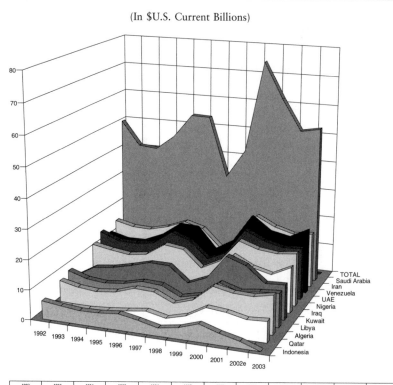

	1992	1993	1994	1995	1996	1997	1998	1999	2000	2001	2002e	2003
▥ Indonesia	6.1	5.2	4.6	4.8	5.4	4.2	2.7	3.7	5.9	3.8	2.3	
▢ Qatar	2.9	2.7	2.7	3.2	3.9	4.8	3.4	5.1	8.7	8.1	6.7	7.1
▢ Algeria	8.4	7	6.4	7.1	9.2	8.9	5.9	7.9	13.4	12	11.8	13.1
▨ Libya	9.6	7.7	7.1	7.7	9.3	8.9	5.7	7.3	12.3	10.1	11	11.4
▨ Kuwait	5.9	9.4	10.3	11.7	13.5	13.3	8.2	10.9	18.9	16.6	11.5	11.8
▢ Iraq	0.5	0.4	0.4	0.5	0.7	3.5	5.6	9.9	17.2	13.9	12.3	15.5
▢ Nigeria	12.7	11.5	10.6	11.5	15.7	14.8	9.1	12.4	20.1	18	17.2	18
■ UAE	15.2	12.7	12.6	13.5	18.1	15.8	10.2	13.3	21.9	18.9	17.3	17.7
■ Venezuela	12.8	11.2	11.2	14	18.7	18.3	11.1	15	24.5	19.8	18.5	21.9
▢ Iran	15.5	14	13.8	15.4	18	16.3	10.1	13.9	23	19.9	18	18.7
▨ Saudi Arabia	50.7	42.5	41.9	46.9	54.9	54.7	34.2	43.9	75.3	63.1	52.6	53.8
■ TOTAL	*140.4	*124.3	*121.4	*136.3	*165.5	*163.5	*106.2	*143.2	*241.2	*204.2	*179.6	*191.5

Source: Adapted by Anthony H. Cordesman from projections by the EIA in various editions of its "OPEC Revenues Sheet"; and from Cambridge Energy Associates (CERA), "OPEC Tilts to Market Share," *World Oil Watch*, Winter 2002, p. 28.

Chart 3.21
Beyond Market Forces: Oil Is a Conflict-Driven Business: Politics, War, and the Trends in the Price of Saudi Arabia Light Crude: 1970–1999

($U.S. Current and $U.S. 1997 Constant)

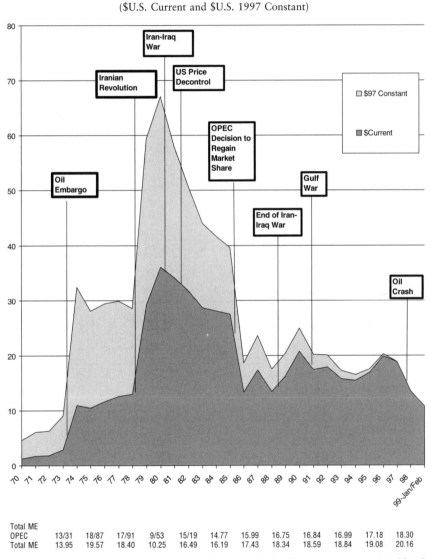

Total ME												
OPEC	13/31	18/87	17/91	9/53	15/19	14.77	15.99	16.75	16.84	16.99	17.18	18.30
Total ME	13.95	19.57	18.40	10.25	16.49	16.19	17.43	18.34	18.59	18.84	19.08	20.16

Source: Adapted by Anthony H. Cordesman from Cambridge Energy Associates, *World Oil Trends 1998*, Cambridge, MA, 1998, p. 26.

135

Chart 3.22
The Impact of Oil Wealth on the Saudi GDP and Government Expenditures: 1970–1999

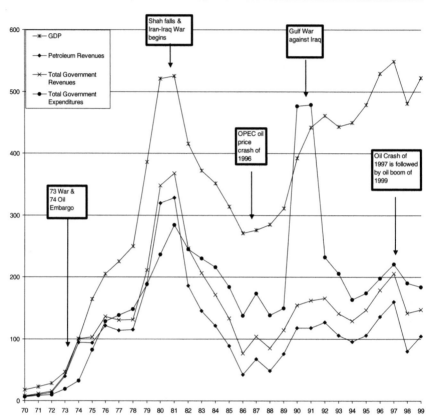

Note: The Saudi budget cycle was changed in 1990, and the period from 1990–1991 is reported as a single year.
Source: Adapted by Anthony H. Cordesman from Saudi Arabian Monetary Agency, *36th Annual Report-1421H (2000G)*, Riyadh: SAMA, 2001, pp. 343–346, 360–361, 393–395.

41 percent in 1970 to 59 percent in 2000, and will probably rise to well over 70 percent by 2020.

These problems are further compounded by labor migration and the slow breakdown of the region's traditional family, clan, and tribal system, which is based on villages and the extended family. They are also compounded by hyperurbanization, shift away from agriculture, and the need to absorb an increasingly well educated population of women both for social reasons and to create productive economies that are globally competitive.

Virtually all Southern Gulf states are heavily dependent on foreign labor at a time when many of their own younger citizens lack not only jobs but also the training and work ethic to get them. In many cases, these problems are reinforced by poor immigration policies that are routinely violated by the toleration of illegal immigrants, the issue of visas for money, and the existence of laws that require major benefit packages for native labor, thus making it difficult to hire or fire native labor. Some countries are trying to solve the problem with erratic purges of foreign labor, but most still lack consistent policies.

At present, many MENA oil-exporting states can get by in spite of these problems. If low or low-to-moderate oil revenues should suddenly become the normal long-term case again, the resulting cut in government revenues will force many such countries to cut their budgets and development plans in ways that result in significant economic, social, and political trade-offs. The International Monetary Fund stated in May 1998 that the decline in oil export revenues "would pose a serious risk to the growth outlook" for the Persian Gulf region, "and particularly for the region's largest oil exporters such as Saudi Arabia and Kuwait . . . if sustained." This warning is just as true today, and it is clear from the economic history of the region, and virtually every current projection of future oil revenues, that population growth will outpace increases in oil revenues, and cut per capita oil wealth indefinitely into the future.

- Chart 3.23 shows the rate of the youth explosion in Iran, and the critical impact it will have during 2000–2050. Even with one of the lowest rates of population increase in the Gulf, Iran will become a nation of over 100 million by 2030, which compares with 40 million at the time of the Shah's fall from power.

- Chart 3.24 shows similar data for Iraq. It shows an extremely rapid rate of growth in spite of war and sanctions. Iraq is also projected to continue rapid growth through 2030, which will present major problems for reconstruction and nation building.

- Chart 3.25 shows the impact of population growth and the "youth explosion" in Saudi Arabia. Saudi Arabia not only is the region's most critical energy exporter, it is the country with one of the most critical population problems. Saudi Arabia already has real oil revenue per capita about one-fifth of its peak in 1980. Current projections of Saudi exports and export earnings show little chance of a recovery in real dollar terms through 2030.

- Chart 3.26 shows the increase in jobs required to deal with population growth in 2003. This number will often double by 2030, and would double again if women were employed on globally competitive terms.

- Chart 3.27 shows the overall level of dependence on foreign labor in the Gulf region, a dependence that blocks job creation for native youth and lowers labor costs to the point where many native youths will not accept jobs and the

Chart 3.23
Case Examples: Population Growth and the Youth Explosion in Iran

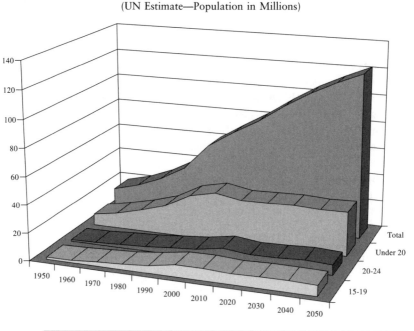

(UN Estimate—Population in Millions)

	1950	1960	1970	1980	1990	2000	2010	2020	2030	2040	2050
□ 15-19	1.6	2	3.1	4.1	5.8	9	8.9	7.6	8.2	8.2	7.8
■ 20-24	1.4	1.7	2.5	3.5	5.1	6.4	9.5	7.4	7.7	8.5	7.8
□ Under 20	8.2	11.5	16	21.5	31.4	35.3	31.8	32.2	32.9	31.9	32.3
■ Total	16.9	21.7	28.8	39.1	58.4	70.3	80.8	93.5	104.5	113.5	121.4

Source: Adapted by Anthony H. Cordesman from data provided by the United Nations.

resulting drop in social status. This undermines the creation of a modern work ethic, and pushes youths toward radicalism.

- Chart 3.28 uses Saudi Arabia as a case study. It also shows that in many cases, abolishing foreign jobs will not create local jobs because many are maid and housework jobs for women.

- Chart 3.29 shows the MENA region is incapable of competing in global terms because of its low rates of employment and productive use of women. This is crippling in many countries because they have reverse the norm. Rather than undereducated women, they have social structures where women have far fewer social outlets than men but the opportunity to learn. The result is that

Chart 3.24
Case Examples: Population Growth and the Youth Explosion in Iraq

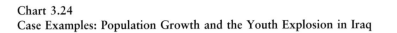

(UN Estimate—Population in Millions)

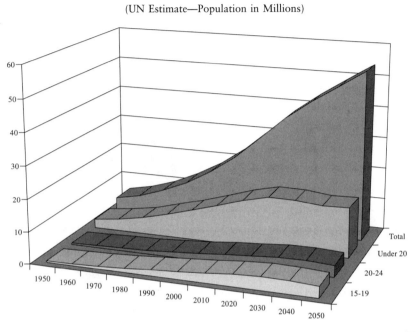

	1950	1960	1970	1980	1990	2000	2010	2020	2030	2040	2050
☐ 15-19	0.54	0.72	0.98	1.4	1.9	2.5	3	3.8	4.2	4	3.6
▨ 20-24	0.45	0.6	0.82	1.1	1.6	2.1	2.9	3.5	4.1	4.2	3.7
▨ Under 20	2.9	3.9	5.3	7.3	9.6	12	14.6	16.5	16.3	15.4	15.7
▨ Total	5.2	6.8	9.4	12.9	17.3	22.9	29.9	37.1	43.1	48.4	53.6

Source: Adapted by Anthony H. Cordesman from data provided by the United Nations.

women are becoming the best-educated part of the labor force, but only to have their productivity largely wasted.

- Chart 3.30 shows that some MENA countries are so dependent on foreign male labor that it has created a serious imbalance in the distribution of the sexes, and the potential for social unrest.

- Chart 3.31 shows the dynamics of urbanization and the decline in agriculture, making the MENA region heavily dependent on food imports, breaking up traditional social patterns and the security of the extended family, and pushing labor toward market-driven jobs to survive.

- Chart 3.32 reflects similar trends in the labor force.

Chart 3.25
Case Examples: Population Growth and the Youth Explosion in Saudi Arabia

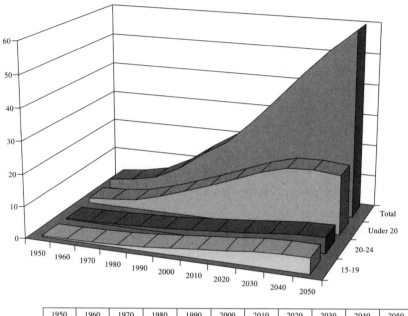

(U.S. Census Bureau Estimate—Population in Millions)

	1950	1960	1970	1980	1990	2000	2010	2020	2030	2040	2050
☐ 15-19	0.32	0.41	0.57	0.91	1.4	2.1	2.9	3.6	4.5	4.9	4.9
■ 20-24	0.27	0.35	0.49	0.87	1.2	1.8	2.6	3.2	4.1	4.8	5
☐ Under 20	1.7	2.2	3.1	5.2	8	10.8	13.9	17	19.2	19.5	18.7
■ Total	3.2	4.1	5.7	9.6	15.4	20.3	27.6	36.1	44.8	52.7	59.7

Source: Adapted by Anthony H. Cordesman from data provided by the U.S. Census Bureau.

- Chart 3.33 indicates the overall rate of urbanization by country.
- Chart 3.34 shows that urbanization and flight from the land have led to a net decline in arable land, made worse by the shift of water to urban populations. This internal competition for water would be much sharper if MENA economies successfully diversified and increased industrial use of water, although the industrial use of water generally makes desalinized water economic while industrial use does not.
- Chart 3.35 shows a rough estimate of both direct and disguised unemployed (employment with little or no productive output). Unfortunately, MENA countries are unwilling to report accurately in these areas, and generally fail to analyze and report on disguised unemployment—a problem that casts severe doubt on the quality and value of economic analysis and planning in virtually every MENA country.

Chart 3.26
The Search for Jobs: CIA Estimate of Number of Young Males Entering the Labor Market Each Year

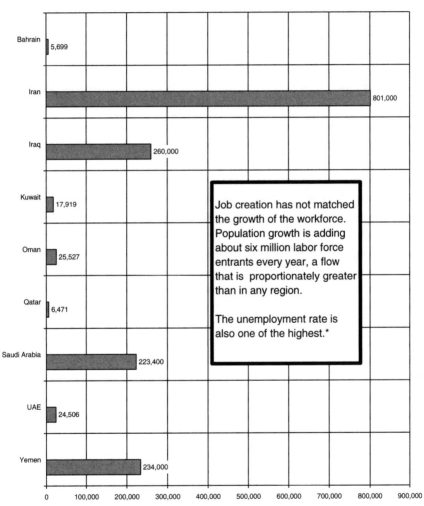

Bahrain 5,699

Iran 801,000

Iraq 260,000

Kuwait 17,919

Oman 25,527

Qatar 6,471

Saudi Arabia 223,400

UAE 24,506

Yemen 234,000

Job creation has not matched the growth of the workforce. Population growth is adding about six million labor force entrants every year, a flow that is proportionately greater than in any region.

The unemployment rate is also one of the highest.*

0   100,000   200,000   300,000   400,000   500,000   600,000   700,000   800,000   900,000

*From *Arab Human Development Report 2202*, p. 10.
Source: Adapted by Anthony H. Cordesman from CIA, *World Factbook 2002*.

Chart 3.27
Foreign Population in Selected Countries in the Gulf

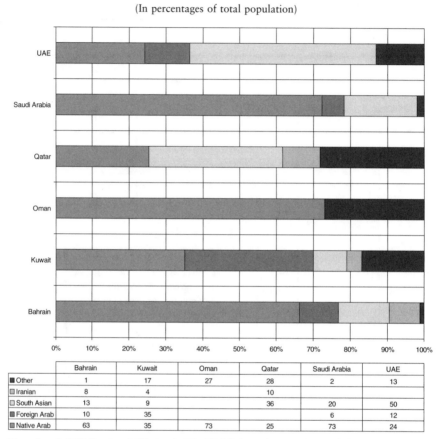

(In percentages of total population)

	Bahrain	Kuwait	Oman	Qatar	Saudi Arabia	UAE
■ Other	1	17	27	28	2	13
▨ Iranian	8	4		10		
☐ South Asian	13	9		36	20	50
■ Foreign Arab	10	35			6	12
▨ Native Arab	63	35	73	25	73	24

Note: Iran is 51% Persian, 24% Azeri, 8% Gilaki/Mazandarani, 7% Kurdish, 2% Lurm, and
    2% Turkoman; Iraq is 75-80% Arab, of which some 55% are Shiite and 45% Sunni, and
    20-25% Kurdish and other minority.
Source: Adapted by Anthony H. Cordesman from CIA, *World Factbook 2002*; and IISS,
    Military Balance 2002–2003.

ABILITY TO FUND INVESTMENT TO INCREASE OIL AND GAS PRODUCTION

As is discussed in more detail in a later chapter, these uncertainties surrounding future demand and future oil and gas export revenues do more than
affect regional stability in ways that could lead to oil interruptions. They may
also be creating serious long-term problems in financing the expansion of

Chart 3.28
The "Youthening" of Saudi Arabia—Case Example: Estimate of the Distribution of the Total Native and Foreign Population by Age and Sex in 2000

(In Thousands)

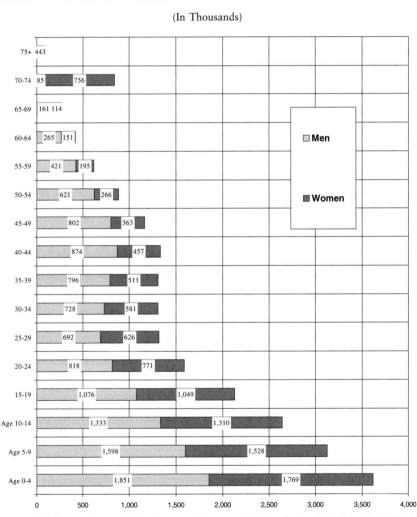

Source: U.S. Census Bureau, "IDB Summary Demographic Data for Saudi Arabia," May 2001, www.census.gov/cgi-bin/ipc/idbsum?cty=SA.

Chart 3.29
Women as a Percentage of the Labor Force: Pace of Social Change

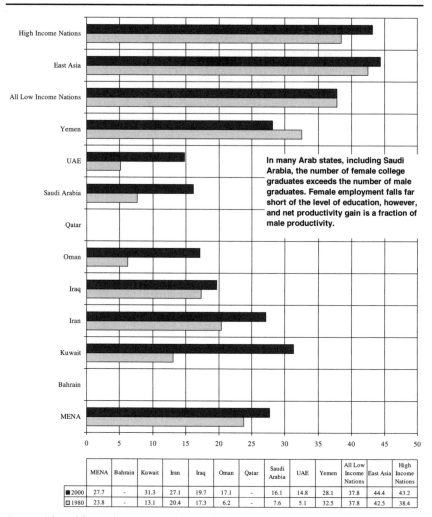

In many Arab states, including Saudi Arabia, the number of female college graduates exceeds the number of male graduates. Female employment falls far short of the level of education, however, and net productivity gain is a fraction of male productivity.

	MENA	Bahrain	Kuwait	Iran	Iraq	Oman	Qatar	Saudi Arabia	UAE	Yemen	All Low Income Nations	East Asia	High Income Nations
■2000	27.7	-	31.3	27.1	19.7	17.1	-	16.1	14.8	28.1	37.8	44.4	43.2
□1980	23.8	-	13.1	20.4	17.3	6.2	-	7.6	5.1	32.5	37.8	42.5	38.4

Source: Adapted by Anthony H. Cordesman from World Bank, *World Development Indicators 2000*, pp. 46–48; and World Bank, *World Development Indicators 2002*, pp. 52–54.

MENA oil and gas production capacity. Unfortunately, an examination of current estimates of energy investment costs indicates that there is little recent effort to estimate the cost of the required future regional and country-specific investment requirements beyond relatively near-term projects, to determine how well countries can finance development on their own through cash flow, loans, and various cashback or production-sharing arrangements.

Chart 3.30
Foreign Labor Impact on Sex Ratio Issues: Men as a Percentage of the Total
Population in 2003

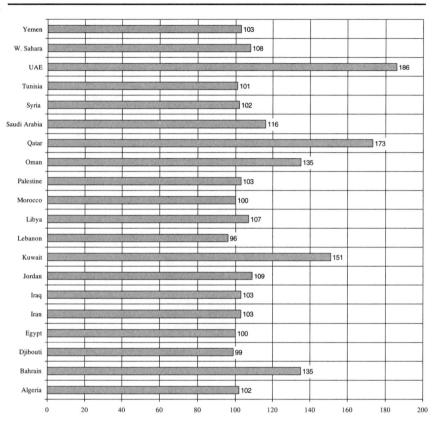

Yemen	103
W. Sahara	108
UAE	186
Tunisia	101
Syria	102
Saudi Arabia	116
Qatar	173
Oman	135
Palestine	103
Morocco	100
Libya	107
Lebanon	96
Kuwait	151
Jordan	109
Iraq	103
Iran	103
Egypt	100
Djibouti	99
Bahrain	135
Algeria	102

Source: Adapted by Anthony H. Cordesman from United Nations, *World Population Prospects: The 2002 Revision*, New York: United Nations, ESA/WP 180, 2003.

The International Energy Agency (IEA) made a major effort to examine these issues in 2003, in a study called *World Energy Investment Outlook: 2003 Insights*. This work, however, is a global study of all energy resources and is necessarily limited in covering the Middle East.[5] It also uses nominal costs for investment that seem to badly understate the recent cost of exploration and development activity in the MENA region. The United States badly needs to give this kind of "what if" modeling high priority and to consider just how much investment and reform is needed in each key producer country.

Two critical factors could affect the ability to fund investment in increased oil and gas production. One is the growing limits on the budgets

Chart 3.31
Massive Ongoing Pressures for Social Change: Massive Urbanization and Sharp Decline in the Role of Agriculture

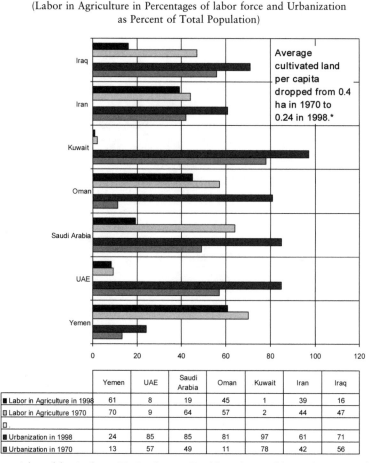

(Labor in Agriculture in Percentages of labor force and Urbanization as Percent of Total Population)

	Yemen	UAE	Saudi Arabia	Oman	Kuwait	Iran	Iraq
■ Labor in Agriculture in 1998	61	8	19	45	1	39	16
▨ Labor in Agriculture 1970	70	9	64	57	2	44	47
▢ .							
■ Urbanization in 1998	24	85	85	81	97	61	71
▨ Urbanization in 1970	13	57	49	11	78	42	56

Source: Adapted by Anthony H. Cordesman World Bank, *World Development Indicators 2000*, pp. 26–28.

and investment capabilities of MENA energy exporting states caused by the lack of economic diversification and moderate oil prices. The second is the slowly increasing structural economic problem caused by rising populations, high welfare and entitlement programs, high military and arms expenditures, and low long-term revenues.

Market forces and state-driven energy investment may still be enough. Most Middle Eastern states have been relatively successful in using state

Chart 3.32
Percentage of Urbanization and Percentage of Labor Force in Agriculture:
Shaping the Pace of Social Change in the MENA Region

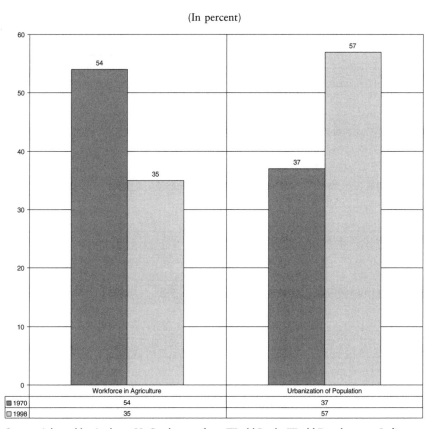

(In percent)

	Workforce in Agriculture	Urbanization of Population
■ 1970	54	37
□ 1998	35	57

Source: Adapted by Anthony H. Cordesman from World Bank, *World Development Indicators 1998* and *2000*.

revenues to fund energy investments in the past. It now seems likely, however, that their cash flow and savings will not be adequate to meet both their other spending and investment needs and energy investment needs. Foreign investment and the domestic private sector may have to assume a much larger share of the burden if the region is to produce anything like the energy output projected in estimates by the IEA and U.S. Department of Energy (DOE). Relying on market forces might still lead to enough cost-effective investment, particularly given the oil industries history of investing in reserves, future market share, and development even in periods of low oil income.

Chart 3.33
Arab Development Report Estimate of Urbanization

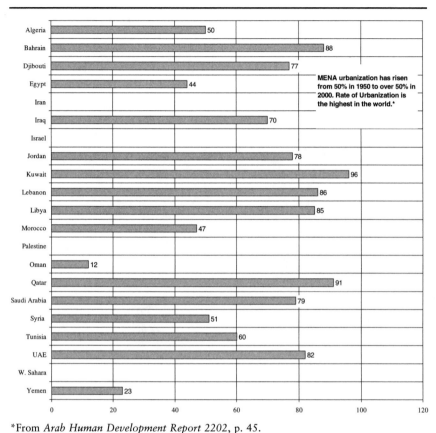

*From *Arab Human Development Report 2202*, p. 45.
Source: Adapted by Anthony H. Cordesman from *Arab Human Development Report 2202*,
p. 143.

The era of being able to safely rely on state oil and gas revenues to fund other state expenditures and investments may well be over. Middle Eastern governments do not need to abandon state industries, state investment, and state control over energy resources, but fundamental reforms are needed to increase the ratio of foreign and domestic private investment. There currently, however, is no Middle Eastern country where market forces are allowed to operate without serious state interference. However, only a few oil-exporting countries—Bahrain, Egypt, Qatar, and Oman—are making

Chart 3.34
Arab Development Report Estimate of Decline in Arable Land Per Capita

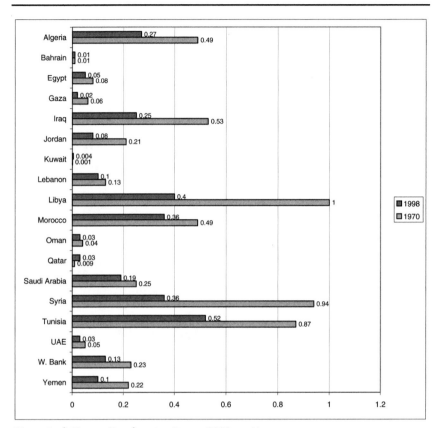

*From *Arab Human Development Report 2202*, p. 44.
Source: Adapted by Anthony H. Cordesman from *Arab Human Development Report 2202*, p. 143.

serious progress. This helps explain why nearly all oil-producing countries in the Middle East are currently examining ways in which to privatize some aspects of its energy investment and obtain foreign investment.

At this point in time, there is no meaningful way to predict whether Middle Eastern oil-exporting states will persist in these plans if oil and gas revenues rise, how successful they will be in obtaining the energy investment and other capital they need, how much money any given country

Chart 3.35
Overdependence on Nonproductive Government Jobs Has a Cost: Estimated Comparative Direct and Disguised Unemployment Rate in the Middle East— A Rough Estimate

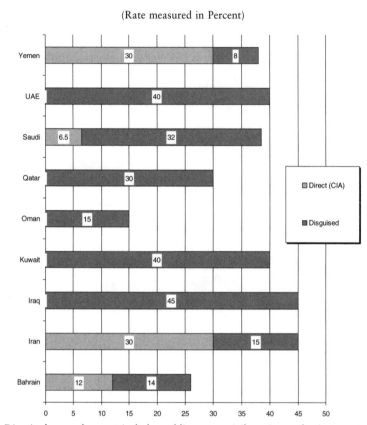

(Rate measured in Percent)

Note: Disguised unemployment includes public sector, civil service, and private sector jobs with no useful economic output.
Source: Rough estimate by Anthony H. Cordesman based on CIA and World Bank estimates for 2002.

requires, and how well investments will be managed. Middle Eastern regimes tend to backpeddle on reform the moment oil revenues rise to moderate levels, and many face resistance from nationalists, pan-Arab socialists, state-oriented technocrats, and Islamists. Virtually all states want to maximize revenues, but also have powerful elements that want to conserve resources for the future.

Chapter 4

Current Energy Developments: The Trends by Subregion and Country

As has been discussed earlier, the efforts to model future energy developments in the Middle East and North Africa (MENA) described in the previous chapters are based on projections of market forces and not on an analysis of country energy development plans and national ability to implement them. There is no way to avoid this. Only a handful of countries in the MENA region announced plans for modernizing and expanding their energy production and exports, and these only for limited periods in the future. Similarly, a risk assessment of the countries involved would require a net assessment of all of the strategic, military, political, economic, demographic, and social issues that affect each country. This is a level of analysis that is scarcely practical in a regional overview and one in which the risk assessment would usually still have to be based largely on speculation.

It is possible, however, to provide an overview of what MENA states have said about the energy developments in their country, and to give a brief summary of the key factors shaping a given country's stability and ability to develop its energy resources. Like all summary risk analysis, such judgments are inevitably filled with broad generalizations and uncertainties, and grow progressively more uncertain as they move into the future. They do, however, illustrate the key issues involved, and provide a rough indication of whether major exporters will be ready and willing to respond to market forces.

THE IMPORTANCE OF THE GULF REGION

While the preceding analysis has dealt with the Middle East and North Africa as a region, most of MENA energy reserves and production are concentrated in the Gulf. The MENA region as a whole may have more than 65 percent of the world's proven oil reserves and 35 percent of its gas reserves, but over 94 percent of these oil reserves are in the Gulf. Similarly, the U.S. Department of Energy (DOE) estimates that the Gulf averaged 20.8 million barrels per day (MMBD) worth of exports in 2000. This equaled 28 percent of all world exports versus 30 percent for the entire Middle East. the DOE estimates that the Gulf will average 35.8 MMBD in exports by 2025, which will equal 38 percent of all world exports compared to 44 percent for the entire MENA area.[1]

Many Gulf oil-exporting nations are expected to reach future production levels equal to entire regions. The Energy Information Administration (EIA), for example, estimates that Saudi oil production capacity will rise from a little over 10.2 MMBD in 2001 to 23.8 MMBD in 2025. This is a larger output than is projected for all members of the Organization of Petroleum Exporting Countries (OPEC) outside the Gulf combined, whose total production capacity is estimated at 16.6 MMBD. To put this increase in Saudi production in a broader perspective, the entire former Soviet Union—Russia, Central Asia, and the Caspian—is estimated to have a capacity of 19.7 MMBD. Latin America will have a capacity of 12.3 MMBD, Asia will have 4.1 MMBD, and Africa will have 10.5 MMBD. The United States is estimated to have a capacity of 9.4 MMBD, and Mexico 48 MMBD. Canada will have 4.1 MMBD, even with tar sands included.[2] Moreover, production costs in the Gulf will average 15–30 percent of those of virtually all other producers.

Gulf Oil Exports

As has been discussed in previous chapters, there are important uncertainties in these estimates (Gulf OPEC production capacity increased from 18.7 million barrels per day in 1990 to 20.6 million barrels per day in 2001). If one compares the estimates in the EIA reference case estimate with the high-low range in other scenarios, Gulf production capacity will rise to 21.7 MMBD in 2005 (19.98–23.5), 28.7 MMBD in 2010 (20.8–28.4), 33.0 (23.1–34.5) MMBD in 2015, 38.9 (27.4–43.21) MMBD in 2020, and 45.2 (32.1–52.1) MMBD in 2025. This is a potential increase from 28 percent of all world production capacity in 2000 to 36 percent in 2025.[3]

The EIA estimates that the Gulf contains around 674 billion barrels of proven oil reserves, and 1,923 trillion cubic feet (TCF) of natural gas reserves (35 percent of the world total). At the end of 2002, Gulf countries maintained about 22.3 MMBD of oil production capacity, or 32 percent of the world total. In addition, Gulf countries also normally maintain nearly a 90 percent share of the world's surplus oil production capacity, although the Iraq War has reduced excess world oil production capacity to only around 0.7–1.2 MMBD, all in the Gulf region.[4]

In 2002, eight Gulf countries (Bahrain, Iran, Iraq, Kuwait, Oman, Qatar, Saudi Arabia, and the United Arab Emirates [UAE]) produced about 25 percent of the world's oil, and Gulf countries had estimated net oil exports of 15.5 MMBD. Saudi Arabia exported the most, with an estimated 7.0 MMBD (45 percent of the total). Iran had estimated net exports of around 2.3 MMBD (15 percent), followed by the United Arab Emirates (2.1 MMBD—13 percent), Kuwait (1 MMBD—5 percent), and Bahrain (0.01 MMBD—0.1 percent). Gross oil imports to the Organization of Economic Cooperation and Development (OECD) countries from Persian Gulf countries averaged about 10.6 MMBD or some 27 percent of the OECD's total gross oil imports.

The EIA estimates that industrialized countries imported 9.7 million barrels per day from the Gulf region in 2001, and these imports represented some 58 percent of all Gulf exports. The EIA also estimates that OPEC exports to industrialized countries will be about 11.5 million barrels per day higher in 2025 than in 2001, and that more than half of this increase is expected to come from the Gulf region.[5]

The EIA estimates that North America's petroleum imports from the Gulf will almost double during 2001–2025—from 2.9 MMBD to 5.8 MMBD.[6] This increase is estimated to occur in spite of the fact that more than one-half of North America's imports in 2025 are expected to come from other regions and particularly from Atlantic Basin producers and refiners. The EIA projects that the United States will make significant increases expected in crude oil imports from Latin America, including Venezuela, Brazil, Colombia, and Mexico, and from West African producers like Nigeria and Angola. In the case of Europe, moderate decline in North Sea production is expected to increase, Western European imports from Persian Gulf producers and from OPEC member nations in northern and western Africa. Substantial increases in imports from the Caspian Basin are also expected. Finally, industrialized Asian nations are expected to increase their already heavy dependence on Gulf oil and depend almost exclusively on Gulf exports.

In spite of such increases in the amount of Gulf oil going to industrialized states, the EIA estimates that the share of total Gulf exports going to the industrialized nations will fall by about 12 percent, from 57 percent in 2001 to 45 percent in 2025. This shift will occur because of the high rate of economic growth the EIA projects for developing nations, especially in Asia. Total OPEC petroleum exports to developing countries are expected to increase by more than 18.0 million barrels per day during 2001 and 2025, with three-fourths of the increase going to the developing countries of Asia. The developing countries of the Pacific Rim are expected to almost double their total petroleum imports between 2001 and 2025. The EIA estimates that China alone is likely to import about 6.6 million barrels per day from OPEC by 2025, virtually all of which is expected to come from Gulf producers.[7]

The International Energy Agency (IEA) does not project a trend for the Gulf per se, but its definition of the "Middle East" excludes Egypt and North Africa, and Syria—a minor producer and exporter—is the only non-Gulf nation included in the IEA totals. The IEA projects Middle Eastern oil supply as increasing from 21 MMBD in 2000, in its reference case, to 26 MMBD in 2010, 38 MMBD in 2020, and 51 MMBD in 2030.[8] These estimates track, in broad terms, with those of the EIA.

As has been discussed earlier, the EIA and IEA estimates are shaped by demand-driven models, and do not reflect many of the real-world constraints affecting major energy suppliers and exporters. Many experts in the oil industry feel the levels of future production and exports estimated by the EIA, and other governmental groups like the IEA, are too high. Few, however, dispute the broad accuracy of such trends. Virtually all feel that the Gulf will become steadily more important with time, not only as a percentage of total production and exports, but also as a "swing" producer whose ability to increase production and exports will stabilize world prices.

It is also clear that the Gulf states will be absolutely critical to both compensating for the depletion of oil in reserves outside the Gulf and in expanding production. As Chapter 5 describes in more detail, this is a matter of investment and production costs, and the price of oil in future world markets, and not simply the size of Gulf reserves.

Gulf Gas Exports

As has been discussed in Chapter 1, the Gulf also has major gas reserves, and is becoming a major exporter of liquefied natural gas. While the Russian Federation dominates the world's reserves with 1,680 trillion cubic feet, or 27.6 percent of the world total, EIA analysis of the energy resources of the Persian Gulf indicates that it contains huge reserves (2,293 TCF) of natural gas, with Iran and Qatar holding the world's second and third largest reserves (behind Russia), respectively. Iran alone has 15 percent of the word's gas reserves and Qatar and the UAE have another 18.5 percent. In total, the Gulf has over 39.6 percent of the world's reserves. The rest of the Middle East adds less than another 1.26 percent.[9] As has been discussed in Chapter 1, these reserves will become increasingly important over time to serve domestic gas consumption and gas exports.[10] The EIA projects major new gas developments in the Gulf region. Saudi Arabia resolved a long-standing offshore Persian Gulf border dispute with Kuwait in 2000, making possible the development of the 13-TCF Dorra gas field in the waters between Iran, Saudi Arabia, and Kuwait. Qatar's gas is located in the North Dome field, which contains 380 TCF of in-place and 239 TCF of recoverable reserves, which EIA estimates is the largest known non-associated gas field in the world. Qatar has two liquefied natural gas (LNG) exporters: Qatar LNG Company (Qatargas), and Ras Laffan LNG Company (Rasgas). Its $10 billion Dolphin Project is expected to supply gas from the North Dome to the United Arab Emirates, and from Oman, beginning in 2005.[11]

Iran's huge South Pars field contains 280 TCF of gas (some estimates run as high as 500 TCF), and over 17 billion barrels of liquids. Development of this field is Iran's largest energy project, and has some $20 billion in investment. The EIA reports that natural gas from South Pars is slated to be shipped north via the planned 56-inch, $500 million, IGAT-3 pipeline as well as a possible IGAT-4 line, and then reinjected to boost oil output at the mature Aghajari field, and possibly the Ahwaz and Mansouri fields (which make up part of the huge Bangestan reservoir in the southwest Khuzestan region). South Pars natural gas also could be exported, by pipeline and possibly by LNG tanker.

Phases 2 and 3 of South Pars development began to come on-stream in September 2002, and are producing around 2 billion cubic feet (BCF) per day of natural gas, and 85,000 BBL per day of condensates. On September 29, 1997, Total (now TotalFinaElf) had signed a $2 billion deal (along with Russia's Gazprom and Malaysia's Petronas) to explore South Pars and to help develop the field during Phases 2 and 3 of its development. In July 2000, Italian firm ENI had signed a $3.8 billion deal with Iran to develop the South Pars region for gas. The deal reportedly was the largest between Iran and a foreign company since the 1979 Islamic Revolution.

Iran is also seeking to develop the 6.4-TCF, nonassociated Khuff (Dalan) reservoir of the Salman oil field, which is located across Iran's maritime border with Abu Dhabi, where it is known as the Abu Koosh field. The NIOC is seeking to develop the reservoir to the production of up to 500 MMCF per day of nonassociated gas, along with the 120,000 BBL per day of crude oil now being produced from a shallower reservoir.

In addition, Iran plans to develop the 47-TCF North Pars field development to provide up 3.6 BCF per day of gas production, of which 1.2 BCF per day would be reinjected into the onshore Gachsaran, Bibi Hakimeh, and Binak oil fields. The other 2.4 BCF per day would be sent to the more mature Agha Jari oil field.

- Chart 4.1 shows the EIA reference case's estimate of the future increase in Gulf oil production capacity through 2002. The pivotal role of Saudi Arabia is clearly apparent. So, however, is the importance of the rest of the "Big Five," Kuwait, Iraq, Iran, and the UAE.

- Chart 4.2 shows the EIA's estimate of the increase in Gulf petroleum exports between 2001 and 2025 by total and area of destination. The massive overall increase in exports is clearly apparent. So is the shift toward exports to the developing world and particularly toward Asia, China, and the Pacific Rim.

Chart 4.1
The EIA Reference Case Estimate of Gulf Production and Future Production Capacity

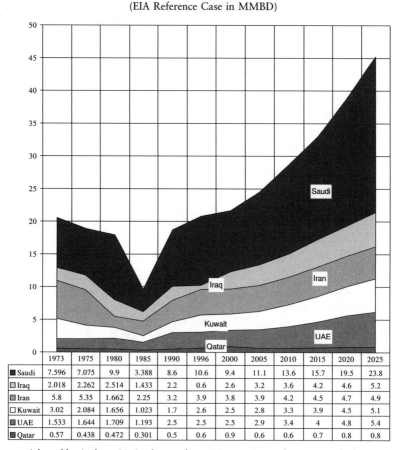

(EIA Reference Case in MMBD)

	1973	1975	1980	1985	1990	1996	2000	2005	2010	2015	2020	2025
■ Saudi	7.596	7.075	9.9	3.388	8.6	10.6	9.4	11.1	13.6	15.7	19.5	23.8
☐ Iraq	2.018	2.262	2.514	1.433	2.2	0.6	2.6	3.2	3.6	4.2	4.6	5.2
▥ Iran	5.8	5.35	1.662	2.25	3.2	3.9	3.8	3.9	4.2	4.5	4.7	4.9
☐ Kuwait	3.02	2.084	1.656	1.023	1.7	2.6	2.5	2.8	3.3	3.9	4.5	5.1
■ UAE	1.533	1.644	1.709	1.193	2.5	2.5	2.5	2.9	3.4	4	4.8	5.4
■ Qatar	0.57	0.438	0.472	0.301	0.5	0.6	0.9	0.6	0.6	0.7	0.8	0.8

Source: Adapted by Anthony H. Cordesman from EIA, *International Energy Outlook 2002*, DOE/
EIA-0484 (2002), June 2002, p. 239; EIA, *International Energy Outlook 2003*, DOE/EIA-0484
(2003), June 2003, p. 239; and EIA, *Monthly Energy Review*, April 1997, pp. 130–131.

COUNTRY TRENDS AND RISKS

Any effort to summarize country plans, trends, and risks presents the
problem that most countries do not have public long-term energy plans,
that the plans they do announce are regularly resolved, and major individual
projects emerge and then go into a constant state of flux that often are not
part of any overall plans. MENA nations respond to market forces, external and internal risk, and new discoveries of energy resources in ways that

Chart 4.2
Estimated Gulf Oil Exports: 2001–2025

(In MMBD)

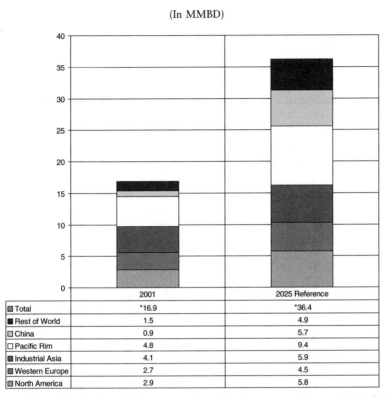

	2001	2025 Reference
Total	*16.9	*36.4
Rest of World	1.5	4.9
China	0.9	5.7
Pacific Rim	4.8	9.4
Industrial Asia	4.1	5.9
Western Europe	2.7	4.5
North America	2.9	5.8

Source: Adapted by Anthony H. Cordesman from EIA, *International Energy Outlook 1998*, DOE/EIA-0484 (1997), April 1998, pp. 175–177; *International Energy Outlook 2002*, June 2002, DOE/EIA-0484 (2002), p. 38; *International Energy Outlook 2003*, June 2003, DOE/EIA-0484 (2003), p. 42; and *International Energy Outlook 2004*, www.eia.doe.gov/oiaf/ieo/index.html, April 2004, Table 8, p. 40.

cannot be anticipated in detail. There are, however, a number of trends that do seem likely to shape the actions of given countries during the period 2004–2030.

Similarly, any summary risk assessment both necessarily oversimplifies the complex factors at work in each MENA country, and ultimately depends on the ability to predict the political, economic, and security dynamics of nations up to thirty years in the future. The recent history of the MENA region makes it all too clear that it is not possible to go beyond short- and midterm judgments and that even these judgments can be nothing more than broad guesses.

Saudi Arabia

Saudi Arabia is one of the largest and most powerful states in the Gulf. According to estimates by the EIA, Saudi Arabia contains 264.2 billion barrels of proven oil reserves, or more than one-quarter of the world's total. The Saudi Arabian Oil Company (Saudi Aramco) claimed in 2004 that Saudi Arabia had a nominal total of 260 billion barrels of proven reserves, or 25 percent of all world reserves.[12] Roughly 131 billion barrels of these proved reserves were stated to be "developed" and in fields that already were in production. It also claimed that it had a total of 700 billion barrels of "discovered reserves" and 200 billion barrels of "undiscovered reserves," and projected that its discovered volume of oil initially in place would reach 700 billion barrels by 2025. It also claimed that it replaced 3 billion barrels of oil production with new reserves in 2004, and added 5 trillion cubic feet of gas to its reserves.[13] On April 2004, Saudi Arabia announced that the kingdom's previous estimate of 261 billion barrels of recoverable petroleum has more than tripled, to 1.2 trillion barrels. Furthermore, Abdallah S. Jum'ah, President of Saudi Aramco, claimed that the kingdom's ". . . estimate of future oil reserves is in the range of 340 billion barrels."[14]

Saudi Arabia is the pivotal oil exporter in the Gulf, the Middle East, and the world. During 2002, Saudi Arabia produced around 8.5 million barrels a day of oil. (It has produced more than 8 million barrels per day since 1991—roughly 30 percent of total OPEC crude production.) According to the EIA, Saudi Arabia had a production capacity of around 10.0–10.5 million barrels a day in 2004. Saudi Aramco estimates a production capacity of 10 MMBD of oil and 9.6 billion cubic feet of gas.[15] Saudi Arabia is also a driving force behind OPEC and in determining whether it can create favorable oil prices. As a result, Saudi production can vary sharply according to global demand for oil and Saudi calculations about which level of production both maintains high oil export revenues in the short run and continued demand for Saudi oil over time.

Saudi Arabia has steadily improved its production capacity and downstream capabilities in response to market forces in the past, and it has sought to retain and expand its oil revenues by keeping prices moderate and preserving both its market share and long-term demand for imports. It has also sought to maintain 2 MMBD of surplus production capacity to maintain its role in shaping the oil market by being its key swing producer.[16] While Russia is emerging as a rival, it has generally been the world's largest producer, and its surplus production capacity has allowed it to act as a "swing" producer that can rapidly increase the supply of exports by 1–2 MMBD, and play a critical role in ensuring and stable supply and more moderate oil prices.[17]

Saudi Oil Production Plans

Saudi Arabia's short-term oil production policy is clear and has not changed since the late 1990s. In October 1999, Oil Minister Naimi stated that Saudi oil policy was based on four facts: (1) the largest oil reserves and among the lowest production costs—around $1–2 per barrel—in the world (the country also has extremely low finding costs, estimated at around 10 cents per barrel); (2) maintenance of significant spare oil production capacity; (3) a national economy closely linked to the oil industry; and (4) a stable political and economic system. Naimi also stressed the importance of "a stable international oil market" where "wide and rapid swings in prices are undesirable." It is also clear that one of Saudi Arabia's long-term goals is to develop its lighter crude reserves, including the Shaybah field located in the remote Empty Quarter area bordering the United Arab Emirates.[18]

Saudi Arabia currently has three projects under way that should increase production capacity by some 1.1 MMBD at a cost of $4–5 billion, and is attempting to change its role as an energy exporter by heavily investing in refinery upgrades and expansions. Currently, it has eight refineries with crude throughput capacity of 1.75 million barrels per day.[19] A $1.2 billion upgrade of the Ras Tanura refinery is nearing completion and its capacity may be further expanded to as much as 1 million barrels per day under longer-term investment plans (through 2007). Saudi Basic Industries Corporation (SABIC) accounts for 10 percent of world petrochemical production. Reduced tariff barriers for petrochemical exports by SABIC are a major motivation behind Saudi Arabia's pursuit of membership in the World Trade Organization (WTO).

Saudi Arabia has also taken aggressive measures to secure market share for its crude oil through refining ventures in the United States, Europe, and Asia. The kingdom took the first step in this direction in 1988, when it acquired a 50 percent stake in Texaco's Star Enterprise joint venture. The newly combined company will have $13 billion in assets, 13 refineries, and 22,000 retail outlets. Despite the recent economic problems in East Asia, Saudi Arabia has continued to look to that region for expansion of its downstream oil investments. Saudi Aramco's ambitious, $3 billion expansion plan in the Philippines, for instance, still seems to be moving forward.

EIA versus Saudi Projections

Saudi Arabia's mid- and long-term energy strategies, and future production capacity, are much less clear. Both the U.S. Department of Energy and the International Energy Agency estimate that the growth in Saudi oil production will outstrip the growth in all of the nations in the former Soviet Union (FSU), in spite of major increases in production by the former Soviet republics in the Caspian and Central Asia. The Gulf states, especially Saudi Arabia, not only have vast reserves, but the lowest costs in the world in terms of incremental production. This explains why the demand-driven models of the EIA and IEA models call for Saudi production capacity to increase by so much between 2001 and 2025.

The EIA estimates that Saudi Arabia will increase its production capacity from 8.6 million barrels per day in 1990, to 10.2 million barrels per day in 2001, 19.5 million barrels per day in 2020, and 23.8 million barrels per day in 2025.[20] The projected increase in Saudi production of 14.4 MMBD from 2001 to 2030 (from 9.4 MMBD to 23.8 MMBD) is equal to 63 percent of a total projected increase of 22.8 MMBD in Gulf production capacity, 55 percent of the total projected increase of 26.1 MMBD in Middle Eastern production capacity, and 32 percent of the 45.3 MMBD increase in world production capacity.[21] In April 2004, the kingdom announced, ". . . We have more than sufficient reserves to increase output. If required, we can increase output from 10.5 million barrels a day to 12–15 million barrels a day. And we can sustain this increased output for 50 years or more. There will be no shortage of oil for the next 50 years. Perhaps much longer."[22]

To put this projected growth in Saudi production capacity in broader perspective, Saudi Arabian production is already equal to all other states in the Gulf combined, and will remain so through 2020 in spite of major increases by Iran and Iraq. The Department of Energy estimates that Saudi Arabia's production will shift from 12.8 percent of world production capacity in 2001 to 13.2 percent in 2005, 14.5 percent in 2010, and then rise to 19.1 percent in 2025.[23]

Yet the fact these estimates are made on the basis of demand-driven models, and not on the basis of Saudi plans, means actual future Saudi production may well be much lower. Like other MENA states, Saudi Arabia has only provided limited detail on its long-term energy strategy regarding future production and export levels, downstream production capabilities, and development of new distribution facilities and ports. It has never had a public debate over the kind of increases in production capacity called for in EIA, IEA, and OPEC estimates.[24]

Saudi Aramco did announce in February 2004, however, that it had plans to maintain production capacity at levels of 10–12 MMBD for the next fifty years (through 2054), and had examined the possibility of producing at levels up to 15 MMBD. Saudi Aramco summarized these fifty-year production scenarios as follows:[25]

Contingent on global market conditions, the Company can readily achieve and sustain a 10 million barrels per day production level through 2054, by relying only on 15 billion barrels of its possible/probable reserves. Future exploration, delineation, and development efforts will certainly push the production plateau well beyond 2054 by expanding the Company's proved reserve portfolio. (Note: the Company's Business Plan calls for a reserves replacement of 15 billion barrels during 2005–2009.)

. . . The Company can achieve and sustain 12 million barrels per day production level through 2054 by relying on 35 billion barrels of its probable/

possible reserves through exploration and development efforts. (The supporting graph shows this increase will occur during 2010–2015.)

A 15 million barrels per day production level can be accomplished and maintained through 2054, by utilizing 68% of the Company's probable/possible reserves. Prudent reservoir management practices, oil-focused exploration efforts and continual emphasis on cutting-edge technologies (including current and future EOR), can certainly extend the plateau period well beyond 2054.

These Saudi statements are a warning that can apply to virtually every other exporting country in the Middle East. Exporting nations may ultimately react to economic forces, and their need to increase oil export earnings, by developing production capabilities far higher than they now plan. At the same time, they may not. As a result, the modeling efforts of the EIA and IEA are most important in indicating that the Saudi share of new and sustained production will be so large that it will be the most critical single factor in limiting the projected price of oil in future world markets.

Even this conclusion, however, has been challenged. There have long been experts who raised serious questions about how long enhanced oil recovery (EOR) can contribute to the growth of proven reserves, and about the quality of the estimates used to estimate reserves. Other experts have questioned how well given states manage their exploration, production, and development and make effective use of the best available technology and practices. A number of states in the MENA area have had significant problems at various times. These include such major producers as Abu Dhabi, Iran, Iraq, Kuwait, and Oman.

Key Uncertainties in Estimates of Saudi and Other MENA Increases in Production: The Simmons Challenge

Matthew R. Simmons has conducted a lengthy investigation of Saudi oil reserves and oil field management practices, as well as of the broader availability of future oil supplies. He feels that most forecasts of production are based on uncertain estimates of reserves, and notes that oil and gas production has peaked in other areas with only limited warning. He also notes that some 20 percent of the world's oil supply comes from only fourteen fields that average sixty years since their discovery.[26] Simmons also claims that major problems exist in the IEA and EIA estimates of OPEC output that can prevent the tracking of production problems.

Simmons focuses on Saudi Arabia as the symbol of what he feels are estimates that are both uncertain and rely far too heavily on continued increases in production from a limited number of major fields. While Simmons is not a petroleum geologist or reservoir engineer, he analyzed a wide range of papers on Saudi fields from the Society of Petroleum Engineers (SPE) that describe problems in producing Saudi fields over the period from 1961 to 2003. Simmons feels these papers reflect steadily growing problems. These include:[27]

- Saudi overreliance on production from a small number of large, but aging oil fields. Saudi Arabia has over 3,200 recognized reservoirs, but 90 percent of its production comes from a small number of fields. The three main fields include Abqaiq (1940), Ghawar (1948–1949), and Safaniya (1951). The more recent major producing fields are smaller and still date back to 1945–1967 (Berri, Zuluf, Marjan, Abu Sa'fah, and Qatif). "Most other formations seem to lack permeability, porosity, aquifer, or all three." Abqaiq peaked in 1973 at 1.095 MMBD, and Berri in 1977 at 787,888 BPD.

- All five major producing Saudi fields use waterdrive to create high levels of oil flow and avoid the normal rate of depletion. Water injection, however, permanently bypasses large pockets of oil.

- Ghawar alone has accounted for 55 percent–60 percent of all Saudi oil produced to date, and still produces 5 MMBD or almost 2 billion barrels a year. Saudi Arabia estimates it still has 125 billion barrels of production capacity left using advanced production techniques. However, some 400 wells have already been drilled in this filed. If advanced EOR techniques do not produce vast amounts of oil from Ghawar, the much more conservative methods of estimating oil reserves developed up to 1975 would indicate that the field only had 60 billion barrels of recoverable reserves and is now 90 percent depleted. There are also problems with tar mats on its eastern flank, some areas require heavy water injection, and others have yet to show any proof they can be produced.

- Saudi Arabia is experiencing production problems with Safaniya, the world's largest offshore field, with watercuts, sand control issues, and production problems in the southern end. Zuluf is its other major offshore field and faces serious production issues. The Marjan complex has H_2S problems.

- Shaybah is the last giant field to be discovered and was discovered in 1967, but its gas cap and contact between oil and water make vertical wells impractical.

- The fields at Qatif, Abu Sa'fah, and Khurais all have their own problems.

- The last major commercial success occurred in 1989. It was the Hawtah field in central Arabia and it produces 200,000 BPD. It has problems with corrosive aquifer water and bacteria contamination.

- The inability to get economic production from vertical wells than are relatively simple and cheap to drill, and reliance on complex, more costly horizontal wells that require much more careful management and that may present risks in terms of their ultimate recovery of oil. These "bottle brush" wells create complex paths through bottom-side water and top-side gas formations to extract the "last thinning columns of easy oil" and may never recover much of the oil in the formation. Overreliance on this technology led to the collapse of production from Oman's Yibal field.

- While technologies like 3-D seismic, horizontal drilling, multilateral well completions, subsea oil production techniques, and other new methods are touted as technical revolutions, "the technology revolution created monstrous decline rates. Proven reserve write-off is likely worldwide." These technologies accelerate extraction, rather than produce the projected increases in recoverable reserves. Prudhoe Bay is a typical example, as are the North Sea giant fields. Once giant fields peak, they usually produce a steady decline, as was the case in eastern Texas.

- A massive drilling effort now requires some 46 drilling rigs, drilling 333 new wells a year. By 2010, Saudi Aramco will need 90 rigs and will have to drill 600 new wells. These wells will all be horizontal and average production per well will drop from 2,010 BPD in 2004 to 1,170 BPD in 2010.

- The methods the U.S. Geological Service (USGS) uses to estimate proven oil and gas reserves are extremely uncertain, and lead to order of magnitude ranges of uncertainty in undeveloped fields. Saudi projections of reserves and future production rely heavily on the content and output of some eighty-five untested oil and gas fields. Saudi Arabia no longer is subject of the strict review of its reserve estimates that took place when outside oil companies ran Aramco, and exaggerated its gas reserves in recent efforts to negotiate major gas development contracts with outside companies. If one applies the older method for estimating Saudi reserves, it would have had only 163.4 million barrels in 1982, rather than the 259.2 billion barrels it now claims.

- Saudi Aramco field production and reservoir models began to fail to predict fluid behavior as early as 1990. New models developed in 2002 remain unproven.

- Saudi Arabia may be forced to shift from producing from high, giant fields to scattered small fields with much less output at much higher costs.

- Saudi oil production could peak as early as 2006–2007 if the "worst case" proves to be true.

It is important to note that Simmons raises many points more as questions than as firm conclusions, and that he uses Saudi Arabia as an example of problems that will affect almost all major oil production efforts throughout the world. Simmons arguments do not, therefore, affect the strategic importance of Saudi Arabia and the MENA areas as much as raise serious questions about all energy forecasts of oil and gas production. Moreover, Simmons is careful to call for further study and for global transparency in producing the best oil reserve and production forecasts, not leap to sudden conclusions.

These are important points and they deserve careful attention at the policy level. It is true that their have been Cassandra-like predictions about oil before, in the Middle East, former Soviet Union, and the world. As the previous chapters have shown, none has proved accurate enough to merit serious retrospective analysis. At the same time, many current production and export forecasts are driven by models and assumptions that do not explicitly analyze technical or geological risk, and assume a predictable level of technological progress. Such assumptions are inherently and inevitably wrong. No matter how long a trend lasts, it will eventually end and usually in ways that produce sharp changes in either a positive or negative trend. The current estimating models of the IEA and EIA do not explore enough variables and lack adaptation to modern complexity theory. They also tend to be re-calibrated regressively, rather than consider future risk. Given the immense increases in midterm energy out put that they project during 2020–2030, this is not an adequate approach to modeling and analysis.

The Saudi Aramco Response

At the same time, it is clear that Saudi Aramco has a very different view of the future, as do virtually all oil companies and government and inter-national agencies. The fact that the *possibility* of drastic error exists in world, MENA, and Saudi energy forecasts does not mean that they are in error, and experts have raised similar arguments in the past. As Saudi Aramco argues:[28]

- It operates on the basis of five basic principles: (1) sustainable performance, (2) maximum hydrocarbon recovery, (3) emphasis on optimal life-cycle eco-nomics, (4) prudent reserves management, and (5) excellence in safety and en-vironmental practices.

- Saudi Aramco practices are equal to, or better than, best practices in the in-dustry. Its estimates of 260 billion barrels of proved oil reserves are conserva-tive and do not include any portion relying on advanced EOR other than pressure maintenance. The standard estimates of reserves set by leading industry exports in the SPE, WPC, and AAPG do include reserves based on such methods.

- Some 131 billion barrels, or 50 percent of Saudi Arabia's 260 billion barrels of proved reserves, are developed, and largely on production. Extensive field performance data, and the relatively high level of development (50 percent), confirm the accuracy of Aramco estimates of proved reserves, and are further confirmed by comprehensive characterization of local, regional, and basin proved reserves.

- Aramco uses SPE, WPC, and AAPG standards for calculating recoverable proved reserves for oil prices, operating methods, hydrocarbon water content, and deepest known hydrocarbon depth, and the same probability criteria (90 percent).

- Reservoir management is based on a sophisticated learning model that is con-tinually improved, and is based on maximum hydrocarbon recovery, reservoir monitoring, low depletion rates, advanced diagnostics, and cutting edge tech-nologies.

- The extent of depletion in existing Saudi fields ranges from 5 percent in newly developed fields like Shaybah to 73 percent in mature fields like Abqaiq. The total depletion is 28 percent as of year-end 2003 (Abqaiq = 73 percent, Ain Der/Shedgum = 60 percent, Ghawar = 48 percent, Berri = 28 percent, Safaniya = 26 percent, Abu Sa'fah = 21 percent, Zuluf = 16 percent, Marjan = 13 percent, Haradh = 10 percent, and Shaybah = 5 percent).

- Saudi depletion rates average 1.0–4.1 percent annually versus 4.2–9.6 percent for most international fields.

- As a case example, Shaybah is currently being depleted at a rate of 1 percent a year, with a production plateau of more than fifty years. It has continued to produce 500,000 BPD since July 1988, and actual production has conformed to Aramco predictions. It will be expanded to 1 MMBD or higher when needed. Horizontal drilling and the shift from simple horizontal wells to maximum reservoir contact wells increased production from 3,000 BPD in 1996, drawing on a distance of 1 kilometer, to 10,000 BPD in 2002, drawing on a distance of 12 kilometers. At the same time, unit development costs dropped by more than 66 percent during 1996–2002.

- Ghawar's development was enhanced by peripheral water injection as early as 1965, and has maintained a comprehensive pressure maintenance program ever since. Rather than decline, technology and prudent reservoir management techniques allowed it to produce 55 billion barrels by the end of 2003. Water cut did increase slowly from under 30 percent in 1993 to 36.5 percent in 1999, but improved practices cut it back to 33 percent in 2003. It has never risen above moderate levels.

- The Ain Dar/Shedgum area of Ghawar has produced 26.9 billion barrels, and currently produces 2 MMBD at a steady water cut of 36 percent. Reservoir pressure has been stable for more than two decades. It still has 13.9 billion barrels of proved reserves, 3.4 billion barrels of probable reserves, 6.8 billion barrels of possible reserves, and 17.1 billion barrels of contingent resources. EOR should allow recovery of 75 percent of the oil initially in place or 51 billion barrels.

- Two giant shut-in fields, Manifa and Khurais, which contain proved reserves of 40.8 billion barrels, have depletion states of 1.2 percent and 1.8 percent respectively. Both fields have been developed and placed on-stream as predicated by Aramco's production and maximum sustainable production capacity (MSC) imperatives.

- Valid exploration, delineation, and development efforts increased Saudi Aramco's estimates of oil initially in place by 17 percent during 1984–2003.[29]

- Exploratory wells have been drilled to confirm the producability of the other fields and expanded use of existing fields, including areas in northwest Saudi Arabia, northern basins along the borders with Iraq, central Saudi Arabia, the Rub' al-Khali, and offshore Red Sea Basin.

- Saudi reserve estimates are confirmed by a USGS survey in 2000 of the top eight regions of undiscovered, recoverable oil resources. The mean estimate of such oil resources was 87 billion barrels for Saudi Arabia, 77 billion for Russia, 53 billion for Iran, 47 billion for Greenland, 45 billion for Iraq, 38 billion for Nigeria, and 21 billion for Kazakhstan.

- Saudi Arabia now projects its estimate of undiscovered oil initially in place to increase from 7,000 billion barrels in 2004 to 9,000 billion in 2025.

- The use of "smart wells," and quad-lateral smart well completion technologies, has already been proven in the Haradh Increment III project and is currently producing 300,000 BPD. Production is projected for fifty years, and water cut levels will only rise to a moderate 22 percent in 2036.

- Simmons relies on reports designed to identify problems that Aramco has largely solved. He is projecting generally from the wrong type of highly specific source.

It is worth noting that Aramco's exploration, reservoir management, and other practices win almost universal praise from U.S., British, and Dutch oil companies—praise they do not give to Kuwait, Iran, Iraq, Oman, and the UAE. U.S. government experts share this opinion. As a result, it seems likely that Saudi Arabia can meet its goals in the near and midterm (through 2025) unless Simmons's calculations are proven correct for reasons that would require significant new discoveries about petroleum geology and oil field management. As has been noted earlier, however, this is *possible* although not *probable*. Moreover, Simmons is certainly correct in warning that IEA and EIA forecasts of Saudi production are unrealistic to the degree that Saudi Arabia has never announced plans to produce at anything like the levels projected by the IEA and EIA.

Saudi Ability to Ship and Transport Oil

Saudi ability to safely ship its oil is also an important strategic issue. Saudi Arabia has attempted to secure its position as an exporter and boost its export capabilities by acquiring new tankers and increasing its overseas crude oil storage capacities. The Saudi fleet currently comprises twenty-three crude tankers and four product vessels. Saudi Arabia also owns and leases storage facilities.

Most of Saudi Arabia's crude oil is exported via the Persian Gulf through the Abqaiq processing facility. In the Persian Gulf, the kingdom's primary oil export terminals are located at Ras Tanura (6 million barrels per day capacity—the world's largest offshore oil loading facility) and Juaymah (3 million barrels per day). In addition, the Yanbu terminal (as high as 5 million BBL per day) serves as the main oil port in the Red Sea, though it is far less profitable than Ras Tanura.

Saudi Arabia operates two major oil pipelines that give it a capability to bypass shipments through the Gulf and the Strait of Hormuz. The 4.8 million barrels per day East-West Crude Oil Pipeline (Petroline) is used mainly to transport Arabian Light and Super Light to refineries in the Western Province and to Red Sea terminals for direct export to European markets. Running parallel to the Petroline is the 290,000 barrels per day Abqaiq-Yanbu natural gas liquids pipeline, which serves Yanbu's petrochemical facilities. The EIA reports that Saudis expanded the Petroline to maintain Yanbu as a strategic option to Gulf port facilities in the event that exports were blocked at that end, and that the Petroline's capacity could be expanded significantly by using so-called drag reduction agents (DRAs).

This could enhance the line's strategic value, but the EIA also reports that Yanbu is a far less economic option for exports than Ras Tanura. Shipments from Yanbu add about five days' round-trip travel time for tankers through the Bab al-Mandab Strait to Asia compared to Ras Tanura through the Strait of Hormuz. In addition, the Petroline is normally utilized at half capacity. Saudi Aramco has begun converting the AY-1 (48-inch) line to natural gas pumping capability. The natural gas will supply Yanbu's petrochemical and power facilities.[30]

The Trans-Arabian Pipeline (Tapline) was mothballed following the Persian Gulf War (after providing only limited service to a refiner in Jordan since the 1970s), and the 1.65 million barrels per day Iraqi-Saudi Pipeline (IPSA-2) was closed indefinitely after the start of the Gulf War.

Saudi Natural Gas Resources

Saudi Arabia's natural gas reserves are estimated at 224.7 trillion cubic feet. Most of these reserves consist of associated gas, which comes primarily from the Ghawar field and the offshore Safaniya and Zuluf fields. The Ghawar oil field alone accounts for one-third of the country's total gas reserves. Most new associated gas reserves discovered in the 1990s have been in fields that contain light crude oil, especially in the Najd region south of Riyadh. Most of Saudi Arabia's nonassociated gas reserves are located in the deep Khuff reservoir, which underlies the Ghawar oil field and which has been expanded steadily over the past decade. In 2002, construction was completed on a $4 billion, 1.4 BCF per day, nonassociated gas-processing plant at Hawiyah, near the Ghawar oil field. Hawiyah represents the largest Saudi natural gas project in more than ten years.[31]

Aramco discovered four new gas fields in 2003. Moreover, the ongoing projects of Hawiyah and Hanadh will enable the respective oil company to increase its natural gas production from 3 to 5 TCF annually. This increase requires an expanded gas pipeline network, and Aramco plans to construct some additional 3,000 kilometers of pipeline by 2006.[32] Nevertheless, many oil company experts believe that Saudi Arabia is still not ready to offer attractive terms for the level of foreign investment it needs in its gas facilities, and is not prepared to address the need for foreign financing of its oil production in the future.

Natural gas development is both a short- and long-term energy issue because of its value as feedstock and because it is critical to reducing the domestic demand for oil. With domestic gas demand expected to grow as much as 8 percent per year through 2007, increasing gas production, particularly nonassociated production, is a priority for the Saudi government. The gas will be used as feedstock for the growing petrochemical industry as well as for electricity generation. In addition, using gas domestically instead of oil could help free up 200,000–300,000 barrels per day of additional crude oil for export within the next two years.

Saudi Need to Increase Domestic Use of Natural Gas

There are no current Saudi plans to export natural gas, but Saudi Aramco projects that domestic gas consumption could exceed 6 BCF per day by 2005, and the EIA reported in June 2003 that Saudi Arabia aims to triple natural gas output (to 15 BCF pr day) by 2009. Most of this demand will come from industrial consumers, power plants, and petrochemical plants located in the Eastern Province (at Yanbu and Jubail), as well as desalination plants and a replacement for burning oil.

To date, Saudi Arabia has not expressed great interest in exporting liquefied natural gas mainly due to doubts regarding economic viability. Saudi oil minister Ali Naimi has said that the kingdom will only investment in major export facilities like gas trains if it finds gas reserves similar to Qatar's North field. Saudi officials have also indicated that building a large natural gas-to-liquids plant is not part of Saudi energy strategy through 2020–2025.[33]

Using natural gas instead of oil domestically frees up additional crude oil for export (OPEC quotas are on production, not exports). Investment in natural gas also provides a substitute for crude burning by electric utilities. In the summer of 1996, high demand by domestic power plants contributed to Aramco's decision to reduce its crude oil deliveries under some term contracts by 5 percent. Domestic demand for gas is rising at a rate of 7 percent per year, and is driving investment in Saudi Arabia's Master Gas System (MGS), which started up in 1982 (prior to that time, all of the country's natural gas was flared). In 1999, Saudi Arabia began an ambitious $4.5 billion expansion of the MSG that continues today.[34]

The need to make massive further increases in gas exploration and development, production, distribution, and use presents investment problems for Saudi Arabia at a time when it must fund oil development, restructure the rest of its economy, and meet rapidly growing civil demands from its rising population. The kingdom also needs technology transfer in the gas sector because Aramco has less experience with gas development than with oil.

Gas development is now slated to consume a large share of Saudi Arabia's energy budget. In late 1999, Aramco decided to invest $45 billion over 25 years on upstream gas development and processing facilities, and Aramco is aiming to add 3–5 TCF of new nonassociated natural gas reserves per year to meet rapid (5 percent annual) gas demand growth. Nonassociated gas development is desirable because it guarantees a steady flow of gas regardless of oil output, which tends to fluctuate. Currently, nonassociated gas accounts for 40 percent of Saudi Arabia's total gas reserves.

As a result, Saudi Arabia has had a steadily growing interest in foreign investment in its gas industry. Crown Prince Abdullah has led a major effort, beginning in March 2000, to obtain foreign investment to help support the expansion of Saudi Arabia's gas industry, but this effort has encountered major problems. Saudi oil minister Naimi officially announced termination of negotiations with foreign energy companies on the $15–20 billion "Saudi Gas Initiative" (SGI) in June 2003. The SGI was supposed to be the first major reopening of Saudi Arabia's upstream hydrocarbons sector to foreign investment since nationalization in the 1970s. The SGI had aimed to increase foreign investment and natural gas development in the country, while integrating upstream gas development with downstream petrochemicals, power generation, and water desalination. SGI had been seen as the key to Saudi Arabia's entire foreign investment strategy.[35]

The EIA reports negotiations broke down over two major stumbling blocks: the extent of gas reserves to be opened to upstream development, and whether or not this should include gas from the Saudi Aramco Reserve Area (SARA); and the rates of return to participating companies (the companies wanted a significantly higher rate than the Saudis were offering).

- Core Venture 1, in South Ghawar, would have been one of the world's largest ($15 billion) integrated natural gas projects, including exploration, pipelines, two gas-fired power plants, two petrochemical plants, two desalination units, and more.

- Core Venture 2 was to involve exploration in the Red Sea, development of the Barqan and Midyan fields on the Red Sea coast in northwestern Saudi Arabia, as well as construction of a petrochemical plant, a power station, desalination capacity, and the like, at a cost of $4 billion.

- Core Venture 3 would have involved exploration near Shaybah in the Rub al-Khali ("Empty Quarter") of southeastern Saudi Arabia, development of the Kidan gas field, laying of pipelines from Shaybah to the Haradh and Hawiyah natural gas treatment plants east of Riyadh, and construction of a petrochemical plant in Jubail, at a cost of $4 billion.

In mid-June 2003, Dubai-based Gulf News reported that Saudi Arabia was considering inviting international oil companies to bid again on the SGI. Companies that had been selected (in 2001) for the three "core ventures" under the SGI were: (1) South Ghawar: ExxonMobil (35 percent), Shell (25 percent), BP (25 percent), Phillips (15 percent); (2) Red Sea: ExxonMobil (60 percent), plus Marathon (20 percent) and Occidental (20 percent); (3) Shaybah: Shell (40 percent), Total (30 percent), and Conoco (30 percent).

This was followed in July by a breakthrough agreement with Shell and Total on joint gas exploration with Aramco, the first time Saudi Arabia had accepted foreign investment since the 1970s. This represented a scaled-down version of Core Venture 3, and covered 209,160 square kilometers of the Empty Quarter. Shell took a 40 percent share and Total and Aramco 30 percent each. Both at the time and later, the major U.S. and British oil companies stated privately that they were not willing to take the risk of bidding on areas where nonassociated gas reserves were so uncertain and the terms were not competitive with other countries in risk-benefit.

While Core Ventures 1 and 2 were abandoned, Saudi Arabia also sent out bid packages for three smaller upstream packages and held discussions with some forty companies. Contract A area is 29,900 square kilometers, Contract B area is 38,800 square kilometers, and Contract C area is 51,400 square kilometers.[36]

In March 2004, the kingdom made gas deals in each area that involved a strikingly new set of partners. Saudi Arabia opened the door on Sunday to fresh natural gas exploration, securing $800 million worth of Russian, Chinese, and European investment that it said would forge new political and economic alliances. Saudi oil minister Ali al-Naimi announced that new deals had been signed with Russia's LUKOIL, China's Sinopec, and a consortium of Italy's Eni and Spain's Repsol YPF. The deals in Contract A, B, and C areas covered a total 120,000 square kilometers in the southeastern edge of Saudi Arabia's Empty Quarter near its border with the UAE. Saudi Aramco took a 20 percent stake in all three ventures.

Saudi oil minister Naimi announced at the signing ceremony, "We already have strong relations with Russia and excellent cooperation in managing market stability. . . . And there is no question in my mind that strengthening economic relations will strengthen other areas of cooperation." The LUKOIL deal was signed less than a year after Saudi Crown Prince Abdullah visited Moscow both to improve Saudi relations with a major competing oil and gas producer and in reaction to U.S. treatment of Saudi Arabia after September 11, 2001. It committed LUKOIL to investing $200 million to explore Contract Area A in southeastern Saudi Arabia. The head of LUKOIL announced that the company expected a minimum rate of return on investment of 12.5 to 15 percent, and that LUKOIL could invest up to $3 billion in the Saudi gas sector if it were to find gas.

The Chinese firm Sinopec signed its deal with Saudi Arabia in response to growing Chinese concerns over dependence on oil and gas imports. Saudi Arabia already ranked as China's top supplier of crude oil, and exported some 13.5 million tons of crude in 2003. The deal gave Aramco a 25 percent stake in a planned $3 billion refinery and petrochemical venture in China, while Sinopec pledged to invest an initial $300 million in drilling wells and shooting seismic surveys in a 38,800 square kilometer block in the Empty Quarter.[37]

The European firms of Eni and Repsol took the biggest block, which had an area of 51,400 square kilometers. Even so, the deals were striking in that they excluded the U.S. oil majors that had been involved in the "Natural Gas Initiative," and only one U.S. company—ChevronTexaco—even bid in the current round. The ChevronTexaco bids did not come close in Contract A area, where Aramco gave LUKOIL a bid score of 218.50 to ChevronTexaco's 108.77, or in Contract B area, where Sinopec got a score of 189.50 to ChevronTexaco's 93.77. The only area where it was roughly competitive was in Contract C area, where it had a bid score of 93.77 compared to 103.50 for Eni and Repsol.

Saudi officials claimed the reasons were economic and not political. There is certainly some truth to this. U.S. and British firms like BP, British Gas, and ExxonMobil did not find that the kingdom provided the necessary disclosure of its data on reserves and costs, believed that it might be greatly exaggerating its estimates of probable nonassociated gas reserves, and felt its cost-benefit calculations were not competitive. They also questioned the commericial feasibility of obtaining non-associated gas from the Khuff gas accumulation. This reserve is very deep, very hot, and has numerous impurities that are difficult to remove. Its value is uncertain, and Abu Dhabi has chosen to import gas from Qatar, rather than develop its own portion of the Khuff reservoir.[38]

The companies also saw little incentive to "buy in" to contracts when they felt that Saudi Arabia's oil minister had little intention of offering truly attractive deals in the future. At the same time, it is clear that the kingdom did have strong geopolitical reasons to turn away from its past dependence on U.S. oil companies, to work out lasting energy relationships with Russia and China, and to send the Bush administration at least an indirect message that the kingdom resented the treatment it had been given since September 11.[39]

Saudi Energy Risk

Saudi Arabia is the most important single case in the world in terms of assessing energy "risk." This is partly because of regional military threats and internal stresses. Saudi Arabia remains the most lucrative single target in the Gulf to any nation seeking to use its military or political leverage to influence the world economy. It faces major economic and demographic challenges for at least the next two decades, and it must its economy and ability to attract private and foreign investment to deal with these issues.[40]

In spite of its conservative religious character, Saudi Arabia also faces a serious terrorist challenge from religious extremists, most notably Al-Qaeda and affiliated neo-Salafi and neo-Wahhabi groups. It must deal with elements of extremism in its own religious and educational system, and it must reform its political and legal structure to provide a more pluralist and modern political system.

As is discussed in Chapter 5, these strategic, political, and economic risks are compounded by financial risks. It simply is not clear that the kingdom can—or should—continue to finance upstream oil and gas production, and the growth and diversification of its downstream sector, with anything like the level of direct and indirect public funding it has relied upon in the past. The kingdom simply has too many other budgetary and investment priorities. It has long suffered from budget deficit problems, except in years of exceptionally high oil revenues. It has never had a public discussion or debate over the costs and financing involved or the possible need for outside private or foreign investment in its upstream oil sector. There are many forces in the kingdom pressing for a more open, consultative, and representative government, and sooner or later such a debate is inevitable.

These pressures on Saudi Arabia do not seem urgent today, although the threat posed by terrorist groups cannot be ignored. The need for political, economic, and social reform will grow steadily, however, as Saudi Arabia's "youth explosion" reaches maturity. This explains why Saudi Arabia has begun reforms to deal with its economic problems. For example, the Saudi government has declared its aim to accede to the World Trade Organization (WTO). The kingdom has announced its intend to join the organization in early 2004. In addition, the Saudi government approved a new income bill in order to attract foreign investors to the kingdom. The new bill cuts the tax rate on foreign investors from 45 to 20 percent.[41] However, Saudi ability to deal with these issues—and to smoothly respond to market forces, in the manner the EIA, IEA, and OPEC currently project—remains uncertain.

There are many areas where reform is still more surface reform than substantive change, and where Saudi Arabia has made a gesture or a beginning that it has yet to demonstrate that it will fully implement. In the past, Saudi Arabia has issued a whole series of five-year plans like "Saudization" that have called for reforms in critical areas, only to fail to implement them at anything like the rate required. Its measures to encourage both the repatriation of Saudi private capital and large scale foreign direct investment have not yet removed many practical barriers that slow the pace of economic liberalization far below the rate that its desirable.

More needs to be done to address problems in the education of young Saudis, both in terms of tolerance and in moving decisively away from the emphasis on rote learning that its one of the greatest single self-inflicted wounds of the Arab world, and one that now makes the idea of a knowledge-based economy little more than a hollow dream. The kingdom has done nothing to address population growth and its demographic problems, and it is unclear that anything else it does can be adequate until it does. It also is just beginning to confront the fact that young Saudi women now are significantly better and more practically educated than young Saudi men, and represent a half of the labor force that must become at least as productive as men.

The very real progress that Saudi Arabia has made in improving the rule of law and expanding the size and powers of the Majlis is important in a nation with no political parties, but the kingdom has not yet provided the degree of transparency in its budgets, and Majlis control over the budget process, that is critical to developing a truly effective popular consensus for reform and to laying the ground work for the creation of political parties and an elected Majlis. Human rights reforms are just beginning, and the press needs to have substantially more freedom.

At the same time, Saudi Arabia is a nation whose more progressive rulers, technocrats, educators, businessmen, and clergy must deal with an extremely conservative population and cannot move quickly, or on Western terms, without creating new problems for internal stability. King Fahd's six-point reform program already challenges Saudi conservatives, and Crown Prince Abdullah's continuing support for the actual implementation of reform has clearly moved more quickly than many conservatives desire. The kingdom can and should move faster, but it must maintain a difficult balance between the demands of its reformers and its conservatives. The United States and the West must recognize that it is the conservatives and not the reformers who almost certainly have the largest share of public opinion.

If Saudi Arabia does sustain the momentum behind reform that it has built up since 2000, it may well be able to achieve mid- and long-term stability. There are, however, several "worst cases" and problems that must be considered in such a judgment as it applies to Saudi stability in the middle and long term:

- The pace of reform must be sustained, and should be accelerated. Saudi Arabia has no slack for a ruler who neglects or slows reform, or pauses in political, social, and economic change, any more than it can afford to slow its improvements in counterterrorism.

- As Crown Prince Abdullah has publicly recognized, Saudi Arabia already has its own poor, slums, and underclass, and many of its schools and public facilities do not meet the needs of its growing poor. Oil wealth no longer provides the money for broad subsidies and the kingdom's infrastructure and services need to be put on a basis that funds services for its growing poor while charging full market value for those Saudis who can afford it. The kingdom must pay growing attention to income distribution and must convert its budget from a patriarchal approach to the entire population to providing welfare for those who are legitimately in need.

- At the same time, reform must phase out patriarchal subsidies, which are not only unaffordable, but discourage a work ethic and Saudi employment. Taxation, market value for utilities and services, and a concentration of entitlements for those in true need must replace the patriarchal system over time.

- Saudi Arabia must redefine the role of its royal family as elections and the expanded role of the Majlis change its political structure. In the process, it must find ways to limit grants and subsidies, ensure that corruption does not take place, and provide the kind of transparency on royal family expenditures that will build public confidence and trust.

- Saudi Arabia must develop ways of repatriating Saudi private capital and getting foreign direct investment that do in fact rapidly expand and diversify its private sector.

- It needs U.S. and Western encouragement for its reforms that focus on practical schedules of action and that reinforce internal Saudi efforts, not efforts to dictate or impose Western approaches.

- Saudi Arabia must transfer part of the funds now used for the military to civil programs, and concentrate more on internal security than foreign threats.

- It is more important for Saudi Arabia to invest in economic diversification and the growth of the private sector than to insist on total state control of the upstream sector.

- Saudi Arabia must prepare for the return of unforeseen and uncontrollable cycles in oil revenues and "bad years." It cannot afford to plan for continued high oil revenues.

- Saudi Arabia must convincingly demonstrate that it is properly managing its oil fields and reservoirs and can, in fact, make and sustain major increases in its oil production capacity and oil exports. The charges now being made that Saudi fields will soon be in decline must be convincingly refuted, and enough technical detail and evidence must be provided regarding oil field development to reassure investors about the kingdom's future.

- Saudi Arabia will face a major mid- and long-term challenge if Iraq does rapidly come online with production capacities of 6 to 9 to 12 MMBD at any point before 2020. This could be compounded by any broader production capacity race in OPEC, and by Iranian efforts to make major production increases. If rises in Gulf production combine with high levels of Russian production and rises in Caspian and other production outside the MENA area, Saudi Arabia cannot count on dominating the market share of oil export revenues to the extent it does today; and this could produce a crisis in financing the state and per capita income.

- Educational reform must do more than change the curriculum. No reform that does not eliminate dependence on rote learning can be effective.

- Saudi Arabia must find ways to give its Shiites full equality in de facto terms in regard to civil rights, opportunity, and legal procedures, and to reduce social tensions between Shiites and Sunnis.

- No amount of educational reform can substitute for job creation and job pull. One great danger in Arab thinking about economic reform is that better education creates jobs. It does not. It may raise the value of jobs, but only economic growth, and particularly private sector growth outside the petroleum sector, creates jobs.

- As King Fahd's six-point reform program recognizes, Saudi Arabia must find its own answer to using women as productively as it does men.

- Saudi Arabia must honestly examine its own demographic crisis and begin to deal with it.

- None of these potential "worst cases" and problems is a "show stopper" in political terms or a reason why the U.S. private sector should not invest in Saudi Arabia. No nation has a secure future, and Saudi Arabia still has ample opportunity to deal with its problems. In fact, its challenges are significantly lower than those of most other oil-exporting nations in terms of mid- and long-term risk management.

No country can afford to prepare for every risk, anymore than it can eliminate risk. There is, however, one set of mid- to long-term problems that Saudi

Arabia must address—difficult as it is for Saudis to do so at the political and cultural level. The UN estimate of Saudi population growth projects massive increases that are still gathering momentum and that will continue to accelerate through at least 2010. The growth in the fifteen- to nineteen-year age group during 1990 through 2030 should be a red flag to every Saudi that a massive social and economic crisis will occur unless reform is sustained, and serious efforts are made to reduce the rate of population growth. This age group grew by 35 percent during 1990–2000 (1.5 million to 2.1 million), and will grow by 84 percent during 2000–2030 (2.1 million to 3.8 million).

As both King Fahd and Crown Prince Abdullah seem to have recognized, the importance of integrating women into a fully productive role in the Saudi economy will ultimately be as important as finding employment for young men. Its importance is indicated both by a current fertility rate of 4.53 percent and the projected decline to 2.28 percent in 2020. If this decline does not take place because women have no other role, Saudi population problems will go from the extreme difficult to impossible problem level. Moreover, women in the working-age population already total over 4.6 million. They will nearly double to 11.7 million by 2030. No Saudi economy can hope to be diversified and globally competitive that does not give Saudi women a role whose productivity is equivalent to that of men.

At the same time, these demographics reinforce the need to convert from a patriarchal nation budget that subsidizes everyone to a welfare budget that aids those truly in need. The data show there has already been a growth in the post–labor force population—those aged sixty-five or older—from 374,000 in 1990 to in 561,000 in 2000. This population is projected to grow nearly five times to 2.6 million in 2030. This is an incredible increase in dependency on pensions and invested capital and social services.

As a result, Saudi Arabia represents a moderate short- to midterm energy risk.

Iraq

Iraq is another Gulf state projected to make major increases in production between 2001 and 2025—in this case the EIA projects that Iraqi production capacity will increase from 2.6 MMBD in 2001 to 5.1 MMBD in 2025—an increase of 2.5 MMBD. Since the fall of Saddam Hussein, various other sources have talked about a much more rapid expansion to levels of 6 MMBD, 9 MMBD, and even 12 MMBD.

If one accepts current methods of estimating proven and potential reserves, Iraq has the oil to reach such production levels—although it would be at least as subject to a reduction in its total reserves as Saudi Arabia if analysts like Simmons are correct. In practice, however, the Iraq War of 2003 has been followed by low-intensity warfare and the sabotage of Iraq's oil facilities and pipelines. These kept Iraq's production levels at 2.4 to 2.6 MMBD through March 2004. It has also opened up internal political and economic issues that could disrupt Iraq's energy development and/or lead to internal violence long into the future.

Iraqi Energy Resources

The EIA summarizes Iraq's role in world energy supplies as follows:[42]

Iraq contains 115 billion barrels of proven oil reserves, the third largest in the world (behind Saudi Arabia and Canada). Estimates of Iraq's oil reserves and resources vary widely, however, given that only 10% or so of the country has been explored. Some analysts (the Baker Institute, Center for Global Energy Studies, the Federation of American Scientists, etc.) believe, for instance, that deep oil-bearing formations located mainly in the vast Western Desert region, for instance, could yield large additional oil resources (possibly another 100 billion barrels or more), but have not been explored. Other analysts, such as the U.S. Geological Survey, are not as optimistic, with median estimates for additional oil reserves closer to 45 billion barrels.

. . . Iraq's oil development and production costs are amongst the lowest in the world (perhaps $3–$5 billion for each million barrels per day), making it a highly attractive oil prospect. However, only 17 of 80 discovered fields have been developed, while few deep wells have been drilled compared to Iraq's neighbors. Overall, only about 2,300 wells reportedly have been drilled in Iraq (of which about 1,600 are actually producing oil), compared to around 1 million wells in Texas for instance. In addition, Iraq generally has not had access to the latest, state-of-the-art oil industry technology (i.e., 3D seismic, directional or deep drilling, gas injection), sufficient spare parts, and investment in general throughout most of the 1990s. Instead, Iraq reportedly utilized sub-standard engineering techniques (i.e., overpumping, water injection/"flooding"), obsolete technology, and systems in various states of decay (i.e., corroded well casings) in order to sustain production. In the long run, reversal of all these practices and utilization of the most modern techniques, combined with development of both discovered fields as well as new ones, could result in Iraq's oil output increasing by several million barrels per day.

. . . In December 2002, the Council on Foreign Relations and the Baker Institute released a report on Iraq's oil sector. Among other things, the report concluded that: 1) Iraq's oil sector infrastructure is in bad shape at the moment, being held together by "band-aids," and with a production decline rate of 100,000 bbl/d per year; 2) increasing Iraqi oil production will require "massive repairs and reconstruction . . . costing several billions of dollars and taking months if not years"; 3) costs of repairing existing oil export installations alone would be around $5 billion, while restoring Iraqi oil production to pre-1990 levels would cost an additional $5 billion, plus $3 billion per year in annual operating costs; 4) outside funds and large-scale investment by international oil companies will be needed; 5) existing oil contracts will need to be clarified and resolved in order to rebuild Iraq's oil industry, with any "prolonged legal conflicts over contracts" possibly "delay[ing] the development of important fields in Iraq"; 6) any "sudden or prolonged shutdown" of Iraq's oil industry could result in long-term reservoir damage; 7) Iraq's oil facilities could easily be damaged during any domestic unrest or military operations (in early February 2003, the Patriotic Union of Kurdistan claimed that Iraqi soldiers were mining oil wells in the north of the country in anticipation of war); and 8) given all this, a "bonanza" of oil is not expected in the near future.

. . . According to the Middle East Economic Survey (MEES), problems at Iraqi oil fields include: years of poor oil reservoir management; corrosion problems at various oil facilities; deterioration of water injection facilities; lack of spare parts, materials, equipment, etc.; damage to oil storage and pumping facilities; and more. MEES estimates that Iraq could reach production capacity of 4.2 million bbl/d within three years at a cost of $3.5 billion, and 4.5–6.0 million bbl/d within seven years. The International Energy Agency, in contrast, estimates a $5 billion cost to raise Iraqi output capacity to 3.7 million bbl/d by 2010, and a $42 billion cost to raise capacity to 8 million bbl/d by 2030.

Iraqi Oil Production

As of November 2003, Iraq's oil ministry called for production levels to rise to 3 MMBD in 2004, but the oil minister also talked of costs of $50 billion to reach production levels of 5 MMBD and compensate for years of underinvestment and cannibalization. It would also require a peaceful environment, and several years of intensive work and investment.[43] Any such estimates, however, are purely speculative. For example, Edward C. Chow, a former Chevron executive and visiting scholar with the Carnegie Endowment for International Peace, estimated on November 2003 that it would cost $20 billion to restore Iraqi production to prewar levels.[44] The United States and Interim Governing Council have since found that the cumulative impact of past mismanagement, the Iran-Iraq War, the Gulf War, sanctions, and fighting and looting in 2003 will require billions of dollars in immediate U.S. aid, although no reliable estimates yet exist of the ultimate cost of fully modernizing Iraq's oil facilities, fixing past neglect, and dealing with reservoir problems.

A great deal has been said about rapid Iraqi energy development over the years without adequate surveys of the state of the industry and the cost of renovation and expansion, without regard to military and political risk, and on the basis of extremely uncertain estimates of reserves and incremental production costs. Yet a number of outside assessments raise serious issues about the present state of Iraq's oil fields and production efforts.[45] They have criticized the Bush administration for spending hundreds of millions of dollars to repair the pipes and pumps that carry Iraq's oil, but not addressing what they fell are serious problems with Iraq's underground oil reservoirs, which might severely limit the amount of oil these fields can produce.

According to such critics, Iraq's large northern Kirkuk field suffers from water seeping into its oil deposits, and similar problems are evident in the major oil fields like Rumaila in southern Iraq. This is not said to be a product of the Iraq War, but rather years of poor management. At the same time, such critics charged that U.S.-led efforts to rapidly return the fields to prewar capacity could cut long-term productivity.

There is some evidence to support this criticism. The UN found before the war that Saddam Hussein demanded high production at a time that UN economic sanctions precluded Iraq from acquiring the sophisticated computer-modeling equipment and technology required to manage older reservoirs properly. Oil experts working for the UN estimated that some reservoirs in southern Iraq "may only have ultimate recoveries of between 15 percent and 25 percent of the total oil" in the field, as compared with an industry norm of 35 to 60 percent.

- Maury Vasilev, senior vice president of PetroAlliance Services, a Russian oil field company that held discussions with Iraq's Oil Ministry in 2000, concluded that "Kirkuk was of particular concern and particular urgency because of the water content in the wells . . . there was a question of how much oil they could recover."

- Fadhil Chalabi, a former top Iraqi oil official, claimed in the summer of 2003 that Kirkuk's expected recovery rate had dropped to 15 percent from 30 percent. The *Times* also quote an unnamed American oil executive as saying in November 2003 that Iraqi engineers told him that they were now expecting recovery rates of 9 percent in Kirkuk and 12 percent in Rumaila without more advanced technology.

- Issam al-Chalabi, Iraq's former oil minister, stated in November 2003, "We are losing a lot of oil. . . . [It] is the consensus of all the petroleum engineers involved in the Iraqi industry that maximizing oil production may be detrimental to the reservoirs." An earlier United Nations report on the Kirkuk field issued in 2000, warned of "the possibility of irreversible damage to the reservoir of this supergiant field is now imminent."

The United States ignored these issues in its initial approach to nation building, and failed to come to grips with them in the period after the war ended in May 2003. The *New York Times* reported in November 2003 that the Energy Infrastructure Planning Group, which senior Bush administration officials established in September 2002 to plan for the oil industry in the event of war, learned that Iraq was still reinjecting crude oil to maintain pressure in the Kirkuk field. It did so even though "Iraqis acknowledged it was a poor practice," and "were unequivocal that that practice had to stop and right away." In October 2003, however, Iraq was still reinjecting 150,000 to 250,000 barrels a day, down from as much as 400,000 barrels a day, but still far higher than oil industry practice.

According to the *New York Times*, the energy planning task force avoided the issue of reservoir development for political reasons. These were partially to avoid charges that the U.S. planned to steal Iraq's oil, and also because the group had secretly decided that the contract for fixing Iraq's oil infrastructure would go to Kellogg, Brown, & Root (KBR), a unit of Halliburton that had an existing Pentagon contract related to war planning and was previously run by Vice President Dick Cheney. It did so, without soliciting bids, making any reserve or reservoir development more controversial.

The *Times* also reported that Wayne Kelley, a Texas oil engineer, and other experts had asked Iraq's oil reservoirs for contractors in July 2003, during a conference. Army Corps of Engineers officials stated that their mission was to restoring war-damaged facilities, not "redeveloping the oil fields," according to a transcript of the meeting. However, Rob McKee, who became senior oil adviser for the Coalition Provisional Authority (CPA) in Baghdad in September 2003, said that the reservoirs would receive attention. "It's bad, but it will not be catastrophic and especially overnight."[46]

The *Times* quoted Wendy Hall, a spokeswoman for Halliburton, the Houston oil services and engineering company managing the Iraqi oil-repair job, as stating Iraq's present production levels and the administration's future oil goals "cannot be sustained without reservoir maintenance." Thamir Ghadhban, a senior adviser to the current Iraqi oil minister, Ibrahim Bahr al-Uloum, was quoted as predicting that production would return to prewar capacity of 3.0 MMBD by the end of 2004; although he also said, "We should do much more than we have in the past" to maintain the reservoirs. . . . We definitely have to put more money into it and bring in consultants."[47]

As of December 2003, the U.S. Army Corps of Engineers had allocated $1.7 billion for maintaining Iraq's oil supply, with funds going to payments for imported fuel and repair of pipes, pumps, and transfer stations. About $2 billion had been approved for oil infrastructure repairs in 2003, including about $40 million to begin the study of the reservoirs. Any actual improvement in managing the reservoirs could, however, take years and be a highly expensive process involving complicated computer simulation and changes in extraction techniques. KBR, as well as others, had made the case that reservoir management was necessary. According to some KBR sources however, these efforts were "pulled and are not being funded." The CPA stated that the financing was not canceled, but "pushed back for a short while."

A rough estimate of Iraqi energy investment costs is provided by the International Energy Agency in a study called "Restoration of Iraqi Oil Infrastructure, Final Work Plan" (July 2003).[48] This study estimates that raising Iraqi production cost to around 3.7 MMBD by 2010 would require a cumulative investment of close to $5 billion, but that government production revenues in a peaceful and stable environment would then be much higher over the 2003–2010 period—at over $20 billion. In contrast, extending production to levels over 4 MMBD would call for major investments in exploration, new production capacity, and new export facilities.

The IEA examined a number of other production scenarios—all assuming peace and stability. A rapid growth case, calling for levels of 9 MMBD in 2030, required investment levels of $54 billion. This was about $12 billion higher that the slower growth rate to 8 MMBD called for in the IEA's reference case projections. Both growth rates are far higher, more rapid, and more expensive than the growth to 5.1 MMBD in 2025 called for in EIA estimates.

Iraqi Energy Export Capabilities

These risks affect Iraq's export capabilities as well as its production capabilities. The EIA reports that many of these capabilities suffered severely during the war. While the CPA is attempting to rapidly repair these facilities, they have been subjected to constant attack and sabotage from former regime loyalists and other hostiles since the fall of Saddam Hussein. The EIA summarized the situation in March 2004 as follows:[49]

> Under optimal conditions, and including routes through both Syria and Saudi Arabia that are now closed, Iraq's oil export infrastructure could handle throughput of more than 6 million bbl/d (2.8 via the Gulf, 1.65 via Saudi Arabia, 1.6 via Turkey, and perhaps 300,000 bbl/d or so via Jordan and Syria). However, Iraq's export facilities (pipelines, ports, pumping stations, etc.) were seriously disrupted by the Iran-Iraq War (1980–1988), the 1990/1991 Gulf War, the most recent war in March/April 2003, and periodic looting and sabotage since then. As of March 2004, Iraq has export capacity as high as 2.5 million bbl/d (around 2.0 via the Gulf and 0.3–0.5 via Turkey). Additional export capacity could be added in coming months, though, via the Gulf, Syria, and Turkey.
>
> The 600-mile, Kirkuk-Ceyhan (Turkey) dual pipeline is Iraq's largest crude oil export line. One, 40-inch line has a fully-operational capacity of 1.1 million bbl/d, but reportedly could handle only around 900,000 bbl/d pre-war. The second, parallel, 46-inch line has an optimal capacity of 500,000 bbl/d and was designed to carry Basra Regular exports, but at last report was inoperable. Combined, the two parallel lines have an optimal capacity of 1.5–1.6 million bbl/d. On August 13, 2003, officials at the Turkish port of Ceyhan said today that Iraq had begun pumping fresh crude oil through the Kirkuk-Ceyhan pipeline for the first time since war broke out in late March 2003. However, the pipeline was operating far below capacity, at perhaps 300,000–400,000 bbl/d, with significant repairs still required. Also, the line was damaged by a bridge ("Al Fatah") that collapsed on it after being bombed by U.S. planes during the war. This will require major repairs, including the drilling of a new tunnel under the Tigris River and the laying of a new pipeline. In addition, the IT-1 pumping station on the Kirkuk-Ceyhan line was damaged by looters, but reportedly is operable manually. The IT-2 pumping station on the same line reportedly was looted and destroyed.
>
> On August 16, 2003, two blasts on the Kirkuk-Ceyhan line once again shut down Iraqi oil flows to Turkey. Officials estimated that it would take 10 days to two weeks in order to repair the line, and also that the shutdown was costing Iraq $7 million per day in lost oil export revenues. The pipeline reopened once again in early March 2004.
>
> At least since 2001 until March 2003, Iraq and Syria were utilizing the 50-year-old Banias oil pipeline in violation of U.N. sanctions. The pipeline,

from Iraq's northern Kirkuk oil fields to Syria's Mediterranean port of Banias (and Tripoli, Lebanon), reportedly was being used to transport as much as 200,000 bbl/d of Iraqi oil, mainly from southern Iraq, to Syrian refineries at Homs and Banias. The oil was sold at a significant price discount and freed up additional Syrian oil for export. Iraq and Syria also had talked of building a new, parallel pipeline as a replacement for the Banias line. In March 2003, flows on the pipeline were halted, although the U.S. Defense Department denied that its forces had targeted the line. In early March 2004, it was reported by Dow Jones that the Iraq-Syria pipeline was ready for use at 250,000 bbl/d.

During the Iran-Iraq War, Iraq also built a pipeline through Saudi Arabia (called IPSA) to the Red Sea port of Mu'ajiz, just north of Yanbu. IPSA has a design capacity of 1.65 million bbl/d, but was closed after Iraq invaded Kuwait in August 1990. In June 2001, Saudi Arabia expropriated the IPSA line, despite Iraqi protests. In June 2003, Thamir Ghadban said that he hoped Iraq would be able to use the IPSA line again. However, the Saudis have stated that they are not willing to do this, having converted the line to carry natural gas to the Red Sea industrial city of Yanbu for domestic use.

In order to optimize export capabilities (i.e., to allow oil shipments to the north or south), Iraq constructed a reversible, 1.4 million bbl/d "Strategic Pipeline" in 1975. This pipeline consist of two parallel 70,000 bbl/d lines. The North-South system allows for export of northern Kirkuk crude from the Persian Gulf and for southern Rumalia crudes to be shipped through Turkey. During the 1990/1991 Gulf War, the "Strategic Pipeline" was disabled after the K-3 pumping station at Haditha as well as four additional southern pumping stations were destroyed. In June 2003, the NOC estimated that it would take "a long time" to repair the K-3 pumping station and resume operations on the "Strategic Pipeline." The whole system also reportedly is in need of modernization.

In February 2004, there were reports that Iraq was negotiating with Iran on possible construction of a 250,000 bbl/d oil pipeline to the Abadan refinery in southwestern Iran. In exchange, Iran would export a similar volume of its own oil in a so-called "swap" arrangement. The Iraqi Oil Minister discussed the pipeline when he visited Tehran in December 2003 and met the Iranian Oil Minister Zanganeh.

It is reported that more damage has been inflicted on vital infrastructure by looting than fighting during the conflict. Between April 2003 and March 2004, there were an estimated 86 attacks on Iraqi oil infrastructure.[50] In order to ensure the security of Iraq's oil infrastructure, the U.S. Army, working with private security consultant ERINYS and local tribal chiefs, has built a force of Iraqi guards. The new force is responsible to protect over 7,000 kilometers of pipeline and almost 300 facilities. Officials argue that the guard force has reduced the number of targets on vital installations. Since the guard force was substantially increased to 12,000 men after December, attacks on pipelines have fallen dramatically—15 incidents of sabotage from 47 in the previous three months.[51]

Iraqi Gas Development

Iraq's status as a gas producer is equally uncertain. The EIA estimates that Iraq contains 110 trillion cubic feet of proven natural gas reserves, along with roughly 150 TCF in probable reserves. About 70 percent of Iraq's natural gas reserves are associated (i.e., natural gas produced in conjunction with oil), with the rest made up of nonassociated gas (20 percent) and dome gas (10 percent). In 2002, Iraq produced 83 billion cubic feet (BCF) of natural gas, down drastically from peak output levels of 700 BCF in 1979.[52]

Before the Iraq War, Iraq announced plans to increase its natural gas output in order to reduce dependence on oil consumption and possibly for export. Iraq was also developing plans to build a liquefied natural gas terminal. These plans called for Iraq to produce 550 BCF within two years after the lifting of UN sanctions, and about 4.2 TCF of natural gas annually within a decade. In December 2003, Iraq renewed a natural gas supply agreement with Kuwait. Under this agreement, which was signed in the 1980s, Iraq would supply natural gas to Kuwait via a 40-inch, 105-mile pipeline. Kuwait and Iraq have also discussed joint development of the Siba natural gas field that straddles the two countries' border near Iran.

Iraq's Future Energy Development Plans

All such plans must wait on the restoration of internal stability in Iraq, and the development of gas is closely linked to oil because most of Iraq's natural gas is associated with oil. The main sources of associated natural gas are the Kirkuk, Ain Zalah, Butma, and Bai Hassan oil fields in northern Iraq, as well as the North and South Rumaila and Zubair fields in the south. The Southern Area Gas Project was completed in 1985, and brought online in February 1990, with a processing capacity of 1.5 billion cubic feet per day. Natural gas gathered from the North and South Rumaila and Zubair fields is carried via pipeline to a 575-MMCF per day natural gas liquids (NGL) fractionation plant in Zubair and a 100-MMCF per day processing plant in Basra. Natural gas also used to be pumped from Rumaila into northern Kuwait via a 40-inch, 105-mile pipeline. The gas was used to supply Kuwaiti power stations and liquefied petroleum gas (LPG) plants, but was halted following Iraq's invasion of Kuwait in August 1990.

Iraq's only nonassociated natural gas production is from the al-Anfal field (200 MMCF per day of output) in northern Iraq. Al-Anfal production, which began in May 1990, is piped to the Jambur gas processing station near the Kirkuk field, located 20 miles away. Al-Anfal's gas resources are estimated at 4.5 TCF, of which 1.8 TCF is proven. In November 2001, a large nonassociated natural gas field reportedly was discovered in the Akas region of western Iraq, near the border with Syria, and containing an estimated 2.1 TCF of natural gas reserves. It is not clear whether the field is associated or nonassociated. Iraq has four other large nonassociated natural gas fields (Chemchamal, Jaria Pika, Khashm al-Ahmar, Mansuriya) located in Kirkuk and Diyala provinces, with total recoverable reserves that may exceed 10 TCF.

The EIA reports that Iraq has a major natural gas pipeline with the capacity to supply around 240 MMCF per day to Baghdad from the West Qurna field. The 48-inch line was commissioned in November 1988, with Phases 2 and 3 of the project never completed due to war and sanctions. The last two phases of the pipeline project were meant to supply Turkey. Iraq's Northern Gas System, which came online in 1983, was damaged during the Gulf War as well as by the Kurdish rebellion of March 1991. The system supplied LPG to Baghdad and other Iraqi cities, as well as dry gas and sulfur to power stations and industrial plants. Iraq also has a Southern Gas System, which came online in 1985.

Iraqi Energy Risk

The previous analysis of energy risks in Saudi Arabia has shown that even a country that has vast oil resources can present a significant degree of risk. These risks are far higher in Iraq, a nation that is still at war and that faces years of difficult political compromises if it is to avoid civil conflict or a return to some form of authoritarian rule. Iraq may well succeed in evolving a more stable mix of politics, economics, and energy production over the next five to ten years, but it faces daunting challenges:

- Iraq faces a long-term population explosion. In spite of sanctions, war, and mass graves, the U.S. Census Bureau estimates that Iraq's population has leaped from 5.1 million people in 1950, and 13.2 million in 1980—at the beginning of the Iran-Iraq War—to some 25 million in 2004. The fertility rate is 4.9 and the birth rate is 2.9 percent. Conservative Census Bureau estimates indicate the population will rise to 30 million in 2010, 37 million in 2020, and 44 million in 2030.

- Jobs are a critical problem, and the problem will grow with time. Some 530,000 young men and women now enter the work force each year at a time when unemployment is 50–60 percent. The figure will rise to over 800,000 per year by 2025. Approximately 40 percent of the population has been affected by the educational problems that began during the Iran-Iraq War, and which became steadily graver after 1990 as a result of the Gulf War and sanctions.

- The current Iraqi leadership has been denied the experience it needs during Saddam's tyranny. Iraq's political problems have been made worse by nearly three decades of dictatorship, nearly continuous war and sanctions, failed command economy, and ruthless political purges. Roughly 70 percent of the population has never known any political leader other than Saddam and the Ba'ath Party. No rival political leaders or parties could develop in Iraq, and its leaders that have returned from exile have not been able to win the trust of the people.

- The Iraqi people have a national consciousness, but are deeply divided. The Iraqi people have no real political experience and there are deep ethnic divisions. While there has never been an accurate recent census, Iraqis seem to be divided into 60 percent Shiite, 20 percent Sunni, 15 percent Kurd, and 5 percent Turcoman and other. Further divisions exist between Sunni and Shiite, by tribe, and between the rural and urbanized populations, and in terms of how religious or secular particular Iraqis are.

- Guilt by association is a major problem affecting the ability to draw on Iraqi talents and skills. The most experienced technocrats, managers, police, and military are all tarred by their association with the former regime.

- There is no history of an adequate structure of law for dealing with security, civil law, crimes, or human rights.

- The economy has long been a state controlled kleptocracy favoring the minority in power and giving guns priority over butter. Few economies in the region have less real-world experience with global competition and the free market.

- The oil sector has been crippled by years of underfunding, lack of technology, state mismanagement, and overproduction of key reservoirs. Many pipelines and large centralized facilities are highly vulnerable to sabotage or terrorism.

- Oil income is Iraq's only significant export income and funds virtually all of the state budget, but is grossly inadequate to meet current and future needs. The U.S. Department of Energy estimates that oil sector earnings in real dollars have gone from real earnings (in 2000 U.S.$) of $58 billion in 1980 to a maximum of $12.3 billion in 2002. They will probably be around $9–12 billion in 2003, and a little over $15 billion in 2004 and $19 billion in 2005. Even with an expansion to 6 MMBD, it is unlikely that real per capita oil income can be more than half what it was in 1980.

- The agricultural sector has been driven by inefficient state planning and subsidies that never resulted in more than half the productivity Iraq should have had and that produced crops with large portions of inedible output. Some 60 percent of food has been imported, and farmers have no experience with financing their crops or marketing them on a competitive basis.

- Foreign investment has been illegal and there has been no real banking system in the Western sense. Industrial employment has been dominated by some 200–250 state industries, of which roughly 48 have been critical employers. None is remotely competitive in global terms, and most cannot survive competition from imports. Massive military industries effectively no longer exist.

- Utilities and infrastructure have been crippled by underfunding that began in 1982–1984, cannibalization, and fragmented organization. Most systems favor urban and Sunni areas and services like water and sewers are grossly inadequate in slums and in many Shiite areas.

- Information has been government dominated at every level. There is no past basis of trust in the media or authority, and Iraqis have had to turn to sources outside their country for anything approaching the truth.

It is hardly surprising under these circumstances that postwar nation building in Iraq has proved to pose major challenges at the political, economic, demographic, social, ethnic, and religious levels. This challenge has been compounded by the fact that virtually every aspect of nation building had to be improvised after the fall of Saddam Hussein's regime in an environment of increasing low intensity combat, and by U.S. officials and contractors with virtually no experience working in Iraq or in transforming a command economy.

If anything, the CBO report of January 2004 titled *Paying for Iraq's Reconstruction* estimates some $50–100 billion will be needed for nation building during 2004–2007. This total does not begin to cover the full cost of creating a new economy and meeting a backlog of human needs. It may still sharply underestimate the scale of the funding required, even if war and sabotage do not add further major burdens. Total reconstruction expenses and government budgets could range from $94 to $160 billion during this period, and oil revenues are estimated to range from $44 to $89 billion, and seem likely to total well under $70 billion.

Iraq's economic and social problems will continue well beyond 2010, even under the best of circumstances. Iraq can also only approach the progress it needs to make if it is not crippled by loan repayments well in excess of $100 billion, and reparations claims that are even larger. One key future issue will be whether a new Iraqi government can find ways to develop Iraq's petroleum production and export facilities in ways that meet the expectations of both its Shiite majority (60 percent-plus), and of key minorities like its Sunnis (less than 20 percent), and Kurds (around 15 percent). Petroleum exports provided something like 80 percent of all government revenues for Iraq's command economy in the past, and were its only meaningful export.

The way in which revenues are divided in the future will be critical to power sharing and internal political stability. This could affect the priority given to the development of largely unexploited reserves in the west (largely in Sunni areas), the major reserves north of Basra (Shiite areas), and pipelines (the Kurds want major amounts of exports to go north and have claimed the right to oil fields around Kirkuk). The Kurdish regional government of northern Iraq is preparing to offer a proposal to reorganize the Iraqi economy on a federal basis. In this proposal the key is the city of Kirkuk, which holds 40 percent of Iraq's oil reserves. The Iraqi Kurds believe that Kirkuk is an indisputable part of Iraqi Kurdistan. Yet the Arab settlers and indigenous Turkmen of Northern Iraq make it clear that they will never give up their rights on Kirkuk. The confessional and ethnic politics are likely to play a major role in shaping the real-world nature of Iraq's petroleum development indefinitely into the future, and will inevitably increase the risk in such development.

As a result, Iraq will be a moderate- to high-risk producer for at least the coming decade, and any accurate assessment of its future role in the world energy market must await a period of far greater political, economic, and military stability.

Iran

Iran is a major energy exporter whose production and export capabilities have been sharply affected by the Iranian revolution, the hostage crisis with the United States that followed, the Iran-Iraq War of 1980–1988, and U.S. sanctions that seek to block U.S. and foreign investment in Iran's energy sector. Iran also remains deeply divided politically between "moderate" and "hard-liner" and over how to restructure and finance its economy and energy sector. There is a significant risk its internal power struggles could turn violent and its inability to agree on realistic incentives to attract foreign energy investment, combined with U.S. sanctions, have limited the modernization and growth of its petroleum sector. Like Iraq, it will be a moderate- to high-risk producer for at least the coming decade.[53]

Iranian Energy Resources

The EIA summarizes the current state of Iran's petroleum industry as follows:[54]

> Iran's domestic oil consumption, 1.3 million bbl/d in 2003, is increasing rapidly (about 7% per year) as the economy and population grow. Iran subsidizes the price of oil products heavily, to the tune of $3 billion or so per year, resulting in a large amount of waste and inefficiency in oil consumption. Iran also is forced to spend around $1 billion per year to import oil products (mainly gasoline) that it cannot produce locally. In early April 2003, as part of an effort to curtail the rise in gasoline subsidy expenditures, gasoline consumption and imports (both of which are growing rapidly), Iran raised gasoline prices by 30%–35%, to around 31–44 cents per gallon. In November 2003, Iran announced that it might even be forced to start rationing gasoline.
>
> It is possible that, with sufficient investment, Iran could increase its oil production capacity significantly. Iran produced 6 million bbl/d in 1974, but has not surpassed 3.8 million bbl/d on an annual basis since the 1978/79 Iranian revolution. During the 1980s, it is believed that Iran may have maintained production levels at some older fields only by using methods that have permanently damaged the fields. Also, Iran's oilfields are—according to Oil Minister Zanganeh—experiencing a depletion rate of 200,000–300,000 bbl/d per year, and are in need of upgrading and modernization. Despite these problems, Iran has ambitious plans to double national oil production—to more than 7 million bbl/d by 2015 or so. The country is counting on foreign investment to accomplish this, possibly as high as $5 billion per year.
>
> NIOC's onshore field development work is concentrated mainly on sustaining output levels from large, aging fields. Consequently, enhanced oil re-

covery (EOR) programs, including natural gas injection, are underway at a number of fields, including Marun, Karanj, and the presently inactive Parsi fields. EOR programs will require sizeable amounts of natural gas, infrastructure development, and financing. Overall, Iran's oil sector is considered old and inefficient, needing thorough revamping, advanced technology, and foreign investment.

Iranian Efforts to Expand Oil Production and Exports

Iran has made progress in dealing with its own internal debates over how to modernize its energy sector, but U.S. sanctions and internal political problems remain. The EIA summarize the current situation as follows:[55]

> Iran is attempting to diversify by investing some of its oil revenues in other areas, including petrochemicals. Iran also is hoping to attract billions of dollars worth of foreign investment to the country by creating a more favorable investment climate (i.e., reduced restrictions and duties on imports, creation of free-trade zones). In May 2002, the country's Expediency Council approved the "Law on the Attraction and Protection of Foreign Investment," which aims at encouraging foreign investment by streamlining procedures, guaranteeing profit repatriation, and more.
>
> This Law, which was sent to the government for implementation in January 2003, represents the first foreign investment act passed by Iran's legislature since the 1978/79 revolution. The legislation was delayed for several years due to disagreements between reformers and conservatives. In June 2001, the Council of Guardians had rejected the bill as passed by the Majlis the previous month. In November 2001, the Majlis had passed a second, heavily amended, version of the bill. Although this version was far weaker than the first bill, the Council of Guardians again rejected it (in December 2001).
>
> . . . President Bush extended the sanctions originally imposed in 1995 by President Clinton for another year in March 2003, citing Iran's "support for international terrorism, efforts to undermine the Middle East peace process, and acquisition of weapons of mass destruction." The 1995 executive orders prohibit U.S. companies and their foreign subsidiaries from conducting business with Iran, while banning any "contract for the financing of the development of petroleum resources located in Iran." In addition, the U.S. Iran-Libya Sanctions Act (ILSA) of 1996 (renewed for 5 more years in July 2001) imposes mandatory and discretionary sanctions on non-U.S. companies investing more than $20 million annually in the Iranian oil and natural gas sectors. In May 2002, the United States announced that it would review an $80 million contract by Canada's Sheer Energy to develop an Iranian oilfield to determine whether or not it violates ILSA.

Although Iran is the second largest oil producer after Saudi Arabia, and holds the world's fourth largest pool of proven oil reserves, its production has dropped by more than a third from a peak of over 6 million barrels per day in 1974 to about 3.4 barrels per day in 2002. Years of political isolation, recurring war, and U.S. sanctions have deprived the oil sector of needed investment. Iran's share of total world oil trade peaked at 17.2 percent in 1972, then declined to 2.6 percent in 1980, but has since recouped to roughly 5 percent. In 2002, earnings from oil and gas made up more than 70 percent of total government revenues, while taxes made up about 20 percent.

After the 1980–1988 Iran-Iraq War, NIOC launched a reconstruction program to restore damaged fields. Since 1994, production has averaged 3.6 million barrels per day, although this is still roughly half of Iran's 1974 levels. The government hopes that foreign finance and technology will help raise Iran's output to 5.6 million barrels per day by 2010 and 7.3 million barrels per day by 2020.

Iranian Oil Production Goals and Investment Requirements

Iranian officials estimate that the country will need to invest as much as $90 billion in its oil industry over the next decade if it is to avert a dramatic drop in oil production, though many estimates go as low as $40 billion. It is estimated that development of new offshore Persian Gulf and Caspian Sea oil fields will require investment of $8–10 billion. In December 1997, Oil Minister Zanganeh stated that the country aimed to boost oil production capacity 200,000–250,000 barrels per day each year. He set a goal of reach 5 MMBD in the next five years, possibly surpassing 6 MMBD by 2010, and reaching 7 MMBD at some point between 2010 and 2020. These goals would more than restore the country's production capacity to the level of over 6 MMBD it achieved in the mid-1970s.[56]

Iran estimated that meeting these goals would require anywhere from $8 billion to $30 billion worth of investment.[57] U.S. government experts, however, are less optimistic. Some experts question whether even 6 million barrels per day is possible, and the majority of industry opinion seems to be that four to five million barrels a day may represent the limit of sustained conventional oil production.

Iran has sought to finance these expenditures with "buyback deals" to get around the fact that the Iranian constitution prohibits granting petroleum rights to any private company on a concessionary basis or direct equity stake. The 1987 Petroleum Law does, however, permits the establishment of contracts among the Ministry of Petroleum, state companies, and "local and foreign national persons and legal entities."

As a result, Iran has offered foreign companies "buyback" contracts, where the contractor funds all investments, receives remuneration from NIOC in the form of an allocated production share, and then transfers operation of the field to NIOC after the contract is completed. This system presents problems for both Iran and any private investor. It offers a fixed rate of return (usually around 15–17 percent), but this means NIOC bears all the risk when oil prices are low, and the NIOC has to sell more oil or natural gas to meet the compensation figure. Private investors and companies have no guarantee that they will be permitted to develop their discoveries, or operate them, and Iran has generally offered contracts with too short a period.

The EIA reported in 2003 that Iranian officials had increasing reservations about the problems in these buyback deals (including charges of corruption, insufficient benefits to Iran, and concerns that the Iranian proposals defining the conditions for buyback deals attract too little investment). Iranian leaders were reported to be considering substantial modifications to its "buyback" model, possibly extending the length of such contracts from the current five to seven years.

Iranian production has also been affected by regional politics and its role in OPEC. Since President Khatami's election, Iran has attempted to coordinate oil policy with Saudi Arabia. Even so, there have been a number of disputes between the two nations. Regarding OPEC production quotas, an agreement was finally reached, delimiting the baseline for Iran's share of OPEC cutbacks at 3.9 million barrels per day, rather than 3.6 million barrels per day as argued by other OPEC member states. Although Iran faced the same 7.3 percent reduction as other member states, in actuality Iran's cuts were smaller due to the amended baseline.[58] As of November 1, 2003, Iran's OPEC production quota was 3.597 MMBD.[59]

Recent Iranian Oil Development Deals

Iran has been able to get some such contracts in spite of these problems and U.S. sanctions. The EIA reported the following developments as of March 2004:[60]

- In October 1998, the first major projects under the buyback scheme became operational. The offshore Sirri A oil field (operated by Total and Malaysia's Petronas) began production at 7,000 BBL per day (Sirri A currently is producing around 20,000 BBL per day). The neighboring Sirri E field began production in February 1999, with production at the two fields expected to reach 120,000 BBL per day.

- In March 1999, France's Elf Aquitaine and Italy's Eni/Agip were awarded a $1 billion contract for a secondary recovery program at the offshore, 1.5-billion-barrel Doroud oil and natural gas field located near Kharg Island. The program is intended to boost production from around 136,000 BBL per day to as high as 205,000 BBL per day by 2004. In April 1999, Iran awarded TotalFinaElf (46.75 percent share), along with Canada's Bow Valley Energy (15 percent share), a buyback contract to develop the offshore Balal field. The field, which contains some 80 million barrels of reserves, started producing at a 20,000 BBL per day rate in early 2003, reportedly reached 40,000 BBL per day in October 2003. In February 2001, ENI-Agip acquired a 38.25 percent share in Balal.

- In October 1999, Iran announced that it made the biggest oil discovery in 30 years, a giant onshore field called Azadegan, a few miles east of the border with Iraq. Reportedly, the Azedegan field contains in-place oil reserves of 26–70 billion barrels, with potential production of 300,000–400,000 BBL per day (and possibly higher) over a twenty-year period. In February 2004, Japanese oil officials signed a preliminary commercial agreement for the development of Azadegan field. First production of the oil field is expected in 2006, with an estimated output of 300,000 BBL per day.

- In November 2000, Norway's Statoil signed a series of agreements with NIOC to explore for oil in the Strait of Hormuz area, to cooperate on developing a natural gas-to-liquids processing plant for four southern onshore fields, and possibly develop the Salman offshore field at a cost of $850 million, with eventual production of 130,000 BBL per day. Iran appears to be accelerating its plans to boost production of natural gas liquids (NGL), as well as liquefied petroleum gas. NGL expansion plans, including a $500 million plan to build two NGL plans on the south coast of Iran, are aimed mainly at making ethane feedstock available for Iran's growing petrochemical industry.

- In May 2002, Iran's Oil Ministry signed a $585 million buyback contract with PetroIran to develop the Foroozan and Esfandiar offshore oil fields and increase production at the fields from around 40,000 BBL per day at present to 109,000 BBL per day within three years. The two oil fields straddle the border with Saudi Arabia's Lulu and Marjan fields.

- In May 2002, Canada's Sheer Energy reached agreement ($80 million to develop the Masjed-I-Suleyman [MIS] field), with the goal of raising production from 4,500 BBL per day to 20,000 BBL per day.

- In April 2003, Shell reported that it was frustrated with the slow pace of negotiations on Bangestan, including numerous changes to terms of the project. The development of the giant Bangestan field had already been delayed several times after an expected award in 2001. Bangestan includes three oil fields (Anwaz, Mansuri, Ab-Teymour) that currently produce about 250,000 BBL per day of oil.

- In September 2003, Russia's Lukoil was granted approval by NIOC to explore for oil in the Anaran block along the border with Iraq. Norsk Hydro is currently in charge of the project.

- In November 2003, NIOC announced the launch of a new tender for sixteen oil blocks. Based on the buyback model, but covering exploration, appraisal, and development for the first time.

- The Cheshmeh-Khosh field, which had been awarded to Spain's Cepsa for $300 million, is likely to be re-awarded to a consortium of Cepsa and the OMV. The two companies are to raise crude production at the field from 30,000 BBL per day to 80,000 BBL per day within four years.

- In early 2004 the Japanese firm Inpex, a government-affiliated oil exploration company, concluded a contract with the Iranian government to develop the Azadegan oil field in two stages, with crude oil production estimated to peak at 150,000 and then at 260,000 barrels per day. Inpex announced on March 5, 2004, that the French oil company Total SA, and four other foreign companies, offered to participate in the project, but Inpex did not announce the names of the four other companies, which included a Malaysian state-run company. The Royal Dutch/Shell group of companies announced that it would not to participate, despite earlier expectations it would do so, and Inpex had sought partnerships with foreign companies with suitable technology and financing capability. The project had an estimated cost of $2 billion, and the deal required the Inpex-led consortium to invest 75 percent of the amount. Inpex sought financing for 40 percent of its 75 percent portion. The investment is expected to be recovered when production in the first stage reaches six and a half years, enabling project participants to decide whether they should proceed to the second stage.[61]

While many deals have been affected by U.S. sanctions to some extent, Iran has probably created more barriers to its success than the United States. Project plans have often been too large, reserve estimates too uncertain, and risk-benefit calculations too unrealistic. There have been arcane internal political debates over foreign ownership and the best way to attract foreign investment, as well as serious internal political instability.

Caspian Energy Issues

Iran is only one element in the complex mix of issues affecting the Caspian Sea and Central Asia, but its role is significant. The U.S. Department of Energy indicates that the Caspian Sea's proven and possible oil reserves could reach 191 billion barrels, along with huge natural gas reserves. Since the breakup of the former Soviet Union, territorial issues have arisen regarding rights to the Caspian's resources.

The main dispute among the five littoral countries has been heavily influenced by the uneven distribution of potential oil and gas reserves in the Caspian Sea. This issue was brought to the international arena when the Iranian military units confronted an Azerbaijani research ship in the Caspian Sea in July 2001.[62] Iran's position is that treaties signed in 1921 and 1940 are still valid, implying that all countries bordering the Caspian must approve any offshore oil developments. In late February 1998, Iranian foreign minister Kamal Kharrazi reiterated Iran's position that any unilateral exploitation of Caspian Sea resources would be illegal. Oil Minister Zanganeh stated that Iran backs national zones extending several miles from the coast and a "condominium" in the middle of the Sea. Iran also has stated (along with Russia) that it opposes laying an oil pipeline across the Caspian Sea floor.

Iranian Energy Export Capabilities

As is the case with its oil production capabilities, Iran has not been able to modernize its export facilities because of the Iran-Iraq War and cash flow problems growing out of its confrontations with the United States, U.S. sanctions, and internal political debates over how to structure and finance its energy sector. All Iranian onshore crude oil production and output from the Forozan field (which is blended with crude streams from the Abuzar and Dorood fields) is exported from the Kharg Island terminal located in the northern Gulf. The terminal's original capacity of 7 MMBD was nearly eliminated by more than 9,000 bombing raids during the Iran-Iraq War. Kharg Island's current export capacity is 5 MMBD, or double Iran's 1996 total crude oil exports of 2.5 MMBD.

Iran installed four single buoy moorings at Ganeveh during the Iran-Iraq War. These provide an additional combined capacity of 1 MMBD. Furthermore, smaller amounts of offshore crude oil production from the southern Persian Gulf are exported from terminals on Lavan Island and Sirri Island. Iran also has unused terminals at Cyrus and Ras Bahregan in the southern Gulf. Iran's role in regional pipelines is a major source of controversy between the United States and Iran. Iran feels it is the natural transit route for oil and gas exports from the Central Asian countries to world markets. U.S. policy opposes pipelines through Iran, the shortest (and most likely the least expensive) path to the open sea. The United States has instead favored multiple routes for Caspian oil and gas through the Caucasus region to the Black Sea or to the Turkish port of Ceyhan, as part of its attempt to isolate Iran and to contain its influence in the region.

NIOC is currently exploring Iran's territorial waters in the Caspian Sea and has sought stakes in several of the various oil field development projects offshore Azerbaijan. Since 1995, Iran has been conducting a five-year exploration program of its sector of the Caspian Sea. However, exploration largely has been limited to shallow waters and primarily has resulted in marginal natural gas finds. In February 1996, Turkmenistan invited Russia and Iran to conduct exploratory drilling in that country's Caspian Sea sector, where oil reserves are estimated at around 100 million barrels. The Azerbaijan International Operating Company (AIOC) is working on another project that will send Caspian oil through Russia for years to come.[63]

Although the five Caspian littoral states could not reach an agreement on division of Caspian Sea's resources, Russia, Azerbaijan, and Kazakhstan have come to a trilateral agreement on subsurface boundaries and collective administration of the Caspian Sea. This agreement, which was signed in May 2003, divided the 64 percent of the northern Caspian into three unequal zones along a median line principle. The agreement gives Kazakhstan 27 percent, Russia 19 percent, and Azerbaijan 18 percent. Turkmenistan and Iran were present during the negotiations but refused to sign the agreement.[64] Thus, the future of Caspian oil remains unclear.

Iran hopes to solve some of its problems in increasing its oil exports by swapping crude oil with its neighbors in the Caspian and Central Asia. Swap arrangements make sense for Iranian domestic purposes, as well as creating the equivalent of Caspian oil exports through Iran. Most of Iran's oil is located in the south, far from major population centers and refineries in the north, meaning that large volumes of oil have to be pumped long distances across Iran. "Swaps" can alleviate this problem, and the U.S. Department of Energy reports that Iran and Kazakhstan agreed to such a swap arrangement for Kazakh crude exports in May 1996. The swap deal was for ten years and set a goal of about 70,000 barrels per day. Much larger swap arrangements could occur in the future. Iran claims that it could handle 750,000 barrels per day in Caspian crude swaps in a short period of time, and up to 1.5 MMBD over time. According to Iran, this would involve "not much investment"—mainly in modifying existing pipelines linking the Tabriz and Tehran refineries with Caspian coastal cities.

Iranian Gas Development

Iran's natural gas development will be a key factor shaping its future energy policy and exports, and possibly its nuclear policy as well. The EIA estimates that Iran contains 812 trillion cubic feet of natural gas reserves—the world's second largest reserves, surpassed only by those found in Russia. The bulk of Iranian gas reserves are located in nonassociated fields. However, Iran's large onshore oil fields contain approximately 120 TCF of associated gas, which is either dissolved in crude or in gas caps.

In 1990, Iran undertook an ongoing gas utilization program that is designed to boost production to 10 TCF per year by 2010, reduce flaring, provide gas for EOR reinjection programs, and allow for increased gas exports abroad. Presently, the majority of Iranian gas is consumed domestically.

Iran's largest nonassociated gas is the South Pars field, which is an extension of Qatar's 241-TCF North field. South Pars was first identified in 1988 and was originally appraised at 128 TCF in the early 1990s. NIOC-sponsored studies indicate that South Pars contains an estimated 240 TCF, of which a large fraction will be recoverable, and at least 3 billion barrels of condensate. Iran's other sizable nonassociated gas reserves include the offshore 47-TCF North Pars gas field (a separate structure from South Pars), the onshore Nar-Kangan fields, the 13-TCF Aghar and Dalan fields in Fars province, and the Sarkhoun and Mand fields.

South Pars is Iran's largest energy project, and development of "Phase 1," which involves production of 900 million cubic feet per day, is scheduled for completion in mid-2004. Understandably, it has attracted considerable interest from foreign companies. In 1997 a consortium led by Total won a $2 billion contract to carry out the now ongoing second and third phases of South Pars development. According to MEED, a consortium comprising Shell, BG (Amoco), Gaz de France, and Petronas (Malaysia), and Russia's state-owned Gazprom were the main competitors for Phases 4 and 5 in the fall of 1999. Elf Aquitaine and Petronas were among the many companies said to be bidding on the later phases of development.[65] More interest from foreign investors might be forthcoming if a clear export route through Turkey or Pakistan were in place.

According to Iran's Oil Ministry, sales from South Pars could earn Iran as much as $11 billion per year over the next 30 years. An analysis by the International Energy Agency notes that Iran has expanded its development plan to a ten-phase plan with the following structure:[66]

Phase	On Stream	Sustainable Peak Production	Gas Production (BCM/yr.)	Foreign Participants
1	July 2003	November 2003	10	—
2, 3	March 2003	October 2002	21	Total, Petronas, Gasprom
4, 5	August 2005	December 2005	21	ENI
6, 7, 8	June 2006	Late 2006	31	Statoil
9, 10	November 2006	Early 2007	21	LG
Total Awarded			104	

Iranian Gas Pipelines and Transport Issues

Although domestic gas consumption is growing rapidly, Iran continues to promote export markets for its natural gas. Iran also hopes to serve as a major transit center for gas exports from Central Asia. Under current plans, NIOC initially hoped to export 450 MMCF per day of gas by 2000, rising to 4,000 MMCF per day by 2005 as its larger, more ambitious projects come online. The NIOC planned to have completed three gas export pipelines to Turkey, Armenia, and Nakhichevan by 2000. Two more lines to Europe and India were planned by 2005, in addition to the possibility of a liquefied natural gas facility for LNG exports to Asia. Implementation of these ambitious plans, however, required substantial international financing and support, both of which have been lacking.

In January 2002, Iran and Turkey officially inaugurated the gas pipeline link between the two countries. The pipeline supplied Turkey with 4 billion cubic meters of natural gas in 2002, and capacity will rise to 10 billion cubic meters a year by 2007. To further relations with Western Europe, Iran and Greece signed a $300-million agreement in March 2002 that entails extending the pipeline from Iran to Turkey into northern Greece.[67] Greece and Turkey agreed on extending the Iran-Turkey natural gas pipeline into Greece. The extension pipeline will be 175 miles long (125 miles in Turkey, 50 miles in Greece) and could be completed by 2005. The pipeline will carry around 17.7 BCF of gas per year. Iran gives great importance to this project since it could transport its natural gas to Southeast Europe and enter the European market.[68]

Iran has increasingly targeted emerging Asian markets like Pakistan and India (rather than Japan and South Korea) for LNG exports. A committee was established in April 1999 to examine the possibility of a gas pipeline from Iran to India via Pakistan. Iran offered to pay more than half of the cost of the proposed natural gas pipeline from the Islamic Republic to India via Pakistan. The Indian government, however, fears that Pakistan might use this pipeline as a political weapon. Because of continuing India-Pakistan tensions, the Indian concerns, and recent advances in pipeline technology, however, Iran may opt instead for a deep undersea pipeline that bypasses Pakistan's territory.[69] In May 1999, British BG proposed construction of a one billion LNG facility on Kish Island to supply gas to India. The proposal calls for construction of LNG production, storage, and export facilities on the Island, located in the Central Gulf. The project is in the prefeasibility stage, and awaits gas supply guarantees by the NIOC and a government assessment of environmental risk factors.

Iranian Energy Risk

As for risk, Iran has not yet demonstrated that it can consistently create the kind of oil and gas development programs that will attract enough foreign investment and technology to meet its ambitious energy development and exploration goals. Far too often, it proposes overambitious and badly formulated projects without adequate analysis of the costs and risks foreign companies must bear and the necessary level of profit it must grant such companies. These problems are compounded by the threat that the United States will try to enforce sanctions on Third World country oil companies, although such threats are increasing less effective.

More generally, Iran has failed to stabilize its political process and modernize its economy. The election of President Khatami has not been followed by the social and economic reforms most Iranians sought, and Iran's hardliners have steadily limited the role of Iran's elected officials and freedom of speech. The Ayatollah Khamenei and Council of Guardians blocked legislation to limit the role of Iran's religious conservatives in 2003, and a new crisis emerged in early 2004 when the council prevented many reform candidates from running for the National Assembly and threatened to destroy the democratic elements of Iran's government. Its political system moved sharply away from true democracy in 2004, compounding all of the faults inherent in a system where hard-line clerics must vet all candidates by openly rigging the choice of candidates for the Majlis to benefit the hardliners and the authority of a religious supreme leader who has yet to demonstrate practical competence in meeting his nation's needs in a single area.

Iran's problems go far beyond its politics. Although its economic problems have recently been eased by years of high oil export revenues, it has failed to make anything like the progress it needs in reforming and diversifying its economy. Years of attempts at economic reform have produced little more than token results, and it is under severe demographic pressure in spite of a relatively low current birth rate by Gulf standards.

At present, Iran must be regarded as at least a moderate to high risk.

Kuwait

Kuwait is another Gulf state that plays a critical role in any projection of the world's future oil supplies. Kuwait contains an estimated 99.0 (including its share of the Neutral Zone) billion barrels of proven oil reserves, or around 8 percent of the world total. The Neutral Zone area or "Divided Zone," which Kuwait shares with Saudi Arabia, holds 5 billion barrels of reserves, half of which belong to Kuwait. The oil produced in the Kuwait-Saudi Neutral Zone is shared equally between the two countries. The KPC owns a 10 percent share in the Arabian Oil Company that operates offshore production in the zone, while Saudi Arabia Texaco operates the onshore production.

The EIA reports that Kuwait contains an estimated 96.5 billion barrels of proven oil reserves, around 8 percent of the world total. It estimates that the Neutral Zone that Kuwait shares with Saudi Arabia holds 5 billion barrels of reserves, half of which belong to Kuwait. Kuwait's oil reserves are located largely in the 70-billion-barrel Greater Burgan area, which comprises three structures: Burgan, Magwa and Ahmadi. The Greater Burgan area is widely considered the world's second largest oil field, surpassed only by Saudi Arabia's Ghawar field. It has been producing oil since 1938. Kuwait has three other fields with proven reserves: Rawdhatain, Sabriya, and Minagish with 6 billion, 3.8 billion, and 2 billion barrels of oil, respectively. All three fields have been producing since the 1950s. The South Magwa field, discovered in 1984, is estimated to hold at least 25 billion barrels of light crude oil with a 35°–40° API gravity.[70] In September 2003, Kuwait announced as much as 1 billion barrels of light oil had been found at the Kara al-Marou field (Western Kuwait). Moreover, in October 2003, the government declared another discovery of light crude oil (42.60 API) at Sabriya.[71]

Kuwait has another major field—Ratqa—that will present problems for Kuwait's future relations with Kuwait. It was once thought to be an independent reservoir, but the EIA reports that it is now known to be a southern extension of Iraq's supergiant Rumaila field. The UN made decisions in Kuwait's favor after the Gulf War in 1991, and a United Nations survey team made a demarcation of the Iraqi-Kuwaiti border that put all eleven of the existing wells at Ratqa within Kuwaiti territory, and Kuwait produces around 40,000 BBL per day from Ratqa. In September 2000, however, Iraq renewed accusations that Kuwait was "stealing" its oil. Iraq claimed that Kuwait was doing this through horizontal drilling on fields straddling the border between the two countries, and that it was losing $3 billion per year worth of oil. Kuwait denied the charges, but it seems likely that the issue will at some point again become a point of contention between the two countries.

Kuwait has recently produced between 2.2 and 2.5 MMBD, including 250,000 BBL per day of Neutral Zone production. Kuwait is one of the two major oil-exporting powers that can rapidly increase production in an emergency, and its role as a swing producer may increase over time. The development of Kuwait's petroleum industry has an important impact on world oil exports. The U.S. Department of Energy estimates that Kuwait will expand its production from 1.7 million barrels per day in 1990, and 2.4 million barrels per day in 2001, to 2.8 million barrels per day in 2005, 3.3 million barrels per day in 2010, 3.9 million barrels per day in 2015, 4.5 million barrels per day in 2020, and 5.1 million barrels per day in 2025.[72]

Kuwait's Uncertain Oil Development

Kuwait's oil wealth should be enough to support the needs of its population with only limited economic reform and diversification. Kuwait's oil industry is the core of its national wealth and economy and indirectly dominates much of its politics. Oil accounts for more than 90 percent of the country's export revenues 80 percent–85 percent of the government's income, and around 40 percent of gross domestic product (GDP). Aside from foreign investments and oil-revenue funded trade, Kuwait has no other meaningful industry. It is also the center of much of the nation's politics. Many of the struggles within Kuwait's ruling elite and within the National Assembly have been over the distribution of oil revenues, oil export policy, or how to develop and modernize Kuwait's oil resources.

Kuwait's ability to fund and implement these plans, however, has become a key issue. Much depends on the extent to which the government actually presses ahead with its plans, and can reform its laws to allow it to obtain the domestic private and foreign investment it needs. Kuwait can only fully develop its oil resources if it makes significant changes in the structure of its oil industry and finds an effective solution to private and foreign investment in some aspects of its oil production development and downstream industries.

This will not be easy. For the last decade, every decision affecting oil exports, oil production capacity, and oil revenues has been a highly visible and important aspect of Kuwaiti political life. Every major proposal or contract has been the subject of intense examination and discussion by the ruling and business elite, the media, Kuwaiti technocrats and intellectuals, the Kuwaiti public, the National Assembly, and the government. So far, the government and National Assembly have failed to reach any important agreement since the end of the Gulf War, and this has not only blocked critical improvements in the use of enhanced oil recovery technology, but threatens to seriously reduce Kuwait's production capacity in the near term.

Managerial and technical difficulties compound these political problems. Kuwait's organization for the development of its oil resources is outdated; Kuwait has no petroleum law; and the emir of Kuwait, Shaikh Jaber al-Ahmed al-Sabah, has ultimate authority over all major decisions relating to oil. The shaikh's principal adviser is the Oil Minister. A Supreme Petroleum

Council was established in 1974 to review all major decisions. This council is chaired by the foreign minister. Its membership includes six other ministers and members of the private sector who are appointed by the emir. This structure encourages internal political debate within the Kuwaiti government, and these problems have been compounded by the government's agreement that the National Assembly must debate and approve every contract.

International oil company participation is now restricted to technical service agreements among the Kuwait Oil Company and BP, TotalFinaElf, and ChevronTexaco. ExxonMobil and Royal Dutch Shell have technical studies agreements for upstream operations.[73] Outside sources report that Kuwait's native technocrats often do a poor job of seeking outside advice, and tend to resist technical innovation. They feel that the system works at the top, but that the quality of Kuwaiti management and planning is weak at middle echelons and that younger Kuwaitis sometimes feel they cannot make a real contribution and have little reason to take their work seriously. Kuwait relies on state investment and is not earning enough to rely on its own resources to pay for both its operating and social needs and must obtain extensive foreign investment. Like Saudi Arabia, these pressures are driving Kuwait and the Kuwait Supreme Petroleum Council toward a new oil strategy.

The government has attempted to modernize Kuwait's oil production through Project Kuwait (a $7 billion), which will entail the doubling of the production capacity of the northern fields to 900,000 barrels per day, to compensate for declines at the mature Burgan field.[74] In mid-1997, the Kuwaiti Supreme Petroleum Council agreed to allow foreign firms to assist in development plans that called for Kuwaiti production to increase from around 2.2 million BBL per day in 2003 to 3.5 million BBL per day in 2005, and 4 million BBL per day by 2020.[75] This involved a number of new projects in western and northern Kuwait, including 300,000 barrels per day from the Neutral Zone. According to the Kuwaiti Oil Ministry, total cost for the related upstream and downstream expansion was expected to total $13 billion between 1995 and 2005.

Upon request from thirty-two members of the fifty-seat parliament, mainly from the Islamic and liberal blocs, Kuwait's National Assembly held a debate on February 8, 2000, on all aspects of Project Kuwait, including the lack of clarity in the relationship between the government and the international oil companies (IOCs). Despite the government's earlier declaration that no new legislation was needed, during the debate, Oil Minister Shaikh Sa'ud Nasir al-Sabah announced that a law would be submitted to parliament to regulate Project Kuwait. However, Shaikh Sa'ud refrained from indicating a time frame for the award of contracts.[76] Shaikh Said resigned before any law was passed, and no action had been taken as of March 2003. In July 2003, parliamentary elections in Kuwait resulted in the defeat of several Project Kuwait opponents as well as the appointment of a new energy minister, Sheikh Ahmad al-Fahd al-Sabah, and Prime

Minister, Sheikh Sabah al-Ahmad al-Sabah.[77] Kuwait, however has delayed any effective action for more than a decade. As a result, there is a continuing moderate risk that Kuwait's energy development will be inhibited in both its growth and efficiency, largely because of internal politics.

Kuwait does, however, have a number of options. Its major production expansion plans focus on the northern part of the country, but proposals exist for other areas. Among the northern fields expected to receive priority development efforts are the Zubair reservoir in the Ratqa oil field, the Zubair and Ratawi reservoirs in the Abdali field, and the Mauddud and upper Burgan reservoirs in the Sabriya and Bahra fields. Combined, the northern fields of Raudhatain, Sabriya, Bahrah, Ratqa, and Abdali are being expanded to 1.25 million barrels per day in capacity by 2005, compared to current output of 400,000 barrels per day.

Onshore and offshore survey work is being undertaken to review existing data on undeveloped fields and to explore for new structures. Kuwait is cooperating with Saudi Arabia in expanding production from the "Divided" or "Partitioned Neutral Zone" shared by the two countries. The Neutral Zone encompasses a 6,200-square-mile area shared equally between Kuwait and Saudi Arabia under a 1992 agreement. It contains an estimated 5 billion barrels of oil and 1 trillion cubic feet of natural gas. Oil production in the Neutral Zone, which is at least 500,000 barrels per day, is exported from area terminals.

Two joint ventures will increase oil output in the area. U.S.-based Texaco and KPC produce from onshore fields at Wafra, South Fawaris, and South Umm Gudair. Texaco plans to boost output in the Neutral Zone's onshore area from around 250,000 barrels per day at present, to 300,000 barrels per day by 2000. Offshore, the Arabian Oil Company (AOC) of Japan produces around 260,000 barrels per day from the Khafji and Hout fields, both of which are connected to Saudi Arabia's Safaniyah, the world's largest offshore oil field.

Kuwaiti Refining and Petrochemicals

Kuwait's refining capacity was damaged severely during the Gulf War. After losing most of its prewar, 820,000 BPD capacity, Kuwait had only 200,000 barrels per day of refinery output by early 1992. Kuwait's $400 million downstream reconstruction program was completed in mid-1994. By 1997, Kuwait's domestic refineries were operating at around their prewar capacity of 886,000 barrels per day. The Kuwait National Petroleum Corporation (KNPC) plans to further expand refining capacity to almost 1 million barrels per day by 2005. This is part of an overall strategy to focus increasingly on relatively high-value product exports. At present, Kuwait domestic refinery capacity is around 773,300 BBL per day, around 100,000 BBL per day less than normal because of damage to Mina al-Abdullah, the country's largest refinery. By mid-2002, Mina al-Ahmadi was operating at around 300,000 barrels per day, and is expected to return to full capacity in 2004.

Kuwait is expanding its investments in petrochemicals. It has been producing fertilizer since the mid-1960s, and had just started building a major complex at Shuaiba when the war began. In mid-1993, Kuwait's state-owned Petrochemical Industries Company (PIC) and Union Carbide Corporation formed a joint venture to build and operate a world-scale petrochemical complex at Shuaiba. Construction of the $2.3 billion facility began in late 1995, and opened on November 12, 1997. PIC and Union Carbide each have a 45 percent share in the project, with the remainder reserved for public offer. The complex includes an ethane cracker capacity of 650,000 metric tons per year (MTY), 450,000 MTY of polyethylene capacity and 350,000 MTY of ethylene glycol production. The complex will primarily serve Asian products markets.

Kuwaiti Energy Export Facilities

Prior to the Iraqi invasion, Kuwaiti terminals had the capacity to load more than 3 million barrels per day of crude oil and around 800,000 barrels per day of refined products. The KNPC has completed major reconstruction efforts on its Mina al-Ahmadi export facility, Kuwait's main crude-oil export port. Kuwait has fully operational terminals at Mina Abdullah (repairs completed in September 1992), Shuaiba (restored by late 1996), and at Mina Saud in the Neutral Zone. Kuwait now has an oil export capacity of over 2 million barrels per day.

Kuwaiti Gas Development

Kuwait is among the top twenty nations in the world in terms of natural gas reserves, but its reserves are not large by Gulf standards. Kuwait estimates that it has 1.5 trillion cubic meters, or 1.1 percent of the world's reserves. Almost all of Kuwait's gas reserves are associated with oil fields, and the Kuwait Production Company carries out all of its natural gas production. Kuwait has established gas gathering facilities and pipelines, but its efforts to find separate gas fields have failed. As a result, gas production has varied with oil production—a trend reflected in the decline in gas production during 1980–1985 and the massive drop in production resulting from Iraq's invasion. Kuwait has been looking for other sources of gas and recently decided to import natural gas from Qatar. A sales and purchase agreement is to be signed between Kuwait Petroleum Corporation and Qatar Petroleum/ExxonMobil.

Kuwait made progress in utilizing its gas for domestic needs and oil production purposes before the Iraqi invasion. The share of Kuwaiti gas that was marketed rose from 42 percent in 1975 to 74 percent in 1989, but massive amounts had to be flared during the first phase of the Gulf War. The Kuwaiti gas industry suffered some war damage. Three of Kuwait's five gas booster stations were damaged, and one was destroyed. However, its LPG plant and bottling unit were not damaged. Gas production and domestic use has since recovered, but Kuwait actually needs more gas than it produces. Though it was an importer of Iraqi gas before the war, for obvious reasons Kuwait is now looking for other sources of gas.

Kuwaiti Energy Risk

The fall of Saddam Hussein's regime has removed the primary security threat to Kuwait. Its internal politics have, however, led to serious underinvestment in its oil field development and use of enhanced oil recovery to the point where Kuwait's oil industry risks serious decline and is a self-inflicted wound. The Kuwaiti National Assembly may be one of the leaders in democratic reform in the region but so far has shown little practical ability to come to grips with economic reality or the nation's most urgent needs.

These problems are compounded by the fact that the petroleum sector provides wealth, but not jobs. Upstream and downstream petroleum operations are among the least labor intensive activities in modern economies, and create some of the fewest lasting jobs per unit of investment capital. Some 65 percent–70 percent of Kuwait's of the population is under the age of twenty-five, and around 90 percent of the employees in its private sector are currently non-Kuwaiti citizens because salaries are relatively low and native Kuwait's have limited job skills and a uncertain work ethic. Roughly 93 percent of Kuwaiti citizens are employed in state-owned enterprises and the government.[78] Some Kuwaiti ministers privately estimate that two out of three such jobs are make work positions with no productive output. The minimum estimate is one out of three.

Like most MENA governments, Kuwait is seeking to create jobs for young natives Kuwaitis. It is trying to attract additional foreign investment. It also is developing a program to privatize state-owned businesses (outside the oil sector) to reduce the strain subsidies put on the national budget. Kuwait has discussed privatizing such key sectors as utilities, ports, oil stations, and telephone service. Privatization, however, can only be competitive in free market terms if massive cuts are made in current employment levels and charges are increased to honestly reflect cost and a reasonable return on investment. There are few indications that Kuwait (or other MENA governments) is prepared to come to grips with this reality or to aggressively create the necessary climate for the growth of the private sector.

As a result, Kuwait is at least a moderate near-term energy risk.

The United Arab Emirates

The UAE is a federation of seven emirates—Abu Dhabi, Dubai, Sharjah, Ajman, Fujairah, Ras al-Khaimah, and Umm al-Qaiwain. Political power is concentrated in Abu Dhabi, which controls the vast majority of the UAE's economic and resource wealth. The two largest emirates—Abu Dhabi and

Dubai—provide over 80 percent of the UAE's income. In June 1996 the UAE's Federal National Council approved a permanent constitution for the country. This replaced a provisional document that had been renewed every five years since the country's creation in 1971. The establishment of Abu Dhabi as the UAE's permanent capital was one of the new framework's main provisions.

UAE Oil Development

The UAE is one of the world's largest oil producers. It currently has 97.8 billion barrels of proven reserves, or nearly 10 percent of the world total.[79] Abu Dhabi holds 94 percent of this amount or about 92.2 billion barrels, and Dubai contains another 4.0 billion barrels. The U.S. Department of Energy estimates that the UAE will increase its production capacity from 2.5 million barrels per day in 2000, to 3.0 (2.6–3.2) million barrels per day in 2005, 3.7 (2.8–4.0) million barrels per day in 2010, 4.4 (3.1–4.8) million barrels per day in 2015, and 5.1 (3.5–5.6) million barrels per day in 2020.[80]

Energy development in the UAE has generally been efficient and market-driven, although Abu Dhabi has failed to make the necessary investment in enhanced oil recovery technology and properly manage its oil reservoirs. The UAE is also in the process of expanding production from Abu Dhabi's giant Upper Zakim offshore field, which has reserves of 98 billion barrels. There have been no additions to the production capacity of this field, which has most of the UAE's proven reserves since 1995. Work is under way, however, to increase capacity from around 2.4 MMBD in 2003 to 3 MMBD by 2005 and 4 MMBD by 2010.[81] In 2003, Abu Dhabi signed contracts worth over $1,000 million with international companies to expand its onshore oil capacity.[82]

The UAE does, however, have some political problems and tensions in dealing with the management of its oil resources. Under the UAE's constitution, each emirate controls its own oil production and resource development. Although Abu Dhabi joined OPEC in 1967 (four years before the UAE was formed), Dubai does not consider itself part of OPEC or bound by its quotas. Consequently, if Dubai were to produce at its full capacity, Abu Dhabi might have to adjust its output in order to keep the UAE within its OPEC production quota.

The UAE still treats oil and gas as state industries. On October 12, 1998, however, the Abu Dhabi National Oil Company (ADNOC) announced a major plan to restructure its management. The plan consolidates ADNOC's operations under five new directorates: exploration and production, gas processing, chemicals, marketing and refining, and shared services (administration). According to *Petroleum Intelligence Weekly,* the plan is the first step in the direction of eventual privatization of major oil assets, beginning with downstream operations. Such privatization might help what has become an increasingly serious problem, at least in Abu Dhabi. ADNOC's reservoir management badly needs modernization, and Abu Dhabi needs to make more effective use of advanced enhanced oil recovery techniques.

UAE Refineries and Petrochemicals

The UAE has two refineries operated by ADNOC. The Ruwais refinery underwent a $100 million upgrade in 1995 and is now operating at 145,000 BBL per day, producing light products mainly for export to Japan and India. After upgrades, Ruwais's total capacity will be around 500,000 BBL per day by 2005. UAE's smaller refinery at Umm al-Nar is now running at 88,500 BBL per day.[83] The UAE has several major petrochemical projects in the development and early stage and will become a major producer in the future.

UAE Natural Gas Development

The U.S. Department of Energy estimates that the UAE's natural gas reserves total roughly 212 trillion cubic feet (TCF), and are the world's fifth largest—4.0 percent of the world's total—after Russia, Iran, Qatar, and Saudi Arabia. About 196.1 TCF of these reserves are located in Abu Dhabi. Sharjah, Dubai, and Ras al-Khaimah contain smaller reserves of 10.7 TCF, and 1.1 TCF, respectively. The UAE's current gas reserves are projected to last for at least 150 years.[84]

Restrictive OPEC oil production quotas and increased domestic consumption of electricity have provided a growing incentive for the UAE to develop its vast gas reserves. Over the last decade, gas consumption in Abu Dhabi has doubled, and is projected to reach 4 billion cubic feet (BCF) per day by 2005. The development of gas fields also increases exports of condensates, which are not subject to OPEC quotas.

In spite of the "oil crash" and its problems with oil revenues in 1998, the UAE spent approximately $10 billion in an effort to expand and modernize onshore and offshore gas extraction and distribution systems, and to transform the Taweelah commercial district into a gas-based industrial zone. One project was the second phase of a $1 billion onshore gas development program (OGD-2) at the Habshan natural gas complex located directly over the huge Bab oil and gas field. According to Middle East Economic Survey, this second phase includes the construction of three or four gas processing trains to process 1 BCF per day of wet sales gas, 300–500 tons per day of natural gas liquids, 35,000–55,000 tons per day of condensate and up to 2,100 tons per day of sulfur. The construction was carried out by France's Technip and Bechtel of the United States at an estimated cost of $1.2 billion, and was completed in early 2001.

Another project linked with OGD-2 is the Asab gas development project, which was completed in 1999. The Asab development processes around 830 million cubic feet per day (MMCF per day) of associated wet gas from the Thamama F and G reservoirs and produce up to 100,000 BBL per day of condensate for processing at the Ruwais refinery. The gas will also support other industries in Ruwais and be reinjected into Asab reservoirs to maintain field pressure. The $700 million project was awarded to Snamprogetti in June 1997 by UAE's Supreme Petroleum Council and was completed in the 1999. A second phase of the project consisted of a $1 billion onshore program at Habshan complex with four trains together producing 1 BCF per day. More capacity is planned for in the third phase in the future.[85]

At least one member of the UAE, however, is becoming a major gas importer. Dubai's gas consumption is expected to grow by nearly 10 percent each year, due to expansions in its industrial sector, a switch to gas by its power stations, and the need for an enhanced oil recovery (EOR) system based on gas injections for its dwindling oil formations. In May 2001, a pipeline from Abu Dhabi to Dubai commenced operations. The pipeline delivers 200 MMCF per day of natural gas.[86]

In February 1998, a deal was announced for the supply of gas from Abu Dhabi to Dubai. The deal reportedly stipulated that Abu Dhabi would sell gas to Dubai for less than $1 per million Btu, a price that undercut other potential suppliers. Dubai's gas deal with Abu Dhabi parallels a separate effort by Dubai to import gas from neighboring Qatar. The planned project, to be managed by an international consortium led by Arco, would deliver between 800 MMCF per day and 1.2 BCF per day of gas to Dubai from Qatar's giant North field. However, this project never really got off the ground, and has been supplanted by the UAE's ambitious Dolphin program.

Phase one of the Dolphin project involves the construction of a subsea pipeline from Ras Laffan in Qatar to a landfall in Abu Dhabi, which will then be extended to Dubai and Oman. In the first phase, the pipeline will supply 3,200 million cubic feet per day of Qatari gas to the UAE and Oman by 2006 via a 450-kilometer pipeline. This equates to 30 billion cubic meters a year, and would account for nearly 10 percent of world gas supplies shipped by pipeline. In a second phase, the pipeline will be extended along the seabed to Pakistan and handle another 1.5 billion cubic feet per day of gas after 2005. The project is estimated to cost $10 billion over the next six to seven years, and could lead the way to greater GCC integration.[87] The proposed extension from Oman to Pakistan remains highly uncertain. This phase of the project is technically uncertain, its costs remain speculative, and it is dependent on Pakistan's ability to afford the natural gas. Pakistan's weak economy might not be able to afford this project.

Oil production and exports, however, will continue to be the core of the UAE's strategic importance. In 2003, the EIA estimated that the UAE would increase its production from 2.5 million barrels per day in 2001, to 2.9 million barrels per day in 2005, 3.4 million barrels per day in 2010, 4.0 million barrels per day in 2015, 4.8 million barrels per day in 2020, and 5.4 million barrels per day in 2020.[88] These figures seem credible.

UAE Energy Risk

While the UAE does have tensions with Iran over the control of three Islands in the Gulf, neither these tensions nor any of its various internal tensions seem likely to seriously inhibit its future energy development. Short- to midterm risks are low, but Abu Dhabi's willingness to modernize its reservoir management and use of enhanced oil recovery technology merit close attention.

Bahrain

Bahrain, Qatar, and Oman are not major oil producers, but any geo-political analysis of the Gulf must consider the risk that the rise of a radical or unfriendly regime could pose in any of these states. Qatar is also a major potential gas producer, with the third largest reserves in the world. All three states play an important role in U.S. power projection. Bahrain is the host to the U.S. Fifth Fleet, Qatar has agreed to allow the U.S. to preposition a brigade set on its soil, and Oman provides prepositioning and port facilities.

The principal risk that Bahrain presents is that the long-standing political tensions between its Sunni elite and Shiite majority could explode into open civil conflict, lead to Iranian covert or overt intervention, and/or bring down its royal family. These problems are compounded by structural economic problems that are the result of the depletion of oil reserves, a growing population, overdependence on foreign labor, and the overconcentration of wealth in the hands of a relatively small elite.

Bahrain has, however, begun a series of political reforms that are easing these tensions. Bahrain also has received substantial economic support from Saudi Arabia, and has modernized its service, financial, and tourism sectors to diversify its economy. Real GDP grew by 4.1 percent in 2001, 4.5 percent in 2002, and is projected to grow at 4.1 percent in 2003 and 3.8 percent in 2004.[89] As a result, energy development risk is in the low to moderate category.

Bahrain has proven oil reserves of 125 million barrels. Bahrain has only one field, Awali, producing this output. Production has been declining at Awali, and in 2002, Awali field produced only 35,000 BBL per day of crude oil.

This situation could change in the future since Bahrain has potential oil reserves in the Gulf of Bahrain. These areas opened to exploration after the International Court of Justice awarded the sovereignty of the Hawar Islands to Bahrain. In late 2001, Bahrain awarded two blocks to Petroms (Malaysia) and one block to ChevronTexaco off the Southeastern coast of the country to start exploratory drilling.[90] In 2002, ChevronTexaco declared, however, that it had failed to find commercially viable opportunities in another concession to the north and west of the mainland.[91]

Sitra is Bahrain's only oil refinery, and has a capacity of 248,900 BBL per day. Sitra, which exports most of its product to India and the Far East, has been in operation since 1936 and has undergone many modernizations. The Bahrain Petroleum Company has announced a $900 million modernization program that will allow Sitra to produce a wider range of petroleum products.[92]

Bahrain produced 300 BCF of natural gas in 2000 and 314 BCF in 2001, all of which was consumed locally. Because Bahrain consumes as much as is produced, Qatar and Bahrain signed a memorandum of agreement in 2002 indicating Bahrain's intentions to purchase natural gas from Qatar.[93]

At present, Bahrain's role in regional energy supply is so limited that it cannot impose a meaningful risk in terms of energy supply. It has, however, taken important steps to both improve its relations with Qatar and move toward political and social reforms that are easing the tension between its Shiite majority and ruling the Sunni elite. Risks are low.

Oman

Oman's oil and gas exports play a role in future global energy balances.[94] Oman's reserves are relatively small. Oman has proven crude oil reserves of 5.5 billion barrels, or only 0.5 percent of the world total. It has a reserve to production ratio of 15 to 7. British Petroleum and Petroleum Intelligence Weekly estimate that Omani oil production averaged 820,000 BBL per day in 1994, 895,000 in 1996, and 905,000 BBL per day in 1998.[95] The EIA estimates that total oil production slipped to just over 700,000 BBL per day in October 2003, down from a high of almost 1 million BBL per day in 1998.[96]

Omani Oil Development

Oman's oil fields are generally smaller, more widely scattered, less productive, and more costly to produce than in other Gulf countries. Most of the country's proven oil reserves are located in the northern and central regions. Most of the crude oil found in these regions is light, with gravities in the 32°–39° API range. Heavier oil is found in southern Oman.

Oman has been more successful in attracting foreign investment to its energy sector than most other Gulf states. Its main oil company, the PDO, is the country's second largest employer after the government. It holds over 90 percent of the country's oil reserves and accounts for about 94 percent of production. The PDO is a consortium comprised of the Omani government (60 percent), Shell (34 percent), Total (4 percent), and Partex (2 percent). It is managed by Shell and operates most of the country's key fields, including Yibal and Lekhwair. Occidental oil is the only other major oil-producing company. There are three other small producers and a number of other oil companies that are actively looking for oil and gas.

Oman cannot afford to conserve its oil resources, and this makes maximizing current export revenues and increasing production a key priority for the Omani government. Fortunately, successful exploration programs over the past several years have resulted in annual reserve increases that have offset production depletions. Some of these "newly" discovered reserves were in fact discovered previously, but were considered uneconomical to develop. Horizontal drilling and other enhanced oil recovery techniques have made production of these reserves more economical in many cases.

The major oil fields in Oman, however, are mature and face future declines in production. Oman has also had serious problems with its Yibal field, which was heavily water injected and where the use of horizontal drilling produced temporary gains. It reached a peak of 250,000 BPD in 1997, but then dropped to under 90,000 BPD in 2001 and around 40,000 BPD in 2004.[97] If new reserves are not discovered, Oman will become a minor oil-exporting nation in the next ten to twenty years. Oman signed a six year contract with Spectrum Energy and Information Technology (UK) to have old seismic studies reevaluated and try to discover new resources.[98]

Omani Refineries and Petrochemicals

In 1982, Oman constructed its first refinery at Mina al-Fahal. Subsequently, the 50,000 barrels per day plant was expanded to 85,000 barrels per day. In January 1997 the Omani government announced that it was considering plans for construction of a new refinery at Salalah, a port city located in the southern tip of Oman. Planned capacity has been set at 50,000 barrels per day. Bids for construction of the project were solicited in March 2002, and JGC Corporation (Japan) was awarded the contract in May 2003. To facilitate this, Oman announced plans in April 2003 to build a $1 billion pipeline that will run the 162 miles between the Oman Refining Company and the new refinery in Sohar. They should both come online in 2006, and the refinery's capacity is expected to be 51,000 BBL per day of gasoline and 30,000 BBL per day each of diesel and fuel gas.[99]

As part of its effort to diversify the economy and to develop domestic value-added industries, Oman is planning to seek foreign investment in petrochemical production. In addition, Oman and India have decided to move forward with a joint venture fertilizer plant. Plans are for the $1.12 billion ammonia/urea complex at Qalhat near Sur to export 1.45 million tons of urea a year to India, and approximately 315,000 tons of ammonia a year to other countries. State-owned Oman Oil Company owns 50 percent of the joint venture, while the two Indian firms, Krishak Bharati Co-Operative and Rashtriya Chemicals & Fertilizers, own 25 percent each.

Omani Natural Gas

The Omani government is attempting to transform Oman into a major natural gas exporter as key element of its economic diversification strategy. The PDO has carried out an extensive exploration program and has consistently increased its natural gas reserves in recent years. According to the *Oil & Gas Journal*, intense exploration raised Oman's proven natural gas reserves from only 12.3 TCF in 1992 to just under 30 TCF in 2002.[100] About one-third of this amount is associated gas, most of which is located in the Natih and surrounding fields. Over 10 TCF of Oman's nonassociated gas is located in deep geological structures, many of which are beneath active oil fields.

The PDO produces the majority of Oman's associated gas, as well as nonassociated gas from Yibal and Lekhwair. In the late 1970s, MPM built a gas pipeline and processing facilities in order to utilize, rather than flare, associated gas. Much of Oman's natural gas is used either for electricity production, for water desalinization, or for reinjection into oil wells.

Oman is considering proposals to build two new gas pipelines. The proposed lines would link Sohar and Salalah to the existing gas network. The 420-mile pipeline from Saih Rawl to Rahud and then to Sohar would be designed to supply a planned aluminum smelter and petrochemicals complex and may meet some domestic power demands. The second 180- to 360-mile pipeline from Saih Nihayda gas field, in northern Oman, to Salalah, in the south, will mainly serve short-term domestic power requirements. Although no timetable has been set for construction, Gasco, a new upstream company mostly owned by OOC, would construct both pipelines.[101]

More broadly, Oman's plans for its future economic development and political stability are heavily dependent on gas export projects whose economics are uncertain. Nevertheless, Oman is moving forward with one major gas export project, a $2.5 billion, 6.6 million ton per year LNG plant at Qalhat, near Sur. The project is under development by the Oman Liquefied Natural Gas Company (OLNGC), which comprises the Omani government (51 percent), Shell (30 percent), Total (5.54 percent), Mitsubishi (2.77 percent), Mitsui (2.77 percent), Partex (2 percent), and Itochu (0.92 percent).

So far, Oman has been able to contract for all the gas it can produce from its first two KLNG trains. In December 1998, Oman LNG signed a twenty-year agreement with Enron to supply 1.6 million tons a year of LNG to India's Dabhol power plant. This raised the total level of production from a previously contracted level of 1.2 million tons a year, and largely offset reductions in the Thai market.[102]

LNG exports constitute a large part of Oman's plan to develop its natural gas sector, and the country is investing in it heavily. In 2002, Oman's total LNG production was 6.6 million tons, of which 6.5 million tons were exported. Since 2000, production has been evenly split between two liquefaction plants (or trains) in Qalhalt, each with a capacity of 3.3 million tons. A third train is expected to increase Oman's total capacity by 50 percent when it comes online in 2005–2006.[103]

Omani Energy Risk

In terms of risk, Oman is one of the smaller oil and gas powers in the Gulf and faces serious future challenges. Oman has one of the highest birth rates in the world, and is still in the early phases of economic development. Oman's population grew by an average rate of 4.2 percent during 1980–1997, and more than doubled from 1.1 million to 2.3 million.[104] The CIA estimated that Oman's population was still growing at a rate of 3.38 percent in 2003.[105] Oman is heavily dependent on foreign labor, but it has a growing problem with the unemployment or underemployment of its native workers.

Oman's economy and stability are overdependent on oil and gas income, and petroleum revenues account for 75 percent of total export revenues and state revenues, and about 40 percent of GDP.[106] Oman's nonoil exports only account for 9 percent of total exports, although they have risen 18 percent since 1996.[107] This helps explain why Oman has never joined the Organization of Petroleum Exporting Countries or the Organization of Arab Petroleum Exporting Countries (OAPEC). It has sought to maintain freedom of action in terms of oil and gas production.

Oman's relationships with many of its neighbors are complicated by its refusal to join either OPEC or OAPEC. It also has had strained relations with Yemen, and its border with the UAE continues to be undefined.

Oman has taken steps to liberalize its investment climate. In November 1994, the government revised its investment law, raising the maximum percentage of foreign ownership from 49 percent to 65 percent. Full foreign ownership was also permitted under special conditions, although there are no actual examples at present. Oman's 1997 budget included a new tax code aimed at providing tax relief to companies with foreign shareholders. Taxes on these firms now have a ceiling of 7.5 percent, the same as for Omani companies. Under the previous tax code, firms with foreign shareholders paid tax rates between 15 percent and 25 percent.

The Omani government has also sought to attract foreign investment, particularly in light industry, tourism, and electric power generation. Foreign investment incentives include a five-year tax holiday for companies in certain industries, an income tax reduction for publicly held companies with at least 51 percent Omani ownership, and soft loans to finance new and existing projects.

However, the EIA reports that Omani nationals now constitute only 10 percent of private sector employment. Oman's population is growing very rapidly, and traditional pursuits like agriculture suffer from overcrowding, over production, and water problems caused by excessive use of aquifers. Job creation in other sectors is still very slow, and many prefer to hire foreign nationals. Oman is also increasing the strains on its budget and investment capabilities by keeping taxes low as an economic stimulus measure. As a result, Oman has sometimes been force to draw on its strategic reserve, which was designed to provide capital for the time when Oman ceased to be a major oil producer.

Oman's economic reforms have also left it with more bureaucratic restrictions than in neighboring Dubai, and Omani labor productivity remains

low. It needs changes in its regulations to exploit tourism, and other prom-
ising sectors of the economy. In October 2002, Oman joined the World
Trade Organization, and further economic reforms may well take place, but
Oman to date has been less realistic about its reform plans that it should
be.[108] It faces an uncertain future because of the lack of a clear successor
to Sultan Qabus, growing demographic pressure, and the fact that its overambitious economic goals may not be possible to implement in ways that
preserve internal stability.

Sultan Qaboos bin Said al-Said has ruled Oman since 1970, when Britain
helped him depose his father in a bloodless coup. The sultan is childless
and sixty years old. Oman did establish rules governing the succession that
were formalized in the 1996 Basic Law, but it is far from clear who will
succeed the sultan and what his competence and experience will be. This
is critical because the sultan still retains power in virtually every aspect of
Oman's government decision making and act as the minister in the finance,
defense, and foreign affairs ministries. This overconcentration of power has
already had an impact in creating internal opposition, and in limiting the
effectiveness of some aspects of Omani economic planning and reform.
There are, however, some elements of political change. The sultan has created two consultative bodies, the Majlis al-Dawla and the Majlis al-Shura,
which make up the Council of Oman. The Majlis al-Dawla is appointed,
but the Majlis al-Shura is elected, and Oman is experimenting with universal adult suffrage.

Oman has relatively good relations with Iran, but could face major problems in any major conflict in which Iran sought to close or limit traffic
through the Strait of Hormuz. Relations with Saudi Arabia have improved
to the point of being correct, but are scarcely warm. Oman has had tensions with Yemen and some aspects of its border with the UAE are not
firmly demarcated.

In spite of these reservations, Oman has long shown it can cope with its
problems and the present mix of short- and midterm risks is not yet serious
enough to qualify Oman as more than a low to moderate energy risk.

Qatar

Qatar's economy depends almost solely on oil and gas revenues, which
account for roughly 89 percent of its export earnings and 72–75 percent
of its government revenues. Oil accounts for around 66 percent of Qatar's
government revenues, and has an impact on production of condensate and
associated natural gas.[109] Most of Qatar's heavy industrial projects are tied
closely to its petroleum sector. They include a refinery with 50,000–60,000
barrels per day capacity, a fertilizer plant for urea and ammonia, a steel
plant, and a petrochemical plant. These industries use gas for fuel. Most
of them are joint ventures between European or Japanese firms and the
state-owned Qatar General Petroleum Company (QGPC).

Qatar has no arable land, irrigated land, or permanent crops and only 5 percent of its territory is suitable for light grazing. Even the limited agricultural production that does take place is extremely wasteful since there are very limited freshwater resources and agriculture must rely on desalinized water, foreign labor, and subsidies. As a result, Qatar's future depends upon its ability to exploit the full downstream potential of its oil and gas resources to maintain and increase oil and gas exports, to increase exports of petroleum-related products, and to develop gas and petroleum fueled industries. This is the only way Qatar can create new jobs for its native labor force, and encourage private investment outside the service industries. Qatar's greatest strength is gas. It has the third largest gas reserves in the world, after Russia and Iran.

Qatari Oil Development

Qatar has proven oil reserves of 15.2 billion barrels. The Dukhan field is Qatar's largest and only onshore oil field. The remaining proven reserves are held in six offshore fields: Bul Hanine, Maydan Mahzam, Id al-Shargi North Dome, Al-Shaheen, Al-Rayyan, and Al-Khalij. It exports almost all of its oil to Asia—Japan is the largest customer. Qatar contains crude oil with gravities in the 24°–41° API range.

Qatar now has a number of oil field developments under way, planning and development activities have improved sharply since a new emir came to power in 1995. Qatar has initiated new policies aimed at increasing oil production, locating additional oil reserves before existing reserves become too expensive to recover. It has invested in advanced oil recovery systems to extend the life of existing fields. The government improved the terms of exploration and production contracts and production sharing agreements (PSAs) in order to encourage foreign oil companies to improve oil recovery in producing fields and to explore for new oil deposits. In November 2003, foreign companies accounted for more than one-third of Qatar's oil production capacity.[110]

The EIA estimates that Qatar's oil production capacity will remain relatively constant, and go from 0.85–0.9 million barrels per day in 2001, to 0.6 million barrels per day in 2005, 0.6 million barrels per day in 2010, 0.7 million barrels per day in 2015, 0.8 million barrels per day in 2020, and 0.8 million barrels per day in 2025.[111] These figures seem credible, and the EIA estimates they could be higher if Qatari plans are successful.

Qatari Gas Development

The key to Qatar's energy future, however, is gas. Qatar's natural gas reserves rank third after Russia and Iran, and the Qatari government believes that the country's economic future is dependent upon developing its vast gas potential. Such development, however, is a challenging task. It costs roughly $1.0 billion to bring one million tons of gas export capacity online, and Qatar has to make hard choices about which project to pursue and when.

According to the IEA, Qatar has proven reserves of 509 trillion cubic feet (TCF). Most of Qatar's gas is located in its North field, which contains 380 TCF of in-place and 239 TCF of recoverable reserves, making it the largest known nonassociated gas field in the world. In addition, the Dukhan field contains an estimated 5 TCF of associated and 0.5 TCF of nonassociated gas. Smaller associated gas reserves also are contained in the Id al-Shargi, Maydan Mahzam, Bul Hanine, and Al-Rayyan oil fields. Additional fields may give Qatar a total producible gas reserve of up to 250.0 trillion cubic feet. This would give Qatar about 5 percent of all the world's gas reserves.

Qatari gas production has risen sharply in recent years, and gas exports and the domestic use of gas have only been heavily marketed since 1991. Qatar produced only 5.9 billion cubic meters in 1988. This rose to 20.0 BCM by 1998.[112] Before 1991, most gas was reinjected, flared, or lost. The Qatari economy has also been boosted by the completion of the $1.5 billion Phase 1 of the North field gas development in 1991. Qatar is now producing about 321 billion cubic feet of gas per year, and this total will rise sharply in the future. The future phases of North field gas development, involving exports via pipeline and/or gas liquefaction, may cost $5–6 billion, and will make Qatar a major gas producer.

The IEA estimates that Qatar's capacity to produce LNG will reach 12.5 million tons by 2005. It estimates that Qatar can sustain this level for more than a decade and has the capability to reach export levels of 17.5 million tons. The IEA estimated that Qatar's contracted capacity to export LNG would reach 8.4 million tons by 2000, and its spare export capacity will be 4.6 million tons by 2005. The projected total upstream cost for Qatar's three LNG trains is $900 million, and downstream costs may reach as high as $3 billion. A consortium of Japanese banks will provide the bulk of this downstream financing, mainly through a $2 billion loan that was finalized in June 1994.

Qatar is focusing on the development of its offshore North field to increase its LNG exports and significantly expand the share of petrochemicals in Qatar's total export trade of crude oil, refined products, and LPG. Qatar currently has two major LNG projects, Qatar Liquefied Gas Company (Qatargas) and Ras Laffan (Rasgas), in development. The Qatargas downstream consortium comprises QGPC (65 percent), TotalFinaElf (10 percent), ExxonMobil (10 percent), Mitsui (7.5 percent) and Marubeni (7.5 percent). The Qatargas LNG plant consists of three trains, each with a capacity of 2 million tons per year (MMTY). A third train was completed in 1999. Current renovations and improvements should expand total capacity to 9.2 MMTY or 446 billion cubic feet (BCF) by 2005. A fourth train is also planned.

Ragas is Qatar's second LNG project. The two major shareholders are QGPC and ExxonMobil. The first train was completed in 1999 and the second followed in April 2000. An additional third and forth trains are planned, and the third is expected to be the largest in the world with a 4.7 MMTY capacity upon completion in 2004. According to RasGas managing director Neil Kelly, "Qatar's LNG will be a force to be reckoned with in world terms."[113]

Qatar is pressing ahead with other high priority gas projects. These include the $300 million gas lift project at Dukhan, and the second phase of the Khuff pipeline development. They also include the construction of a $400 million NGL-4 plant at Mesaieed by QGPC.

One of Qatar's most ambitious projects is the Dolphin Energy Project, an integrated natural gas pipeline grid for Qatar, UAE, and Oman, with a possible subsea extension linking Oman to Pakistan. This pipeline is to provide gas fuel for the UAE and Oman as their gas production declines, and allow them to free oil for exports and for downstream projects. The total project is expected to cost around $10 billion, including the costs associated with the development of more extensive gas distribution networks in the UAE and Oman.

The project has, however, had an uncertain history. The United Offsets Group (UOG), a UAE state-owned corporation supporting the project, signed preliminary memorandums of understanding with Qatar, Oman, and Pakistan in June 1999. ExxonMobil also signed a preliminary agreement in June 1999 for the natural gas supply from ExxonMobil's production capacity in the North field.

Qatar was to begin selling around 730 BCF per year of North field natural gas, starting in 2006, transported through a subsea pipeline linking the North field to Abu Dhabi in the UAE. Links between Abu Dhabi, Dubai, and Oman were be added afterward. The UOG announced in March 2000 that TotalFinaElf and Enron had been selected to implement the project, and each would have an equity stake of 24.5 percent. In May 2001, however, Enron announced in May 2001 that it was pulling out of the project, and UOG acquired Enron's equity stake, which it resold to Occidental Petroleum in May 2002.

The project is scheduled to have an initial capacity of 20 BCM a year, and cost some $3.5 billion. It calls for the construction of an 800-kilometer gas pipeline from Qatar's North field to Abu Dhabi in the UAE that will connect with the existing Jebel Ali pipeline to Dubai. Dolphin Energy projects its investment share at $2.5 billion but Total, Occidental, and the UAE Offsets group may increase their share of the total. Construction is scheduled to begin in 2004, with initial deliveries in 2006.[114] The EIA estimates that Pakistan's participation is now "highly doubtful, due to its financial condition and the possibility of imports from Iran."[115]

Qatar plans to start its biggest gas investment program during 2004–2005. This program will be the $12 billion Qatargas II project. It will export 15 million tons per year of LNG from the Qatar Liquefied Gas Company (Qatargas) to the United Kingdom. The first delivery is projected to begin in 2008.[116] Qatargas is also working on another project with ConocoPhilips (United States). The cost of this project is estimated to be $7.5 billion and it would supply the U.S. market. Its schedule is for the period 2006–2010.[117]

Qatar is also evaluating plans for pipelines to connect Kuwait, Saudi Arabia, the UAE, and Oman, and plans for pipeline or LNG shipments to Israel. These plans, however, have a total potential cost of $20.6 billion, and present serious political, financing, and technical problems. The most practical option is a subsea line to Kuwait through Saudi waters. Kuwait and Qatar signed a protocol for this project in 2002, and for the supply of 7.75 BCM a year over twenty-five years beginning at the end of 2005. The Saudi government gave approval in early 2003, but no Qatari-Kuwaiti government-to-government agreement has yet been reached, and shipments from Iraq to Kuwait may now be more economic.[118]

The EIA reports that Qatar has also been interested in potential development of gas-to-liquid (GTL) projects. Shell signed a contract with Qatar Petroleum in October 2003 for a 140,000 BBL per day GTL facility to be built at Ras Laffan. The first 70,000 BBL per day of capacity is expected to commence operation by 2009, with the rest in 2010 or 2011. If completed, it will be the world's largest GTL plant.[119] Therefore, Qatar will be GTL producer in late 2005. Although the project is still under construction at Ras Laaffan, the Qatar Petroleum and Sasol (South Africa) are working on another project to expand the plant to 120,000 barrels per day. The ChevronTexaco Corporation (United States) will possibly participate in this project.[120]

Qatari Energy Risk

Qatar has settled its border disputes with Bahrain and Saudi Arabia in recent years, and has avoided any confrontation with Iran over the giant offshore gas field the two countries share in the Gulf. It now is home to a major U.S. military presence that deters any foreign threats. Its main source of tension with its neighbors is the result of its tendency to start political feuds and aggressively assert its status and independence.

Qatar is so rich relative to its small native population that it is one of the few MENA states that can subsidize a petroleum-driven, subsidized economy indefinitely. Even so, it is opening up its economy to more efficient operation of its private sector, and has made major progress toward creating democratic institutions, a more effective rule of law, and protecting human rights. Its emir has had health problems, but Qatar has so far shown few signs of political instability, other than jockeying for power among members of the royal family. When its oil exports are combined with the growing exploitation of vast gas resources, effective state planning and management of energy development, and a reasonable pace of political reform, short- to midterm energy development risks are low.

Yemen

Yemen has limited to moderate importance to world energy markets because of its oil and natural gas resources and because of its strategic location overseeing the Strait of Bab el-Mandab, which links the Red Sea and the Gulf of Aden, one of the world's most active shipping lanes. According to U.S. sources, Yemen has 4.0 billion barrels of proven oil reserves, or 0.4 percent of the world's supply, and 16.9 TCF of proven gas reserves, or 0.3 percent of the world's supply.[121] According to Yemen, the country's oil reserves stood at about 5.7 billion barrels in May 2000, and its gas reserves were about 15 trillion cubic feet. President Saleh announced these figures in a televised address to mark ten years of unification between the north and south of the Arab state.[122]

Yemen's oil production rose from 170,000 BBL per day in 1988 to 180,000 BBL per day in 1990, and 350,000 in 1995. It averaged 350,000 BBL per day in 1996, 370,000 in 1997, and 385,000 in 1998. Its production was 440,000 barrels per day in 2000, 438,000 barrels per day in 2001, and 443,288 in 2002.[123] These increases came largely from the Jannah field, where production is projected to rise to 75,000 BBL per day, and the East Shabwa field, where production will increase 50 percent to 30,000 BBL per day.

Yemeni Oil Development

Nabil al-Gawsi, chairman of Yemen's oil ministry's petroleum exploration and production board, stated in May 2000, "We are trying to increase production from these blocks and also from exploration blocks . . . maybe 100,000, 200,000 BBL per day during the coming years." He said Yemen had fifty-nine concession blocks, including the six blocks that were either already producing or would soon start, while twenty-three blocks were under exploration. The rest were open, he added. Gawsi said there were some nineteen foreign firms operating exploration or producing concessions and more than twenty-five subcontractors in the country.[124]

Exploration for additional reserves and the search for new investments from foreign companies has been affected by political instability. Foreign involvement began to decline in 1994, due mainly to the civil war between north and south Yemen, unattractive exploration and production contractual conditions, and the low success rate of new hydrocarbon discoveries. Exploration activity increased again in 1997 after the civil war ended and the government started to offer more attractive contract terms. By mid-1997, approximately twenty exploration agreements were in force with foreign oil companies.

After the border demarcation treaty with Saudi Arabia that was signed in Jeddah on June 12, 2000, new areas were opened for exploration. Four new blocks have been demarcated along the Saudi border. Several companies have already declared their intensions to explore these new fields. In January 2001, Nexen signed a memorandum of understanding with the Yemeni government, covering Block 59, which is located by the Saudi border. In December 2001 the consortium of Austria's OMV, Cespa of Spain, and PanCanadian signed an exploration and production contract for Block 60.[125]

Yemeni Refining and Petrochemicals

Yemen currently has a crude refining capacity of 130,000 BBL per day from two refineries. Yemen signed an agreement in December 2002 with the Hadramawt Refinery Company, backed by Saudi investors, for a $450 million facility with a capacity of 50,000 BBL per day to be completed at Mukalla by 2005. A feasibility study is being conducted for a new 100,000-BBL per day refinery at Ras Issa, located on the Red Sea.

Yemeni Natural Gas Development

Yemen has proven natural gas reserves of 15–16.9 trillion cubic feet, about 0.3 percent of the world supply, and has some potential as a natural gas producer. The bulk of these reserves, in the form of both associated and nonassociated gas, are concentrated in the Marib-Jawf fields, operated by the Yemen Exploration and Production Company (YEPC). However, few facilities for recovering and using associated gas have been installed. All of Yemen's gas production is either reinjected or sold as natural gas liquids.

In early 1996, France's Total and Yemen's General Gas Corporation set up YLNG to operate a $5 billion liquefied natural gas project. The venture, Yemen's largest single energy project, is to develop natural gas from the Marib-Jawf and Jannah fields, and transport it via pipeline to a natural gas processing plant and export terminal in Balhaf on the coast of southern Yemen. The plant will have an export capacity of 5.3 million tons per year (MMTY) of LNG from two 2.65 MMTY trains.

Yemeni Energy Risk

Yemen has made progress toward political reform. It still, however, is politically divided and has a long history of political violence. It is also a country that has been the location of significant terrorist activity. In spite of its progress in energy development, it is an extremely poor country with a rapidly growing population and little success in broader economic diversification and development. Short- to midterm energy development risks are medium to high.

The Levant

The Levant acts as a major route for exporting energy, but its total oil and gas reserves—which include those of Egypt, Israel, Jordan, Lebanon, and Syria—are so limited that they have little strategic importance and impact on the world supply of energy. As has been described in Chapter 2, Egypt is important to energy supply because of the Suez Canal and the Sumed Pipeline. The energy resources of the other states of the Levant are important largely because of their impact on regional stability of the MENA region, and because of the geopolitical impact of the Arab-Israeli conflict.

BP estimates Egypt's oil reserves at 3.7 billion barrels, about 0.4 percent of the world supply. Syria's reserves are 2.5 billion barrels, or 0.3 percent of world supply.[126] Egyptian oil production has slowly declined from around 0.9 MMBD in 1982 to 0.75 MMBD in 2003—when it accounted for about 1.0 percent of world production. Syrian oil production has risen slightly from around 0.52 MMBD in 1982 to 0.58 MMBD in 2003—when it accounted for about 0.8 percent of world production. This gives the Levant a total of 0.7 percent of the world's proven reserves and about 1.8 percent of its total current production. Neither Egypt nor Syria is an OPEC state, and the EIA does not make long-term forecast of their national production.

Egypt continues to discover additional gas, and Israel and Jordan may have small resources. BP estimates Egypt's gas reserves at 22.7 billion cubic meters, about 0.9 percent of the world supply. Syria's reserves are 4.1 billion cubic meters, or 0.2 percent of world supply.[127] Egyptian gas production has risen steadily from around 8.4 billion cubic meters in 1982 to 22.7 in 2003—when it accounted for about 0.9 percent of world production. Syrian oil production has risen slightly from around 1.6 billion cubic meters in 1982 to 4.1 in 2003—when it accounted for about 0.2 percent of world production. This gives the Levant a total of 1.1 percent of the world's proven gas reserves and about 1.1 percent of its total production.

Egypt

Egypt is currently a small exporter of energy, but Egypt's oil export revenues are one of the country's top four main foreign exchange earners, (along with tourism, Suez Canal fees, and worker remittances from abroad). The EIA estimated in January 2004 that Egypt had 3.7 billion barrels of oil reserves and a reserve-to-production ratio of 10:4. Egyptian oil production comes from four main areas: the Gulf of Suez (over 50 percent), the Western Desert, the Eastern Desert, and the Sinai Peninsula. The Egyptian Ministry of Petroleum estimates it has 62.0 trillion cubic feet (TCF) of gas.

Egyptian Oil Development

Successive years of declining crude oil production, and a lack of new major discoveries, have led to a steady deterioration in Egypt's petroleum trade balance. Net petroleum receipts amounted to approximately $1.6 billion in 1996, fell to only $156 million in 1998, and moved into deficit during 1999. Part of the reason was Egyptian payments to foreign partners for their share of gas production. As of February 2000, Egypt was negotiating with international oil companies on a new gas clause that could introduce an amended gas price formula for the production sharing agreements for all upcoming licensing rounds. The gas clause, originally introduced in late 1980s, was designed to encourage exploration for and the development of natural gas in Egypt by offering favorable terms to exploration companies. However, the expenditures contained in the clause are now becoming fully apparent.[128]

Estimates of recent average daily production differ, but are all under 1 MMBD. The EIA estimates that Egypt's crude oil output has fallen in recent years from 920,000 BBL per day in 1995, 922,000 BBL per day in 1996, 856,000 BBL per day in 1997, 866,000 BBL per day in 1998, and 866,000 BBL per day during the first five months of 1999. In January 2004, the EIA reported that Egypt averaged 752,000 barrels per day (BBL per day) in 2003, of which was 620,000 BBL per day is crude oil. Its domestic consumption had risen to 558,000 BBL per day, and net exports were only 194,000 BBL per day. BP estimates that Egypt averaged 921,000 BBL per day in 1994, 924,000 in 1995, 894,000 1996, 873,000 in 1997, 857,000 in 1998, 827,000 in 1999, 781,000 in 2000, 758,000 in 2001, and 751,000 in 2002.[129]

Egypt is hoping that exploration activity, particularly in new areas, will discover sufficient oil in coming years to maintain crude oil production comfortably above a level of 800,000 BBL per day. Crude oil from the Gulf of Suez basin is produced mainly by the Gupco (Gulf of Suez Petroleum Company) joint venture between BP Amoco and Egypt's General Petroleum Corp. Production in the Gupco fields, which have been in operation since the 1960s, has been falling rapidly, though it remains at levels over 300,000 BBL per day. Gupco seems to have been successful in reversing the natural decline in its fields through significant investments in enhanced oil production as well as increased exploration. Production rose to 330,000 BBL per day, and BP Amoco announced a new discovery in the South Ghareb concession in the Sinai that flowed at 18,000 BBL per day by early 1998, with reserves of 25 million cubic meters. Next to Gupco, Egypt's second largest producer is Petrobel (Italian company Eni's Egyptian subsidiary), which produces around 290,000 BBL per day in a joint venture with EGPC. Petrobel is active mainly in the Gulf of Suez and Sinai.

Egyptian Refineries and Petrochemicals

Egyptian petroleum minister Hamdi el-Banbi proposed in the past that Egypt try to deal with this situation by shifting from exports of crude to exports of product, but it is unclear whether Egypt can do this. Egypt's refineries barely meet domestic demand and Egypt imports significant amounts of light product.

Egypt's nine refineries have the capacity to process 726,250 BBL per day of crude. Egypt's future plans include increased production of lighter products, petrochemicals, and upgrading and expanding existing facilities.[130] The Oriental Petrochemicals Company, a local private venture, is planning to build a polypropylene plant in Alexandria that will utilize natural gas from Western Desert fields as feedstock. The plant is expected to cost about $80 million and produce more than 120,000 metric tons of polypropylene annually. Additionally, Phillips Petroleum is looking to establish a joint venture in Egypt to build a polyethylene plant with an annual capacity of 150,000 tons. The plant would use natural gas (ethane) as a feedstock.

Egypt's Role in Energy Transport Routes

In addition to its role as an oil exporter, Egypt has strategic importance to Middle East energy because it controls two routes for the export of Persian Gulf oil: the Suez Canal and the Sumed (Suez-Mediterranean) Pipeline. This currently involves the flow of 3.5 million BBL per day of oil (1.1 million BBL per day through Suez Canal, 2.4 million BBL per day through Sumed Pipeline). The principal destinations are Europe and the United States. Closure of the Suez Canal and/or Sumed Pipeline would force tankers to go around the southern tip of Africa (the Cape of Good Hope), and increase transit time and cost. Such an event now seems very unlikely, but does represent a low-level geopolitical risk.

The Suez Canal Authority (SCA) is continuing enhancement and enlargement projects on the canal, although tanker traffic and revenues have declined over the last decade as a result of the competitive pipelines and alternative routes, such as South Africa. The canal has been deepened so that it can accept the world's largest bulk carriers, but it will need to be deepened further to 68 or 70 feet to accommodate fully laden very large crude carriers (VLCCs). Additional dredging reached a depth of 62 feet in the year 2000. It will need to be deepened further to 68 or 70 feet to accommodate fully laden very large crude carriers. The SCA is also offering a 35 percent discount to LNG tankers as well as some other discounts for oil tankers in order to increase the tanker traffic to its old levels.[131]

The Sumed Pipeline is an alternative to the Suez Canal for transporting oil from the Persian Gulf region to the Mediterranean. The 200-mile pipeline runs from Ain Sukhna on the Gulf of Suez to Sidi Kerir on the Mediterranean. The capacity of the pipeline is 2.5 million BBL per day. An extension of the pipeline is being studied. This extension would traverse the Red Sea from Ain Sukhna to the closest point on the Saudi coast near Sharm al-Shaikh, and then continue to link up with the terminal of Saudi Arabia's main east-west pipeline in Yanbu. Sumed consists of two 42-inch lines, and is owned by Arab Petroleum Pipeline Co., a joint venture of

EGPC, Saudi Aramco, Abu Dhabi's ADNOC, three Kuwaiti companies, and Qatar's QGPC.[132] Egypt and Libya have also announced plans to build a crude oil pipeline. The 600-kilometer (375-mile), 150,000 BBL per day line would transport Libyan crude from Tobruk to Alexandria for refining and sale in Egypt. The pipeline is expected to cost $300 million, and should take three to four years to complete. In exchange, Egypt may export 500 million cubic feet per day of gas to Libya.

Egyptian Natural Gas Development

As a result of increased domestic demand for petroleum products, Egypt is pursuing a policy of substituting natural gas for fuel oil as a means of reducing oil consumption and freeing up more oil for export. Sana'a El Banna, first undersecretary for technical affairs at the Egyptian Ministry of Petroleum, stated that Egypt is "actively trying to maximize natural gas use in order to reduce dependency on liquid fuels."

Egypt's natural gas sector is expanding rapidly, as production nearly doubled between 1999 and 2003. Production averaged 1.6 billion cubic feet per day (BCF per day) at the beginning of 1999, increased to 2.3 BCF per day at the end of year, reached 3.0 BCF per day at the end of 2002, averaged about 3.3 BCF per day in 2003, and is expected to rise to around 5.0 BCF per day by 2007.[133] Proven natural gas reserves have increased significantly in recent years, with major discoveries along the Mediterranean Coast/Nile Delta region and in the Western Desert.

After an intensive period of exploration Egypt's proven gas reserves reached 62 trillion cubic feet (TCF) in November 2003. This compares with 15 TCF in January 1993. Most of this increase has come about as a result of new gas discoveries in the Mediterranean offshore/Nile Delta region, and increasingly in the Western Desert. Offshore activity may also increase in the future. On February 17, 2003, Egypt and Cyprus signed an accord delineating their maritime border. Egypt aims to boost its oil and gas exploration in the Mediterranean offshore. Therefore, Egypt's proven gas reserves are expected to increase rapidly in 2004 due to the continuing oil exploration projects.[134]

In the Nile Delta, which has emerged as a world-class gas basin, recent offshore field developments include Port Fuad, South Temsah, and Wakah. In the Western Desert, the Obeiyed field is an important natural gas area currently under development. Overall, more than half of Egypt's natural gas production comes from just two fields: Abu Madi (on-stream since the 1970s) and Badreddin (since 1990). Abu Qir is the third largest field, and like Abu Madi is considered mature.

The International Egyptian Oil Company (IEOC), a subsidiary of Italy's ENI group, is Egypt's leading natural gas producer. In cooperation with BP Amoco, the IEOC has been concentrating its natural gas exploration and development efforts in the Nile Delta region. The $1 billion development program is expected to yield about 365 billion cubic feet (BCF) annually beginning in 2000. In November 1997, Amoco announced plans to develop the giant Ha'py gas field in the Ras-el Barr concession of the Nile Delta region at an estimated cost of $248 million. The gas, up to 2 TCF annually, was marketed domestically beginning in 2000. The field came online in 2000 and produces an output of 280 million cubic feet per day.[135]

In October 1998, BP Amoco and Eni-Agip signed a gas sales agreement with the Egyptian General Petroleum Corporation (EGPC) and the IEOC for the reserves at the Temsah gas field. Field development is expected to cost $700 million, as production began late 1999. Temsah's gas reserves are estimated at 3.9 TCF, and the gas sales agreement is for 35 MMCF per day initially, increasing to 480 MMCF per day by 2003.[136] Two areas in the Western Desert—Obeiyed and Khalda—have also shown great potential for increasing Egypt's gas production.

The rapid increase in Egypt's natural gas reserves and production has encouraged ambitious plans for gas exports (either by pipeline or liquefied natural gas tanker) to such countries as Turkey, Israel, Jordan, and the Palestinian territories. Pricing issues have complicated these plans—specifically, how much exported gas should cost relative to domestically consumed gas. The International Energy Agency, however, estimates that Egypt may complete five major LNG projects by 2007:[137]

Location	Startup	Cost ($ billions)	Capacity (MTY)	Status	Companies
Idku	2005	1.35	train 1:3.6	under construction	BG, Petrogas, EGPC, EGAS, GDF
	2006	0.55	train 2:3.6	under construction	BG, Petrogas, EGPC, EGAS
	2007	1.5	train 3:4.0	planned	EGPC, BP, ENI
Damietta	2004	1.0	train 1:5.0	planned	EGPC, EGAS, Union Fenosa, ENI
	2006	1.0	train 1:4.0	planned	EGPC/Shell

Egypt also plans to export gas to Jordan. In October 1997, the EGPC and IEOC signed an agreement under which the IEOC will build a $60 million, 140 BCF-per-year natural gas pipeline from the Nile Delta offshore region under the Suez Canal into northern Sinai. In July 1997, Egypt and Jordan started negotiations on a possible gas pipeline across the Sinai and under the Red Sea to the southern Jordanian port city of Aqaba, where the line would link with Jordan's national gas grid. In November 1998, BP Amoco signed an agreement with Egypt and Jordan to build a relatively small capacity gas pipeline across the Sinai and under the Gulf of Aqaba to Jordan. A 270-kilometer gas pipeline to Jordan was inaugurated by King Abdullah and Hosni Mubarak in July 2003, making Egypt's first exports of natural gas possible. Egypt aims to extend this pipeline into Syria, with eventual gas exports to Turkey, Lebanon, and possibly Cyprus. The feasibility of this project, however, is questionable since Turkey has already agreed to buy Russian, Iranian, and Azeri gas.

The natural gas "Peace Pipeline" to Israel was stalled along with the Middle East peace process during the administration of Benjamin Netanyahu. There was increased hope for the project after the election of Ehud Barak in May 1999, but efforts halted again with the outbreak of the second intifada in September 2000. Italy's ENI completed a pipeline that goes up Egypt's Mediterranean coast to El-Arish, which might be perceived as a starting point for the export pipeline to Israel. EIA, however, indicated that contacts between Egypt and Israel on the issue of extending the pipeline resumed in late 2003.[138]

Egyptian Energy Risk

Egypt is a major power in the Arab world and one of the most influential states in the MENA region. It has a moderate secular regime, and is now the most powerful Arab military power, strengthened by its alliance with the United States and U.S. military aid. It has also been a key player in the Arab-Israeli peace process.

Egypt has, however, made little progress in recent years toward political and economic reform and fought a decade-long battle to control Islamic extremists and terrorism. It has large and growing population and—in spite of one economic reform effort after another—has not succeeded in modernizing and diversifying its economy. The EIA reports that the private sector's percentage of the GDP has been growing by around 1.5 percent per year in recent years, at best a third of the required rate.[139]

Egypt's plans for the privatization of state-owned enterprises have moved slowly due to unrealistic calculations of the reforms necessary to make such firms competitive at market prices, the large debts, and massive overstaffing, which current labor regulations make difficult to reform. Although some 40 percent of Egypt's state-owned enterprises have been privatized since 1994, there have been few practical benefits other than reducing the cost of inefficient entities. The government plans to target "strategic" areas for privatization, including telecommunications and other utilities, including the Egyptian Electricity Authority. It does not intend to privatize the EGPC and the new natural gas entity, Egypt Gas (EGAS). Egypt talks a game it does not really play. It is burdened by a large, inefficient state sector ands private sector development has been limited by a variety of state barriers and disincentives.

Egypt also faces the problem of finding a successor to President Mubarak, and moving toward more political pluralism. Its economic reform plans are being implemented too slowly, and it still faces a challenge from Islamic extremism and terrorism. Short- and midterm energy risks are moderate.

Syria

Syria is not a major oil exporter, but could become a major transit route for oil shipments from the Gulf. Syria had about 2.5 billion barrels of proven reserves in 2000, or 0.2 percent of the world supply. The EIA reports that Syria's oil output increased dramatically in the mid-1980s and 1990s, peaking at 590,000 BBL per day in 1996. Since that time, its oil output appears to have begun a steady decline by as much as much as 6 percent per annum, as older fields, especially the 140,000 BBL per day Karatchuk field discovered in 1968, reached maturity. The EIA estimates that total Syrian oil production peaked at 590,000 BBL per day in 1996. It was 570,000 BBL per day in 1997, 546,000 BBL per day in 1999, and 535,000 BBL per day in 2003.[140] Production is expected to fall steadily over the next several years and domestic consumption continues to rise. Syria had net exports of only 257,000 BBL per day in 2002, not counting some 150,000–200,000 BBL per day of oil smuggle in from Iraq. The EIA estimates that Syria could become a net oil importer within a decade.

While Syria's oil exports have had little impact on world energy balances, they have been critical to Syria's economy, accounting for 55–60 percent of Syria's total export earnings. Syria currently exports Syrian Light, a blend of light and sweet crudes produced primarily from the Deir ez-Zour and Ash Sham fields, and heavy Suwaidiyah crude produced from the Soudie and Jebisseh fields. The country also exports fuel oil and other products, including oil sent illegally from Iraq. Syria is a member of OAPEC, although not of OPEC.

Syrian Oil Development

Syria's main oil producer is Al-Furat Petroleum Co. (AFPC), a joint venture established in May 1985 between state-owned Syrian Petroleum Company (SPC) (50 percent share), Pecten Syria Petroleum (15.625 percent), and foreign partners Royal Dutch/Shell (15.625 percent) and Germany's Deminex (18.75 percent). Shell and Deminex have signed a new oil exploration contract with SPC for northeastern Syria.

The SPC's fields include: (1) Karatchuk—Syria's first discovery, located near the border with Iraq and Turkey; (2) Suwaidiyah—a giant heavy oil field located south of Karatchuk in the Hassakeh region and extending into northwestern Iraq; (3) Jibisseh—a major field producing both oil and gas; (4) Rumailan—a small field near Suwaidiyah that produces heavy oil; and (5) Alian, Tishreen, and Gbebeh—three small, depleting fields producing heavy oil. Other major Syrian oil fields include: Maleh (production of more than 50,000 BBL per day); Qahar (40,000 BBL per day); Sijan (35,000 BBL per day); Azraq (30,000 BBL per day); and Tanak (18,000 BBL per day). Jafra, discovered in late 1991, was first expected to have potential for more than 60,000 BBL per day in production. Currently, Jafra is producing only 20,000 BBL per day, however. Besides conventional oil reserves, Syria also has major shale oil deposits in several locations, mainly the Yarmouk Valley stretching into Jordan.

Syria's oil development has been politicized and inefficient. Al-Furat's fields in the northeast—particularly the Deir ez-Zour region, where commercial quantities of oil were discovered in the late 1980s—produced about 350,000–360,000 BBL per day of high quality light crude in 1997–1998, a significant decline from 405,000 BBL per day in 1994. Al-Furat's main oil field is al-Thayyem, although production there has been declining since 1991. Another important field, Omar/Omar North, began production in February 1989 at 55,000 BBL per day.

Shortly thereafter, operator Shell was pressed by the cash-strapped Syrian government to step up production (against Shell's advice) to 100,000 BBL per day. The result was serious reservoir damage, and in April 1989, output plummeted to 30,000 BBL per day. Currently, Omar produces about 15,000 BBL per day from natural pressure and 30,000 BBL per day from water injection. Other al-Furat fields include: (1) al-Izba, with light oil production of 55,000 BBL per day; (2) Maleh, with output of about 50,000 BBL per day of 34° API gravity oil; (3) Sijan, at about 30,000 BBL per day; and (4) Tanak, producing around 18,000 BBL per day.

In 1996, Al-Furat began a five-year production cutback schedule of 10,000 BBL per day annually, but production has fallen even faster. Production from fields run by the SPC peaked in the late 1970s at more than 165,000 BBL per day.

Syria's economic reforms have either failed or moved too slowly in virtually every respect, and oil is no exception. Oil exploration activity in Syria has been slow in recent years due to unattractive contract terms by the SPC, and poor exploration results. For these reasons, only four companies (Elf, Shell, Deminex, and Marathon) out of fourteen operating in the country in 1991 remain in Syria at present. Since June 1996, when Mohammed Maher Jamal, a geologist, replaced Nader al-Nabulsi as minister of oil and mineral wealth (as part of an anticorruption drive), exploration has picked up somewhat, although drilling activities are limited to a small number of companies. In November 1997 a new 12,000-BBL per day oil well ("Al-Kashmeh") began production near the Syrian-Iraqi border. The well represents a joint venture between the SPC and the Irish company Tullow. In October 1998, however, Tullow withdrew its concession and closed operations in Syria, citing reduced oil revenues due to low oil prices. Similarly, officials at TotalFinaElf announced their intentions to scale back their Syrian operations in May 2002, and ConocoPhilips announced in February 2004 that it was ending its operations in Syria.[141]

Only about 36 percent of the country's estimated 800 potential oil and gas structures have been drilled. No major new oil reserves have been discovered since 1992. Without significant new discoveries in the next few years, Syrian and foreign oil company officials (including Shell, the main foreign operator) believe that the country could become a net oil importer as early as 2005. The last time Syria was a net oil importer was in 1987 (Syria bought from Iraq until April 1982, when it switched to Iran as an ally and oil supplier and closed the 1.1–1.4 MBBL per day capacity IPC pipeline from Kirkuk to Banias). The Syrian government has reacted and the Syrian Petroleum Company decided to launch a new round of oil exploration licenses in early January 2004. Ten oil blocks are opened to international oil companies for exploration.[142]

Syria markets all of its crude oil, including that produced by foreign companies, through its state marketing company Sytrol. Prices for Syrian Light and Suwaidiyah blends are tied to the price of dated Brent and are adjusted monthly. At present, Sytrol has term contracts with more than twenty companies, including Agip, Bay Oil, ChevronTexaco, ConocoPhilips, Marc Rich, OeMV, Royal Dutch Shell, TotalFinaElf, and Veba.

Syrian Energy Export Routes

Syria's major oil export terminals are at Banias and Tartous on the Mediterranean, with a small tanker terminal at Latakia. Banias can accommodate tankers up to 210,000 DWT, and has a storage capacity of 437,000 tons of oil in 19 tanks. Tartous can take tankers up to 100,000 DWT, and is connected via a pipeline to the Banias terminal. Latakia can handle oil tankers up to 50,000 DWT. The Syrian Company for Oil Transport (SCOT), a sister of the SPC, operates all three terminals.

SCOT is also in charge of Syria's pipelines. Main internal pipelines are: (1) a 250,000 BBL per day export pipeline from SPC's northeastern fields to the Tartous terminal with a connection to the Homs refinery; (2) a 500,000 ton per year refined products pipeline system linking Homs refinery to Damascus, Aleppo, and Latakia; (3) a 100,000 BBL per day spur line from Al-Thayyem and other fields to the T-2 pumping station on the old Iraqi Petroleum Company (IPC) pipeline; (4) a spur line from the Al-Ashara and Al-Ward fields to the T-2 pumping station.

A thaw in relations between Iraq and Syria before the Iraq War led Iraq to export oil once again through the IPC pipeline in Syria. On July 14, 1998, Syria and Iraq signed a memorandum of understanding on reopening the pipeline. Both the Iraqi and Syrian sections of the IPC pipeline were reportedly ready for operation in early March 2000. While Syria was using parts of it to transport its own crude oil to Mediterranean terminals, the UN will have to approve any Iraq oil exports through Syria.[143]

Syrian Natural Gas Development

Syria's proven natural gas reserves are estimated at 8.5 trillion cubic feet, which does not equal even 0.1 percent of the world supply, and are located mainly in eastern Syria, while population is centered in western and southern Syria. Most (73 percent) of these reserves are owned by the SPC, and approximately 54 percent of the country's gas production is associated gas.[144] In, 2002, Syria produced about 205 billion cubic feet of natural gas, a slight decline from the 213 BCF produced in 2000.[145] In 1998, Syria produced about 208 billion cubic feet of natural gas, an approximately five-fold increase over the past decade. It plans to increase this production even further in coming years, as part of a strategy to substitute natural gas for oil in power generation in order to free up as much oil as possible for export. A number of new gas-fired power projects are currently under construction or being planned.

The Syrian government has enacted a new law to establish the Syrian Gas Company (SGC). The company will be an independent public company, and will take over all gas-related responsibilities and operations that have been handled by the state owned Syrian Petroleum Company.[146]

The SPC currently is working to increase Syria's gas production through several projects. The Palmyra area in central Syria is the site of much of this activity, including development of the Al-Arak gas field, which came on-stream at the end of 1995. Two other "sweet gas" fields in Palmyra include Al-Hail and Al-Dubayat, both of which came online in 1996, while two "sour gas" fields—Najib and Sokhne—began production during 1998. Syria may, however, have somewhat larger reserves than most current estimates. The Syrian Petroleum Company is expected to award contracts for a $750–800 million project to develop the nonassociated gas fields in the Palmyra region. Syria declared that it would give its decision by the end of January 2004. At least five major international oil companies submitted their bids for the contract, including a joint venture between Total (France), Sumitomo Corporation (Japan), and Japex (Japan), as well as Occidental Petroleum Corporation (United States), PetroCanada, and Petrofac International. The project is planned to produce 9 million cubic meters a day of gas for domestic consumption and to supply the Lebanese market.[147] In early 2004, Syria will start exporting 1.5 million cubic meters per day of gas to Lebanon under an agreement signed in late 2001.[148] In addition, Syria signed agreements with Egypt, Jordan, and Lebanon in early 2001 for an onshore pipeline network that would connect the four. An agreement was signed in January 2004 among the respective countries for the extension of the pipeline from Egypt to northern Jordan into Lebanon through Syria. However, the construction had not begun as of April 2004.[149]

Syrian Energy Risk

Syria remains a dictatorship under Bashir Asad, and has made little progress in serious economic reform although it is trying to create a climate that can attract more foreign investment. Syria is also seeking to improve its relations with the European Union (EU) and to join the WTO. So far, however, early hopes that Bashir would offer political and economic reform after he succeeded his father on June 10, 2000, have produced cosmetic results at best. There has been some improvement in the banking industry, but scarcely enough. Privatization efforts have been replaced with ineffective efforts to make public companies more efficient, and the private sector remains crippled by over regulation and an administrative jungle. The government remains repressive in terms of politics, the economy, and human rights and faces a massive demographic challenge in terms of employment and raising per capita income.

Syria faces a continuing risk of involvement in the Arab-Israeli conflict, and is treated as a sponsor of terrorism by the United States. The present instability of Iraq compounds Syria's problems. Until Syria achieves significant political and economic reform, it will remain a moderate energy risk.

Jordan

Jordan has no meaningful oil resources of its own, and its importance in Middle Eastern energy is largely political. Jordan has relied on Iraqi oil for most of its needs (around 106,000 barrels per day in 2002).[150] Jordan's oil imports from Iraq before the Iraq War were worth around $500 million, and were permitted by the United Nations under a special dispensation from the general UN embargo on Iraq. Jordan has discussed the possibility of reducing this dependence by importing oil from Saudi Arabia and Kuwait, but no agreements have been concluded. The United States has been active in encouraging any move by Jordan away from Iraqi oil.

There are possibilities that Jordan's energy status could change. In February 1998, Jordan signed an agreement with Shell Oil to extract crude oil from the country's abundant (possibly as high as 40 billion tons) oil shale resources, but later dropped the project. Canada's Suncor conducts limited exploration digging in the Lajjun area, southwest of Amman. Jordan has looked into burning oil shale directly to generate electricity. Several tests of the physical and chemical characteristics of Jordan's shale oil resources have shown them to be of high quality. Other features of the shale oil include the likelihood of relatively easy mining due to a small overburden (the amount of dirt and rock), as well as proximity to water sources and other necessary infrastructure. The economics of these ventures, however, are tenuous unless substantial rises continue in world oil prices.

If Iraq does reemerge as a stable supplier to Jordan, it may construct a pipeline. In 1998, Jordan and Iraq agreed on construction of a joint oil pipeline with an initial capacity of 100,000 BBL per day. Such a pipeline would have considerable value to Jordan because it now receives nearly all its oil from Iraq, via 1,500 of tanker trucks. These trucks cost Jordan an estimated $60 million per year in damaged roads, traffic, and environmental damages. The proposed 400-mile, $250–300 million pipeline would carry oil from Iraq to the existing Zarqa refinery northeast of Amman, as well as to the new refinery in Aqaba.[151] What is not clear is whether a new Iraqi government will have the same incentive to subsidize Jordanian oil that Saddam Hussein's government had while Iraq was under sanctions.

Jordan's state Natural Resources Authority (NRA) has been promoting exploration within the country, which has been relatively unexplored until now. In October 1995, the NRA signed agreements with Malaysia's Petronas and Houston-based Trans-Global Petroleum for possible exploration of northern and central Jordan. To help attract foreign investment, the Jordanian government has plans to privatize its oil sector. In October 1995, the country set up the state-owned National Petroleum Co. (NPC) to handle upstream oil and gas exploration and development. The intent is for the NPC to operate as independently as possible, and eventually to be privatized.

It is unlikely that any of these developments will make Jordan a major energy producer, but the U.S. Department of Energy estimates that Jordan might become a major center for oil exports. It feels that a comprehensive settlement of the Arab-Israeli conflict could affect Middle East oil flows significantly because Jordan's geographic location between the Arabian peninsula and the Mediterranean coastal states of Israel and Lebanon offers a potential alternative route for exports of Gulf oil to the West. At present, these oil exports must travel either by ship (through the Suez Canal or around the horn of Africa), by pipeline from Iraq to Turkey (capacity 0.8–1.6 million BBL per day), or via the Sumed (Suez-Mediterranean) Pipeline (capacity 2.4 million BBL per day).

Utilization of the Trans-Arabian Pipeline (Tapline) could offer another potentially economic alternative. The Tapline was originally constructed in the 1940s with a capacity of 500,000 BBL per day, and was intended as the main means of exporting Saudi oil to the West (via Jordan to the port of Haifa, then part of Palestine, now a major Israeli port city). The establishment of the state of Israel resulted in the diversion of the Tapline's terminal from Haifa to Sidon, Lebanon (through Syria and Lebanon). Partly as a result of turmoil in Lebanon, and partly for economic reasons, oil exports via the Tapline were halted in 1975. In 1983, the Tapline's Lebanese section was closed altogether. Since then, the Tapline has been used exclusively to supply oil to Jordan, although Saudi Arabia terminated this arrangement to display displeasure with perceived Jordanian support for Iraq in the 1990–1991 Gulf crisis.

Jordan is also a potential customer for Egyptian gas. The Jordanian government awarded a contract in June 1998, to build a 170-mile natural gas pipeline from fields in Egypt's Nile Delta region across the Sinai and under the Red Sea to Aqaba. In July 2003, King Abdullah and Hosni Mubarak inaugurated the Egyptian portion of the Egypt-Jordan pipeline that reached to the Jordanian port Aqaba. The gas is to be used as a replacement for the diesel and fuel oil now used to generate electricity. Construction began on the Jordan section of pipeline, which will be 393 kilometers long. The project is a part of a greater interregional project to export Egyptian gas to Jordan and then to Syria and Lebanon by 2006.[152]

Jordan is not a significant player in world energy supply, and has little impact on energy risk. It does, however, face serious demographic and economic pressures, and may not receive low-cost energy supply from Iraq in the future. Coupled to the problems created by the Israeli-Palestinian conflict, risk is moderate to high.

Israel

Israel now depends almost exclusively on imports to meet its energy needs. Israel has attempted to diversify its supply sources and to utilize alternatives like solar and wind energy. In general, however, Israel has relied on expensive, long-term contracts with nations like Mexico (oil), Norway (oil), the United Kingdom (oil), Australia (coal), South Africa (coal), and Colombia (coal) for its energy supplies. It currently imports about 300,000 barrels of oil per day.[153]

Improved relations with the Arab world encouraged Israel to pursue other, cheaper sources, particularly Egypt, before the collapse of the peace process in September 2000. In 1997, Israel received about 20 percent of its oil supplies from Egypt, although this share has reportedly fallen since. In November 1998, then–national infrastructure minister Ariel Sharon said that the major decision on Israel's energy supply for the twenty-first century had been delayed by one year. This allowed more time to secure supply sources for natural gas, Israel's preferred fuel for several reasons (including environmental and financial), as opposed to coal. Israel hopes to significantly expand (to 25 percent) natural gas in its energy mix by 2005.[154]

Israeli Dependence on Oil Imports

The Israeli energy sector remains largely nationalized and state-regulated, ostensibly for national security reasons. Little progress on energy sector privatization has been made since the late 1980s, when Paz Oil Company (the largest of three main oil-marketing companies in Israel) and Naphtha Israel Petroleum (an oil and gas exploration firm) were sold to private investors.

Israel has virtually no oil output. Oil exploration in Israel itself has not proven successful in the past (current Israeli oil output is less than 1,000 barrels per day), although drilling is being stepped up. Oil was discovered near the Dead Sea town of Arad in August 1996, and is currently flowing at the rate of about 600 barrels per day.

In the future, Israel might have more importance as an oil shipment route. The U.S. Department of Energy estimates that a comprehensive settlement of the Arab-Israeli conflict could significantly affect Middle East oil flows.

Israel's geographic location between the Arabian Peninsula and the Mediterranean Sea offers the potential for an alternative oil export route for Persian Gulf oil to the West. At present, these oil exports must travel either by ship (through the Suez Canal or around the horn of Africa), by pipeline from Iraq to Turkey (capacity 1–1.2 million BBL per day), or via the Sumed (Suez-Mediterranean) Pipeline (capacity 2.5 million BBL per day).

Utilization of the Trans-Arabian Pipeline (Tapline) offers another potentially economic alternative. The Tapline was originally constructed in the 1940s with a capacity of 500,000 BBL per day, and intended as the main means of exporting Saudi oil to the West (via Jordan to the port of Haifa, then part of Palestine, now a major Israeli port city). The establishment of the state of Israel resulted in the diversion of the Tapline's terminus from Haifa to Sidon, Lebanon (through Syria and Lebanon).

Partly as a result of turmoil in Lebanon, oil exports via the Tapline were halted in 1975. In 1983, the Tapline's Lebanese section was closed altogether. Since then, the Tapline has been used exclusively to supply oil to Jordan, although Saudi Arabia terminated this arrangement to display displeasure with perceived Jordanian support for Iraq in the 1990–1991 Gulf War. Despite these problems, the Tapline remains an attractive export route for Persian Gulf oil exports to Europe and the United States. At least one analysis indicates that oil exports via the Tapline through Haifa to Europe would cost as much as 40 percent less than shipping by tanker through the Suez Canal.

The Iraq War might also affect Israel's energy supplies, if a new Iraqi government establishes good relations with Israel—a questionable assumption. The EIA reports that there has been discussion of "reopening" the old oil pipeline from Mosul in northern Iraq to Haifa. This pipeline was built in the 1930s, and carried 100,000 BBL per day at its peak, but has been closed since Israel's establishment in 1948. The new regime in Iraq, however, has sparked Israeli interest in importing Iraqi oil from the Kirkuk field for use in the Haifa refinery.[155] This may or may not be prove feasible. (The Iraqi section of the pipeline is completely rusted and the Jordanian section was sold as scrap metal several years ago.) It would require hundreds of millions of dollars to repair/rebuild, even if this was politically feasible. Jordan has also strongly denied any interest in rebuilding the pipeline at the present time, stating that "the pipeline no longer exists in Jordanian territory."[156]

Israel now has only one main operational oil pipeline, known as the "Tipline," built in 1968 to ship Iranian oil from the Red Sea port of Eilat to Haifa (via the Mediterranean port of Ashkelon). As of March 2003, the Eilat-Ashkelon Pipeline Company (EAPC) reportedly was working to reverse flows on the 1.2-million-BBL-per-day line, so that oil would run from the Mediterranean to Eilat. Russia's Tyumen Oil Company reportedly was interested in the possibility of pumping Russian crude leaving Black Sea ports through the Israeli line to Eilat, where it could be loaded onto tankers for shipment to markets in Asia.

Israeli and Palestinian Gas Development

Israel has looked seriously at importing gas from several countries. Israel and Egypt, for instance, have discussed a possible "peace pipeline" to transport large volumes of Egyptian natural gas across the Sinai Peninsula (or alternatively, under water) directly to Israel. Whether or not this deal will ever take place, however, is complicated by several factors, both economic and political. For one, Egypt has shown signs that it places higher priority on Turkey as a potential customer. In December 1996, Egypt signed a deal with Turkey making it the most important market for Egyptian gas exports, and raising suspicions that Egypt would abandon its "peace pipeline" to Israel. Israel has also considered natural gas supplies from non–Middle Eastern sources, such as Russia, though a pipeline would be expensive. LNG supplies from Algeria, Australia, Nigeria, Norway, and Qatar also have been discussed, with a possible LNG regasification facility to be built in shallow waters offshore of Ashkelon, Israel. Such a plant would also be expensive.

Israel's need for such gas imports may, however, be sharply diminishing. During 1999–2002, several energy companies (Israel's Yam Thetis group, Isramco, BG, and U.S.-based Samedan) had discovered significant amounts of natural gas off the coast of Israel (and even more off the Gaza Strip). Initial estimates of 3–5 trillion cubic feet in proven reserves would be enough potentially to supply Israeli demand for years, even without natural gas imports, although this now seems optimistic.[157]

Israel's new offshore gas reserves belong mainly to two groups: (1) the Yam Thetis group (comprising the Avner Oil, Delek Drilling, and Noble Affiliates' Samedan subsidiary); and (2) a BG partnership with Isramco and others. In August 2000, Isramco/BG announced that it had discovered a large gas field 12 miles offshore at its Nir-1 well. The field reportedly contains gas reserves of 274 BCF, and represents the third gas field discovered offshore Israel during 2000 (the largest two being Mary and Noa, with combined reserves of nearly 1.5 TCF). In early September 2001, Isramco announced that BG was abandoning the Tommy, Orly, Shira, and Aya concessions after analyzing geological and geophysical findings.

Gas has also been discovered in areas that lie in Palestinian territorial waters off the Gaza Strip. The EIA reports that British Gas, which first struck gas in this area with its Gaza Marine-1 well in August 1999, has signed a twenty-five-year contract to explore for gas and set up a gas network in the Palestinian Authority. In December 2000, BG successfully completed drilling a second gas well offshore Gaza. The drilling confirmed findings from the Marine-1 well, which had flowed at 37 million cubic feet per day, indicating possible reserves of around 1.4 TCF. BG plans to invest $400 million in its offshore Gaza gas finds, which could be used to supply Israel, along with other sources. These plans, however, have so far been blocked by the Israeli government. The exact reasons are not clear but may include a desire to deny the Palestinians the funding or to use the gas deal as a political lever.

Israeli Energy Risk

Israel is actively at war with the Palestinians, is subject to constant terrorist attacks, and could see its present structure escalate to include other Arab states. Near- and midterm energy risks are high.

North Africa

North Africa's energy exports do not approach the strategic and economic importance of the Gulf, but it does play a major role in supporting European markets and its exports have a far greater impact than their size as a percentage of world exports would otherwise indicate. BP estimates that Algeria had a total of 9.2 billion barrels worth of reserves in 2002 (0.9 percent of world holdings), Libya had 29.5 billion barrels (2.8 percent), and Tunisia had 0.3 billion (less than 0.5 percent). This was a total of 39.0 billion barrels or 3.7 percent of total world supply.[158]

Algerian oil production slowly increased from average annual levels of 1.3 MMBD in 1992 to 1.6 MMBD in 2002. It averaged 1.659 MMBD in 2002, or 2.0 percent of world production. Libyan oil production decreased from average annual level of 1.47 MMBD in 1992 to 1.38 MMBD in 2002: 1.8 percent of world production. The limits to Libyan production were in part the result of UN sanctions. Tunisia declined from annual levels of 110,000 barrels a day in 1992 to 76,000 in 2002: 0.1 percent of world production.[159]

If these figures are combined, the EIA reports that North Africa had a total production capacity of 2.8 MMBD in 1990 and 3.3 MMBD in 2001—about 4.2 percent of world capacity. The EIA reference case estimate indicates that North African production capacity will rise to 3.4 MMBD in 2005, and projects a range of 3.2–3.5 MMBD in its low and high oil price scenarios. The figures are 4.0 (3.5–4.2) MMBD for 2010, 4.3 (3.8–4.7) MMBD for 2015, 5.0 (4.45–5.3) MMBD for 2020, and 5.7 (4.6–6.1) MMBD for 2025. In 2025, North Africa will account for an estimated 4.5 percent of world production capacity, according to the EIA reference case estimate.[160]

The fact that Europe is North Africa's major customer is indicated by the fact that BP reports that North Africa exported 2.62 MMBD of petroleum per day in 2002. Some 1.77 MMBD went to Europe, 283,000 went to the United States, 116,000 barrels to Asian and Pacific states, and 103,000 barrels went to Canada. Exports to other regions averaged less than 100,000 barrels.

The EIA estimates that North African oil exports totaled 2.6 MMBD in 2001, or 4.6 percent of the world total. The EIA projects that this total will be grow to 4.8 MMBD in 2025, or 5 percent of the world total.[161] This is a far smaller level of energy exports than from the Gulf. Nevertheless, North Africa will still be an important part of the world market, and its exports will remain of major importance to Europe. North African exports will also be large in comparison with most other regions. The EIA estimates that by 2025, North Africa's exports will slightly exceed the estimated total exports of West Africa (4.7 MMBD), the Caribbean Basin (4.5 MMBD), the North Sea (4.3 MMBD), and Asia (2.1 MMBD). They will be only marginally smaller than the exports from Latin America (5.4 MMBD), and roughly half the combined total of Russia, Central Asia, and the Caspian (9.9 MMBD).[162]

North Africa also is a major gas exporter. BP estimates that Algeria had a total of 4.52 trillion cubic meters or 159.7 trillion cubic feet of gas reserves in 2002 (2.9 percent of world holdings), Libya had 1.31 trillion cubic meters or 46.4 trillion cubic feet (0.8 percent), and Tunisia had negligible reserves. This is a total of 5,83 trillion cubic meters or 206.1 trillion cubic feet—3.7 percent of total world supply.[163] North Africa serves key markets in Southern Europe, and North Africa is also an important gas exporter to Europe.[164]

Algerian gas production increased from average annual levels of 55.2 billion cubic meters in 1992 to 80.4 billion cubic meters in 2002: 3.2 percent of world production. Libyan gas production decreased from average annual levels of 6.1 billion cubic meters in 1992 to 5.7 billion cubic meters in 2002: 3.2 percent of world production. The limits to Libyan production were in part the result of UN sanctions.[165] As is the case for other regions, the rare no EIA or IEA projections of gas exports that match the projections of petroleum exports.

The fact that Morocco, Algeria, Libya, and Tunisia make up much of the southern coast of the Mediterranean gives them added strategic importance to Europe. So does the problem posed by emigration from these countries to nations like France, Spain, and Italy. The end of the Cold War has largely ended the regional arms race and much of the terrorist threat from Libya, but many Europeans see internal instability in North Africa as posing a much more tangible future demographic threat than the region ever posed during the Cold War.

Both Algeria and Libya have serious internal stability problems. There is no way to know how long the political crisis and civil war in Algeria will last, or whether the low-level Islamic uprisings in Libya will ever reach more serious levels of civil conflict. Furthermore, it is possible that political unrest in Egypt might add a new North African dimension in terms of a threat to oil movements through the Suez Canal and Sumed pipeline.

- Chart 4.3 shows the EIA reference case projection of the increases in North African oil production during 2001–2025, and provides an illustrative projection of possible oil interruption scenarios.

Chart 4.3
Estimated North African Oil Production Capacity

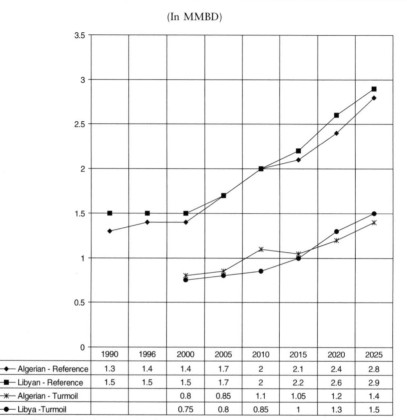

(In MMBD)

	1990	1996	2000	2005	2010	2015	2020	2025
◆ Algerian - Reference	1.3	1.4	1.4	1.7	2	2.1	2.4	2.8
■ Libyan - Reference	1.5	1.5	1.5	1.7	2	2.2	2.6	2.9
✳ Algerian - Turmoil			0.8	0.85	1.1	1.05	1.2	1.4
● Libya -Turmoil			0.75	0.8	0.85	1	1.3	1.5

Source: Adapted by Anthony H. Cordesman from EIA, *International Energy Outlook 1998*, DOE/EIA-0484 (1997), p. 239; *International Energy Outlook 2002*, June 2002, DOE/EIA-0484 (2002) p. 239; and *International Energy Outlook 2003*, June 2003, DOE/EIA-0484 (2003), p. 235.

- Chart 4.4 projects total North African oil exports, showing that Europe remains a dominant market.

Algeria

Algeria is a deeply troubled country that has been in a political and economic crisis since the late 1980s, and that began a brutal civil war in 1992, after the country's ruling military junta nullified a popular election that promised to bring the Islamic Salvation Party to power. The war has cost over 100,000 lives, but has largely been won by the junta, and there have been efforts at reform.[166]

Chart 4.4
Estimated North African Oil Exports: 2000–2025

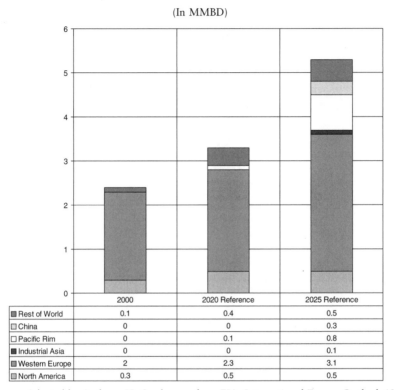

(In MMBD)

	2000	2020 Reference	2025 Reference
■ Rest of World	0.1	0.4	0.5
☐ China	0	0	0.3
☐ Pacific Rim	0	0.1	0.8
■ Industrial Asia	0	0	0.1
■ Western Europe	2	2.3	3.1
☐ North America	0.3	0.5	0.5

Source: Adapted by Anthony H. Cordesman from EIA, *International Energy Outlook 1998*, DOE/EIA-0484 (1997), April 1998, pp. 175–177; *International Energy Outlook 2002*, June 2002, DOE/EIA-0484 (2002), p. 38; *International Energy Outlook 2003*, June 2003, DOE/EIA-0484 (2003), p. 42; and *International Energy Outlook 2004*, April 2004, DOE/EIA-0484 (2004), p. 40.

The junta arranged the elections of President Abdelaziz Bouteflika on April 15, 1999, for a five-year term. Bouteflika has since attempted to implement plans for national reconciliation and economic reforms like deregulation and privatization, often in ways that seem to create problems with the junta (a pattern of conflict between the junta and various presidents that has been a problem in Algerian politics for several decades). President Bouteflika offered amnesty to rebel groups on July 13, 1999. He then held a national referendum on September 16, and a large majority approved the offer. The government then claimed that nearly 80 percent of rebels (including members of the Islamic Salvation Army) accepted amnesty, but violence continued, and the most violent groups have carried out significant attacks.

President Bouteflika replaced Prime Minister Ahmed Benbitour with Ali Benflis in August 2002, and the FLN picked up significant strength in a May 2002 election. The FLN has since become divided, however, by tensions between the president and the former prime minister, and between the president and the army. President Bouteflika will stand for reelection in April 2004, and the result is uncertain.

Algeria has remained an important oil and gas state in spite of its civil war. Official estimates of Algeria's proven oil reserves remain at 11.3 billion barrels, but they are expected to rise significantly as a result of recent oil discoveries, plans for more exploration drilling, improved data on existing fields, and use of enhanced oil recovery systems. Algeria also has at least 160 TCF of gas reserves. Algeria's National Council of Energy believes that the country still contains vast hydrocarbon potential and the government and its state-owned Sonatrach have made major efforts in recent years to exploit this situation.

Algerian Oil Development

Algeria's Saharan Blend oil, 45° API with 0.05 percent sulfur and negligible metal content, is among the best in the world. Algeria's has a reserve to production ratio of 18:8.[167] The EIA estimates that Algeria produced an average of 1.75 million barrels a day in 1990, 1.16 million in 1993, 1.20 million in 1995, 1.28 million in 1997, and 1.4 million in 2000. Algeria's crude oil production quota was set at 782,000 BBL per day as of November 1, 2003, significantly below the country's crude oil production capacity of 1.2 million BBL per day. The EIA estimates that Algeria produced an average of 1.86 million barrels per day (BBL per day) in 2003, of which 1.17 million BBL per day was crude oil, 0.45 million BBL per day was lease condensates, and 0.25 million BBL per day was natural gas liquids. Domestic oil was 1.65 million BBL per day.[168]

The U.S. Department of Energy estimates that Algeria will increase its oil production capacity from 1.6 MMBD in 2001 to 1.7 million barrels per day in 2005, 2.0 million barrels per day in 2010, 2.1 million barrels per day in 2015, 2.4 million barrels per day in 2020, and 2.8 million barrels per day in 2020.[169]

Algeria plans to increase its crude oil exports over the next few years by making a rapid shift toward domestic natural gas consumption and through increases in oil production by Sonatrach and its foreign partners. Approximately 90 percent of Algeria's crude oil exports go to Western Europe, with Italy as the main market followed by Germany and France. The Netherlands, Spain, and Britain are other important European markets. The United States makes up a significant portion of the remaining 10 percent of Algerian crude exports.[170]

There have been significant oil and gas discoveries during the last six years, largely by foreign companies. Under a government program first launched in April 1996, Sonatrach and its foreign partners attempted—with only some success—to increase Algeria's crude oil production to 1.5 million barrels per day by 2000. The program included provisions for 300 exploration wells to be drilled between 1996 and 2000, half by Sonatrach and the other half by foreign companies. In 1998 the resulting efforts led to fifteen new discoveries by some nineteen different international oil companies.[171]

Sonatrach and its partners will drill over 200 exploration wells and will invest $20.8 billion, of which some $16.4 billion is intended for field development in the period between 2000 and 2005. Sonatrach will be responsible for 54.8 percent of the $20.8 billion estimated cost, while the foreign partners will account for 30.5 percent and Sonatrach and the partners will jointly share the remaining 14.7 percent.[172]

The largest foreign investor is the Anadarko Petroleum Company of the United States. Its production is now only 300,000 BBL per day, but it hopes to raise production to as much as 500,000 BBL per day by 2005. In the last decade, Anadarko has discovered fourteen fields in Algeria with reserves totaling more than 2 billion barrels.[173] In January 1999, Oryx Energy Company signed a five-year, $28.8 million exploration deal with Sonatrach. Oryx will carry out seismic and drilling activities in the Timissit area of southeastern Algeria. In September 2003, Petrobas (Brazil) signed a contract with Sonatrach to explore for oil in Algeria. A similar contract was also signed by Algeria and China's CNPC.[174]

The French firm Elf (now TotalFinaElf) returned to Algeria in 1999 for the first time since 1971 by buying a 40 percent stake in Arco Rhourde al-Baguel field, with an eventual production capacity estimated at 120,000 BBL per day.[175] AmeradaHess and Sonatrach announced a joint company merger in 2000 to be called Sonahess. This joint operating company merger will invest $500 million over five years to enhance recovery from 30,000 to 45,000 BBL per day. In 2002, Sonatrach agreed to six new exploration contracts.[176]

The current OPEC quota for Algeria is 782,000 million barrels per day. The Algerian government has been demanding from OPEC to increase its quota in line with the country's production capacity increases, which reached 1.2 MMBD at the end of 2003, will hit 1.5 MMBD by 2005, and 2.0 MMBD by 2010.[177]

Algerian Gas Development

Algeria ranks among the top ten nations in the world in terms of proven gas reserves, with 160 trillion cubic feet or 2.5 percent of the world supply. It accounted for one-fifth of EU's natural gas imports in 2000. The EIA estimates that Algeria produced 2.84 TCF in 2003, consumed 0.79 TCF, and exported 2.05 TCF.[178]

The ratio of its proven gas reserves to annual production is 50.7 percent.[179] Sonatrach estimates that Algeria's ultimate gas potential is around 204 TCF, of which 135.5 TCF is recoverable. Algerian officials indicated that natural gas production will reach 166 BCM by 2004, up from the current level of 125 BCM.[180] Algeria's largest gas field is the supergiant Hassi R'Mel, which initially held probable and possible reserves of 95–105 TCF and proven reserves of about 85 TCF. Hassi R'Mel produces 1.35 BCF per day, one-fourth of Algeria's total dry gas production.

Algeria has had a long-standing policy to develop its gas reserves as a source of domestic energy and as a raw material for the petrochemical industry. As of mid-1997, approximately 95 percent of the country's electricity was generated by gas.

Algeria currently has four LNG plants, with a design capacity of 2.95 BCF per day. Sonatrach's total upgrading program has boosted the country's LNG capacity to 3.29 BCF per day. Algeria is a leading gas exporter, exporting 60 billion cubic meters a year, and almost all of its exports go to Europe.[181] Algeria has special strategic importance, however, because its pipelines allow it to ship gas directly to Europe. These gas pipelines could also suddenly take on far more importance if any disruption took place in Russia's gas exports.

Algeria's natural gas pipeline export capacity of 1.38 trillion cubic feet per year includes 988.6 billion cubic feet per year via the Transmed pipeline to Italy and 300.2 BCF per year via the new Maghreb-Europe Gas (MEG) line to Spain and beyond to Portugal via an extension. As of 2002 Algeria's total natural gas export capacity was over 2 TCF per year, and it's expected to raise to 3 TCF per year or more by 2010.[182]

The 667-mile Transmed pipeline links the Hassi R'Mel gas field to Mazzara del Vallo in Sicily. Transmed comprises segments through Algeria (342 miles), Tunisia (230 miles), under the Mediterranean (96 miles) to Sicily, and then on to Slovenia. The Hassi R'Mel-Oued Saf-Saf link to the Tunisia border originally consisted of two parallel 48-inch lines. With the signing of a revised gas supply contract, however, the three international links have been augmented with several 48-inch and 24-inch lines as well as at least four compressor stations.

Until recently, the Algerian segment of the Transmed pipeline had a slightly higher capacity (1.5 BCF per day) than the Tunisia-Italy link (1.15 BCF per day). Most of the gas from this line is taken by Italy's main gas utility Snam, which is under contract to buy 680 BCF per year from 1997 until 2018. Tunisia purchases about 39 BCF per year, with 14 BCF per year committed until 2020 under a deal signed in March 1997, and the rest bought on spot basis and in lieu of transit fees. Slovenia's Sozd Petrol is committed to 21 BCF per year until 2007 under a contract signed in January 1990. Petroleum Economist reports that Algeria plans to expand the capacity of the Transmed line by 212 BCF per year.[183]

The 1,013-mile, $2.5 billion MEG pipeline was jointly financed by Sonatrach and Spain's Enagas, the line's main customers. MEG is made up of five sections: 324 miles from Hassi R'Mel to the Moroccan border, 326 miles from Morocco to the Strait of Gibraltar, 28 miles across the strait at a depth of 1,312 feet, 168 miles from the Spanish coast to Cordoba, Spain, where it ties into the Spanish transmission network, and 168 miles to Portugal. The Algerian section of MEG was built by U.S.-based Bechtel and consists of a 48-inch line with a design capacity of 695 million cubic feet per day.

In late 2001, Spain's Cepsa and Algeria's Sonatrach agreed to install a new natural gas pipeline, the Medgaz, linking Algeria directly to Spain. It will have a capacity of 7 BCM per year when it opens in 2005. The capacity is projected to increase to 16 BCM per year by 2020.[184] In September 2002, the consortium of partner companies completed a study of the line's feasibility, but the construction did not start in 2003 as had been expected. Sonatrach signed another deal in 2001 with Italy's Enel and Germany's Wintershall on a possible natural gas pipeline running from Algeria under the Mediterranean Sea to Sicily and onward through Italy to France.[185] In 2002, Sonatrach and BP signed a deal to develop natural gas production in the in Amenas region. This $1.8 billion deal is projected to go online in 2005 and is expected to produce around 900 million cubic feet per day of "wet" natural gas.[186] These efforts are part of four major Algerian pipeline projects, and one Libyan project that are helping to increase the impact of Algerian gas exports along with the growth of LNG production and exports:[187]

Pipeline	Origin–Destination	Capacity	Length (km.)	Year	Cost ($ billions)
GME	Algeria–Spain via Morocco	expansion (+3)	1,620	2004	0.2
Medgas	Algeria–Spain	8	1,100	2006	1.4
Galsi	Algeria–Italy	8	1,470	2008	2.0
Trans-Saharan	Algeria–Nigeria	10	4,000	After 2010	7.0
Green Stream	Libya–Italy	8	540	2005	1.0

Algerian Energy Risk

Energy development is still the only sector of Algeria's government that operates efficiently, and it has been under sporadic attack as the result of Algeria's civil war. While the struggle between Algeria's corrupt military junta and vicious Islamic extremists seems to have shifted in the government's favor, Algeria's civil government also remains far too much of a façade, hiding de facto rule by military leaders.

Economic reform is weak and falling far behind population growth and Algeria's "youth explosion." The EIA estimates that unemployment is officially around 30 percent, but is probably much higher, and is estimated at around 50 percent for the "under-thirty" age group. There is violence by Islamic fundamentalists and serious labor unrest; and the economy relies on a large black market that the EIA estimates may be as large as 20 percent of the country's GDP.

Algeria has made some progress. Algeria signed a cooperation pact with the European Free Trade Association in December that encouraged expanded and liberalized trade with EFTA members (Iceland, Liechtenstein, Norway, and Switzerland). In late 2001, Algeria and the EU reached an association agreement, and the deal was ratified by the European Parliament in October 2002. Under the accord, Algeria is to cut tariffs on EU agricultural and industrial products over the next ten years. In exchange, the EU will eliminate duties and quotas on many Algerian agricultural products. Algeria is also pursuing membership in the World Trade Organization.

The EIA reports, however, that Algeria has made little progress in the structural reforms and fiscal discipline it needs to compensate for fluctuating oil revenues and a steady long-term decline in per capita energy export revenues. The EIA is particularly negative in regard to Algeria's efforts to reform its energy sector:

> In January 2004, the International Monetary Fund (IMF) issued its annual "Article IV" assessment of the Algerian economy, urging that the government proceed with privatization and banking reform, while lowering tariffs aimed at protecting domestic industry and reducing dependence on hydrocarbons. The IMF praised the Algerian government for its strong macroeconomic discipline, while pointing out that high oil prices provide Algeria with an opportunity to make progress on implementing reforms and addressing the country's many problems.
>
> . . . To date, however, little progress in this regard appears to have been made. For instance, an important hydrocarbons reform bill, which among other things would "corporatize" state oil company Sonatrach, had gone nowhere.
>
> . . . In late 2001, an important new hydrocarbons reform bill was introduced, but progress stalled in 2002 and 2003. The bill would open Algeria's all-important energy sector to private (including foreign) investment, although state oil and gas company Sonatrach most likely would remain in public hands. The law faces opposition from trade unions and others, and already has been watered down somewhat from its original form, while Energy and Mines Minister Chekib Khelil has stated that "it is not necessary to privatize" Sonatrach. One study, by Bayphase, estimates that Algeria's oil and gas sectors will require total capital investment of $50–$73 billion over the next 10 years.

. . . In February 2003, a two-day strike among oil and gas workers was launched in protest of the proposed legislation. Algeria is scheduled to hold Presidential elections in April 2004, meaning that any new reform initiatives will probably have to wait until mid-2004. Meanwhile, it is likely that Algeria will pursue expansionary economic policies.

Short- and midterm energy risk are moderate to high.

Libya[188]

Libya's strategic importance lies largely in the fact that it is a significant energy exporter. Libya currently has twelve oil fields with reserves of 1 billion barrels or more and two others with reserves of 500 million to one billion barrels. The U.S. Department of Energy estimates that Libyan production capacity will gradually increase from 1.7 million barrels per day in 2005 to 2.0 million barrels per day in 2010, and 2.6 million barrels per day in 2020. Libya produces high-quality, low-sulfur ("sweet") crude oil at very low cost (as low as $1 per barrel at some fields).[189]

At the same time, Libya has been involved in five major clashes with the United States and has been under sanctions for major acts of terrorism. The worst was the 1988 bombing of Pan Am flight 103 over Lockerbie, Scotland, that killed 270 people. On April 15, 1992, the United Nations imposed economic sanctions on Libya for refusing to extradite two Libyan nationals accused of carrying out the bombing of Pan Am flight 103. These sanctions included the grounding of all air traffic to and from Libya, a reduction in diplomatic relations and a ban on all arms sales to the country.

The United States imposed additional sanctions on Libya on August 5, 1996. The U.S. Iran-Libya Sanctions Act (ILSA) of 1996 extends U.S. sanctions on Libya to cover foreign companies that make new investments of $40 million or more over a twelve-month period in Libya's oil or gas sectors. These sanctions were renewed for five years on July 27, 2001.

This situation is, however, being resolved and key issues like Libya's compensation for its acts of terrorism, putting an end to military adventures and its support of terrorism, and giving up its search for weapons of mass destruction seem to have been resolved.

President Qadhafi transferred two key suspects in the Lockerbie bombing on April 5, 1999. They stood trial in the Netherlands under Scottish law. In return for releasing the suspects, UN sanctions on Libya were suspended for ninety days, after which Secretary-General Annan reported to the Security Council on Libya's cooperation. Annan reported his findings on Libya to the Security Council on July 2, 1999. According to Annan's report, Libya has, so far, complied with the provisions set forth by the Security Council. In response, the United Nations suspended economic and other sanctions.

Libya has complied with the remaining requirements, including the compensation of victims' families after the guilty verdict in the Pan Am 103 trial. The United States continues to adopt a tough stance toward Libya, and British and French moves toward rapprochement with Libya further isolate the United States.[190] U.S. and Libyan talks have eased the tensions between the two countries, however, and Libya indicated in May 2002 that it would pay $2.7 billion to the families of the victims (about $10 million per family). France has also renegotiated its compensation agreement for the victims of Libya's attack on UTA flight 772, and has convicted six people in absentia for the crime. In late April 2003, Libya's foreign minister stated that Libya "has accepted civil responsibility for the actions of its officials in the Lockerbie affair." If Libya completes its claims settlements with the United States and France, all sanctions are likely to be lifted. The United States has already permitted some of its firms to negotiate with Libya in preparation for this event.

Relations between the United States and Libya are improving in other ways. The United States no longer estimates that Libya is a major source of terrorism. The claims over the destruction of Pan Am flight 103 seem to have been settled, and Libya declared in December 2003 that it would give up its programs for developing weapons of mass destruction and allow unconditional inspections. This has raised the hopes that the U.S. government will lift sanctions.[191]

Libyan Oil Development

The U.S. Department of Energy estimates that Libya's ability to increase its oil production (and exports) has been hampered by sanctions, mainly due to a ban on needed enhanced oil recovery equipment. Moreover, Libya's state-operated oil fields are undergoing a 7–8 percent natural decline rate, and Libya depends heavily on foreign companies and workers. Despite these problems, Libya generated $10.8 billion in oil export revenues in 2002 with a forecast of $12.9 billion in 2003. Nearly all (about 90 percent) of Libya's oil exports are sold to European countries like Italy (580,000 BBL per day in 1996), Germany (258,000 BBL per day), Spain, and Greece.

The EIA summarizes the present state of Libya's oil industry as follows:[192]

> Overall, Libya would like foreign companies help to increase the country's oil production capacity from 1.4 million bbl/d at present to 2 million bbl/d over the next five years, at a cost of perhaps $6 billion. This would restore Libya's oil production capacity to the level of the early 1970s. During the 1970s, the country's revolutionary government imposed tough terms on producing companies, leading to a slide in oil field investments and oil production. In May 2000, Libya invited around 50 foreign oil and gas companies to a meeting to discuss exploration and production sharing agreements. In order to achieve its oil sector goals, Libya will require as much as $10 billion in foreign investment through 2010. Around $6 billion of this is to go towards exploration and production, with the rest going towards refining and

petrochemicals. In addition, NOC has earmarked $1.5 billion for oil infrastructure investment. In January 2002, NOC appointed Abdel-Hafez Zleitni as its new chairman, with the specific mission to work on attracting foreign investment into the country's oil sector. Combined with the selection of reform-minded Prime Minister Shukri Ghanim, some privatization of the country's oil sector, particularly the downstream sector, now appears more likely than it has in the past.

The suspension of UN sanctions may offer Libya the means to revitalize its older fields. Sanctions have prevented the development of older fields run by NOC by banning the import of spare parts needed to maintain the fields and enhance production. Several fields operated by NOC affiliates are suffering from low pressure, which has held back production. The procurement of equipment for these fields is likely to be a priority. However, the situation is complicated by the fact that most of these fields were originally developed by U.S. firms and will need U.S.-manufactured spare parts.[193]

The decline in Libya's older fields has been offset by fresh discoveries by European operators. Spain's Repsol is now producing about 140,000 BBL per day in the Murzuk basin in the southwest, and announced discoveries in early 1999 that indicated potential reserves of 100–200 million barrels. British firm Lasmo is developing its Elephant discovery in the same region and is due to produce the first oil there in 2000, with output rising to 150,000 BBL per day in 2002. Other international groups active in the upstream oil sector include Italy's Agip, Canadian Occidental, Canada's Red Sea Oil Corporation, Dublin-based Bula Resources, and France's Elf Aquitaine.[194]

Oil export revenues account for about 95 percent of Libya's hard currency earnings. In 2000, oil production stood at 1.5 million BBL per day, down from over 3 million BBL per day in 1970. Libya would like to boost production by at least 1–1.5 MMBD, but sanctions have caused delays in a number of field development and enhanced oil recovery projects, as well as deterred foreign capital investment. Faced with a mature oil reserve base, Libya's challenge is to maintain production at older fields while at the same time bringing new fields online. Reserve replacement, however, has been slipping since the 1970s.

A lifting of the U.S. embargo would boost the country's current oil production, which is now about 1.4 million barrels per day. Several U.S. oil companies are eager to start operations in Libya, and the Libyan government wants to expand its exploration and production sharing agreements. Much of Libya remains unexplored and there are more than 90 exploration blocks on offer. The Libyan government intends to boost the oil production capacity beyond 2 million barrels per day by 2010.[195]

Libyan Gas Development

Sanctions have also affected Libyan gas production. The U.S. Department of Energy estimated Libya's proven natural gas reserves at 46.4 trillion cubic feet in 2003. Libya believes the country's actual gas reserves to be considerably larger, possibly 50–70 TCF. Large new discoveries have been made in the Ghadames and El-Bouri fields, as well as in the Sirte basin.

Continued expansion of gas production remains a high priority for Libya for two main reasons. First, Libya has aimed to use gas instead of oil domestically, freeing up more oil for export. Second, Libya is looking to increase its gas exports. Libya also produces a small amount of liquefied petroleum gas, most of which is consumed by domestic refineries. Natural gas consumption has been rising at a 10 percent annual rate since 1990. Besides gas used for injection into oil fields, most of this consumption has been by the petrochemical industry at Ras Lanuf, and by electric power sectors. In recent years, several power plants have switched from fuel oil to natural gas, and four new gas-powered plants have been built recently. The Department of Energy reports that considerable potential exists for a large increase in Libyan gas exports to Europe.

Agip has promoted linking the reserves of both Egypt and Libya to Italy by pipeline. An agreement in principle to link Egypt and Libya's gas grids was reached in June 1997, following a visit to Libya by Egyptian president Husni Mubarak. Yet another proposal is to build a pipeline from Egypt and Libya to Tunisia and Algeria, from where it would hook up with the existing pipeline to Morocco and Spain.

During the fist half of 2003, Libya produced nearly 1.5 million BBL per day, an increase from 2002 levels but still only two-fifths of the 3.3 million BBL per day produced in 1970. Libya aims to increase oil output capacity by 175,000 BBL per day in 2004 with the help of European companies. In spite of UN and U.S. sanctions, international oil companies have continued to explore Libyan fields, and UN sanctions were suspended in April 1999, after two of the suspects in the Lockerbie bombing were turned over for trial. Libya is courting foreign oil companies, which view Libya as an attractive oil province due to its low cost of oil recovery, its proximity to European markets, and its well-developed infrastructure.

The EIA estimates that Libyan oil production will gradually increase from 1.5 million barrels per day in 1990 to 1.7 million barrels per day in 2005, 2 million in 2010, 2.2 million in 2015, 2.6 million in 2020, and 2.9 million in 2025.[196]

Potential exists for a large increase in Libyan gas exports to Europe. A joint venture between Eni (Italy) and NOC (Italy) on the $4,500 million Western Libyan Gas Project (WLGP) is reportedly moving ahead. Eni and NOC will produce 30,000 million cubic meters a year of gas and 60,000 barrels per day of condensate by 2005.[197] The gas is to be delivered via a 370-mile underwater pipeline (called "Green Stream") under the Mediterranean to southeastern Sicily and the Italian mainland.[198]

Low energy prices and sanctions have delayed gas pipeline projects in the past, but this situation may begin to change. A 160-kilometer pipeline is planned between Homs and Tripoli, and Sirte Oil Company signed a $200 million contract with MAN Oil & Gas of Germany in 1998 to build a 142 kilometer pipeline between Zuetina and Benghazi.[199]

The suspension of UN sanctions in April 1999 has led to progress in Libya's natural gas export program. In October 1999, the Russian company Zarubezhneftegazstroi signed a $182 million contract to build a 117-kilometer section of Libya's Khums-Tripoli pipeline. Libya is planning the pipeline as a step toward a gas network that will eventually run across its entire territory and connect with both Tunisia and Egypt.

In 1971, Libya became the second country in the world (after Algeria in 1964) to export liquefied natural gas. Since then, Libya's LNG exports have been of little importance, largely due to technical limitations which do not allow Libya to extract LPG from the LNG, thereby forcing the buyer to do so. Libya's LNG plant, at Marsa El Brega, was built in the late 1960s by Esso and has a capacity of about 100 billion cubic feet per year, but due to technical limitations only about one-third of this is available for export, mainly to Enagas of Spain. The EIA reports that efforts to refurbish and upgrade the El Brega LNG plant in order to deal with the LPG separation problem have been delayed since 1992. If they were completed, the EIA estimates that Libyan LNG exports could triple.

Libyan Energy Risk

Libya is experiencing political and economic change. It has experienced economic growth over the past three years. Real gross domestic product grew by around 6.5 percent in 2000, 3.1 percent–4.3 percent in 2001 and 1.2 percent in 2002. Real GDP growth of 2.1 percent is expected in 2003, and inflation remains under control.

Despite this economic growth, Libya's unemployment rate remains high. The U.S. government also notes that other problems exist: "Libya's relatively poor infrastructure (i.e., roads and logistics), unclear legal structure, often-arbitrary government decision making process, a bloated public sector (as much as 60% of government spending goes towards paying public sector employees' salaries), huge public works programs (i.e., the 'Great Man Made River' project), and various structural rigidities all have been impediments to foreign investment and economic growth."[200]

Nevertheless, Libya may be moving toward a variety of economic reforms and a reduction in the state's direct role in the economy. In January 2002, Libya announced its intention to open up its economy and to attract foreign capital to the country, while devaluing the official exchange rate on its currency, the dinar, by 51 percent as part of a move toward unification of the country's multitier (official, commercial, black-market) foreign exchange system. Among other goals, the devaluation aimed to increase the competitiveness of Libyan firms and to help attract foreign investment into the country.

In January 2002, Libya cut its customs duty rate by 50 percent on most imports in part to help offset the effects of its currency devaluation. In June 2003, President Qadhafi said that the country's public sector had failed and should be abolished, and called for privatization of the country's oil sector, in addition to other areas of the economy. Libya's parliament also selected former trade and economy minister Shukri Muhammad Ghanim, a proponent of privatization, as prime minister that same month.

Libya has continuing problems with antiregime and Islamic extremist groups, and has a long history of erratic leadership and sudden reversals in policy. If it consistently pursues it current policies of moderation and seeking foreign investment and technology, however, energy risk will drop from moderate-high to moderate-low.

Chapter 5

Supply, Demand, Financing, and the Future of Energy in the Middle East and North Africa

The key to understanding the future of energy production and exports in the Middle East and North Africa (MENA) is to accept the complexity of the issues involved and the fact that major uncertainties are unavoidable in making any projections of what will or will not happen at both the national and regional level. There is no easy way to separate short- and long-term issues or to separate geopolitical risks from energy issues, and the impacts of given issues differ sharply by nation.

The previous chapters have discussed estimates of future production and export trends based on market driven models, the various security risks affecting the MENA region, and the sources of internal instability that have a major impact. At the same time, it is clear that the following additional issues will have a long-term impact on MENA energy supply that will extend well beyond 2030:

- The future demand for oil and gas exports, future export prices, and the resulting flow of income into the region.

- The future economics of gas and liquefied natural gas (LNG) exports, and the impact of changes in gas liquids technology.

- The ability to fund the required investment to maintain and increase oil and gas production capacity, and the extent to which surplus of swing capacity will both moderate prices and ensure against sudden rises in oil and gas prices if a limited interruption should take place in Middle Eastern oil and gas exports.

- The future patterns of investment flows from inside and outside the region, and the region's willingness and ability to create a climate in which outside and private investment can meet the region's needs.

- The ability to create the improved mix of pipelines, ports, and other facilities necessary to ensure the secure and efficient delivery of large amounts of energy.

FUTURE DEMAND FOR OIL AND GAS EXPORTS, FUTURE EXPORT PRICES, AND THE RESULTING FLOW OF INCOME INTO THE REGION

Many of the short-term problems in predicting energy demand and regional energy production and exports have been discussed earlier. It is clear from the history of past trends that major shifts can take place that are not predictable even a year in advance, and that national medium- and long-term energy development plans are often in considerable disarray. War, crises, weather, global economic conditions, and changes in export capabilities all combined to produce major changes in the level of demand and supply for MENA oil exports, and sometimes can do so in a matter of days. It is scarcely surprising, therefore, that uncertainty grows with time.

This is reflected in the history of various forecasts by the U.S. Department of Energy (DOE), the International Energy Agency (IEA), the Organization of Petroleum Exporting Countries (OPEC), and other sources. They have changed along with forecast of global economic development and changes in forecasts of what MENA states plan and can do to develop their energy resources and export capabilities. For example, conventional wisdom called for sharp medium- and long-term increases in Middle Eastern oil and gas exports, and a steady increase in oil and gas prices and export revenues, until the Asian crisis began in the fall of 1997. This conventional wisdom was based on the assumption of high levels of sustained economic growth, driven largely by Asia.

The 1998 estimates of the EIA—which were developed before the "oil crash" of late 1997—indicated that Asia would import about 24.2 million barrels of oil a day (MMBD) from the entire Middle East by 2020, and 23.9 million barrels a day from the Gulf. Asia would import about 54 percent of total projected Middle Eastern exports in 2020, which would reach 44.5 million barrels a day. Asia would consume 57 percent of total Gulf exports of 41.8 million barrels a day. This would have meant an increase from 8.7 million barrels a day in 1995 to 15.1 million barrels a day, or 74 percent. The IEA and OPEC had somewhat different numbers, but projected similar trends.

To put these estimates in broader perspective, the MENA region provided 47 percent of all world exports in 1996, and the Gulf provided 41 percent. According to the 1998 EIA projections, Asian demand was to be part of a global increase in demand that would lead to massive overall increases in Middle Eastern and Gulf oil production capacity. The EIA estimated that Gulf production would increase from 18.7 million barrels per day in 1990, and 20.9 million barrels per day in 1996, to 21.6 (10.6–11.8) million barrels per day in 2000, 24.4 (10.6–14.1) million barrels per day in 2005, 28.6 (10.6–17.2) million barrels per day in 2010, 38.4 (13.5–24.1) million barrels per day in 2015, and 49.8 (18.2–33.7) million barrels per day in 2020. This was a potential increase in the role of Gulf production from 28 percent of all world production in 1996 to 42 percent in 2020.

Only a year later, the economic recession in Asia, and the "oil crash," led to significantly lower estimates. The EIA estimated in 1999 that Gulf production would increase from 22.8 million barrels per day in 1997, to 23.9 (23.5–24.2) million barrels per day in 2000, 28.1 (25.8–30.2) million barrels per day in 2005, 29.6 (27.1–35.4) million barrels per day in 2010, 34.9 (28.6–42.8) million barrels per day in 2015, and 42.2 (35.3–52.3) million barrels per day in 2020. This projection would increase the role of Gulf production from 29.6 percent of world production to 37.6.

At the time the EIA made the 1999 forecast, however, many experts thought that Asian economic recovery, and that of other developing regions, would occur much more slowly than was the case during 1999. Furthermore, many experts felt that economic reforms would go much deeper and do more to prevent future economic problems. The result was a recovery that was both quicker and less stable than most experts predicted.

Forecasts can differ sharply, even in more "normal" periods. Chart 5.1 compares recent EIA projections of Gulf oil production capacity for the year 2020 that were made during 1998–2003. The estimates differ sharply. The 1998 estimate is high because it is based on work actually done during 1997, and reflects the impact of the high growth estimates of that year. The 1999 estimate is low, reflecting the much more negative estimates made during the economic "meltdown" in Asia in 1998. The 2000–2001 estimates reflect the relatively rapid global economic recovery. The 2002 estimate is high because of the optimistic forecasts made during the boom year of 2001, while the 2003 estimate is low because it reflects the impact of the end of the information technology (IT) boom in the United States and a global recession in many other areas. The end result is a nearly 50 percent difference between the minimum and maximum estimated total for Gulf production capacity over a five-year period.

It is interesting to note that all of these forecasts failed to anticipate nonmarket forces like the actual impact of UN sanctions on Iraq in all of the years before 2003, and assumed Iraq's oil development during 2000–2020 would be driven purely by market forces. The EIA estimates of Saudi production also varied so sharply because the modelers used Saudi Arabia to provide the margin of additional production that their models indicated the market required on a global level. Saudi Arabia became the de facto "swing state" of world petroleum capacity. This kind of volatility, however, is typical of the EIA made by other sources such as the IEA and OPEC. It

Chart 5.1

Comparative EIA Reference Case Estimates of Gulf Oil Production Capacity by 2020

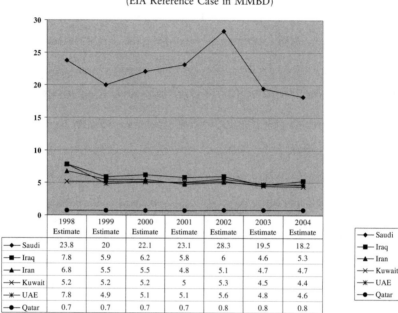

(EIA Reference Case in MMBD)

	1998 Estimate	1999 Estimate	2000 Estimate	2001 Estimate	2002 Estimate	2003 Estimate	2004 Estimate
◆ Saudi	23.8	20	22.1	23.1	28.3	19.5	18.2
■ Iraq	7.8	5.9	6.2	5.8	6	4.6	5.3
▲ Iran	6.8	5.5	5.5	4.8	5.1	4.7	4.7
✕ Kuwait	5.2	5.2	5.2	5	5.3	4.5	4.4
✱ UAE	7.8	4.9	5.1	5.1	5.6	4.8	4.6
● Qatar	0.7	0.7	0.7	0.7	0.8	0.8	0.8

Source: Adapted by Anthony H. Cordesman from EIA, *International Energy Outlook*, 1998, 1999, 2000, 2001, 2002, 2003, and 2004 editions.

is unavoidable unless the modeler assumes it is safe to ignore actual current global economic trends and make an independent guess at the future.

Chart 5.2 provides a historical comparison of estimates of Gulf exports by destination. It shows that similar uncertainties inevitably occur in the estimates of export flows, although the variation in total flows is somewhat less dramatic. It is important to note that the variations in the amount of Gulf exports to each region are generally greater than the variations in total demand.

They also interact with more than general market forces. The estimates made about the availability of exports from other regions in any given year, plus assumptions made about the trend in regional economic growth and importer demand, sharply affect where the model sends Gulf exports and

Chart 5.2
Comparative Estimates of Gulf Oil Exports in 2020

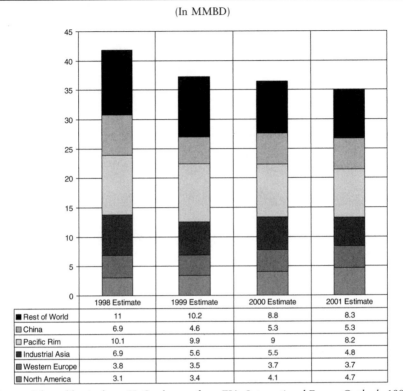

(In MMBD)

	1998 Estimate	1999 Estimate	2000 Estimate	2001 Estimate
■ Rest of World	11	10.2	8.8	8.3
▨ China	6.9	4.6	5.3	5.3
▢ Pacific Rim	10.1	9.9	9	8.2
■ Industrial Asia	6.9	5.6	5.5	4.8
■ Western Europe	3.8	3.5	3.7	3.7
■ North America	3.1	3.4	4.1	4.7

Source: Adapted by Anthony H. Cordesman from EIA, *International Energy Outlook*, 1998, 1999, 2000, and 2001 editions.

the estimate of how much is involved. In short, basic uncertainties about the global market in terms of both supply and demand produce steadily greater uncertainties in any estimate of both the source and destination of exports as time progresses.

The EIA forecasts do take such uncertainty explicitly into account, and examine high and low oil price cases as well as the reference case. As has been touched upon earlier, these cases examine worlds in which high prices lead most producers to limit the rate at which they increase oil production and oil capacity, and another world in which low oil prices produce lower oil revenues and push oil exporters to increase capacity and exports. One can argue the economic rationale for each case.

Chart 5.3
Comparative EIA Estimates of MENA Oil Production Capacity in 2020 under Different Oil Price and Economic Conditions

(EIA Reference Case in MMBD)

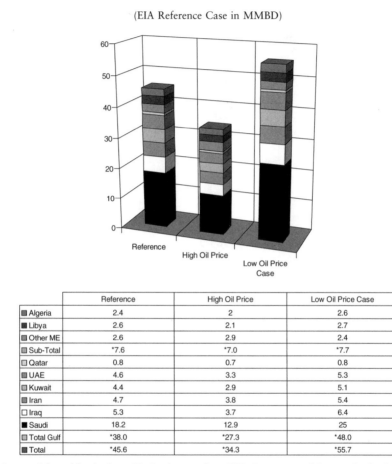

	Reference	High Oil Price	Low Oil Price Case
▨ Algeria	2.4	2	2.6
■ Libya	2.6	2.1	2.7
▨ Other ME	2.6	2.9	2.4
▨ Sub-Total	*7.6	*7.0	*7.7
☐ Qatar	0.8	0.7	0.8
▨ UAE	4.6	3.3	5.3
▨ Kuwait	4.4	2.9	5.1
▨ Iran	4.7	3.8	5.4
☐ Iraq	5.3	3.7	6.4
■ Saudi	18.2	12.9	25
☐ Total Gulf	*38.0	*27.3	*48.0
■ Total	*45.6	*34.3	*55.7

Source: Adapted by Anthony H. Cordesman from EIA, *International Energy Outlook 2004*, www.eia.doe.gov/oiaf/index.html, April 2004, pp. 213–215.

These cases have a major impact on the estimate over time. This is shown in Chart 5.3, where total MENA production capacity in 2025 is 44.9 MMBD in the high oil price case and 63.2 MMBD in the low oil price case—a difference of more than 40 percent. Chart 5.4 traces these differences over time for estimated actual production in the Gulf. It is clear that the range of uncertainty grows with time—this time the highest estimate for 2025 is 62 percent larger than the lowest.

Chart 5.4
Comparative EIA Estimates of Actual Persian Gulf Oil Production under Different Oil Price and Economic Conditions

(in MMBD)

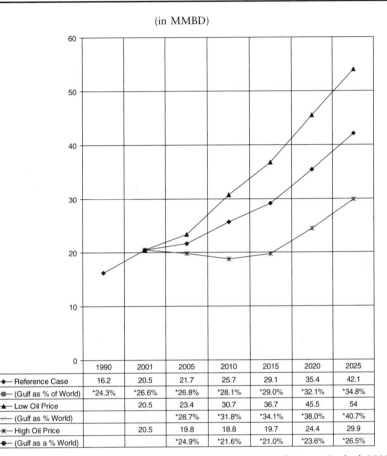

	1990	2001	2005	2010	2015	2020	2025
—◆— Reference Case	16.2	20.5	21.7	25.7	29.1	35.4	42.1
—■— (Gulf as % of World)	*24.3%	*26.6%	*26.8%	*28.1%	*29.0%	*32.1%	*34.8%
—▲— Low Oil Price		20.5	23.4	30.7	36.7	45.5	54
—✕— (Gulf as % World)			*28.7%	*31.8%	*34.1%	*38,0%	*40.7%
—✳— High Oil Price		20.5	19.8	18.8	19.7	24.4	29.9
—●— (Gulf as a % World)			*24.9%	*21.6%	*21.0%	*23.6%	*26.5%

Source: Adapted by Anthony H. Cordesman from EIA, *International Energy Outlook 2003*, DOE/EIA-0484 (2003), June 2003, p. 239; and EIA, *International Energy Outlook 2004*, www.eia.doe.gov/oiaf/ieo/index.html, April 2004, pp. 216–218.

It is not possible to use the results published for models to directly compare estimates for the Gulf or MENA region. Chart 5.5, however, compares the estimates of total OPEC production made in five major sources. Chart 5.6 provides a similar comparison for future oil prices. The highest price for 2025 is 73 percent higher than the lowest.

The range of different results does not mean there is something wrong with any given forecast or models; they reflect legitimate uncertainty. If

Chart 5.5
Comparative Estimates of OPEC Oil Production by Source

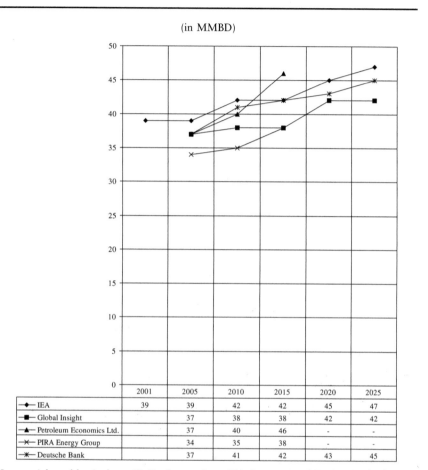

(in MMBD)

	2001	2005	2010	2015	2020	2025
◆ IEA	39	39	42	42	45	47
■ Global Insight		37	38	38	42	42
▲ Petroleum Economics Ltd.		37	40	46	-	-
✕ PIRA Energy Group		34	35	38	-	-
✳ Deutsche Bank		37	41	42	43	45

Source: Adapted by Anthony H. Cordesman from EIA, *International Energy Outlook 2003*, DOE/EIA-0484 (2003), June 2003, p. 45.

current modeling has any major limit, it may lie in the fact that modeling should also examine a scenario based on producer/exporter plans and capabilities rather than simply demand-driven cases. The reality is that modelers and models can illustrate rational futures but cannot possibly predict what actually happens. Furthermore, the differences between estimates shown in Charts 5.1 to 5.6 reflect several key factors, not easily modeled, but which must be considered in evaluating the impact of different future levels of MENA energy supply:

Chart 5.6
Comparative Estimates of World Oil Prices

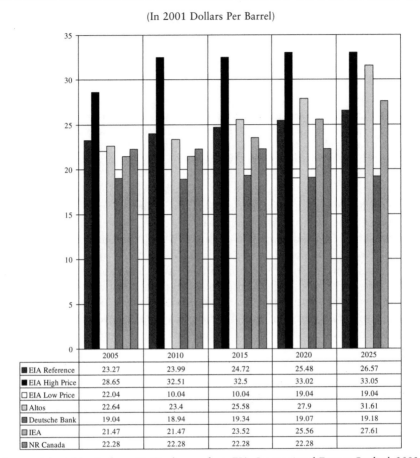

(In 2001 Dollars Per Barrel)

	2005	2010	2015	2020	2025
■ EIA Reference	23.27	23.99	24.72	25.48	26.57
■ EIA High Price	28.65	32.51	32.5	33.02	33.05
□ EIA Low Price	22.04	10.04	10.04	19.04	19.04
□ Altos	22.64	23.4	25.58	27.9	31.61
■ Deutsche Bank	19.04	18.94	19.34	19.07	19.18
□ IEA	21.47	21.47	23.52	25.56	27.61
■ NR Canada	22.28	22.28	22.28	22.28	

Source: Adapted by Anthony H. Cordesman from EIA, *International Energy Outlook 2003*, DOE/EIA-0484 (2003), June 2003, p. 43.

- Producer/exporters cannot predict the demand market any better than importer/users can predict supply. This tends to lead to cautious investment in production and export facilities when the global economy is weak and more investment when it is strong. However, many producers need to maximize energy export revenues in times of low prices and invest in increased capacity without paying close attention to the economic forecasts made at the time.

- MENA energy production and exports are not simply volatile in the short run, they are volatile in the long run. National decision makers must constantly revise their energy plans to take account of changing conditions and forecasts.

This made it extremely difficult to predict just how important the failure of any one exporter in increase capacity will be, particularly because another may increase capacity in response to the same information and conditions.

- At the same time, the demand market must also adapt to long-term as well as short-term volatility. It can do this in a number of ways, and with steadily lower cost and greater flexibility over time. For example, the demand side can increase energy efficiency, shift to less energy intensive activities, use different forms of energy, and/or pay more and raise prices.

- Many oil companies challenge the basic validity of market-driven models on the basis that MENA countries and other exporters cannot or will not pay for the level of export capacity projected in demand-driven models because they cannot afford to spend the capital required in anticipation of possible need, and will wait on demand to rise and then invest only if demand shows that the resulting increase in revenues will justify the investment.

These are not minor issues when one considers the level of global dependence on MENA oil, the impact of war or economic conditions on energy development plans, and the impact of future energy interruptions. It is easy to establish the overall importance of the MENA region, but almost impossible to then make meaningful detailed estimates of how important given developments could be in the future. It is clear that Saudi Arabia remains the world's most important energy exporter, but not whether Saudi success or failure in meeting any given future target for production and export capacity will be critical. History has already shown that a major exporter like Iraq can off-line for an extended period and the market soon adapts.

As has been explained in Chapter 2, the modeling of energy interruptions also shows that most credible interruptions are likely to be limited in scope. They would have an impact on global importer economic growth, but not a critical one. Most low-level interruptions would not produce effects that are more serious than the swings produced by market forces. Interruptions are only more critical than the impact of market forces if the interruption is so massive and/or prolonged that it could only result from a major war involving key exports or some political crisis that produced a regional oil embargo.

In addition, the history of the market shows that the short-term economic interests of importers may not be their long-term interests. Interruptions and market swings may drive importers to take actions that reduce both their dependence on imports and their vulnerability to oil interruptions. Past oil interruptions and supply and price volatility have reduced importer dependence on MENA oil, made them learn how to adapt to sudden changes in supply and price, and forced them to diversify their sources of energy and improve conservation. Models assume that the world works best when goods are provided in ways that establish a reliable and steady state equilibrium between supply and demand. The real world does not come close to functioning in this manner. It is far more adaptable and secure when goods are provided in ways that *do not* establish a reliable and steady state equilibrium between supply and demand.

THE IMPACT OF A PROLONGED PERIOD OF LOW OIL AND GAS REVENUES ON REGIONAL STABILITY

As has been discussed in Chapter 2, there is no credible way to estimate the further uncertainties that could be caused by war or internal unrest other than to consider a few worst case scenarios like a new MENA oil embargo, a closing of the Strait of Hormuz, the loss of Saudi production or a Saudi failure to increase oil production capacity, and a sustained loss of exports from one of the other "big five" MENA exporters.

Even these cases can vary so much in date, intensity, and duration that they can do little more than illustrate the obvious: limit fluctuations in supply are not critical, and are possibly even desirable; large-scale interruptions or losses of exports, particularly sudden ones, are critical and very undesirable. The problem is that there is no way to anticipate which kind of case will actually occur in the future, and meaningful modeling must wait on reality to establish suitable parameters and priorities.

A Slow Energy Development Scenario

There is another set of contingencies, however, that could have a major impact on MENA export capability over time. Most MENA exporters have so far been able to either fund the development of their own energy facilities, or to obtain outside capital for well-planned projects if they have not been at war or under sanctions. The four MENA nations that have been most affected by war or sanctions—Algeria, Iran, Iraq, and Libya—have all managed to maintain a reasonable level of exports, and carry out enough development to sustain their exports—although Iraq has faced periods of low or no exports and production.

Chapter 3, however, has shown that capital will become harder and harder to generate from within most MENA economies during the years to come, and that sustained periods of low production and/or oil revenues could have a serious cumulative impact on regional stability. Virtually all of the major oil producers already have serious short-term budget deficits or financing problems. All face serious future demographic pressures. All must make massive investments in greatly expanded infrastructure and social (entitlements) programs if they are to meet popular expectations and maintain internal stability. They must also invest in major job creation programs and the diversification of their economies.

Three MENA oil exporters are likely to have a combination of high oil revenues and small populations that means they will be able to obtain enough oil and gas export revenues so that they can fund both energy investment and all of their other expenditures indefinitely into the future. These countries include Kuwait, Qatar, and the United Arab Emirates (UAE)—although even in these cases overdependence on foreign labor and a lack of job opportunities already present problems. In every other case, MENA energy exporters face very serious problems, and some—such as Algeria, Bahrain, Egypt, Iran, Iraq, and Yemen—are already under serious stress. Oman and Saudi Arabia are scarcely far behind.

Chart 5.7 provides a historical case study that illustrates just how much oil revenues can swing in a real-world contingency, and how much they can impact on a region where many countries both draw 80 percent or more of their government revenues from energy export earnings and finance much of their economy through such revenues. During the period shown in Chart 5.7, Algeria, Bahrain, Egypt, Iran, Iraq, Libya, Oman, Saudi Arabia, Syria, and the eastern emirates of the UAE all came under severe economic pressure. All cut back or delayed major energy projects and some, like Saudi Arabia, had major cashflow and budget problems in spite of Saudi budget cuts. It also became clear during the crash in oil prices in 1997–1999 that even Abu Dhabi, Dubai, Kuwait, and Qatar made serious adjustments in their budgets when oil revenues were low.

The pressures to follow a similar path in any period of low or moderate oil revenues will grow steadily for at least a decade even if these countries began to carry out successful economic reform. They will grow indefinitely if they do not. Moreover, low oil revenues mean less spillover of revenues into the economies on non-oil-exporting Middle Eastern states, less aid, and fewer payments from foreign workers. Their impact will go beyond the borders of the MENA oil-exporting states and have a broader impact on regional stability.

The MENA Cash Squeeze

During the next five to fifteen years, each of the MENA exporting states will face a growing dilemma in deciding between funding domestic programs and energy investment. The problems that will result are obvious. MENA states have to spend money to get money: reductions on energy spending may provide more money for internal security and meeting popular demands in the short run, but may mean lower oil revenues in the middle and long term. Regimes that come under severe stress, however, always put short-term stability and survival first. Moreover, states can also cut back on long-term maintenance, marginal modernization, and the rate of investment in new facilities. This will either produce a long-term decline in revenue or forgo the opportunity of future revenue, but at a political cost many states may find acceptable in order to find short-term sources of money.

There are other methods MENA states can employ to obtain money that would either compound their energy funding problems or interfere with the

Chart 5.7

EIA Estimate of OPEC Earnings in 1998 by Major Country under Different Price Assumptions in "Oil Crash" Did Not Occur

(In $U.S. 1990 Constant Billions)

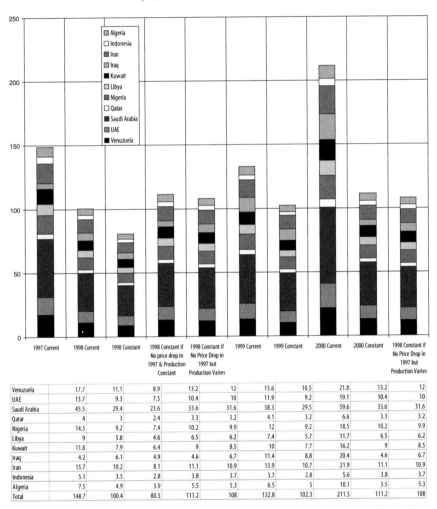

	1997 Current	1998 Current	1998 Constant	1998 Constant if No price drop in 1997 & Production Constant	1998 Constant if No Price Drop in 1997 but Production Varies	1999 Current	1999 Constant	2000 Current	2000 Constant	1998 Constant if No Price Drop in 1997 but Production Varies
Venuzuela	17.7	11.1	8.9	13.2	12	13.6	10.5	21.8	13.2	12
UAE	13.7	9.3	7.5	10.4	10	11.9	9.2	19.1	10.4	10
Saudi Arabia	45.5	29.4	23.6	33.6	31.6	38.3	29.5	59.6	33.6	31.6
Qatar	4	3	2.4	3.3	3.2	4.1	3.2	6.6	3.3	3.2
Nigeria	14.5	9.2	7.4	10.2	9.9	12	9.2	18.5	10.2	9.9
Libya	9	5.8	4.6	6.5	6.2	7.4	5.7	11.7	6.5	6.2
Kuwait	11.8	7.9	6.4	9	8.5	10	7.7	16.2	9	8.5
Iraq	4.2	6.1	4.9	4.6	6.7	11.4	8.8	20.4	4.6	6.7
Iran	15.7	10.2	8.1	11.1	10.9	13.9	10.7	21.9	11.1	10.9
Indonesia	5.1	3.5	2.8	3.8	3.7	3.7	2.8	5.6	3.8	3.7
Algeria	7.5	4.9	3.9	5.5	5.3	6.5	5	10.1	5.5	5.3
Total	148.7	100.4	80.5	111.2	108	132.8	102.3	211.5	111.2	108

Source: Adapted by Anthony H. Cordesman from data provided by the EIA as of June 2000.

economic reforms they need to deal with their social, economic, and demographic problems. One is to draw down on any capital accounts accrued for future energy investment. Another is to drawdown on the money in banks and stock markets for "loans." A third is to increase taxes and the burden on the private sector, and a fourth is to try to obtain private capital. In each case, such methods have been used in the past. In each case, they have helped to contribute to the economic problems in the region and its slow rate of growth.

Much will obviously depend on the size of future oil revenues and the rate individual MENA countries do or do not reform and diversify their economies. Chart 5.8 provides a rough and now dated estimate of future oil export revenues, but this chart is still valid in illustrating the fact that no one can now predict how much pressure and when MENA budgets could come up against enough of a cash squeeze to seriously limited the rate of

Chart 5.8
Petroleum Finance Institute Estimate of Middle Eastern and North African Oil Revenues by Country: The Range of Future Oil Revenues in 1998–2020

(in U.S. $Constant Billions)

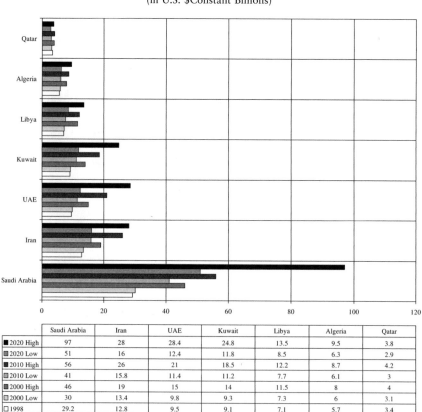

	Saudi Arabia	Iran	UAE	Kuwait	Libya	Algeria	Qatar
■ 2020 High	97	28	28.4	24.8	13.5	9.5	3.8
▨ 2020 Low	51	16	12.4	11.8	8.5	6.3	2.9
■ 2010 High	56	26	21	18.5	12.2	8.7	4.2
▨ 2010 Low	41	15.8	11.4	11.2	7.7	6.1	3
■ 2000 High	46	19	15	14	11.5	8	4
□ 2000 Low	30	13.4	9.8	9.3	7.3	6	3.1
□ 1998	29.2	12.8	9.5	9.1	7.1	5.7	3.4

Total oil exports = 2,734 thousand barrels per day.
Source: Adapted by Anthony H. Cordesman from projections by the Petroleum Finance Corporation.

increased oil and gas production and export capability. Moreover, internal violence and/or war might interact with demographic and economic pressures, and produce much more serious budget, capital flow, and oil revenue problems in given countries. All that can be said is that it seems almost certain that some MENA countries will see intensified terrorism, experience at least low-level civil war, or clash with each other between now and 2025–2030.

Future Patterns of Investment Flows from Inside and Outside the Region

One potential solution to the problems the MENA region faces is to seek outside or private investment in energy facilities—although this inevitably means that regimes again must give up export revenues in some form. This helps explain why many energy-exporting countries in the MENA area are currently examining ways in which to obtain increased foreign or domestic investment in some form, and some are examining ways to privatize some aspects of their energy facilities.

So far, many of these proposals have run up against a MENA country unwillingness to offer the most lucrative investment opportunities in the form of control over upstream crude oil and gas production or reserves, postcolonial fears of foreign ownership of energy resources, an unwillingness to offer realistic risk premiums in defining return on investment (ROI), resistance from national oil companies, and the host of petty barriers most MENA countries maintain that create disincentives to both foreign and domestic investment.

Some MENA countries have shown the region can succeed in attracting such investment or suitable loans by presenting realistic economic proposals. Qatar is a good example. Others are developing ways to attract foreign investment through complex buyback and other arrangements that avoid giving foreign firms direct control over their energy resources. Some countries, such as Saudi Arabia, have opened up their refinery and petrochemical sectors to private investment.

Saudi Arabia is also in the process of opening up its minerals industry to local and foreign private investments. Furthermore, in January 2004, Saudi Arabia approved a new income tax bill that cuts the tax rate on foreign investors from 45 to 20 percent in order to attract foreign investors.[1]

At this point in time, however, no MENA country is on a path where it has fully privatized a major aspect of its crude oil and gas production, and few have created opportunities for private or foreign investment in important aspects of any of their energy production and export facilities. In many cases, MENA countries do not charge market prices for—or realistically tax—fuel oil, gasoline, or even for the oil and gas feedstock provided to downstream users. Many—like Iran and Saudi Arabia—have ambitious domestic gas distribution programs that do not plan to charge enough to properly recover their pipeline and distribution costs, much less charge the kind of prices that would make up for the alternative of exporting the gas.

The problem of attracting domestic capital, and repatriating what many experts estimate is between $800 billion and $2 trillion worth of MENA capital held overseas, is one that affects every aspect of MENA economic development, not just energy.[2] So far, no MENA country has carried out all of the reforms needed to provide the incentives for the necessary flow and repatriation of private capital, although many have made progress in reducing past barriers. Many governments have talked the talk, and have workable plans. The problem is that MENA regimes have great problems in walking the walk, and acting decisively on their plans. This may change in the future, as governments come under more and more pressure, but there is no way to predict where or when.

Historically, the MENA area has done badly in attracting foreign investment relative to other regions, although it is slowly getting better. There is no way to accurately estimate the scale of such investment in energy facilities to date, except to note it has been limited, that it has been far more limited than MENA countries have hoped, and that most countries have relied on foreign loans rather than investment in obtaining foreign capital.

The problems that have limited foreign investment have been diverse and varied by country. Key problems have been that the terms for investment have been too complex and too filled with financial and political risk, negotiations have been cumbersome and ineffective, and MENA nations have sought to obtain investment in projects in the less desirable sectors of their energy economy and/or for overambitious projects of massive scale. The potential is there, but it is no easier to predict what the reality will be during 2004–2030 than it is for private investment, and the region continues to confuse a few flagship projects with serious structural reform.

- Chart 5.9 shows that the Middle East and North Africa did an extremely poor job of attracting direct foreign investment once the initial "oil boom" was over.

- Chart 5.10 shows that this situation did not improve during the period in the 1990s when foreign investment in "emerging markets" was relatively easy to obtain.

- Chart 5.11 shows how small the dollar flow to the MENA area was in absolute and comparative terms, although it did improve with time.

- Chart 5.12 reinforces this point by showing foreign investment flows as a percentage in 2001.

- Chart 5.13 shows this point is equally valid if the data are compared in dollar terms.

- Chart 5.14 shows that the patterns in foreign direct investment are even more erratic when examined by MENA country. Recent work by the UN Conference on Trade and Development (UNCTAD) also shows that the MENA area continues to lag behind the rest of the world, and there is no sustained up-

Chart 5.9
The Positive Trend in Foreign Direct Investment in the Middle East Reversed
after the Oil Boom Years

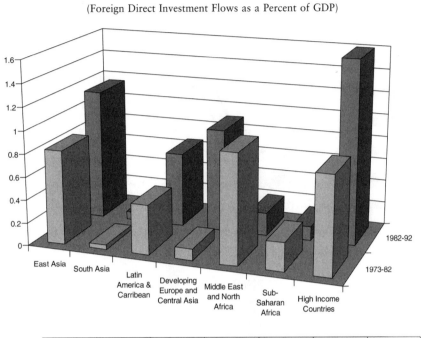

(Foreign Direct Investment Flows as a Percent of GDP)

	East Asia	South Asia	Latin America & Carribean	Developing Europe and Central Asia	Middle East and North Africa	Sub-Saharan Africa	High Income Countries
1973-82	0.82	0.04	0.43	0.1	0.95	0.25	0.85
1982-92	1.15	0.07	0.65	0.9	0.2	0.125	1.6

Source: Adapted by Anthony H. Cordesman from World Bank, *Global Economic Prospects and the Developing Countries*, 1996, p. 22.

ward trend. MENA foreign direct investment (FDI) fell by 35 percent relative to 2001, to a regional total of $4,800. It is also clear that the performance of Saudi Arabia, the country most critical to regional energy development and one that had made increasing FDI a critical goal, had some of the worst performance of any nation in the region.[3]

THE ABILITY TO FUND MENA ENERGY DEVELOPMENT IN AN UNCERTAIN FUTURE

Many in the oil industry discount these problems on the grounds that most MENA states have been relatively successful in using state revenues to fund energy investments in the past. It now seems likely, however, that

Chart 5.10
Net Foreign Direct Investment as a Percentage of GNP

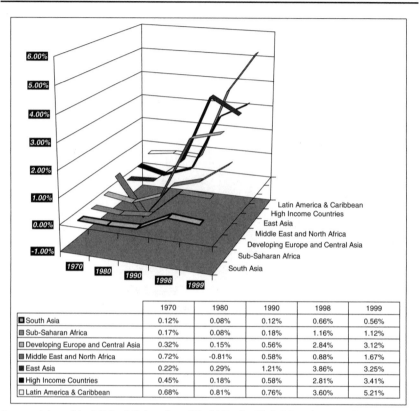

	1970	1980	1990	1998	1999
▣ South Asia	0.12%	0.08%	0.12%	0.66%	0.56%
▨ Sub-Saharan Africa	0.17%	0.08%	0.18%	1.16%	1.12%
▨ Developing Europe and Central Asia	0.32%	0.15%	0.56%	2.84%	3.12%
▪ Middle East and North Africa	0.72%	-0.81%	0.58%	0.88%	1.67%
▪ East Asia	0.22%	0.29%	1.21%	3.86%	3.25%
▪ High Income Countries	0.45%	0.18%	0.58%	2.81%	3.41%
☐ Latin America & Caribbean	0.68%	0.81%	0.76%	3.60%	5.21%

Source: Adapted by Michael Cohen from World Bank, *Global Development Finance*, 2000, pp. 236–264.

a combination of foreign investment and domestic private investment must assume a much larger share of the burden if the region is to produce anything like the expanded oil, gas, and product exports estimated in Chapter 1. In some cases, relying on market forces and the resulting oil revenues may still provide enough capital to rely on state investment if export revenues are high. However, it seems doubtful that a combination of market forces and export revenues will enable most MENA states to use state funds to finance the expansion of their export capabilities at the levels projected by the EIA and IEA.

A study by the International Energy Agency also indicates that the future level of energy investment required could be truly massive. This study projects the total investment needed to meet the world's energy needs between 2001 and 2030 at $16 trillion. These costs are based on the IEA's

Chart 5.11

The Trend in Total Foreign Direct Investment in the MENA "Flat Lined" During 1990–1999

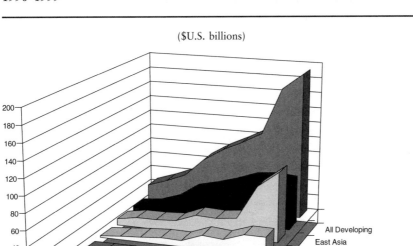

($U.S. billions)

	1990	1991	1992	1993	1994	1995	1996	1998	1999
▣ Sub-Saharan Africa	0.9	1.6	0.8	1.6	3.1	2.2	2.6	3.7	3.4
◼ Middle East and North Africa	2.8	1.8	2.2	4.2	3	-0.3	2.2	5.1	8.1
▣ South Asia	0.5	0.5	0.6	0.8	1.2	1.8	2.6	3.7	3.4
☐ Europe and Central Asia	2.1	4.4	6.3	8.4	8.1	17.2	15	24.4	24
▣ Latin America and Caribbean	8.1	12.5	12.7	14.1	24.2	22.9	25.9	69.3	89.4
◼ East Asia	10.2	12.7	20.9	38.1	44.1	51.8	61.1	64.2	61.5
▣ All Developing	24.5	33.5	43.6	67.2	83.7	95.5	109.5	170.9	192

Source: Adapted by Anthony H. Cordesman from World Bank, *World Debt Tables*, 1996, p. 17; *Global Development Performance*, 1997, p. 29; *World Development Indicators*, 1999, p. 262; *Global Development Finance*, 2000, pp. 236–264; *World Development Indicators*, 2003, p. 330.

reference estimates of 2002, and some 51 percent of the projected investment will be required simply to maintain the present level of supply and deal with depletion. The study also warns that the risks involved in such investment are formidable and changing, that much more capital must come from private and foreign sources than in the past, and that financing the required investments in developing countries with be the greatest challenge.[4]

Chart 5.12
Foreign Direct Investment Inflows as a Share of GDP by Region in 2001

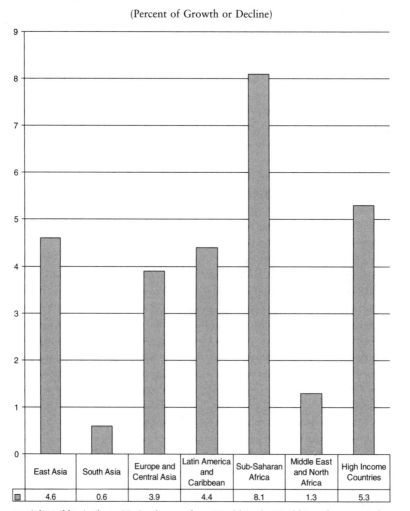

(Percent of Growth or Decline)

	East Asia	South Asia	Europe and Central Asia	Latin America and Caribbean	Sub-Saharan Africa	Middle East and North Africa	High Income Countries
	4.6	0.6	3.9	4.4	8.1	1.3	5.3

Source: Adapted by Anthony H. Cordesman from World Bank, *World Development Indicators*,
2003, p. 312.

The IEA estimates that the total cost of the global investment in the oil
industry necessary to pay for an increase in global oil production from 45
MMBD in 2001 to 120 MMBD in 2030 will be almost $3.1 trillion, with
$2.2 trillion or 72 percent devoted to exploration and development for con-
ventional oil. Investment in nonconventional oil (including gas-to-liquids) is
estimated to total $205 billion, or 7 percent of total oil investment.

Chart 5.13
Size of Foreign Direct Investment Inflows by Region in 2001

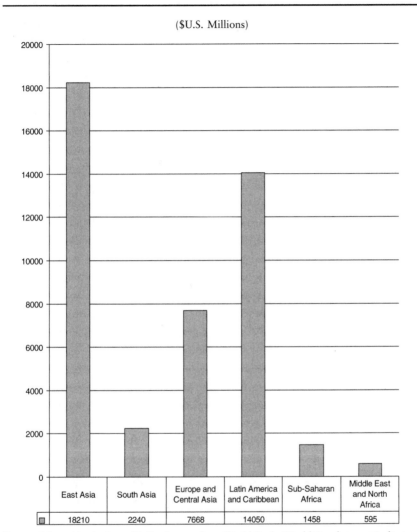

($U.S. Millions)

	East Asia	South Asia	Europe and Central Asia	Latin America and Caribbean	Sub-Saharan Africa	Middle East and North Africa
	18210	2240	7668	14050	1458	595

Source: Adapted by Anthony H. Cordesman from World Bank, *World Development Indicators*,
2003, p. 332.

These costs are extremely conservative, and do not seem to reflect the
costs of new exploration and EOR techniques. They could easily understate
the true market costs by 50 percent. As has been touched upon earlier,
massive additional investments will also be needed in tankers and pipelines,
costing some $260 billion or 8 percent of the total. Investment in addition
crude oil refining capabilities will total $410 billion or 13 percent. Some

Chart 5.14
Size of Foreign Direct Investment Inflows by MENA Country in 2000–2002

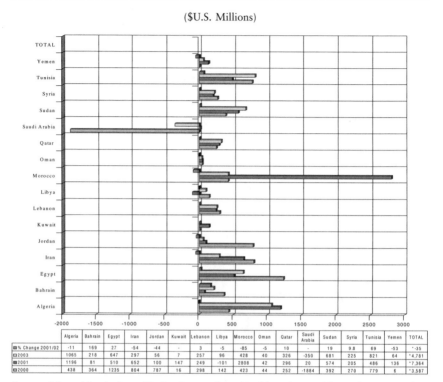

($U.S. Millions)

	Algeria	Bahrain	Egypt	Iran	Jordan	Kuwait	Lebanon	Libya	Morocco	Oman	Qatar	Saudi Arabia	Sudan	Syria	Tunisia	Yemen	TOTAL
% Change 2001/02	-11	169	27	-54	-44	.	3	-5	-85	-5	10	.	19	9.8	69	-53	*-35
2003	1065	218	647	297	56	7	257	96	428	40	326	-350	681	225	821	64	*4,781
2001	1196	81	510	652	100	147	249	-101	2808	42	296	20	574	205	486	136	*7,364
2000	438	364	1235	804	787	16	298	142	423	44	252	-1884	392	270	779	6	*3,587

Source: Adapted by Anthony H. Cordesman from World Bank, *World Development Indicators*, 2003, pp. 330–332; and Tom Evertt-Heath, "Deciphering the FDI Figures," *MEED*, October 2, 2003, p. 10.

66 percent of all such investment must occur in developing countries like the MENA region although 45 percent of the investment will be necessary meet the needs of the United States and other industrialized countries of the Organization of Economic Cooperation and Development (OECD).[5]

These investment costs could be much higher if the MENA region is not a stable supplier and cannot attract the necessary follow of investment. They depend heavily on the development of new supply, much of it offshore, from MENA countries, which are projected to provide more than two-thirds of the global increase in oil production between 2001 and 2030—even if significant increases occur in the production of nonconventional oil from Canada and Venezuela. If investment in the Middle East did not succeed, the cost of meeting rising world oil demand through 2030 would be 8 per-

cent higher, even though total consumption would be 8 percent lower because of rising oil prices.[6]

The cost of global investment in the natural gas supply chain is also estimated at about $3.1 trillion between 2001 and 2030, with more than half
going to exploration and development. This investment will be needed to
both compensate for the natural decline or depletion of existing gas fields
and to meet a near doubling of global demand equal to some 300 billion
cubic meters (BCM) a year—roughly equivalent to the present total gas
production capacity of all OECD European countries. The IEA estimates
that annual global investment spending on gas must increase from around
$80 billion in the 1990s, and $95 billion in the current decade, to roughly
$120 billion annually between 2020 and 2030.

Global investment in transmission and distribution networks, underground storage, LNG liquefaction plants, ships, and regassification terminals is estimated at $1.4 trillion. The investment in LNG is estimated to
be much higher than in previous years because of a six-fold increase in interregional LNG trade will be more than offset by further cuts in unit costs.
Roughly half of the interregional trade in gas is projected to be in the form
of LNG by 2030.[7]

The IEA estimated that public companies will not be able to finance such
development in many developing countries, and that the private sector will
have to provide a growing share of the necessary investment:[8]

> In many cases, only the largest international oil and gas companies, with
> strong balance sheets, will be able to make the required multi-billion dollar
> investments. Long-term take-or-pay contracts in some form will remain nec-
> essary to underpin most large-scale projects. The lifting of restrictions on
> foreign investment and the design of fiscal policies will be crucial to capital
> flows and production prospects, especially in the Middle East, Africa, and
> Russia, where much of the increase in global production and exports is ex-
> pected to occur. . . . As a result of these factors, there is a great risk that in-
> vestment in some regions and parts of the supply chain will not always occur
> quickly enough.

MENA Oil Development and Investment

The IEA makes it clear in its analysis that there are many different ways
to estimate the costs of future energy development and many different
energy and global economic scenarios that can emerge between 2001 and
2030—the period covered by its analysis. It also does not provide a break
out that provides figures for the MENA region. It issues a separate estimate for the Middle East and for all of Africa, with no individual cost data
for North African countries. The estimate of the investment costs for oil
production and infrastructure for the Middle East alone, however, total
$525 billion for 2001–2030, which requires investment to rise from an

estimate annual average of $12 billion during 2001–2010 to an annual average of $23 billion in 2020–2030.[9]

These estimates are heavily dependent on much of the increase coming from nations like Saudi Arabia, and a relatively slow rise in the cost of finding new production capacity in spite of a gradual shift to offshore production. As has been mentioned earlier, the cost factors the IEA uses are also extremely conservative. The IEA estimates that Saudi Arabia has an incremental production development cost of $0.6 per barrel per day (BPD) from its onshore fields. In contrast, the average capital cost of onshore capacity in the Middle Eastern OPEC countries is around $4,600 per BPD, compared with $10,200 worldwide per BPD, and around $22,000 per BPD in the North Sea.

As is the case with the EIA, the IEA estimates that much of the growth in world energy supplies that underlies the growth of the world economy will come from low cost Middle East oil, and that the growth in MENA oil exports will dominate global growth in oil exports during 2001 and 2030. This is based on IEA estimates that the Middle East retains 66 percent of the world's proven oil reserves of some 686 billion barrels, of which Saudi Arabia, Iran, and Iraq have 464 billion.

As has been discussed in detail in previous chapters, the IEA estimates that Middle Eastern production of crude oil and natural gas liquids will surge to 28.3 MMBD in 2010 and 52.4 MMBD in 2030, an annual average rise of 3 percent. This, however, is only part of the investment story. The IEA estimates an average annual decline of around 5 percent in existing production. This means that some 65 MMBD of incremental production capacity must be found between 2001 and 2030, and some 60 percent of this must be found to replace depleted capacity. This again illustrates the exceptional strategic importance of nations like Saudi Arabia and Iraq, with massive unexploited reserves, versus those exporting nations that either have declining reserves or high and steadily rising incremental production costs.[10]

The IEA only estimates totals for Africa, but much of the increase in oil production will come from Algeria and Libya, as well as states like Nigeria and Angola. The IEA estimates that oil sector investment in Africa will have to total some $360 billion during 2001–2030, or an average of over $12 billion a year. About 85 percent will be needed for oil exploration and development, in order to raise African production from 8 MMBD in 2002 to 13 MMBD in 2030. Another $42 billion will be needed to double the capacity of Africa's refining industry to 7.3 MMBD by 2030. These estimates are based on oil exploration and development costs of $1.7 to $4.5 per BPD, and the lowest costs are the onshore development costs in North Africa states like Algeria and Libya.[11]

There are, of course, many uncertainties in these estimates, and they assume—as in most projections in the previous chapters—that MENA nations respond efficiently to market forces and are not affected by external or internal instability and conflicts. The IEA has, however, run projections that illustrate what will happen if investment in the Middle Eastern share of global oil supply only maintains existing production levels. This "restricted investment scenario" is contrasted with the reference case in Table 5.1.

Like all of the estimates discussed earlier, one key message of Table 5.1 is that the strategic importance of energy exports from the MENA area is not sensitive to credible scenarios based on anything approaching current conditions relating to the impact of market forces, global demand, and the availability of alternative sources of energy and technology. At the same time, the restricted investment case does shown what could happen either as a result of inadequate investment or regional instability and conflict.

Table 5.1
The Role of the Middle East in Global Oil Supply in Different Investment Scenarios

Category	2000	2010	2020	2030
Price in $ Per Barrel				
Reference	28	21	25	29
Restricted Investment	—	27	30	35
Regional Demand in MMBD				
OECD				
Reference	47	52	56	60
Restricted Investment	—	49	52	53
Non-OECD				
Reference	28	37	48	60
Restricted Investment	—	36	46	57
Total World Oil Demand (MMBD)				
Reference	75	89	104	120
Restricted Investment	—	85	97	110
Total World Oil Supply (MMBD)				
Middle East OPEC				
Reference	21	26	38	51
Restricted Investment	—	24	27	31
Rest of World				
Reference	54	62	66	69
Restricted Investment	—	61	70	79

Source: International Energy Agency, *World Energy Investment Outlook, 2003 Insights*, Paris: IEA, 2003, pp. 179–182.

World oil demand only grows by 1.2 percent per year in the restricted investment case, and total demand is 110 MMBD in 2030, versus 120 MMBD in the reference case because of higher oil prices. The total share of oil in world energy balances drops from 38 percent to 35 percent because of increased conservation and a shift to other fuels.[12] The OECD cuts oil demand most—by 10 percent—because it is best able to find substitutes. The former Soviet Union (FSU) and Eastern Europe cut demand by 8 percent and developing countries by 6 percent. Ironically, the net cost of global investment in oil production rises by 3 percent in spite of the lower production levels because of the higher costs of production.

The impact on the Middle East is more on supply and on oil revenues than on demand. Middle Eastern oil production still increases from 21 MMBD in 2001 to 31 MMBD, but the total is 10 MMBD lower by 2030 than in the reference scenario. Middle Eastern OPEC nations also drop from 45 percent of supply in 2030 to 28 percent, with a major (6 percent) increase in the share of unconventional oil, in production from other OPEC countries (5 percent). The rate of depletion outside the Middle East also increases significantly. Middle Eastern countries also lose a great deal of oil revenue—a total of $400 billion over the period 2001–2030.[13]

It is important to note that in examining the Restricted Investment case, the IEA does mention political and military instability as major risks, in addition to the risk of underinvestment. It also identifies eight major market related risks:[14]

- *Reassure availability.* If reserves prove to be smaller than expected or difficult to recover because of operational difficulties, the need to find and develop new resources would be greater. Such new projects would not be developed so quickly as those projected in the reference scenario, since investors would have lower confidence in resource availability and the associated risks would make projects less attractive.

- *Infrastructure.* Inadequate infrastructure could constitute another barrier. If access to production sites is difficult, or roads, railways, pipelines, or export facilities are not available, upstream projects could be delayed or canceled.

- *Labor availability.* Operational and financial performance could be affected by a shortage of qualified labor.

- *National financing constraints.* In countries with national oil companies, financing new projects could become a problem where the national debt is already high and considerations of national sovereignty discourage reliance on foreign investment. The call of the national budget on future oil revenues could increase new financing costs. Strong guarantees could be difficult to find or involve a high insurance premium. Sovereign risk in many Middle Eastern countries is still high. A combination of these factors could delay or prevent investments.

- *Foreign investment policies.* The producing countries' policies on opening up their oil industries to private and foreign investment, the legal and commercial terms on offer and the fiscal regimes will have a major impact on how much capital Middle East producers will be able to secure.

- *Oil prices.* Prices will affect the ability of producing countries to finance investments from their own resources and, therefore, their need to turn to private and foreign investment.

- *Oil pricing and depletion strategy.* Governments could choose to delay development of production capacity in order to achieve higher profits by driving up international prices. Some may slow the development of their resources in order to preserve them for future generations.

- *Competition for financial resources.* In countries with state-owned companies and a rapidly growing population,[15] education, health, and other sectors of the economy could command a growing share of government revenues and constrain capital flows to the oil sector. Even in countries open to foreign investment, and therefore less dependent on government revenues, the needs of an expanding population could lead governments to increase taxes, lowering the profitability of projects and so deterring investment.

The importance of these risks obviously varies on a country-by-country basis, but it is all too clear from the previous analysis that none of them can be disregarded.

MENA Gas Development and Investment

The IEA raises similar issues relating to gas. As has been discussed in previous chapters, the IEA projects a major increase in world gas production. These projections are summarized in Table 5.2. The IEA estimates that the total cumulative investment necessary to meet these production levels between 2001 and 2030 will be $3,145 billion. Out of this total, $280 billion must go to the Middle East, with $140 billion for exploration and development, $65 billion for transmission and storage, $64 billion for new LNG facilities, and $12 billion for distribution. Once again, the IEA does not break out a separate total for North Africa. The cost for all of Africa is projected to total $226 billion, with $153 billion for exploration and development, $34 billion for transmission and storage, $37 billion for new LNG facilities, and $3 billion for distribution.[16]

The Middle East share of gas development will be far smaller than its share of oil development, but it will grow the most quickly of any region in absolute terms. The Middle East will also be the largest component for LNG investment, and the IEA estimates that roughly 70 percent of the investment in Middle Eastern gas ($196 billion) will go primarily for exports to the United States and other OECD countries, while 35 percent will go for exports to non-OECD governments ($84 billion). As a result, the capital requirements will grow rapidly, averaging some $10.6 billion a year by 2020–2030; they will average $8.8 billion a year over the period from 2001 to 2030, roughly twice the spending level in 2000, and an average of $4.7

Table 5.2
The IEA Estimate of the Role of the MENA Region in Global Gas Production:
1990–2030

Region	1990	2001	2010	2030
OECD North America	643	783	886	990
OECD Europe	210	306	300	276
OECD Pacific	27	42	65	125
Total OECD	880	1,131	1,251	1,391
Russia	640	580	709	914
Other transition economies	196	161	205	308
Total Transition Economies	835	742	914	1,222
China	17	34	55	115
East Asia	77	150	213	409
South Asia	29	62	89	178
Latin America	61	101	217	516
Middle East	99	252	421	861
Africa	70	134	246	589
Total Developing Countries	354	723	1,241	2,667
Total Non-OECD	1,190	1,464	2,156	3,889
World	2,070	2,595	3,407	5,280
Middle East as % of World Increase in Middle East over previous decade in %	—			

Source: Adapted from International Energy Agency, *World Energy Investment Outlook, 2003 Insights*, Paris: IEA, 2003, p. 189.

billion of this total with need to be invested in the upstream sector. The rate of decline in existing gas fields that must be compensated for in order to meet these goals is projected at an annual rate of 4 percent.[17]

These costs are not proportionate to the scale of the increase in Middle Eastern gas production because, as is the case with oil, Middle Eastern gas production has some of the lowest incremental costs of any region in the world—around $0.2 per MBTU or $7.5 per thousand cubic meters of gas produced. The Middle East cannot export to many of its customers by pipeline, however; and the IEA estimates that about 18 percent of all investment will go to liquefaction plants, although many plants will come online early in the period and annual average costs will drop from $1.9 billion during 2001–2010 to $1.2 billion during 2010–2020, rising back to $1.6 billion during 2020–2030.

Investment in transmission capacity will average $2 billion a year and go largely to domestic consumption. As has been discussed earlier, domestic gas consumption has become a major regional source of energy and way of freeing oil for export. Gas provided some 45 percent of primary energy needs in 2001 (211 BCM), with about a third going to power generation. Total regional use of gas is expected to double by 2030, largely to meet the needs of the power sector. At the same time, exports are projected to increase far more quickly and rise from 242 BCM in 2001 to 861 BCM in 2030. Iran is expected to lead these exports, along with five other Gulf countries. Iran, Iraq, Kuwait, Qatar, Saudi Arabia, and the UAE have 97 percent of all of the Middle East's proven gas reserves.

If the IEA is correct, this means a fundamental shift in the impact of Gulf and Middle Eastern oil production. Exports *outside the region* are projected to rise from 30 BCM in 2001 to over 360 BCM by 2030, and from 13 percent of total production to 42 percent. These increments will come largely from Iran, Qatar, Oman, and the UAE, with some from Yemen in the medium term and with Iraq becoming an exporter in the longer term. Most will be in the form of LNG, although new export pipelines may be built to Europe and Asia.

As for investment risks, they are almost identical to those discussed earlier for oil. The investment challenge is somewhat greater for gas, however, because Iran is the key to the rapid increase of gas exports and Iran presents special political problems, in terms of both internal instability and U.S. sanctions. In addition, the technical and financial risks are less familiar, and because large-scale LNG projects have a somewhat higher risk premium in terms of gas and war. There also are problems for private investment because most local banks do not have a history of large loans. The one exception is Saudi Arabia, but loan exposure rarely rises about $500–500 million per project. The IEA also notes that the Middle East does not have a history of charging fair rent for the pipeline and distribution cost of gas and this too affect the willingness of the private sector to invest.[18]

The IEA does not provide a great deal of detail on North Africa in its estimate of future gas investment needs. It does note, however, that three out of four of the nations responsible for almost all of Africa's gas production in 2001 were North African: Algeria (84 BCM), Egypt (23 BCM), Libya (6 BCM)—a total of 113 BCM versus 16 BCM for Nigeria. Production is expected to increase from 134 BCM in 2001 to 589 BCM in 2030. The total investment cost is projected at $216 billion, and average annual capital costs as rising from $3 billion in 1991–2000 to $4.8 billion in 2001–2010 to $10 billion in 2020–2030. Upstream development will dominate these costs, with average annual exploration costs rising from $2.8 billion during 2001–2010 to $7.5 billion during 2020–2020. More than $26 billion will be needed, however, to build liquefaction facilities during 2001–2030, and raise capacity from 47 BCM to 230 BCM.

The IEA also projects that exports will rise from 64 BCM in 2001 to 145 BCM in 2010, to 212 BCM in 2020, and 299 BCM in 2030. LNG production is expect to rise four-fold during 2001–2030, a rise of 140 MTY of additional liquefaction capacity. Exports to Europe by pipeline are expected to triple from 30 BCM in 2001 to 90 BCM in 2030. The basic risks again are similar to those discussed earlier under oil with the exception that corruption is seen as a far higher risk in African gas projects than in Middle East oil and gas projects.

ENERGY DEVELOPMENT VERSUS HUMAN DEVELOPMENT: A GROWING CONFLICT IN PUBLIC INVESTMENT AND EXPENDITURE PRIORITIES

The previous chapters have shown that there will be a growing conflict between the needs of MENA states to provide services for a growing population and invest in economic reform and diversification, and the need to expand energy production capacity, energy infrastructure, and energy export facilities. It is also a grim reality, as the *Arab Development* reports make clear, that the history of economic reform in the MENA region is the history of good plans and intentions and faltering or failed executions.[19] MENA regimes suffer from additional problems. They tend to backpeddle on reform the moment oil revenues rise to moderate levels, and many face resistance from nationalists, pan-Arab socialists, state-oriented technocrats, and Islamists. Virtually every state wants to maximize revenues, but also has powerful elements that want to conserve resources for the future.

What is clear is that the era of being able to safely rely on state oil and gas revenues to fund maintenance and modernization is at least at risk. Many MENA governments may not have to abandon state industries, state investment, and state control over energy resources, but fundamental changes will be needed to find ways to attract foreign and domestic private investment or many states will have energy expansion and development problems.

One key problem in estimating how serious the resulting problems will or will not be is that there are no reliable analyses and forecasts of the costs necessary to provide all of the increases in petroleum and gas facilities that are planned or required to meet the demand for exports and increased production capacity. It is clear, however, that massive investment will be required in ports, pipelines, supporting utilities, and tanker fleets.

At present, infrastructure investment also takes place on a country-by-country basis in response to those market forces that affect a given MENA region, with little overall regional cooperation. Joint development efforts are increasing but there are also major political and governmental barriers to the efficient development of export facilities, in developing common facilities for exports and infrastructure. The pipeline politics of the Caspian and Central Asia are the most obvious cases in point, but the lack of clear future plans to move oil out of Iraq and the limits on the cooperative plans for infrastructure development in the Southern Gulf affect much larger amounts of oil and gas. The lack of any cooperative plans for pipelines from the Gulf to ports in the Indian Ocean is particularly striking.

In short, it is no safer to assume that present policies and market forces create an "invisible" hand that ensures that national distribution effort will be both adequate and secure than it is to make such assumptions about production capacity. Much more detailed analysis is needed to examine the real-world probabilities that the market can fund the necessary energy transportation and distribution systems and the implications that the kind of massive increases in energy production projected in Charts 5.1 to 5.3 have for Middle Eastern and North African pipelines, ports, distribution facilities, and tanker fleets. Similar analysis is needed of their impact on energy vulnerability.

Chapter 6

Geopolitics, Domestic Development, and the Future of Energy in the Middle East

It is tempting to conclude this analysis with yet another set of policy recommendations about reducing dependence on imported energy, finding alternative energy sources, or encouraging reform in the Middle East and North Africa (MENA). These are all noble goals, but it is time to be realistic about the nature of world energy supplies and what can and cannot be done without a major (and currently totally unanticipated) breakthrough in energy technology or massive dislocation of the global economy. More than thirty years have passed since the oil embargo of 1973, and countless similar policy recommendations have come and gone with little real-world effectiveness.

The forces involved in shaping world energy balances—and the overall trends in energy exports in the MENA region are simply too vast and too complex for slogans and simple solutions to work, particularly because natural market forces already are constantly in play at a global level in an effort to find new energy sources or reduce dependence on energy imports whenever this is economically possible. As the United States has learned from experience, the Bush administration is no more able to articulate an energy policy that has the slightest chance of significantly reducing U.S. strategic dependence on MENA energy exports than were the Ford or Carter administrations, and the same has been true of the rest of the Organization of Economic Cooperation and Development (OECD) and of virtually every nation in Asia. The assumption that either governments or policy planners can alter this level of reality is roughly equivalent to the assumption that one can sculpture an iceberg with the *Titanic*.

Moreover, the previous chapters have shown the MENA region is experiencing a level of political, social, economic, and demographic change on a scale so large that no energy policy can now be both national and effective. An effective energy policy must also address MENA energy developments to the extent this is possible. The most obvious solution is to encourage political and economic reform, but experts in the region and outside nations have done so for decades. The reality is that they have only had limited impact, and some trends—particularly demographic pressure and the threat of terrorism—are growing worse not better.

Complexity and regional inertia are no reason to abandon efforts to encourage reform, and one must clearly distinguish between the long list of problems examined in this book and the conclusion they will inevitably lead to some form of regional crisis. There is still a good prospect that many MENA states will "muddle through" in the sense that no crisis will occur that has a lasting impact on the region's energy development. Outside nations can assist in this process although the key to change must come from within MENA states and intellectuals have already spent far too long trying to export both the causes and the solutions to their problems. Outside efforts can have limited and gradual impact. Responsibility for success, however, lies with the leaders and peoples in each MENA state, and any effort by them to deny this, or wait for outside aid, is a certain recipe for failure.

There is still a reasonable chance that Middle Eastern and North African energy production and exports will continue to cumulatively meet growing world demand at an acceptable price. There is also a chance that no period of regional political turmoil or conflict will be long or broad enough to produce the kind of major supply and price problems that go beyond the unpredictable swings in supply and price that are the result of market forces. In fact, "muddling through" is the most probable future.

Such an "optimistic" future scarcely means there will be no panics, no shortfalls, no price rises, and no crises. It does mean that the level of past problems and crises will not grow drastically worse, that the MENA region will cope with its problems well enough to develop enough energy exports, and that history will repeat itself in ways that the West and other importers can live with.

THE KEY FORCES SHAPING THE REGIONAL GEOPOLITICS OF ENERGY

The fact remains, however, that there are serious threats that could threaten regional stability and the security of energy exports and other credible futures. As has been discussed earlier, some of these risks are increasing. Proliferation and long-range strike systems can greatly increase the damage that regional conflicts might do to energy supply. Revolutions and conflicts will increasingly occur in an environment where the overall volume of exports will continue to increase and where the impact of interruptions or price increases may have more drastic effects on the world economy.

The tragic events of September 11, 2001, have become a symbol of the threat posed by terrorism and Islamic extremism. These threats, however, have never been directed primarily at the West. They are rather threats to every regime in the MENA region that is seeking to move forward through economic, political, and social reform. Islamic extremism and terrorism interact with the region's economic and demographic problems, and cases like Iran have shown that such radicalization can have a lasting impact on national energy development. Whether the end result has a more negative impact than the secular militarism of a nation like Iraq is something only time can tell.

The second intifada is another factor—like proliferation and Islamic extremism—that may have a medium- or long-term impact on energy development. Arab and Iranian hostility to the United States because of U.S. support for Israel has grown steadily since the second intifada began in September 2000. This threatens U.S. strategic partnerships with key Arab states like Egypt and Saudi Arabia and interacts with the problem of terrorism and Islamic extremism to create a potential "clash of civilizations" between the West and MENA region.

There could also be another kind of future in which economic problems prove more serious than conflict. A prolonged period of moderate increases in demand and low prices could create another future in the MENA region. Such a future could lead to systematic underinvestment in maintaining and expanding energy investment over time, creating new problems when Asia and the world economy recover. It also could lead to a situation where the "oil wealth" of the past turns into de facto "oil poverty."

Governments would lack the export revenues needed to maintain subsidies and entitlements and investment. This would interact with internal political and succession problems, growing demographic problems, cultural change and the problem of Islamic extremism, and a long-standing failure to diversify the economy. The oil-exporting states already face a world where oil revenue is well under 50 percent of the peak of the oil boom in per capita terms. This figure could drop to 35 percent by 2000–2005, particularly if oil and gas production and reserve findings continue to increase in other regions.

All these risks have serious implications for energy policy. The West cannot shape an energy or political policy that makes the necessary changes in the MENA region from the outside. The key changes necessary to achieve security and internal stability must come from within. Reducing population growth, economic reform that shifts reliance to the private sector, replacing subsidies and patriarchal government with a free economy and more of the elements of a modern state are all decisions that must be made from within individual MENA states. They cannot be imposed from the outside and there is no regional solution.

Western and Asian governments can help, however, particularly in terms of aiding regional military security and in trying to bring an end to the Arab-Israeli conflict. They can only deal with internal stability problems, however, if they are willing to commit themselves to a slow and consistent policy of persuasion in encouraging regional political and economic reform and helping MENA nations expand and diversify their economies. Western and Asian investment may ultimately accomplish far more in this area than governments, but only if economic and demographic reform inside the region moves forward enough to allow the MENA region to fully join the world economy. The plain truth is that no combination of outside policies can protect a failed regime or a failed nation from the consequences of its own actions.

POSSIBLE FUTURES

The MENA region must undergo fundamental changes. A stable future depends on key political events like the success of the Arab-Israeli peace process, the moderation of the Iranian revolution, the creation of a stable and peaceful Iraq, and an end to the civil war in Algeria. Many key leaders are aging and the highly personal patriarchal systems of government they have established are unlikely to survive them. Regional stability depends on the survival or succession of stable and progressive regimes in key states like Bahrain, Egypt, Jordan, Libya, Kuwait, Morocco, Oman, Saudi Arabia, and the UAE.

A stable future also depends on the ability of the region to fund and actually implement the level of energy development that it, and the world, need over the coming decades. There are strong indications that this will require major changes in the way most countries finance their energy development and in the role of foreign investment. These issues have been discussed in the energy sections of this analysis, but even the most successful development of the region's energy resources may not fully meet its economic needs and bring regional stability.

A stable future requires MENA exporting states to be willing to implement sustained economic reform, to come to grips with the need to reduce population growth, and to reduce dependence on foreign labor. The region must either further reduce its population growth rate or breed itself into poverty. Similarly, every oil-exporting state must improve the management of its economy, diversify, and shift to far greater reliance on free markets, or risk economic collapse.

The pressures and challenges the region, and on its individual states, can create many possible futures. One such future is that the region will do enough to "muddle through," largely preserving the status quo. In this case, political change will be limited and economic growth will barely keep up with population growth, if at all. Internal tensions will grow worse, civil conflict will continue, and some low-level fighting will take place between states.

Another possible future is that most exporting states will react in a positive manner, and will steadily implement the reforms they need in ways that avoid sudden political and domestic shocks. This kind of future is still open to the Southern Gulf oil-exporting states and Libya. The political, demographic, and economic pressures on Algeria, Iran, Iraq, and Syria are so great that even partial success—"muddling through"—may be difficult.

The high-risk future involves a mix of different variables that can interact in very unpredictable ways. These variables include a succession crisis or internal instability in Saudi Arabia, instability in Iran and a transfer of power to revolutionary extremists, and continued reaches and authoritarianism in Iraq. They also include the problems in the Arab-Israeli peace process and the continuing civil conflict in Algeria and Libya.

The most likely future is not one type of future for the region, but rather a mix of such futures that varies sharply by country. Most MENA states have, after all, muddled through for decades with considerable success. Many "problem states" have remained problems for the same period. A number of Middle Eastern and North African states are seriously debating reforms and beginning to implement them. The fact that there are many risks and problems is by no means a prophecy that most things that can go wrong will go wrong.

Scenario 1: Moving toward Growth and Stability

The MENA region scarcely faces a Malthusian nightmare. Moderate political leadership, basic economic reforms, and aggressive efforts to reduce population growth and/or overdependence on foreign labor could move virtually every MENA state toward sustained real economic growth in terms of both its GDP and per capita income within five to ten years. Rough working estimates by the World Bank indicate that sustained growth could average twice the population growth rate in half a decade—although these estimates were made at a time when it was assumed that Asian economic demand would keep oil prices moderate to high.

Economic and demographic reform will not be easy in any part of the Middle East, but it would be least difficult to implement in the Southern Gulf, and would affect three key oil-exporting states: Kuwait, Saudi Arabia, and the UAE. Iran would require a definitive shift toward political moderation to implement effective reform, and Iraq would require a fundamentally different form of leadership elite that could focus on national development and provide more equity to Iraq's Shiite majority and Kurdish minority.

North Africa presents more difficult challenges. Algeria would have to solve its political crisis and put a firm end to its civil war. Libya would require both a fundamentally different leader and a leadership grounded in reality. North Africa has much less average oil and wealth per capita, and its average per capita income has dropped from a peak of $2,000 in 1985, in constant 1995 dollars, to around $1,600 in 1997. By contrast, the average per capita income has dropped from a peak of $3,600 in 1985 to around $2,700 in 1997.[1]

Morocco and Tunisia have, however, at least begun the process of political and economic reform, and Algeria's plans provide a basis for action are a beginning. The Egyptian private sector has made serious progress, and is an indication of just how much the right kind of reform might accomplish.

While the Arab-Israeli states are peripheral to the geopolitics of energy, much depends on the ability to end the second intifada and rebuild the peace process. There is enough political linkage between tensions caused by the second intifada, and the ability to concentrate on development in the rest of the region, so that it is far from clear that a best case scenario can really take place in the region's energy exporters without a success and stable Arab-Israeli peace.

At the same time, such a peace must also be accompanied by coherent economic reform. Israel may be much wealthier than its Arab neighbors, with a strong and vibrant private sector, but state and political interference and a swollen public sector are as much enemies to Israel as to Iran or any other Arab state. Jordan has talked about and planned economic reform, but has not implemented it. Syria's economy is mired in a state-dominated past. The Palestinians lack governance and have no real economy. Lebanon is a glorified Ponzi scheme—all construction and infrastructure, and no real productivity and exports. Major changes would be required in the leadership and political elites of at least Syria and the Palestinian Authority.

It should be noted this "best case" scenario has several other requirements. Nations must avoid new major conflicts or civil wars, and military expenditures and arms imports must remain relatively low. (They have shrunk from about 17 percent of gross national product in 1985 to around 8 percent today, and from around $28 billion in 1985, in constant 1995 dollars, to around $14 billion.)[2]

The other states of the MENA region also need to follow Iran's lead in making aggressive efforts to reduce population growth—which ultimately may have to be kept well below 2 percent. The region must privatize and reform in ways that allow countries with minimal foreign investment to attract well over $1 trillion in added private and foreign investment between 1998 and 2010, at least $500 billion of which must go into energy investment, infrastructure, utilities, and water.

At the same time, the West needs to be careful about focusing too exclusively on peace, democracy, improved human rights, and/or reductions in corruption to solve the region's basic problems. These are important human values, and progress in these areas is necessary to achieve progress in other areas. The previous analysis has shown, however, that the most important changes necessary to achieve the "best case" are economic and demographic reform. In fact, there is little about the history of the MENA region to indicate that it matters very much whether a country has a president, dictator, socialist leader, king, or shaikh. The results are remarkably similar in terms of overall development and the resulting impact or per capita wealth.

Scenario 2: Muddling Through

As has been mentioned earlier, the "muddling through scenario" is likely to be the real-world case for most states. Some countries—Israel, Kuwait, Qatar, and the UAE—will probably either make enough progress to partially resolve their development problems or earn enough oil wealth to minimize their impact. Egypt, Iran, Morocco, Oman, Saudi Arabia, and Tunisia require substantially better leadership and efforts at reform, but can probably muddle through with some degree of growth or minimal further strain. Algeria, Bahrain, Lebanon, and Syria are more marginal cases, politically, economically, and demographically. They are likely to muddle downward as muddle through. Iraq, Libya, the Sudan, and Yemen are high-risk cases.

Muddling through does not imply that there will not be low-intensity and civil conflict, terrorism, and individual failed states. It does mean that regional states will continue to need to maximize their oil and gas export revenues, and will find the necessary investment in expanded production. There may be occasional blips or interruptions in some aspect of oil exports, and it is questionable whether sufficient capital will go into development to reach the U.S. Department of Energy's estimates of oil production listed earlier. In broad geopolitical terms, however, "muddling through" means the MENA region would be a reasonably reliable supplier over time, and become even more dependent on imports from outside the region—ensuring a need to recycle petrodollars or petroyen.

Scenario 3: Failed States

True worst case scenarios are pointless. Not only is everyone already dead at the start of such scenarios, but they have never been born. In the case of the MENA region, such worst case scenarios include the prolonged internal collapse of a major exporter like Saudi Arabia, wars that cause prolonged total interruptions in all Gulf oil exports, nuclear or weapons-of-mass-destruction attacks on critical exporting facilities, plus the odd meteor or earthquake. Such futures are possible—particularly over a period as long as 1998 to 2030. However, such futures are scarcely *probable* and they virtually defy meaningful cost-effective contingency planning.

Other "worst case" risks are more probable, and are still quite serious. These contingencies can cause the kind of energy "crisis" that can have a slow and cumulative effect in raising real energy prices and slowing global economic growth. They can cause serious human tragedies in parts of the MENA region, and lead to serious short-term panics or cuts in growth. Such contingencies include a mix of events in which regional states fail to deal with their internal problems, become involved in serious regional conflicts, or "institutionalize" problems that block effective investment and development of their resources. These cases include:

- The second intifada becomes a systematic, long-term breakdown in the Arab-Israel peace process with a backlash that limits U.S. ability to deter and terminate conflict in the Gulf, increases terrorism and Islamic extremism throughout the region, and limits outside investment.

- The failure of Iranian political and economic reforms and of Iran's oil and gas development.

- Nation building in Iraq fails. The resulting turmoil limits Iraqi exports and increases in export capacity, and the U.S. and British invasion of Iraq fails to bring a stable peace or effective economic and energy development.

- Internal civil conflict or tension becomes serious in Saudi Arabia, or there is a shift to a kind of Islamic extremism that discourages further increases in oil export capacity and tries to use oil exports as a political weapon.

- State sponsored or proxy terrorism affects some mix of MENA states, possibly using weapons of mass destruction, of a kind that would have a major impact on energy investment and/or the willingness and capability to export.

- Regional proliferation takes place at a level that leads to a major arms race and creates a structure of deterrence sufficiently uncertain to make investment a major risk, possibly coupled to some actual use of a few weapons against oil-exporting countries, with the resulting panic.

- A new, intense, and prolonged civil war in Algeria and/or Libya takes place that affects exports or blocks effective investment and development of export capacity.

- Naval/air conflicts occur in a critical "bottleneck" in areas like the Strait of Hormuz that have a serious short-term impact the flow of tankers.

- Prolonged U.S. economic sanctions that affect energy investment in key exporting states.

- A failure by the West to sustain the necessary power projection forces, regional political pressures that make them difficult or impossible to use, and a regional failure to develop any effective regional security structure.

It is important to realize that the risks in such "worst case" scenarios are not that any one problem is probable in the form that is listed above, but rather that the cumulative probability that one or more events of the *kind* listed above will occur over the period before 2030. The resulting range of uncertainty is not a reality that planners and forecasters like, but it is a mathematical fact of life—and a constant historical reality. When it comes to risk assessment in the MENA region, the cumulative probability that one of many less probable events will actually occur over time is generally higher than the probability that one of a small set of more probable events will occur.

Notes

CHAPTER 1

1. Energy Information Administration (EIA), *International Energy Outlook 2003*, DOE/EIA-0484 (2003) (Washington, DC, May 2003), pp. 18–27.

2. *BP Amoco Statistical Review of World Energy 1999* (London: BP Amoco, 1999), p. 4; *BP Statistical Review of World Energy 2003* (London: BP, 2003), p. 4.

3. EIA, *International Energy Outlook 2003*, p. 185.

4. EIA, *Annual Energy Outlook 2004*, DOE/EIA-0383(2004) (Washington, DC, January 2004), p. 68.

5. Matthew R. Simmons, "The Saudi Arabian Oil Miracle," Washington, DC, CSIS, February 24, 2004.

6. *BP Statistical Review of World Energy 2003*, p. 3.

7. Simmons, "Saudi Arabian Oil Miracle."

8. EIA, *International Energy Outlook 2003*, p. 40.

9. U.S. Geological Survey, *World Petroleum Assessment 2000*, available at usgs.gov/energy/worldenergy/dds-60.

10. International Energy Agency (IEA), *World Energy Outlook 2002: Insights* (Paris: IEA, 2002), p. 97.

11. High as these figures are, they are scarcely the maximum; the low price case estimate is substantially higher. U.S. Department of Energy (DOE) estimates that total oil production capacity of Persian Gulf members of the Organization of Petroleum Exporting Countries (OPEC) will increase from 22.4 MMBD in 2001 to 25.8 MMBD in 2005, 31.8 MMBD in 2010, 38.4 MMBD in 2015, 46.6 MMBD in 2020, and 54.4 MMBD in 2025. Put differently, Gulf OPEC oil production capacity will increase from 26.9 percent of total world capacity in 1990, and 28.3 percent of world capacity in 2001, to 36.0 percent of world capacity in 2015, and

41.6 percent of world capacity in 2025. These figures would be even higher if other non-OPEC "Gulf" oil-producer powers like Oman and Yemen were included.

While the Gulf dominates this increase, the EIA also estimates significant increases in oil production capacity in North Africa. Algeria and Libya are estimated to increase their production from 3.3 MMBD in 2001 to 3.5 MMBD in 2005, 4.2 MMBD in 2010, 4.7 MMBD in 2015, 5.3 MMBD in 2020, and 6.1 MMBD in 2025. If the entire MENA region is considered, oil production capacity will increase from 22.9 MMBD in 1990 and 27.5 MMBD in 2001 to 31.2 MMBD in 2005, 38.1 MMBD in 2010, 44.9 MMBD in 2015, 54.2 MMBD in 2020, and 63.1 MMBD in 2025. This would mean that total MENA oil production capacity would increase from 33.0 percent of total world capacity in 1990, and 34.7 percent of world capacity in 2001, to 36.9 percent of world capacity in 2005, 39.8 percent in 2010, 42.0 percent in 2015, 45.8 percent in 2020, and 48.2 percent in 2025.

12. EIA, *International Energy Outlook 2003*, p. 237.

13. Ibid.

14. Ibid.

15. IEA, *World Energy Outlook 2002: Insights*, pp. 91–93; EIA, *International Energy Outlook 2003*, p. 185.

16. IEA, *World Energy Outlook 2002: Insights*, pp. 91–93. For a detailed comparison of different estimates, see EIA, *International Energy Outlook 2003*, p. 45.

17. EIA, *International Energy Outlook 2003*, pp. 235–240.

18. *BP Statistical Review of World Energy 2003*, p. 6.

19. Ibid., p. 18.

20. Ibid., p. 6.

21. EIA, *International Energy Outlook 2003*, p. 42.

22. Ibid., p. 237.

23. *BP Statistical Review of World Energy 2003*, p. 17.

24. Ibid.

25. EIA, *International Energy Outlook 2003*, p. 42.

26. EIA, *Annual Energy Outlook 2004*, p. 68.

27. IEA, *World Energy Outlook 2002: Insights*, p. 106.

28. Ibid., p. 107.

29. Ibid., p. 103.

30. Ibid., p. 109.

31. See www.eia.doe.gov/fueloverview.html#i, accessed August 8, 2003.

32. "Overview of U.S. Petroleum Trade," *EIA Monthly Energy Review*, July 2003, p. 15, Table 1.7.

33. Ibid.

34. EIA, *EIA Short Term Energy Outlook*, August 2003, Table HL-1.

35. EIA, *Annual Energy Outlook 2003*, pp. 80–84.

36. EIA, *Annual Energy Outlook 2004*, p. 95.

37. EIA, *Annual Energy Outlook 2003*, pp. 80–84.

38. Ibid.

39. Ibid.

40. Ibid., p. 47.

41. *BP Statistical Review of World Energy 2003*, p. 20.

42. EIA, *International Energy Outlook 2004*, www.eia.doe.gov/oiaf/ieo/index.html, April 2004, Table 11, p. 49.

43. Ibid.; EIA, *International Energy Outlook 2003*, p. 49.

44. *BP Statistical Review of World Energy 2003*, p. 20; EIA, *International Energy Outlook 2003*, p. 49.

45. EIA, *International Energy Outlook 2003*, p. 50.

46. IEA, *World Energy Outlook 2001: Insights*, p. 141.

47. Ibid.

48. EIA, *International Energy Outlook 2003*, p. 55.

49. *BP Statistical Review of World Energy 2003*, p. 9.

50. Ibid., p. 25.

51. EIA, *International Energy Outlook 2003*, p. 186.

52. Ibid., p. 185.

53. Ibid., p. 186.

54. Ibid.

55. IEA, *World Energy Outlook 2002: Insights*, p. 141.

56. See EIA, *International Energy Outlook 2003*, pp. 57–68.

57. See ibid., pp. 68–70.

58. IEA, *World Energy Outlook 2002 Insights*, p. 117.

59. Ibid.

CHAPTER 2

1. CIA, *World Factbook 2001*.

2. U.S. State Department, Bureau of Verification and Compliance, *World Military Expenditures and Arms Transfers, 1989–1999*. The Middle East does not include North African states other than Egypt.

3. Richard F. Grimmett, "Conventional Arms Transfers to Developing Nations, 1993–2000," Washington, DC, Congressional Research Service, RL31529, August 2001.

4. *New York Times*, December 18, 2003.

5. There have also been cases of state-sponsored attacks. These include the Libyan bombings of Pan Am flight 103 over Scotland in 1988 and the bombing of UTA flight 772 over Chad in 1989. The bombing of Pan Am flight 103 killed 259 people on board and 11 people on the ground, and the bombing of UTA flight 772 killed 171 people on board.

6. For historical background on Bin Laden, see Kenneth Katzman, "Persian Gulf: Radical Islamic Movements," Washington, DC, Congressional Research Service, 96-731-F, August 30, 1996.

7. EIA, "Persian Gulf Fact Sheet," April 2003, available at www.eia.doe.gov/emeu/cabs/pgulf.html.

8. Ibid.

9. This text is adapted from ibid.

10. This text is adapted from ibid.

11. This text is adapted from ibid.

12. EIA, "Persian Gulf Fact Sheet."

13. Ibid.

14. EIA, *International Energy Outlook 2003*, p. 235.

15. Ibid.

16. Ibid.

17. IEA, *World Energy Outlook 2002*, p. 96.

18. EIA, *International Energy Outlook 2003*, p. 42.

19. IEA, *World Energy Outlook, 2002*, pp. 108–109.

20. Ibid., pp. 118–119.

21. EIA, *Annual Energy Outlook 2004*, p. 93.

22. This analysis is taken from EIA, "Energy Price Impact on the Economy," April 2001, available at www.eia.doe.gov/oiaf/economy/energy_price.html.

23. U.S. Department of Energy (DOE), "Strategic Petroleum Reserve Profiler," August, 2003, available at www.fe.doe.gov/programs/reserves/spr.

24. EIA, "Rules of Thumb for Energy Interruptions," December 11, 1997, is virtually identical to "Rules of Thumb for Energy Interruptions," October 18, 2002, in spite of changes in oil flows, inflation, and world economic conditions. See www.eia.doe.gov/emeu/security/rule.html.

25. EIA, "Rules of Thumb for Energy Interruptions," October 18, 2002, in spite of changes in oil flows, inflation, and world economic conditions. See www.eia.doe.gov/emeu/security/rule.html.

CHAPTER 3

1. This analysis can only touch upon some of the human development issues involved. For more depth, see the excellent work in the *Arab Human Development* reports, especially UN Development Programme (UNDP), Arab Fund for Economic and Social Development, *Arab Human Development Report 2003: Building a Knowledge Society* (New York: UNDP, 2003). Additional country-by-country background can be found in the annual *Human Rights* report of the U.S. State Department.

2. EIA, "OPEC Revenues Fact Sheet," June 2003, available at www.eia.doe.gov/emeu/cabs/opecrev.html; and data provided to this author by the EIA.

3. Ibid.

4. There are considerable uncertainties in this estimate. The figures shown are this author's estimate, based on various editions of the CIA, *World Factbook*; World Bank, *World Development Indicators*; IISS, *Military Balance*; and IMF, *World Economic Outlook*.

5. IEA, *World Energy Investment Outlook 2003: Insights*.

CHAPTER 4

1. EIA, www.eia.doe.gov/oiaf/ieo/tbl_14.html.

2. EIA, *International Energy Outlook 2003*, p. 235.

3. Ibid., pp. 235–240.

4. This text is adapted from EIA, "Persian Gulf Oil and Gas Exports Fact Sheet," April 2003, available at www.eia.doe.gov/emeu/cabs/pgulf.html.

5. Web summary of *International Energy Outlook 2003*, available at www.eia.doe.gov/oiaf/ieo/oil.html.

6. EIA, *International Energy Outlook 2004*, available at www.eia.doe.gov/oiaf/ieo/index.html, April 2004, Table 8, p. 40.

7. Web summary of *International Energy Outlook 2003*, available at www.eia.doe.gov/oiaf/ieo/oil.html.

8. IEA, *World Energy Investment Outlook 2003: Insights*, p. 181.

9. EIA, *International Energy Outlook 1998,* DOE/EIA-0484 (1998) (Washington, DC: EIA, April, 1998), p. 51.

10. This text is adapted from EIA, "Persian Gulf Oil and Gas Exports Fact Sheet."

11. Ibid.

12. The Saudi claims regarding proved reserves follow industry standards set by the SPE/WPC/AAPG, and verified by Aramco, but exclude reserves attributable to enhanced oil recovery to provide a more conservative figure. They do include reserves attributable to pressure maintenance.

13. Mahmoud M. Abdul Baqi and Nansen G. Saleri, *Fifty-Year Crude Oil Supply Scenarios: Saudi Aramco's Perspective* (Washington, DC: Saudi Aramco, 2004).

14. Saudi Aramco, May 7, 2004, www.saudiaramco.com

15. Abdul Baqi and Saleri, *Fifty-Year Crude Oil Supply Scenarios.*

16. For additional details, see IEA, *World Energy Investment Outlook 2003,* pp. 160–161.

17. EIA country analysis, "Saudi Arabia," accessed January 21, 2004, pp. 1–3.

18. EIA country report, "Saudi Arabia," June 2003, available at www.eia.doe.gov/emeu/cabs/saudi.html.

19. Ibid.

20. EIA, *International Energy Outlook 1999,* DOE/EIA-0484 (1999) (Washington, DC: EIA, March 1999), p. 201.

21. EIA, *International Energy Outlook 2003,* Table D-1.

22. *The Arab News,* "Saudi Oil Is Secure and Plentiful, Say Officials," April 29, 2004.

23. EIA, *International Energy Outlook 1999,* p. 201.

24. IEA, *World Energy Investment Outlook 2003: Insights,* pp. 161–162.

25. Abdul Baqi and Saleri, *Fifty-Year Crude Oil Supply Scenarios.*

26. Simmons, "Saudi Oil Miracle."

27. Ibid.

28. Abdul Baqi and Saleri, *Fifty-Year Crude Oil Supply Scenarios.*

29. For further discussion, see the work of Herman Fransen; Bhushan Bahree, "Saudis Assert They Have Enough Oil to Double Output," *Wall Street Journal Online,* February 24, 2004; Tom Dogget, "Saudi Says to Be Big World Oil Supplier Past 2050," *Reuters,* February 24, 2004; Jeff Gerth, "Forecast of Rising Oil Demand Challenges Tird Saudi Fields," *New York Times,* February 24, 2004.

30. EIA country report, "Saudi Arabia."

31. Ibid.

32. United Kingdom Trade and Investment, www.trade.uktradeinvest.gov.uk/oilandgas/saudi_arabia/profile/overview.shtml.

33. Edmund O'Sullivan, "Saudi Gas: How Empty Is the Empty Quarter?" *Middle East Economic Digest,* March 5–11, 2004, pp. 4–6.

34. EIA country report, "Saudi Arabia."

35. *Middle East Energy Survey* 45–47, November 25, 2002, pp. A9–A11.

36. IEA, *World Energy Investment Outlook 2003,* p. 234; and Oliver Klaus, "Starting Over," *MEED,* October 2, 2003, pp. 51–52.

37. O'Sullivan, "Saudi Gas," pp. 4–6.

38. Ibid.

39. Edmund O'Sullivan, "Saudi Gas: How Empty Is the Empty Quarter?" *Middle East Economic Digest,* March 5–11, 2004, pp. 4–6.

40. For good recent economic and energy summaries, see the country analyses of the EIA, the reporting of the Saudi American Bank (SAMBA), the Saudi Arabia Monetary Agency (SAMA), and Klaus, "Special Reporting," pp. 37–62.

41. Saudi Arabia General Investment Authority, www.sagia.gov.sa/ innerpage.asp?section=newsandevents.

42. EIA country report, "Iraq," August 2003, available at www.eia.doe.gov/ emeu/cabs/iraq.html.

43. Glen C. Carey, interview with Iraqi oil minister Ibrahim Mohammed Bahr al-Uloum, "Iraq Keeps Eye on Goal of 3 Million Barrels a Day," *USA Today,* November 20, 2003.

44. Jeff Gerth, "Oil Experts See Long-Term Risks to Reserves," *New York Times,* November 30, 2003, p. A1.

45. Ibid.

46. Ibid.

47. Ibid.

48. For additional details on estimated Iraqi investment cost relative to given production levels over time, see IEA, *World Energy Investment Outlook 2003,* pp. 164–166.

49. EIA country report, "Iraq," August 2003 and March 2004.

50. Ibid., March 2004.

51. *Middle East Economic Digest,* March 12–18, 2004, p. 6.

52. The analysis of Iraqi gas in this section is adapted from ibid.

53. This analysis draws heavily upon EIA country report, "Iran," November 200, available at www.eia.doe.gov/emeu/cabs/iran.html.

54. EIA country report, "Iran."

55. Ibid.

56. *Reuters,* December 4, 1998, 12:19; *Middle East Economic Digest,* January 22, 1999, pp. 10–12.

57. *Middle East Economic Digest,* January 22, 1999, pp. 10–12.

58. Ibid., March 26, 1999, p. 4.

59. EIA Analysis, "OPEC Brief," November 6, 2003.

60. EIA country report, "Iran." This summary differs somewhat from the details in an early summary by the IEA. See IEA, *World Energy Investment Outlook 2003,* p. 162.

61. Associated Press (AP), March 5, 2004, 07:48 EST, available at http:// aolsvc.news.aol.com/news/article.adp?id=20040305074909990001.

62. EIA report, "Caspian Sea Region," January 2004, available at www.eia.doe.gov/emeu/cabs/casplaw/html.

63. *Reuters,* February 25, 2000, 08:02.

64. EIA report, "Caspian Sea Region."

65. "Special Report: Oil and Gas," *MEED Weekly Special Report,* October 29, p. 7.

66. IEA, *World Energy Investment Outlook 2003,* p. 234.

67. EIA country report, "Iran."

68. EIA country report, "Greece," January 2004, available at www.eia.doe.gov/ emeu/cabs/greece/html.

69. *Oil and Gas Journal,* October 4, 1999, p. 25.

70. This text is adapted from EIA country report, "Kuwait," March 2003, available at www.eia.doe.gov/emeu/cabs/kuwait.html.

71. EIA country analysis, "Syria," April 2004.

72. EIA, *International Energy Outlook 2003,* p. 235.

73. *Middle East Economic Digest,* January 22, 1999, p. 12.

74. EIA country report, "Kuwait."

75. *Middle East Economic Digest,* January 22, 1999, p. 12.

76. *Middle East Economic Survey* 43, no. 7 (February 14, 2000): A11–A12.

77. EIA country report, "Kuwait," April 2004.

78. Statistics are taken from EIA country report, "Kuwait."

79. EIA country report, "UAE," December 2002, available at www.eia.doe.gov/emeu/cabs/uae.html.

80. EIA, *International Energy Outlook 2003,* Table D1.

81. IEA, *World Energy Investment Outlook 2003,* pp. 164–166.

82. *Middle East Economic Digest* 48, no. 2 (January 9–15, 2004): 41.

83. EIA country report, "UAE."

84. Ibid.

85. Ibid.

86. Ibid., February 2004.

87. *Middle East Economic Digest,* June 25, 1999, pp. 2–3; *Middle East Economic Digest,* January 15, 2004, p. 41.

88. EIA, *International Energy Outlook 2003,* Table D1.

89. EIA country report, "Bahrain," October 2003, available at www.eia.doe.gov/emeu/cabs/bahrain.html.

90. Ibid., September 2002.

91. Ibid., October 2003.

92. Ibid., September 2002.

93. Ibid.

94. *BP Amoco Statistical Review of World Energy 2001,* pp. 4, 20.

95. *Middle East Economic Digest,* January 22, 1999, p. 18.

96. EIA country report, "Oman," October 2003, available at www.eia.doe.gov/emeu/cabs/oman.html.

97. Simmons, "Saudi Arabian Oil Miracle."

98. EIA country report, "Oman."

99. Ibid.

100. Ibid.

101. Ibid., April 2000.

102. *Middle East Economic Digest,* January 22, 1999, p. 16.

103. EIA country report, "Oman," October 2003.

104. World Bank, *World Development Indicators 1999,* p. 43.

105. CIA, *World Factbook 2003;* EIA country report, "Oman."

106. EIA country report, "Oman," October 2003.

107. Ibid., April 2000.

108. Ibid., September 2002.

109. This section draws heavily upon interviews; the country analysis of the Energy Information Administration; John Duke Anthony, "Qatar's Economic and Energy Policies in Perspective: A Discussion with OPEC President and Qatar's

Minister of Energy and Industry, H. E. Abdallah Bin Hamad Al-Attiyeh," Washington, DC, U.S.-GCC Corporate Cooperation Committee, 1997; and various reporting in *Middle East Economic Digest* and *Middle East Economic Survey.*

110. EIA country report, "Qatar," November 2003, available at www.eia.doe.gov/emeu/cabs/qatar.html.

111. EIA, *International Energy Outlook 2003,* Table D1.

112. *BP Amoco Statistical Review of World Energy 2003,* p. 23.

113. *Middle East Economic Digest* 43, no. 45 (November 12, 1999): 4.

114. IEA, *World Energy Investment Outlook 2003,* pp. 234–235.

115. EIA country report, "Qatar."

116. *Middle East Economic Digest,* January 9–15, 2004, p. 39.

117. Ibid.

118. IEA, *World Energy Investment Outlook 2003,* pp. 234–235.

119. EIA country report, "Qatar."

120. *Middle East Economic Digest,* January 9–15, 2004, p. 39.

121. *BP Amoco Statistical Review of World Energy 2003,* pp. 4, 20.

122. *Reuters,* May 21, 2000, 13:42.

123. EIA country report, "Yemen," May 2003, available at www.eia.doe.gov/emeu/cabs/yemen.html.

124. *Reuters,* May 21, 2000, 13:42.

125. EIA country report, "Yemen."

126. *BP Statistical Review of World Energy 2003,* pp. 4, 6.

127. Ibid., pp. 22–23.

128. *Middle East Economic Survey* 43, no. 6 (February 7, 2000).

129. *BP Statistical Review of World Energy 2003,* p. 6.

130. EIA country report, "Egypt," January 2003, available at www.eia.doe.gov/emeu/cabs/egypt.html.

131. Ibid.

132. EIA country report, "World Oil Transit Chokepoints," available at www.eia.doe.gov/emeu/cabs/choke.html#SUEZ.

133. EIA country report, "Egypt," January 2003 and February 2004.

134. *Middle East Economic Digest,* January 9–15, 2004, p. 34; *Middle East Economic Survey,* February 24, 2003, p. 19.

135. EIA country report, "Egypt," January 2003.

136. EIA country report, "Egypt," July 1999.

137. IEA, *World Energy Investment Outlook 2003,* p. 241.

138. EIA country report, "Egypt," February 2004.

139. Ibid.

140. EIA country report, "Syria," March 2003, available at www.eia.doe.gov/emeu/cabs/syria.html.

141. Ibid.

142. *Middle East Economic Digest,* January 2–8, 2004, p. 15.

143. EIA country report, "Syria," April, 2000.

144. *Middle East Economic Survey,* October 27, 1997. Also see *Middle East Economic Survey* 42, no. 52 (December 27, 1999), and 43, no. 1 (January 3, 2000): A10.

145. EIA country report, "Syria," March 2003.

146. *Middle East Economic Survey,* April 7, 2003, p. 12.

147. *Middle East Economic Digest,* January 2–8, 2004, p. 15.

148. *Middle East Economic Survey,* February 17, 2003, p. 24.

149. EIA country analysis, "Syria," April 2004.

150. EIA country report, "Jordan," March 2003, available at www.eia.doe.gov/emeu/cabs/jordan.html.

151. Ibid.

152. *Middle East Economic Digest,* January 30–February 5, 2004, p. 14.

153. *New York Times,* December 11, 1998, pp. C1–C2.

154. This section draws heavily on EIA country report, "Israel," April 2003, available at www.eia.doe.gov/emeu/cabs/israel.html.

155. *Middle East Economic Survey,* April 7, 2003, p. 12.

156. EIA country report, "Israel."

157. Ibid.

158. *BP Statistical Review of World Energy 2003,* p. 4.

159. Ibid., p. 6.

160. EIA, *International Energy Outlook 2003,* pp. 235–237.

161. EIA, "Worldwide Petroleum Trade in the Reference Case: 2001 and 2025," June 2003, available at www.eia.doe.gov/oiaf/ieo/tbl_14.html.

162. Ibid.

163. *BP Statistical Review of World Energy 2003,* p. 4.

164. EIA, *International Energy Outlook 1998,* p. 51.

165. *BP Statistical Review of World Energy 2003,* p. 6.

166. See EIA country report, "Algeria," January 2003 and February 2004, available at www.eia.doe.gov/emeu/cabs/algeria.html.

167. *BP Amoco Statistical Review of World Energy 2003,* p. 7.

168. See EIA country report, "Algeria," January 2003 and February 2004.

169. EIA, *International Energy Outlook 2003,* p. 235.

170. See EIA country report, "Algeria," January 2003 and February 2004.

171. For further details, see IEA, *World Energy Investment Outlook 2003* pp. 168–171.

172. *Middle East Economic Survey* 42, no. 45 (November 8, 1999): A1–A2.

173. Ibid., March 31, 2003, p. A14.

174. EIA country report, "Algeria," February 2004.

175. BBC Summary of World Broadcasts, September 28, 1999, 06:08.

176. EIA country report, "Algeria," January 2003.

177. *Middle East Economic Digest,* January 9–15, 2004, pp. 32–33; EIA country report, "Algeria" February 2004.

178. See EIA country report, "Algeria," January 2003 and February 2004.

179. *BP Amoco Statistical Review of World Energy 2003,* p. 20.

180. *Middle East Economic Survey* 42, no. 45 (November 8, 1999): A2.

181. *Middle East Economic Digest,* January 9–15, 2004, p. 33.

182. EIA country report, "Algeria," January 2003.

183. Ibid., August 1999.

184. *Middle East Economic Digest,* January 9–15, 2004, p. 33.

185. EIA country report, "Algeria," January 2003.

186. Ibid.

187. IEA, *World Energy Investment Outlook 2003,* pp. 241–243.

188. Substantial portions of this analysis are taken from the country analysis provided by the U.S. Department of Energy. See EIA country report, "Libya," July 2003, available at www.eia.doe.gov/emeu/cabs/libya.html.

189. EIA, *International Energy Outlook 2003*, pp. 235–237.

190. *Middle East Economic Survey* 42, no. 48 (November 29, 1999): A12.

191. *Middle East Energy Digest,* January 2–8, 2004, p. 3.

192. EIA country report, "Libya."

193. For further details, see IEA, *World Energy Investment Outlook 2003,* pp. 168–171.

194. *Middle East Economic Digest,* April 23, 1999, p. 2.

195. Ibid., January 9–15, 2004, p. 37.

196. EIA, *International Energy Outlook 2003*, p. 235.

197. *Middle East Economic Digest,* January 9–15, 2004, p. 37.

198. EIA country report, "Libya."

199. EIA, *International Energy Outlook 1998*, pp. 36, 175–178.

200. EIA country report, "Libya."

CHAPTER 5

1. Saudi Arabia General Investment Authority, January 14, 2004, available at www.sagia.gov.sa/innerpage.asp?section=newsandevents.

2. Tom Evertt-Heath, "Deciphering the FDI Figures," *MEED*, October 2, 2003, p. 10.

3. Ibid.

4. IEA, *World Energy Investment Outlook 2003: Insights,* pp. 25–27.

5. Ibid., pp. 27–30.

6. Ibid., pp. 29–30.

7. Ibid., pp. 30–31.

8. Ibid.

9. Ibid., pp. 155–156.

10. Ibid., pp. 156–159.

11. Ibid., pp. 167–170.

12. Ibid., pp. 179–182.

13. Ibid., pp. 181–184.

14. Ibid.

15. The Middle East's population is expected to grow by more than 2 percent per year between now and 2030—the fastest growth of any WEO region.

16. IEA, *World Energy Investment Outlook 2003: Insights,* pp. 187–188.

17. Ibid., pp. 188–190, 227–232.

18. Ibid., pp. 188–190, 231–232.

19. For the latest report, see UN Development Programme, "Arab Fund for Economic and Social Development," *Arab Human Development Report 2003.*

CHAPTER 6

1. Estimate based on ACDA working date and *World Military Expenditures and Arms Transfers, 1996* (Washington, DC: U.S. Government Printing Office, 1997), Table 1.

2. Ibid.

Index

Note: Page numbers in *italic* type indicate figures or tables.

About the Author

ANTHONY H. CORDESMAN is a Senior Fellow and holds the Arleigh A. Burke Chair in Strategy at the Center for Strategic and International Studies. He is an analyst for ABC News and a frequent commentator on National Public Radio. He is the author of numerous books on security issues and has served in a number of senior positions in the U.S. government.